STODDERT'S WAR

Secretary of the Navy Benjamin Stoddert (1751–1813)

". . . We shall unquestionably have war—perhaps a long one . . . We are equal to the Contest—& shall assuredly be the victors. There is a spirit in America which rises with dangers & difficulties—this spirit will carry us triumphantly through whatever we undertake."

Stoddert to John Templeman, 29 June 1798

Studies in Maritime History
William N. Still, Jr., Editor

———

STODDERT'S WAR:

Naval Operations During the Quasi-War with France, 1798–1801

by MICHAEL A. PALMER

University of South Carolina Press

To Carol

Published in Columbia, South Carolina, by the
University of South Carolina Press

FIRST EDITION

Manufactured in the United States of America

Library of Congress Cataloging-in-Publication Data

Palmer, Michael A.
  Stoddert's war.

  (Studies in maritime history)
  Bibliography: p.
  Includes index.
  1. United States—History—War with France, 1798–1800
—Naval operations. 2. Stoddert, Benjamin, 1751–1813.
I. Title. II. Series.
E323.P35 1987   973.4'5   87-5024
ISBN 0-87249-499-3

CONTENTS

Illustrations

Maps

PREFACE

UNRATTLING HISTORY

The undeclared naval war with France was a formative event in American naval history. The conflict catalyzed the creation of the Department of the Navy and virtually ensured its bureaucratic permanence. During the war the old veterans of the Continental Navy and the American privateers of 1775–1783 passed to the next generation the mantle of naval leadership. Yet the Quasi-War has remained relatively forgotten. While books on the American Civil War or the Second World War would fill a small library, only one military history concerned exclusively with the Quasi-War has appeared since 1801—Gardner W. Allen's *Our Naval War with France* (1909).[1]

The nature of the Quasi-War, a *guerre de course,* is primarily responsible for the paucity of historical interest. War against commerce remains the exception to Thomas Hardy's maxim: "War makes rattling good history. . . ." The *guerre de course* has become the stepchild of a history born of Salamis, Lepanto, Trafalgar, Jutland, and Midway. To naval historians reared on the works of Alfred Thayer Mahan, slowly developing campaigns characterized by dispersion, avoidance of battle, patrolling, and convoying hold few attractions. With decision achieved in the cumulation of small encounters significant only in their aggregate, irregular warfare on the seas has been too often ignored. Jutland is the symbol of the Great War at sea, not the German submarine campaign that nearly brought Great Britain to her knees. Likewise, the symbol of the Quasi-War has become the singular victory of the American frigate *Constellation* over the French *l'Insurgente.*

In *Our Naval War with France,* Gardner W. Allen virtually ignores the two most significant aspects of the Quasi-War: operations, and the European context within which the struggle was waged. His study concerns itself primarily with ". . . some of the most stirring exploits in the history of the navy. . . ." A compilation of tactical actions, the work contains only a sprinkling of strategy, and no operational analysis. Naval operations involve the planning, organization, and direction of specific campaigns, intermediate between the tactical realm of battles, and the strategic realm at the highest level of military and political decision making. The operational fruits of the Quasi-War were the safe passage of escorted convoys of merchantmen and the elimination of pirates and privateers from major shipping routes. Such results make "unrattling" history, but the realities of the war made the United States Navy a stopgap force meant not to destroy French battle fleets, but to safeguard the growing commercial interests of the young republic.

And American naval operations of the Quasi-War cannot be understood in isolation. When the ships of the United States Navy made landfall in the Caribbean, they entered a European theater where the war had been underway since 1793. The Royal Navy deployed four to five times more men-of-war in the West Indies than the Americans. British ships chased and fought the same French cruisers and privateers. Both navies escorted each others's merchantmen. American warships operated from British bases. And most importantly, as this study demonstrates, British policies and shifts in deployment within the Antilles had dramatic effects on American operations.

As an operational history, this work is primarily a study of command. The central figure is Secretary of the Navy Benjamin Stoddert. His was a speculative nature to which intrigue came rather naturally. Stoddert's willingness to risk his ships, in the face of the enemy and the elements, led to an aggressive war waged in the Caribbean. His bureaucratic and administrative dexterity kept naval operations under his control. The Quasi-War was largely Ben Stoddert's war. But directing distant operations from the departmental office in Philadelphia (or later Washington), Stoddert relied on his commodores and commanders. The ultimate success or failure of the secretary's best-laid plans depended upon the capabilities of his subordinates. They are, accordingly, judged critically, primarily for their command attributes and initiative, and less for their personal bravery or seaman's skills.

In writing this history, I have benefited from a research tool not available to Allen three-quarters of a century ago. Between 1935 and 1938 the Navy Department published a seven-volume collection of documents on the Quasi-War, under the able direction of Dudley W. Knox. Whatever the shortcomings of these volumes by the standards of modern documentary editing, they contain a wealth of information that no researcher, unwilling to devote his adult life to but a single enterprise, could hope to assemble. After seven years of study with Knox's volumes on my desk as ready reference, I would be the last to deprecate Allen's work. He was an excellent scholar, naval historian, and writer. But the main purpose of documentary editing is to provide the material for new histories. The labors of Knox and his staff deserve such an effort. And I hope that in offering this history of the Quasi-War I have made the account of a less than action-packed conflict, in the Mahanian sense, interesting without falling into the highlighted narrative style of past historians. The names of famous men and ships fill the pages of this work, but the text remains critical, and the routine operations that are the true story of the war, and of the navy that fought it, are not ignored.[2]

In preparing earlier drafts of this work, irregularities in spelling and capitalization apparent in many quotations were so extensive that they detracted from the text. The first few appear quaint, but words consistently miscapitalized by modern standards and the continual inclusion of the notation [sic] serve little purpose. I have corrected spelling and applied modern rules of capitalization in quotes, except in a few cases where effect is intended. Punctuation was not altered.

M.A.P.
Springfield, Virginia
August 1986

ACKNOWLEDGMENTS

There are many people whom I need to thank for their assistance in writing this book. My wife Carol has come to know the war, its ships, and personnel rather well. Her encouragement, faith, patience, and clerical and editorial assistance were indispensable. My parents deserve recognition as well, for their support took many forms. At Temple University, where the Quasi-War served as the topic for my dissertation, Russell F. Weigley, who fostered my interest in naval history, and Waldo H. Heinrichs and David Davis provided guidance and encouragement that helped produce a work in which publishers showed interest, and which brought me to the attention of the Naval Historical Center in Washington. I must thank Rear-Admiral John D. H. Kane, USN (Ret.), former Director, Dean Allard, the Navy's senior historian, and especially William S. Dudley at the Center for providing me with the opportunity to sharpen my skills as a naval historian. I consider myself blessed to be working in my chosen field with such fine colleagues. The assistance of fellow Historical Research Branch staffers was a great help. Dr. Dudley, the branch head, and his assistant Michael J. Crawford, offered constant encouragement and a willingness to sit through one more tale of the Quasi-War. E. Gordon Bowen-Hassell gave freely of his understanding of the character of the veterans of the Continental Navy with whom he is so well acquainted. Tamara Moser Melia provided excellent editorial assistance and advice. Lieutenant Mary-carol Hennessey was always willing to go the extra mile to be of assistance. Photographic Section's Charles Haberlein was a great help in the selection of illustrations. Nancy Miller, presently with the National Archives, was my key to the Center's Operational Archives's reference files. Katherine Bowman, John Vajda, and Barbara Lynch were forever opening the door to the Navy Department Library's Rare Book Room where so many treasures lie. I must also thank the staff of Temple University's Paley Library, the

Acknowledgments

manuscript section of the Library of Congress, and the old Navy and Old Army Branch at the National Archives. Special thanks go to Marc S. Gallicchio, whose personal interest lie very far from the Quasi-War, but who found the time to review the manuscript nonetheless.

Special thanks go to William N. Still Jr., the editor of the University of South Carolina Press's new maritime series, who with Kenneth J. Scott and Warren Slesinger proved extremely helpful, constructively critical, and assisted me in at last bringing my work to press.

I also wish to express my appreciation to the Mariners' Museum in Newport News, Virginia, and to the Public Record Office, Kew, Richmond, Surrey, for permission to reproduce copyrighted materials. All illustrations appear courtesy of the United States Navy Department except "USS *Delaware* seizing *le Croyable*" and "The *Boston* vs. *le Berceau*," which appear courtesy of the Mariners' Museum, Newport News, Virginia.

M.A.P.

STODDERT'S WAR

INTRODUCTION

"DEVASTATION OF THE AMERICAN COMMERCE"

An undeclared and limited conflict, the Quasi-War did not begin on any specific day with any particular event. For the American navy, the "war" did not begin until the spring of 1798 when its first ships put to sea. But for the nation's merchants, the struggle began much earlier. To protect America's trading vessels, the men who sailed them, and the cargoes they carried, Congress established the United States Navy and empowered the president to employ it against the maritime forces of the French republic.

France was America's first and most important ally during her revolution. The treaties of 1778, and French economic and military assistance, helped to secure the political independence of the thirteen rebelling colonies. But independence guaranteed neither security nor prosperity. The United States remained surrounded by European colonial territories. American ships, carrying goods not prohibited by European mercantilists, sailed sea-lanes controlled by European navies. The post-Revolutionary decade was one of economic depression for the American commercial community.

For release from the Old World's economic shackles, many Americans looked to a renewed European struggle. An Anglo-French war in 1778 had given Americans their political independence; perhaps another would bring commercial independence as well. A New York merchant wrote his Jamaican correspondent in 1787: "Should a war (O, horrid war!) take place between Britain and France, will not your ports be open to us, and our commerce with you as a neutral be an object of consideration?"[1]

The hopes of such Americans for war were to be more than fulfilled. In 1793 the wars of the French Revolution and Napoleon began, twenty-three years of global conflict that provided Americans with enormous opportunities. Between 1792 and 1816 American exports rose from

3

$21,000,000 to $82,000,000; imports rose from $32,000,000 to $143,000,000. The tonnage of American vessels engaged in foreign trade increased from 564,000 to 1,732,000. The percentage of United States flag ships entered and cleared from American ports rose from 62 to 77.[2]

Faced with the increased shipping demands of the war, both Britain and France relied ever more heavily on the commerce of neutrals, especially the United States. In this reliance, however, there was not only opportunity for the Americans, but also danger. The New World was an integral part of the European power system and pressures would be exerted upon the United States that would strain its neutrality, threaten its ability to reap fully the benefits of its position, and perhaps drag it into war.

Indeed, real dangers faced the United States, a young, weak nation in a hostile world. To survive and prosper Americans had to walk a narrow path between the belligerents. Between 1793 and 1796 American states-men demonstrated their diplomatic adroitness. The Jay Treaty lessened frictions with Great Britain in the Northwest and on the seas. The Pinckney Treaty settled troubles with Spain in the west and south. Diplo-macy temporarily halted Barbary depredations in the Mediterranean, but not before the passage of the naval act of 27 March 1794. Demonstrating its willingness to fight given proper conditions, Congress authorized the construction of six powerful frigates, the warships that provided the backbone of the navy during the war with France.[3]

Reconciliation with Britain, however, complicated America's ties with France. The Jay Treaty proved to be too much for a relationship already strained by differing conceptions of neutrality and variant interpretations of the treaties of 1778. From the start of the war in Europe in 1793, the French tried to bully the United States into a more pro-French alignment with threats, periodic harassment of commerce, and interference in Amer-ican domestic politics. After the ratification of the Jay Treaty, 30 April 1796, the policy of the Directory steadily increased in bellicosity.

In the decree of 2 July 1796, the directors declared that France would treat neutrals in the same manner that they suffered Britain to treat them. Whatever the fairness or legality of the decree vis-à-vis the United States, considering that the Treaty of Amity and Commerce of 1778 remained in force, its major fault was practical. The decree contained no provisions for determining what constituted like treatment. Could French admiralty tribunals in the Indian Ocean or the Caribbean he expected to know how British courts were treating a given neutral? The decree was an invitation to excess.[4]

Following John Adams's defeat of Thomas Jefferson in the presidential election of 1796, the French responded with the decree of 2 March 1797. The Directory renounced the principle "free ships make free goods," contained in Article XXIII of the Treaty of Amity and Commerce, and the list of contraband was extended beyond Article XXIV. Also, failure to produce proper forms and clearances for the ship, the cargo, and the crew became grounds for seizure and condemnation. The latter stipulation the Americans considered "the most extensive and the most seriously destructive. . . ." Vessels engaged in legitimate neutral trade carried papers for ship and cargo, and the French had the right to demand, under the terms of Article XXV of the treaty, that American ships carry a *rôle d'équipage,* a list of the crew giving names and nationality. But the French had never insisted American ships carry a *rôle d'équipage* during the Revolution, nor during the four years of war preceding the decree. Virtually no American ships bothered to carry such a list, as the French well knew. Nor were the Americans given any time to comply. The decree took effect immediately, making all Yankee ships and cargoes fair game for French cruisers and privateers. The decree was a declaration of commerce war, a *guerre de course,* and the Adams administration in Philadelphia perceived it as such. The official American response noted:

> The result of these regulations has been the most extensive and universal devastation of the American commerce. Not only vessels bound to and from the enemies of France, but vessels bound to and from her allies, and to and from her own ports, have been seized and confiscated.
>
> The inevitable consequence has been, that direct commerce between the two nations is almost annihilated, and that the property of American citizens has been taken to a much larger amount than would have been possible in a state of actual war.[5]

The decrees of the Directory had a major impact upon American commerce and the country's political leadership. Congress called for a report on European spoliations of American trade. Secretary of State Timothy Pickering forwarded documents to the legislature, however, that made evident the severity of the French depredations. Over 300 ships had been seized in the Caribbean alone since July 1796. With the issuance of the decree of 2 March 1797, the situation could only deteriorate.[6]

The American response followed the Roman adage, "If you want peace, prepare for war." The naval act of 1 July 1797 empowered the president to man and employ the frigates *United States* and *Constitution* 44 guns, and *Constellation* 36, three of the six begun in 1794. But while preparing for war, the administration sought peace. In July a diplomatic mission composed of Elbridge Gerry, John Marshall, and Charles Cotesworth Pinckney sailed for France. Simultaneously many French diplomats realized that their policies were proving counterproductive. Unfortunately, advocates of a new American policy were swept from power in the coup of 4 September 1797. The renewed French hardline towards the United States found expression in yet another decree issued 18 January 1798. Henceforth, a ship carrying any British goods as cargo would be considered "*bonne prise.*" News of the decree reached Philadelphia in early March, boding ill for the success of the peace mission. In early April dispatches from the envoys arrived in the capital. A French demand for a *doceur*—a $220,000 bribe—before the negotiations began aborted the initiative. Publication of the official letters led to a wave of anti-French feeling. Since known as the XYZ Affair, the rebuff of the American envoys left the United States with few options.[7]

The Adams administration faced a serious challenge. From her global empire, France could strike at American trade on all seas. Of approximately 5,000 American vessels involved in foreign trade in 1797, more than 300—over 6 percent—were lost to French cruisers and corsairs. Imports fell from $81,000,000 to $75,000,000; exports from $67,000,000 to $51,000,000. Exports to the Caribbean (where American commerce was hit hardest) declined from $24,135,939 in 1796 to $19,637,764 in 1797. Insurance rates that averaged 6 percent in 1796 rose to between 15 and 25 percent a year later. By September 1800, when a diplomatic accord was finally reached, French seizures, captures, detentions, condemnations, and confiscations of American ships, cargoes, and crews involved 2,309 vessels and would ultimately leave the Federal government to sort out 6,479 claims. Such losses threatened America's new found commercial prosperity, the revenue base upon which the Hamiltonians had structured the government, and the political support of the Federalists themselves. With no diplomatic options immediately available, the administration resigned itself to the necessity of a military response. The Gallic *guerre de course* would be met on the seas by the men and ships of the United States Navy.[8]

1

UNDER THE WAR DEPARTMENT

-----

1. "Well Disposed *but* . . . Unqualified Hands"

Nominal responsibility for military administration in the spring of 1798 rested with Secretary of War James McHenry. The War Department under McHenry and his predecessors, Henry Knox (1789–1794) and Timothy Pickering (1795–1796), had overseen the nation's naval affairs since the passage of the act of March 1794 authorizing the construction of six frigates during the Algerine crisis. Work on three of the frigates halted not long after McHenry became secretary in February 1796. Progress on the others continued at a slow pace. Nevertheless, by early 1798 McHenry's administration of his department, and especially of naval affairs, had come under the critical scrutiny of Congress. As relations with France deteriorated, and expansion of both the army and the navy became likely, doubts about McHenry's suitability for office increased.[1]

Captain John Barry, commanding the forty-four gun frigate *United States* outfitting in the Delaware at Philadelphia, complained about McHenry's maladministration to a New Jersey Congressman in January 1798. Barry, who blamed McHenry for the retarded preparation of the frigate, condescendingly admitted that "there ought to be some allowance made for young beginners." The veteran captain suggested, however, that a separate naval department be established. A short time later, McHenry found himself the target of a Congressional inquiry and an assault from both political enemies and friends.[2]

To the Adams administration, McHenry was becoming a liability. Mismanagement resulting in delays and waste of public funds served only the opposition. Robert Goodloe Harper, Federalist Congressman from South Carolina, wrote Alexander Hamilton urging him to offer himself as McHenry's replacement. Oliver Wolcott, secretary of the treasury, likewise came to believe that Hamilton would have to become *"Secy of War in fact,"* for McHenry's "good sense, industry & virtues, are of no avail, without a certain address & skill in business which he has not & cannot acquire." Hamilton, McHenry's Svengali, resisted such calls, preferring to work behind the scenes. He had no illusions about the secretary of war's abilities, however, having written in 1795 that McHenry "would give no strength to the administration but he would not disgrace the office. . . ." But Hamilton came to realize that his man was "loaded beyond his strength," and that "whatever may be the props the administration of the war department cannot prosper in the present *very well disposed* but *very unqualified hands.*" Nevertheless, McHenry held on as secretary of war until 31 May 1800 when Adams demanded his resignation, not for bureaucratic ineptitude, but for political machinations with Hamilton behind the president's back.[3]

In order to provide for more effective naval administration, and to remove some of the burden from McHenry in the forlorn hope that so relieved he would prove capable of competently managing the remainder, Congress recommended that "a Commissioner of Marine" be established within the War Department to oversee naval affairs. McHenry was not adverse to the idea, and went a step further, adding his voice to those suggesting that a separate department be created.[4]

Congress gave McHenry's suggestion due consideration. Relations with France were deteriorating. There was talk of forming a provisional army of 25,000 men. A bill to authorize the president to build, purchase, or lease as many as a dozen vessels to carry not more than twenty-two guns each was making its way through the House. At a stroke, the number of ships to oversee would triple. On 16 April, the Senate passed a bill to establish a separate naval department. In the House, the major debate took place on 25 April. Proponents of the measure argued that it would insure more effective administration, save money, follow European precedent, and demonstrate to the nations of the Old World the seriousness with which Americans considered their national defense. Opponents argued that the nation's military was too small to justify separate departments. A division of labor would more likely lead to waste. As for European examples, they were to be avoided rather than emulated. As a compromise, the opposition returned to the concept of a commissioner of marine subordinate to the secretary of war. But the navalists had their way. The bill passed by six votes. On 30 April 1798, the second anniversary of the ratification of the Jay Treaty, President John Adams signed "An act to establish an executive department, to be denominated the Department of the Navy."[5]

Adams and Pickering conducted the search for the new cabinet officer, seeking a prominent Federalist merchant. American naval officers, with their rather limited wartime experience, lacked many of the administrative skills possessed by their army brethren. The Continental Navy had been too small; the service of its officers too parochial. Nor were shipwrights considered eligible. The holder of the post would do more than run the navy. As a cabinet member he would be one of the president's advisors in the formulation of national policy. Shipping merchants were representative of Federalist supporters and leading figures in their communities. They owned and operated fleets of ships built of the same materials, and armed, manned, commanded, and maintained in a fashion similar to navies. Moreover, being successful businessmen, merchants could be expected to value the public's money. On 1 May 1798 John Adams nominated as secretary of the navy George Cabot, a distinguished and successful Federalist from Massachusetts. The Senate, of which Cabot was a former member, concurred, ratifying the selection on 3 May. It then fell to Pickering both to notify Cabot of the president's offer and to convince the nominee to accept the position.[6]

Pickering knew first hand the difficulties involved in finding suitable cabinet officers willing to serve. He had been secretary of war in August 1795 when Edmund Randolph resigned as secretary of state. Washington gave Pickering responsibility for the nation's diplomatic affairs while a replacement was sought. By November, the president had despaired of finding a successor for Randolph, and considering the State Department more important, he convinced Pickering to take over that post, serving instead as war secretary pro tem until a replacement for that office could be found. Washington's fourth choice, McHenry, accepted. It was February 1796, however, before he reached Philadelphia and relieved Pickering of his dual duties. As for Cabot, he had refused an appointment to serve as one of the ministers sent to France in July 1797. Pickering considered another refusal likely. Nevertheless, he wrote Cabot a personal letter imploring him to make the necessary sacrifices and serve in Adam's cabinet. But while Cabot had the time and wealth, the forty-seven-year old believed he lacked the strength. "Suffer me to ask," he wrote Pickering, "how a man who has led a life of indolence for twenty years can be rendered physically capable of these various exertions."[7]

Cabot's return letter, dated 11 May, reached Philadelphia from Brookline, Massachusetts, on the 18th. Secretary of the Treasury Wolcott noted in a letter to Hamilton: "Mr. Cabot will not accept the naval department & I almost despair of obtaining a tolerably fit character. . . . Will you be so good as to turn the thing in your mind, & mention a number of suitable characters." But Adams and Pickering had already settled on their second choice, Benjamin Stoddert, a prominent Maryland Federalist.[8]

Under the War Department

Pickering took a personal interest in finding a suitable candidate for the new naval department. Since maritime issues were the major points of contention between France and the United States, he realized that as head of the State Department he would have to work closely with any secretary of the navy. And if the latter lacked administrative competence, as had McHenry, the unborne burdens would fall on Pickering's shoulders. Pickering knew Stoddert well. Both men were veterans of the Continental Army. During the Revolution Stoddert had served as secretary of the Continental Congress's Board of War, of which Pickering was a member. Stoddert's business partner, Uriah Forrest, was a friend of John Adams. In fact, in 1795 Pickering had suggested Forrest for consideration as secretary of war, but to head the navy, Pickering recommended Stoddert and Adams agreed. On Friday, 18 May 1798, the president placed the Marylander's name before the Senate, which confirmed the nomination on Monday. The following day Pickering addressed a short note to Stoddert informing him of his appointment and enclosing a commission from Adams.[9]

2. "A More Fortunate Selection"

Benjamin Stoddert accepted the appointment to the newly created cabinet post. Though a second choice, his selection brought no discredit to the administration. Henry Cabot Lodge, in his biography of George Cabot, wrote that "neither the administration nor the country was embarrassed by [Cabot's] refusal since . . . Mr. Stoddert, proved himself in every respect an able and efficient officer." Charles Goldsborough, who served Stoddert as clerk for over two years, wrote of the first secretary of the navy: "A more fortunate selection could not well have been made. To the most ardent patriotism, he united an inflexible integrity, a discriminating mind, great capacity for business, and the most persevering industry." Harold and Margaret Sprout in *The Rise of American Naval Power, 1776–1918*, considered Stoddert one of the few Americans with "a clear grasp of the naturally strong strategic position of the United States, and at least a partial knowledge of the function and utility of capital ships in a system of strategy calculated to make the most of our geographical isolation." And Robert Greenhalgh Albion in *Makers of Naval Policy, 1798–1947*, judged "the intelligent serene" Stoddert one of the three greatest secretaries of the navy with Gideon Welles and James Forrestal.[10]

Benjamin Stoddert's grandfather came to Maryland from Scotland late in the seventeenth century. James Stoddert became a prominent tobacco grower and landowner. Son Thomas, fourteen at his father's death, eventually inherited the family holdings, and slaves, as older brothers died heirless. He married Sarah Marshall of Marshall Hall and son Benjamin was born in 1751. Thomas Stoddert died in 1761.[11]

Raised as a merchant rather than a tobacco grower, Benjamin Stoddert spent his apprenticeship in pre-Revolutionary Philadelphia with fellow Marylanders William Trueman Stoddert, a cousin, and good friend James Wilkinson. War in 1775 brought an end, if only temporarily, to Stoddert's career. In January 1777 Wilkinson, then a lieutenant colonel in Thomas Hartley's Additional Continental Regiment recruiting in Maryland, offered Stoddert, "the valued friend of my youth and age," a commission as captain. Stoddert accepted and served with the regiment during the Philadelphia campaign of 1777. He was wounded at the battle of Brandywine, so badly according to his great granddaughter, that he was troubled until his death in 1813. After the fall of the capital, the Board of War ordered Hartley's depleted regiment to York, Pennsylvania, where Congress had relocated. There, during the winter and spring of 1778, Stoddert made the political connections that twenty years later led to his selection as secretary of the navy.[12]

In York, Stoddert found "Jamie" Wilkinson, now a brigadier general and secretary of the Board of War. Through Wilkinson, Stoddert became acquainted with the members of the board—its head, Major General Horatio Gates, Major General Thomas Mifflin, Colonel Timothy Pickering, and Richard Peters. Gates, the hero of Saratoga, had substantial Congressional support for an invasion of Canada. Stoddert, observing the value of political connections for a young officer aspiring for promotion, that is the example of Wilkinson, added his voice to that of those calling for a northern offensive, going so far as to assume a middle name—Canada![13]

But Stoddert's politicking proved pointless. Gates and Wilkinson quarreled, only Stoddert's intervention preventing a duel. Congress dropped the plan for a Canadian invasion. Wilkinson resigned as secretary of the Board of War. Gates, at his own request, was reassigned by Congress to New York. Pickering asked Stoddert if he would agree to serve as secretary for the board. The Marylander agreed, but Congress had its own nominee. In June, the British evacuated the capital; Congress prepared its return to Philadelphia. Benjamin Stoddert was left with nothing to show for his efforts than a new middle name.[14]

For Hartley's regiment, the summer and autumn of 1778 were months of frontier fighting against Indians along the upper Susquehanna River. Brutal campaigning tested Hartley's men. He reported to Congress: "the officers of my regiment behaved well to a man. All the party will acknowledge the greatest merit and bravery of Capt. Stoddert. I cannot say enough in his favor, he deserves the esteem of his country." But for Stoddert, the immediate future held not "esteem," but further disappointment. Congress ordered Hartley's shattered regiment consolidated with several others, redesignated the 11th Pennsylvania, and merged into the Pennsylvania Line. For Stoddert, the senior regimental captain and the next due for promotion, the Congressional action dashed all hopes of quick advance. He resigned in April 1779.[15]

Stoddert's wartime service, however, had not yet come to an end. He served as a deputy forage master general of the Continental Army under Clement Biddle, James Wilkinson's father-in-law. The civilian appointment carried the pay, rations, and title—but not the rank—of major. From his short tenure under Biddle, Stoddert earned the "Major" by which he was frequently thereafter known, and he renewed his contacts with the Board of War. In August, the board's secretary resigned and Pickering again asked for and secured Stoddert's agreement to serve. This time Congress assented, voting unanimously for approval on 1 September 1779.[16]

For seventeen months Stoddert served the Board of War, resigning in February 1781 after Congress directed the establishment of new civil executive departments. Stoddert gained important administrative experience and extended his political connections.[17]

After resigning, Stoddert returned to Maryland, married Rebecca Lowndes, daughter of Bladensburg merchant and tobacco-trader Christopher Lowndes, and moved to Annapolis where he served as President of the Maryland Council until the end of the war.[18]

The Revolution over, Stoddert at last felt free to begin his mercantile career. He formed a partnership with two other Maryland veterans— Uriah Forrest and John Murdock—and began trading tobacco from Georgetown, a small town along the Potomac where the Stodderts had long owned land. With the peace, the tobacco trade revived and Georgetown's economy boomed. For the partners these were halcyon days.[19]

On his own and in partnership with Forrest, Stoddert began to speculate in both land and the purchase of public securities, that is the paper issued by the Continental and state governments during the Revolution. With the new Federal government's decision to assume the old debts and to locate the permanent capital at the junction of the Potomac and the Eastern Branch (Anacostia), Stoddert's continued good fortune seemed secure. The "Major" was one of the men to whom Washington and Thomas Jefferson turned to purchase in secret land for the District of Columbia. Forest and Stoddert were incorporators of the Bank of Columbia, the first in the District, and the latter served as president until the spring of 1798.[20]

But speculation ultimately proved Stoddert's demise. The financial collapse of Robert Morris in 1797 precipitated a sharp fall in land values. Lots in the District purchased by Morris and his partner, but still unpaid for, were thrown onto a depressed market. Over 200 parcels had been purchased from Forrest and Stoddert. The latter personally held notes from Morris totaling $86,000. To complete Stoddert's rather sudden reversal of fortune, the Georgetown boom went bust. War in Europe, altered patterns of trade, the collapse of the tobacco market, a shift to the production of cereals, and a silting Potomac brought an end to the halcyon days.[21]

By May 1798, when Stoddert received Pickering's letter enclosing a commission as secretary of the navy, the Marylander's fortunes were waning. It is not clear from existing documents whether Stoddert's shift from merchant to land speculator was accidental or intentional. He was aware of the market changes that were taking place. He retained a hope until the end of his life that Georgetown would revive as a trading center. But by 1798 Stoddert's economic future was irrevocably tied to the rise and fall of district land values. His holdings were significant, but his debts, with realty prices depressed, greater. Unless land values rose, or the town's trade recovered, Stoddert could at best keep one step ahead of his creditors, selling off property to pay his debts as they came due.[22]

Stoddert's eventual economic demise, however, was by no means certain. Nor were his financial problems so pressing as yet that they would have attracted much notice. In 1798 Stoddert appeared to be a well-off Federalist. He had his old connection to Pickering and newer ties to Washington to recommend him. He had served in the Senate of Maryland in the early 1790s with McHenry. Would Stoddert accept? The salary, $3,000, was not much of an incentive. His personal financial situation should have demanded his attention. Stoddert would have been better off had he followed Cabot's example and declined the appointment. The talk in the capital, in fact, was that Stoddert, "a man of good sense," would turn down the president. And Stoddert had reservations. He wrote his brother-in-law, Benjamin Lowndes: "I hate office—have no desire for fancied, or real importance—& wish to spend my life in retirement, & ease— without bustle of any kind." But Stoddert felt that to refuse Adams would be "cowardly at such a time as this." He was confident of his ability. He had managed ships in peace, "why should I not be able to direct as well those of war?" Nevertheless, displaying his speculative nature, Stoddert at first considered his acceptance a "30 to 1" chance. But assured by his pregnant wife Rebecca that she would not mind living in Philadelphia for two years, and by her brother that Stoddert's logging operation at Beaver Dam would be attended to, the Marylander decided to answer once again the call of his nation and "accept the appointment . . . with determination to discharge to the best of my power, the duties of it. . . ."[23]

14

Under the War Department

Adams and Pickering at last had their man, a self-confidant, energetic, forty-six-year-old, willing to shoulder the responsibilities of office. With his record and experience, Stoddert was well suited not only to administer the navy, but also to serve as an advisor to the president. In that capacity Stoddert stood above many of his fellow cabinet officers, especially Pickering and McHenry. After turning over the presidency to Thomas Jefferson in March 1801, Adams wrote Stoddert, who alone had stood with the chief executive against the intraparty machinations of Alexander Hamilton, "I am and ever shall be, I believe, world without end, your friend. . . ."[24]

3. "Better Arrangements"

The bill of 30 April creating the Navy Department marked more than a simple transfer of authority for naval matters from the War Department. The act consolidated under the control of a single cabinet officer many of the responsibilities dispersed throughout the executive branch because of McHenry's administrative incompetence. These responsibilities involved not only the implementation of the various naval acts passed by the spring of 1798, but also questions of policy and deployment. As France and the United States drifted towards war, Congress moved to create a permanent naval establishment. The nation needed a coherent policy to shape that development. Strategic and operational decisions needed to be made relative to the conduct of the war, whether it remained undeclared or escalated into a full-scale, declared war. Until Benjamin Stoddert reached Philadelphia, responsibility for these decisions rested not only with Secretary of War James McHenry, but also with Secretary of the Treasury Oliver Wolcott, Jr., Secretary of State Timothy Pickering, and President John Adams.

Adams considered the navy his "hobby horse." His interest in naval affairs was as old as the nation itself. Adams drew up the regulations for the Continental Navy in 1775 and these same rules were resurrected under the naval act of 1 July 1797. But while the president possessed an interest in naval affairs, matters of state left him little time to involve himself in the day to day operations of the navy. It was with relief that Adams learned of Stoddert's acceptance. Throughout the remainder of his term, the president left naval administration and policy development to the Marylander.[25]

Pickering's involvement in naval affairs began in January 1795 when he replaced Henry Knox as secretary of war. For over a year Pickering oversaw work on the six frigates begun in 1794. Relinquishing responsibility for the War Department in February 1796, Pickering nevertheless kept a hand in the nation's naval business because of both interest and necessity. McHenry frequently turned to his predecessor for advice, and well into the spring of 1798, Pickering concerned himself with the selection of officers for the service. Adams turned to Pickering, after all, and not McHenry to find a competent secretary of the navy. Moreover, Pickering had his own naval force to administer. Under the terms of the treaty of 1796 ending the Algerine crisis, the United States agreed to construct a frigate and supply a large quantity of specie and naval stores for the Dey. Responsibility for implementing the treaty fell to Pickering at the State Department. He oversaw the building and outfitting of the frigate *Crescent* 36, and the transport of stores and tribute to Algiers. In the spring of 1798 Pickering was busy outfitting a squadron of a half-dozen ships for the Mediterranean. He, like Adams, simply lacked the time to devote to America's naval expansion.[26]

Oliver Wolcott at the Treasury Department bore significant naval responsibilities as well. He wrote Hamilton, "The purchase, building & providing of the ships falls upon me, & you know that my other duties are enough to employ a mind more active & vigorous than I possess." In addition, Wolcott had his own naval establishment. Ten new Revenue Service cutters were at sea, outfitting, or building by the spring of 1798. The naval act of 1 July 1797 authorized the president to employ the revenue cutters as a naval force if expedient. By the following spring such use seemed likely. For that reason, new cutters were being built stronger to enable them to perform dual roles. But while Wolcott understood that his cutters needed to be larger and more heavily armed than the older ships they were replacing, he was unable to make detailed recommendations and suggested that local treasury officials rely on merchants for advice. Wolcott admitted that they "must be better judges of what would be the most suitable construction of an armed vessel than I can pretend to be. . . ." For Wolcott, Stoddert's arrival would be a double blessing. The treasurer would be able to free himself from the shared burdens of naval administration, and turn to Stoddert for advice on the management of the revenue cutter fleet.[27]

As for McHenry himself, no one was more eager to see Stoddert reach the capital. The secretary of war came face to face with his own incapacities in early May. Several ships were nearly ready to sail and their commanders required instructions. McHenry saw "no chance" of a navy secretary arriving in time to assume responsibility, so the orders would have to issue from the War Department. The intensity of both the diplomatic and domestic political situations concerned McHenry. It was obviously the intent of Congress in building a navy that it be used to protect

American commerce, but the instructions would have to be limited and framed in such a manner as to "preserve the executive from any future accusation of having by its orders involved the country in a war." For advice McHenry wrote Hamilton in New York.[28]

Hamilton's reply, dated 17 May, expressed a correct understanding that the various naval bills passed thus far contained no special powers for the executive regarding employment. Hamilton recommended that Adams ask Congress to delimit those powers it wished to assign to the president. In the meantime, there was little American warships could do except repel attacks and defend American ships within the jurisdictional limits—one marine league. McHenry's first instructions, issued 22 May, included much of Hamilton's advice but were more detailed and, in fact, were drawn up at the direction of Adams who took upon himself the decisions regarding deployment.[29]

As Hamilton had noted, despite the numerous naval acts passed by Congress, no powers beyond those inherent in the Constitution had yet been given to the executive. Not until late May did the House agree to a limited extension of war powers. On 28 May 1798, Adams signed the bill and the same day express riders and dispatch boats rushed new instructions to American warships. Drawn up by Adams, the new orders directed his commanders "to seize take and bring" into American ports armed French vessels that had committed, were committing, or intended to commit depredations against American commerce off the coast. Captured merchantmen were to be retaken. These circumscribed instructions limited American naval operations until early July 1798, by which time Stoddert had assumed control.[30]

McHenry learned of Stoddert's acceptance from the new navy secretary himself. The two Marylanders had known each other from the time of their service in the state Senate in the early 1790s. Stoddert wrote McHenry the same day he informed Pickering of his acceptance: "I put in thus early my claim on your friendship for all the assistance I shall need and it will be a great deal." He expected to travel north in about a week, leaving his pregnant wife and six children to follow later.[31]

McHenry was anxious to see Stoddert arrive, not only to rid himself of naval responsibilities, but also because he was eager to travel to New York to examine proposals for the port's fortification and, most importantly, to meet with Hamilton. The secretary of war expected Stoddert to reach Philadelphia by 10 June and intended to wait for him. By the 11th, however, Stoddert had yet to arrive and McHenry departed for New York. In the latter's absence, Adams charged Timothy Pickering with the duties of the Department of War, which still included, of course, the nation's naval affairs.[32]

On the afternoon of 12 June, Stoddert reached the capital. One of his first visitors was William Hindman, a Federalist Congressman from Mary-land, friend to both Stoddert and McHenry. Hindman found Stoddert at his lodgings at 8th and Chestnut streets, less than a block from the offices set aside for the Navy Department. Hindman noted that the new secretary was "anxious to be geered & enter upon the duties of his office. . . ." Stoddert intended to wait upon President Adams the following morning. In the meantime, the first order of business was to review the numerous applications for clerkships and select a staff. Stoddert expected the process to take several days.[33]

Despite his eagerness to begin work, Stoddert did not take on the duties of his office until 18 June, and not officially until the 19th when Adams administered to him the oath of office. Pickering continued as interim secretary of war. Stoddert spent most of his time attending to the private affairs that he had warned McHenry might take as much as a week. Stoddert had to locate a house to rent in town for his large family. There were also pressing financial matters. In March 1798 Stoddert, then presi-dent of the Bank of Columbia, had appointed Clement Biddle his attorney in the city to handle his business affairs. It is probable that only on his arrival in the capital did Stoddert learn the full extent of Robert Morris's financial collapse. No doubt, Stoddert was one of Morris's visitors in "the Prune," the debtor's prison on Prune Street in Philadelphia. If such a meeting did take place, perhaps Morris, a former secretary of marine during the Revolution, had some naval advice for the man who was in a sense his successor.[34]

Despite the terrible financial news that greeted Stoddert on his arrival in the capital, he could not long ignore his duties. The day after his arrival, Adams signed an act that embargoed trade with France and her colonies. Abrogation of the treaties of 1778 would soon follow; a declaration of war seemed imminent. Stoddert waded into the "business of my department" in the midst of a deteriorating diplomatic situation and rapid naval expan-sion. He noted that the absence of McHenry in New York, where he was followed a few days later by Wolcott, "kept back" his work. Relying on the clerks of the absent cabinet officers, Pickering's advice, and the relevant correspondence on naval affairs, Stoddert struggled with the respon-sibilities of his new department. The experience was unsettling; he wrote in mid-July: "It was unfortunate, that in conferring the appointment of secretary of the navy upon me, the President could not also confer the knowledge necessary . . . to possess . . . I have been obliged to act—& under great disadvantage—without having a moment to think,—I shall soon have time to make better arrangements. . . ."[35]

2

"PAYING RESPECTS"

———

1. Defending the Coast

The restrictions imposed on American naval operations by the act of 28 May 1798 gave to the initial phase of the Quasi-War a defensive character. Following the XYZ Affair, the Adams adminstration only gradually and cautiously converted public outrage towards France into legislative authority to strike at a former ally. This national mood was reinforced by losses to privateers active off the American coast and fear of invasion. Adams, assessing the situation of France in 1798, concluded that no "formidable invasion" of the United States was possible, but he did expect privateers and cruisers to prey on American coastal commerce. He also believed it possible that a small French squadron with troops could appear off the coast where they "might lay some of our cities under contribution."

A more likely scenario involved an invasion originating not in Europe, but in the Caribbean. French agents had fomented servile revolt throughout the West Indies as a method of striking against Great Britain. As important and knowledgeable a man as Henry Knox, former secretary of war, believed that an attack on the American south might be launched from Hispaniola. Corsairs operating from the island had seized hundreds of well-built American ships. Winds and currents would carry even poorly sailed and navigated vessels to the southern coast. Arrival of an ex-slave armada might precipitate a bloody servile uprising. Agents were already rumored at work. The Federalists, partly from fear, partly in an attempt to weaken Republican political support in the south, whipped up this mood, one journalist writing: "Take care, you sleepy southern fools, your negroes will probably be your masters this day twelve month." To prevent an invasion should it ever be launched, and to drive off French privateers and cruisers from the coast of the United States became the first task of the United States Navy.[1]

Within this context of defensive-mindedness and Congressional restrictions, Adams, through McHenry, shaped the navy's initial operations. The first warship ready for sea, Captain Richard Dale's *Ganges* 24, sailed from Philadelphia to patrol between the western tip of Long Island and Cape Henry, covering the major ports between New York and Norfolk. When Captain Thomas Truxtun had outfitted and manned his command, the Baltimore frigate *Constellation* 36, he cruised between Cape Henry and the St. Marys River, the southern border of the United States and Spanish Florida. Having established a southern, central, and, by default, still unprotected northern sector, McHenry turned over control to Stoddert, who retained this basic coastal division. The northern patrol sector was soon established extending from Georges Bank to the eastern tip of Long Island, protecting the important New England fisheries and the major ports between Portsmouth, New Hampshire, and Long Island Sound. Between May and November 1798 the bulk of the American navy was deployed defensively within these three coastal sectors.[2]

The effort expended patrolling the coast during 1798 was worthwhile, even though no invasion was coming and few privateers were captured off the American shore. Simple possession of a naval force served to scare most French privateers away from America's Atlantic outlets. Also, the activity was useful for the ships and men of the navy. As warships were outfitted and sent to sea, usually for the first time, they patrolled off a friendly coast only days from their home ports. Officers and men had time to work out the daily routines of naval life on board strange new ships. Captains exercised their crews, many of whom, even if good seamen (which most were not), were without military experience. All of this was accomplished in an atmosphere where little threat of combat existed. While this proved a disappointment for many officers and men, it was ultimately fortunate, for many of the navy's ships put to sea as anything but well-honed fighting machines. Even the limited experience gained in these early patrols was worth the effort, especially the establishment of routines for convoying. The months between May and November 1798 became a necessary shakedown period for the navy. Its commanders had much to learn about themselves, their men, their ships, and their enemy.[3]

2. *The Stopgap Navy*

Richard Dale was appointed to command the *Ganges* 24, on 11 May 1798, that same day being advised by McHenry that the ship was to be at sea "in the course of a week." That was expecting much, for the *Ganges* had become a warship only eight days earlier, having been purchased in Philadelphia by agents of the government for $58,000. Previously, as her name might imply, she had been an East Indiaman, a merchant ship designed to carry cargo, not guns. But the choice to purchase and convert the *Ganges* for use in the naval service was wisely made. The ship was only three-years-old, of fair size, and well able to mount over twenty cannon, a number of which she already carried. While hopes that the ship would be ready for sea within a week were unfounded, and exemplified McHenry's poor understanding of naval affairs, if anyone could get *Ganges* out to sea with alacrity it was Dale, who had been her master in her former service. Dale knew the *Ganges* thoroughly, a knowledge that combined with his Revolutionary War experience stood the former merchantman in good stead.[4]

During the Revolution, Dale had a varied, if at times unlucky, career. Captured by the British on three occasions, he landed in the infamous Mill prison twice. His most notable experiences were with John Barry in the *Lexington* and in the *Bonhomme Richard,* where Dale served as John Paul Jones's first lieutenant.[5]

In 1794 George Washington named Dale captain of one of the six frigates begun that year as a response to the depredations of the Algerines. When work on his ship was halted in 1796, Dale had already resumed his career as a merchant master. His recall to the naval service of the United States in 1798, along with his ship, was symbolic of the situation facing the country. The logical response to the French *querre de course* against American commerce would take a naval form, but in early 1798 there was no American navy. The last ship of the Continental Navy was sold off in 1785 and the ships of the state navies met their end with the adoption of the Federal Constitution. Of the six frigates begun in 1794, only three were anywhere near completion, and three frigates, however powerful, were not sufficient to challenge the French on the seas.[6]

Both the executive branch and the Congress understood that additional ships would be needed to supplement the frigates. While newly constructed ships, smaller than frigates, were desired, such vessels could not be ready well into 1799. But a large number of ships were needed immediately, in 1798, and as a stopgap the administration decided they would have to be purchased. The *Ganges* was one of the first.[7]

Warships were not available at short notice on the eighteenth-century market. The divergence of warship and merchantman design of vessels rating below frigates, however, did not preclude the use of the latter in a naval role. The difference between war and merchant vessels in the machine age is clear and distinct, but variations in the age of sail did not prevent the speedy conversion of a cargo-carrier into a weapon of war. As a rule, merchant ships were cut to carry guns and were occasionally armed.

During the course of the Quasi-War the United States relied heavily on converted ships. Eight merchantmen were purchased and modified: the ships *Ganges* 24, *George Washington* 24, *Baltimore* 20, *Montezuma* 20, *Delaware* 20, and *Herald* 18; and the brigs *Norfolk* 18, and *Augusta* 14. The citizens of Norfolk, Manchester, Petersburg, and Richmond, Virginia, purchased an additional brig by subscription for the government, the *Richmond* 18.[8]

These transmuted trading vessels varied greatly in size and performance. The ship *Herald,* for example, measured 279 tons and carried 140 men and 22 guns. The larger *George Washington* 24, actually mounted 32 cannon, measured 629 tons, and was manned by a crew of 220. These dimensions are comparable to the smaller class of frigates completed during 1799, such as the *Adams* 28, which carried 28 guns, measured 530 tons, and was crewed by 220 men. No wonder contemporaries, and some historians, refer to the *George Washington* as a frigate.[9]

The performance of the vessels differed from ship to ship. The *George Washington, Montezuma,* and *Herald* were considered dull sailers. The others performed adequately, while the *Augusta* was judged a fine brig. Four were so unsuited for naval service that the department decided to sell them off during the war, the *Montezuma* in 1799, and the *Norfolk,* only two years old but rotting badly, in 1800. Circumstances intervened to prevent the final sale of the *George Washington* and *Herald* before the war's end. Nevertheless, none of the purchased ships were worth keeping, and all were eventually turned over to the auctioneer.[10]

There were two main causes for the uneven quality of the vessels. First, in haste to buy a stopgap navy, the government paid for ships ill-suited for conversion. In some cases, such as the *Ganges*'s, a skilled and trusted man with naval experience could be relied upon to pass fair judgment on the qualities of a ship; in the latter case, one he would have to command himself. But in other instances, naval agents earning commissions were too ready to suggest purchase. Also, many of the men appointed to captain the ships lost sight of the limitations of their commands. Not built for war, the ships were not expected to excel as warships, but few captains were eager to admit that theirs was but a hastily transformed cargo ship. Yearning for glory in action with the French, many captains hauled on board extra ordnance in an attempt to increase broadside power. A few ordered extensive remodeling in an effort to make a vessel better fit their conception of what a warship ought to be; remodeling that exceeded the demands of utility, yet work local navy agents were often eager to perform. Too frequently commanders lost sight of the original goal of quick conversion and outfitting for sea, and the result was the ruination of whatever sailing qualities many ships possessed.

An illustrative incident occurred in the fall of 1799. In June, Stoddert decided that the *Herald,* a dull and unsuccessful ship, would be sold. As a replacement he purchased the *Augusta* brig at Norfolk, which he ordered to Boston where the crew and equipment of the *Herald* would be transferred to her.

Captain Thomas Truxtun and Norfolk naval agent William Pennock examined the *Augusta* at Norfolk and judged her "nearly perfect in hull, masts and spars . . . and the best calculated vessel for a West India cruiser ever built in Norfolk." Admittedly, both the Truxtun and Will Pennock were close friends of the *Augusta's* owner, Moses Myers. Despite the evident overstatement, the Norfolk brig was superior to the *Herald.* On arrival at Boston, however, Stoddert learned that the *Augusta* had "lost all her good qualities." Both the commander of the *Herald,* Lieutenant Charles C. Russell, and the Boston navy agent, Stephen Higginson, declared the brig unfit, recommending alterations to the *Herald* instead. To Stoddert, something seemed "strange." When Myers heard of the trouble in Boston he took the view that "Russell expected he was to have a brig of 500 tons to carry 36 pounders and would rather sacrifice his judgement to his pride in going out in a ship to a brig. . . ." Stoddert had reached the same conclusion, writing Higginson that the *Augusta* was "not so large and therefore not so agreeable to Captain Russell as the *Herald.*" Stoddert refused to allow the proposed modifications of the ship and threatened to replace Russell in command if he refused to go out in the *Augusta.* Stoddert also noted that he "understood the *Herald* was a good vessel until she was ruined by alterations in her," a direct slap at Higginson who had performed the modifications.

Stoddert, however, was forced to "yield" to the Bostonians, clearly against his wishes, under political pressures not defined in the secretary's correspondence. He made clear that he did so "not with a good grace." Minor alterations were allowed, but in the "cheapest mode" and as soon as practicable. Russell remained in command. The *Augusta* Stoddert ordered to Philadelphia to be examined anew by Joshua Humphreys under Stoddert's own eye. The secretary remained convinced that the *Herald* would "prove to be a dull vessel and . . . the *Augusta* . . . a fine cruiser." And so it proved to be. The brig Humphreys judged fit for service. *Augusta* rendered excellent service in the Caribbean. The *Herald* remained dull and as unsuccessful as ever.[11]

From the *Augusta-Herald* affair, one can get some idea of the amount of unnecessary and even counterproductive alterations of purchased vessels. In all but a few cases Stoddert, and McHenry and Wolcott before him, had to trust the local navy agent and vessel commander. Rarely was there a second opinion to guide the secretary. Yet Stoddert was forced to acquiesce and allow waste and delay in wartime for partisan political gain. That it went against his character is clear, for the incident was not forgotten. After the affair, Stoddert no longer addressed correspondence to his Boston agent Stephen Higginson personally, as he had since June 1798. Henceforth letters from the Navy Department were sent to Stephen Higginson & Co. And Stoddert had his revenge on Russell as well. When the *Herald* (in the secretary's eyes at least) was slow returning to duty, Russell was relieved of command and ordered to report to the *Experiment*, a schooner smaller than the *Herald* or *Augusta*, where the former commander would find himself serving under another lieutenant. Russell managed to sail before these orders caught up with him and thus escaped Stoddert's wrath. After the war, however, Russell was not included among the lieutenants retained under the peace establishment. His career was over.[12]

Overarming was another related problem plaguing the young American navy. While warships normally carried additional cannon beyond their official rates, smaller ships, especially converted merchantmen, were not meant to mount more than a few, if any, extra guns. Yet by the time the *George Washington* 24, put to sea, she carried thirty-two guns; the *Baltimore* 20, twenty-four; the *Delaware* 20, twenty-four; and the *Herald* 18, twenty-two.

As merchant vessels, the ships were designed to carry weight low, in their holds. Carrying heavy guns on their decks, let alone extra cannon, changed the lines of many ships. What may have been a fine sailing vessel with cargo, could prove to be a dull sailer with cannon. There were no good reasons for the ships to be overarmed. The purchased vessels were not expected to stand up and fight the warships of the French navy; that was the job of the frigates. The converted ships were to engage the small, fast, lightly armed French privateers—speed, not firepower, was needed. Stoddert recognized that extra cannon frequently inhibited the ships from performing their missions. He took the sensible position that a vessel ought to carry only as many guns as it could without affecting its sailing qualities. The rating of a ship was not sacrosanct; every gunport did not have to be filled. Stoddert wrote James Sever, the first captain of the *Herald* 18, that his ship would be better off carrying sixteen guns and fewer men than the twenty-two cannon Sever had dragged on board.[13]

Captain's reports confirmed the results of overarming. The over-gunned *Montezuma,* chasing small, speedy privateers under full sail, was unable to work her main deck guns and was reduced to reliance on musketry. Captain Alexander Murray complained that his guns rode "too low."

Stoddert was concerned enough that he wrote a shipwright in Alexandria, under contract to the navy, that the ship being built "carry 18-9 pounders to advantage, and no more . . . I mention these particulars because our Capts. are frequently fond of overloading their vessels with useless guns. . . ."[14]

Despite their shortcomings, the purchased ships played an important role at a critical time for the United States Navy. Of the twenty-two ships of the service operational at any time during 1798, eight were former merchantmen, filling the gap between the three frigates completed during the year and the small revenue cutters pressed into the naval service. While the frigates provided the backbone of the navy, the converted ships furnished the muscle.

* * *

The honor of becoming the first operational warship of the reborn American navy fell to the *Ganges*. Although unable to sail within the week McHenry hoped for, Captain Richard Dale's drive to ready his ship must be admired in the light of subsequent delays that plagued the outfitting and refitting of ships over the course of the war. Dale made no unnecessary alterations in the *Ganges,* and left the capital with over 200 men and twenty-six 9-pounders before the end of May.

After dropping down the Delaware from Philadelphia, Dale sailed into the bay on 30 May 1798. The weather was poor, a fresh northeast wind driving rain onto the deck. But Dale had heard of a French privateer about, and foul weather was not going to keep him from sea. He wanted not only to be the first out, but also the first to meet and beat the French.

Dale was disappointed. "Some *dam rascal*" leaked word of the *Ganges* sailing, and the privateer, if one had existed, fled. Dale's crew also disillusioned him: "A number of them shipped for seamen, is not much better than landsmen." Without any Frenchmen to pursue, there was little to be done except patrol, activity that cooled Dale's ardor. The *Ganges* sailed between Cape Henry and Long Island, within a marine league of the coast, with lookouts' eyes strained for the masts of a French vessel behaving "unlawfully."[15]

3. The New Frigates

While Dale cruised off Delaware Bay his third week out of Philadelphia, another captain was leaving the Chesapeake to take up station along the southern coast. Dale and Thomas Truxtun first met in Lorient, France, in October 1780, when Truxtun was master of the privateer *Independence* and Dale was the first lieutenant in John Paul Jones's *Ariel* 20, of the Continental Navy. The *Ariel* had been dismasted and nearly lost in a gale and returned to port to find Truxtun's privateer flying a broad pendant, forbidden by Congressional regulations on privateers in the presence of ships of the national navy. When Truxtun refused to lower the pendant, Jones dispatched two boat loads of armed men, commanded by young Richard Dale, to force acquiescence. Truxtun yielded, though only temporarily. The pendant was soon flying again, for the privateer master held little esteem for the Continental Navy.

There was some irony that Truxtun, the privateersman, now became the first captain to take to sea one of the new frigates, the pride of the young service. Truxtun was the most junior of the six captains originally appointed to command in 1794. Those senior to him all had held national commissions during the Revolution. Truxtun, who had not, was included because of his fine reputation for command and skill earned both during the war and over the following decade. He was one of perhaps a dozen Americans who could determine his longitudinal position at sea without the use of a chronometer (then neither widely used nor available) but through observation of the position of the moon relative to the sun or a fixed star. It was an involved and difficult process of calculation beyond many mariners. Truxtun followed up his appointment with the publication that same year of a book on navigation which he was kind enough, and proud enough, to send to his fellow captains. He also developed a theory for the masting of ships that he suggested for the frigates, but which proved unacceptable to the other commanders. In 1797 he wrote a book on signals, which was adopted for the navy's use. Truxtun gave much thought to the infant navy of the United States and believed that it was extremely important that the service benefit from strong leadership and as much uniformity as could be established. He did this not in spite of the feelings he had exhibited at Lorient, but because of them. He was determined that the new navy, and especially his ship and person, would demand, deserve, and receive the respect that he had withheld from Jones in 1780.[16]

The *Constellation* 36, cleared the Virginia Capes on 23 June 1798. McHenry's orders instructed Truxtun to patrol the coast between Cape Henry and the St. Marys. Like Dale, Truxtun was eager to "pay my respects" to the "piratical Junto" threatening American commerce. His zeal, a source of trouble on several later occasions, was already evident. He wrote his friend Charles Biddle that although authorized to strike only at French cruisers, should the *Constellation* "meet a fat merchantman, or a neutral covering French property, it will seem hard to let such pass." Evidently, the privateersman in Truxtun was dying hard.[17]

Whatever his hopes for early action, Truxtun discovered that more mundane tasks awaited his talent of command. Ship and crew had to be exercised, and only time and hard work could make of the two an efficient sailing and fighting instrument. As with all of the new frigates, great size made heavy demands on captains who had never commanded anything as large. Like Dale, Truxtun found no Frenchmen. Instead patrolling and convoying took up the *Constellation's* time as Truxtun slowly rid the crew of certain of its members, "rotten inanimate animals that found their way into the ship."[18]

All such men were not easily discovered. Early in July rumors of "mutinous assemblies" reached Truxtun's ears. Indiscipline even spread to the marines when one leatherneck insolently assailed his sergeant and tried to wrestle a pistol from him. On 2 July, a Monday, the Articles of War, normally read on Sunday, were read to the assembled crew. The marine was flogged at the gangway. Coincidently, as Truxtun was reading the articles to his crew, Stoddert was writing the captain a letter warning him of a "spirit of mutiny" in the frigate. The secretary of the navy enclosed with his letter one given him by the Speaker of the House, written by a crewman in the *Constellation,* that spoke of unrest and possible mutiny.[19]

The troubles in the ship were caused in part by men unaccustomed to naval discipline, and in part by Truxtun's style of command. He was not a brutal captain; he preferred withholding rum rations to flogging men. But Truxtun was demanding and held himself in high esteem. He realized that he was driving his crew too hard, for he gradually relaxed certain conditions in the *Constellation,* but only as he regained his grip on the crew's loyalty.[20]

The "spirit of mutiny" that drifted as far away as Philadelphia Truxtun found to have been helped along by a seaman named Hugh Williams. Truxtun's search of troublemakers in the frigate led to his discovery in August that Williams was in fact John Watson, one of the mutineers who slew the infamous Captain Hugh Pigot and seized His Majesty's frigate *Hermione* 32, off Puerto Rico in September 1797. Watson was put ashore as soon as possible and turned over to the British for court-martial.[21]

The *Constellation,* one of six frigates laid down in 1794, would soon be joined at sea by the *United States* 44, outfitting at Philadelphia, and the *Constitution* 44, at Boston. These frigates were destined to become the objects of much acclaim earned by their service during the War of 1812. It was during the Quasi-War, however, that many of the various problems that plagued them were worked out.[22]

The implementation of Congress's decision to build six frigates in 1794 fell to the then secretary of war, Henry Knox, a landlubber. Knox recognized his own limitations and absence of naval expertise and turned to more experienced friends and acquaintances for advice. Fortunately, despite his lack of naval competence and the political favoritism evident in the rewarding of contracts, the shipwrights to whom the responsibility for design and construction fell were competent men.

Joshua Humphreys, a Philadelphia Quaker, emerged as the central figure in the American shipbuilding program of 1794, becoming chief naval constructor that May. Humphreys was not the preeminent American shipwright he is often made out to be. Although a capable practitioner of his craft, he was not even the foremost Philadelphia shipwright. He owed his appointment to the location of his yard in the capital, his interest in building warships, his work on and construction of ships for the Continental Navy, and his cousin John Wharton's friendship with Knox.[23]

Humphreys's main impact on the early American navy was theoretical, rather than practical. He assumed that an American navy would be small, with ships no larger than fifth rates—frigates. Given their cruising and scouting roles in naval warfare, frigates usually engaged the enemy in single ship encounters. In such contests "it would be an equal chance by equal combat, that we loose [sic] our ships. . . . Unable to match European numbers, a small American Navy would face eventual extermination. Lacking quantity, an American force would need quality, frigates strong enough to "overmatch" European frigates, but fast enough to escape from European ships of the line. "Frigates will be the first object and none ought to be built less than 150 feet keel to carry 28 32-pounders or 30 24-pounders on the main gun deck and twelve pounders on the quarter deck. Those ships should have scantlings equal to 74's [the standard third-rate ship of the time]. . . ." One author terms Humphreys's conception a "pocket battleship theory"; "pocket ship of the line" might be a more fitting if somewhat cumbersome appellation. Essentially, the American frigates were designed for the role that latter-day battlecruisers filled during the Dreadnought era, that of supercruisers. Humphreys's thinking was in that sense revolutionary.[24]

The actual design of the frigates remained, however, evolutionary. While the design of ships of the line reached a stage of equilibrium during the period 1763–1815, the standard liner being the third-rate seventy-four, frigates continued to be built larger, stronger, and faster sailing, reaching stasis only with the American fifth-rates. British frigates of the 1790s were mostly twenty-eight and thirty-two-gun ships, measuring between 600 and 1,000 tons. Even the larger frigates that faced the Americans in the War of 1812 were significantly weaker than those of the United States. Comparisons with the British, however, can be misleading, for they lagged behind other maritime powers in some areas of ship design. The French were the first to build a frigate mounting 24-pounder cannon, the *Pomone* 44, 1,239 tons, completed shortly before the beginning of war in 1793.

Most French frigates were weaker than the *Pomone,* but larger and stronger than British-built models. Even the *Pomone,* however, cannot be compared with an American forty-four, although the forty and thirty-six gun French frigates were capable of challenging the smaller American thirty-six gun frigates.[25]

When completed, the American frigates were to be the strongest fifth-rates on the seas. The forty-fours, 1,576 tons, were to carry thirty 24-pounders on the gundeck and twenty-two 42-pounder carronades on the quarterdeck and forecastle. The thirty-sixes, 1,287 tons, were to carry twenty-eight 18-pounders on the gundeck, and twenty 32-pounder carronades on the quarterdeck and forecastle. The frigates were able to mount so many guns for two reasons. First, greater length allowed more ports and cannon on the gundeck. Second, the frigates had a unique spardeck construction. Normally the quarterdeck and forecastle of frigates were connected by narrow gangways on either side of the ship that permitted passage between the fore and aft decks without descending onto the crowded gundeck. But on the American frigates, the gangways were wide and strong. Cannon could be mounted on them, essentially creating a second gundeck. The American frigates possessed great defensive strength as well as firepower. They were constructed of live oak, a wood superior to both New England white oak and English oak for warship construction. Tough live oak frames, equal in dimensions to those of British ships of the line, would earn for the *Constitution* the nickname "Old Ironsides."[26]

So, as Truxtun cleared the Virginia Capes with the first of these new ships to sail, he was in command of a formidable fighting vessel. But just as the quality of his crew was suspect, so too was that of his ship. The lore that surrounds the early American navy has masked a number of problems that made the frigates the subject of contemporary criticism. Stoddert, for example, took office unconvinced of the superiority of the American designs and considered it still to be determined if they were better "than the size adopted by the British nation."[27]

Size was the main problem. A wooden vessel could bear a limited amount of strain and that extreme was nearly reached with the long, sharp hulls of the American ships. The frigates tended to "hog" or "humpback," the ship's hull bending in such a manner that the bow and stern were lower than the amidships. Such continual motion gradually worked the timbers apart, and during the first cruise of the *Constellation* Truxtun noted that both her decks and outside works were coming asunder and needed to be caulked anew. He attributed the condition to the caulking of the ship during winter, but the problem was rooted in design and construction. The *Constellation* was too narrow for her length, and ultimately would be rebuilt and widened by fourteen inches.[28]

The deep draught of the frigates was another design-related problem. The *Constellation,* one of the smaller, drew twenty-two feet of water, making it impossible for her to enter any American port south of the Chesapeake. The narrowness of the ships also limited storage space. Truxtun wrote: "the *Constellation* being so uncommonly sharp, we have in proportion to that sharpness, less room in the hold, than frigates of other nations." He found it impossible to stow the six months of provisions he was expected to carry. "Three or four months' full allowance of provisions and water, is as much as this ship will carry, and then she will be very much down in the water for sailing fast."29

The problems Truxtun discovered during his first voyage were rooted in design. There were costs to be paid in any scheme where speed, space, and power competed. None of the problems were, however, so insurmountable that the frigates could be judged failures. In fact, the existing difficulties, while design-related, were being exacerbated by inexperienced American officers who were their own worst enemies. While all were veteran seamen, none had ever commanded so large a vessel. Charged with overseeing both the construction and outfitting of their ships, captains such as Truxtun held discretionary power to spar, rig, and arm them as they saw fit. With myriad variables at play in fitting out the frigates, no two were alike. One historian of the early navy writes that "some of the American naval officers appear as surprisingly pompous and opinionated amateur ship designers, whose ill-judged decisions spoiled the reputations of many well modeled ships." Captain John Barry, for example, had a roundhouse constructed on the quarterdeck of the *United States* (rumor had it to house his wife better in port), giving the ship a nice poop deck for a captain to strut, a fine cabin for a commodore, but somewhat different sailing qualities than her sisters the *Constitution* and *President.* The *United States* would eventually earn the sobriquet "Old Waggoner."30

Truxtun was responsible for a great many of his own problems. The extreme heeling of the *Constellation* was the result of the more than ample sparring that he bragged about. His frigate carried substantially longer masts and yards than her sister, the *Congress.* Truxtun also overgunned the ship, further increasing the tendency of the frigate to roll and straining the timbers. Instead of 18-pounders, Truxtun mounted 24-pounders, each weighing an extra 1,200 pounds, totaling sixteen additional tons for the entire suite. In his first major engagement he found that his oversparred, overgunned frigate heeled to such an extent in the strong wind, that the lee guns could not be worked, forcing him to run under his opponent's lee, not a favorite maneuver in the age of sail.31

Truxtun's example demonstrates the extent to which captains could cause themselves additional problems. He outfitted his frigate in such a manner that she was top-heavy and at risk in battle. The added weight also affected the ships's draught (the much larger *Constitution* drew only twenty-three feet), and strained the construction of the vessel. Time and experience would allow the frigates to achieve their full potential. Isaac Hull, a lieutenant in the *Constitution* during the Quasi-War, commanded that ship in 1812 knowing well her strengths and weaknesses. Also, by 1812, it was clear that the authorized armament of the frigates placed too great a strain on the midsection. Neither cannon nor carronades were mounted by that time in the three gunports amidships on the spar deck. There were a great many such lessons to be learned during the course of the war with France.[32]

4. First Blood

While Dale and Truxtun patrolled the American coast protecting merchantmen but never catching a glimpse of a French vessel, a ship destined to be the first to meet the French neared the end of her preparation for sea. Purchased on 5 May 1798 in Philadelphia, the *Hamburgh Packet* was another merchant vessel impressed into the naval service. Renamed the *Delaware,* the ship measuring 321 tons was placed under the command of forty-six-year old Stephen Decatur, Sr., a Philadelphian whose early service was also in privateers. Stoddert, who by then had taken up the reins of the Navy Department, ordered Decatur late in June to take the *Delaware* 20, and join Dale's *Ganges* patrolling the coast between Long Island and Cape Henry.[33]

After quelling a disturbance among black sailors quarantined in French ships being held near Fort Mifflin, Decatur finally sailed south leaving the river on the evening of 6 July 1798. Early the following morning he ran across an American merchant ship, the *Alexander Hamilton.* A French privateer had waylaid the ship off Little Egg Harbor, New Jersey, on the morning of 6 July. Looking for booty, rather than prizes, the French allowed the American vessel, carrying a cargo of wine and brandy from New York to Baltimore, to continue on its way, minus seven cases of wine and sundry items.[34]

When the *Alexander Hamilton* ran across the *Delaware,* Captain Wyse of the plundered ship took his complaint to Decatur. Eager to meet the French, Decatur listened attentively as Wyse explained the attack on his vessel and gave the details of the courses both he and the privateer had taken on departing. Decatur decided to backtrack along Wyse's course, sailing north along the Jersey shore. Soon, four schooners were sighted ahead. In doubt about the *Delaware's* ability to run down a speedy schooner, and uncertain about whether any of the four were French privateers, Decatur adopted a ruse. He maneuvered his ship cautiously, attempting to make the *Delaware* appear to be a wary merchantman, a role the ex-*Hamburgh Packet* was well suited to play.

One of the schooners quickly broke from the others, eager to plunder a new victim. But as the French drew near they discovered their error: the twenty-four 9 and 6-pounders and the 180 crewmen about the deck and rigging gave the *Delaware* a look no merchant ship possessed. In their haste to escape, the French erred again. They assumed the warship to be English, the Americans having heretofore no navy of their own. The schooner sheered off and headed towards Egg Harbor, hoping to escape by taking shelter in American waters. Decatur followed hard in pursuit with his quarry now cornered between the *Delaware* and the coast. After a "pretty long chase" and several shots from the American sloop of war, the French schooner struck.

Decatur got a boat away and sent a crew to take possession of the first prize of the reborn United States Navy. As the French captain climbed to the deck of the *Delaware,* he at last realized that his pursuer was not an English man-of-war violating American waters, but a warship flying the Stars and Stripes as her national ensign, rather than a *ruse de guerre*. As did most vanquished French commanders during the Quasi-War, the master of *la Croyable* remonstrated against his capture, complaining that the two republics were not at war. Decatur remained unmoved by the French pleas; he reminded his prisoner that the French had been making war on Americans for some time, and now the Yankees would take care of themselves. Much embarrassed by his capture, the French captain told Decatur that he would have gone down fighting had he known the *Delaware* to have been American. Decatur replied that he would "have been gratified if he had stood on board his vessel and fought her!"[35]

Thanks to Decatur's cunning, the navy of the United States had its first victory. Mounting only twelve guns with a crew of seventy, *la Croyable,* 107 tons, stood no chance in an engagement with the stronger *Delaware*. The significance of the victory lay in the surprised French reaction to the armed American response to the *guerre de course,* a reaction that would be repeated time and again throughout the war. There was also meaning in Decatur's conduct, marked by aggressiveness and quick thinking. Fortunately for the navy, many other American officers shared Decatur's spirit and enterprise; unfortunately, many did not.[36]

3

"OLD NAVAL OFFICERS"

-----

1. The Father of the Navy: Ailing John Barry

At dawn on 8 July 1798, Decatur made his way up the Delaware towards New Castle with his prize. Ahead in the early morning mist loomed a large frigate he recognized as the *United States* 44, commanded by the navy's senior captain, John Barry. Decatur hailed the ship, bringing Barry to the deck, and told the tale of his victory. The officers of the frigate lined the side of their ship, among them Stephen Decatur, Jr., a midshipman. Barry offered congratulations but he envied the elder Decatur's good fortune. The *United States* was under orders to cruise the same waters as the *Delaware*. Though plagued by delays, Barry had actually dropped down the river before Decatur. While the latter was making his show of force off Fort Mifflin, Barry's carpenters were feverishly at work mounting the last of the frigate's cannon. But despite their efforts, they saw the *Delaware* sail past on its way to the Capes and the rendezvous with *la Croyable*. For Barry there would be no capture, nor the share of the prize money that would have come his way as commodore had he managed to leave the river.[1]

From the first, ill-fortune stalked the *United States*. Near disaster marked her launching, and she suffered hull damage and had to be careened. During the summer of 1797, yellow fever swept through Philadelphia, struck the men on the frigate, and brought all outfitting to a halt. There followed a bitter winter and more delays. With the coming of spring work resumed and preparations neared completion, but an annoyed Barry found his mighty frigate still unarmed.[2]

Barry's problems were atypically severe, but they were indicative of conditions facing the American military establishment, and particularly the navy, throughout what McHenry termed "a season of difficulty." In 1794 the War Department had contracted with foundries to produce heavy cannon for fortifications and naval guns and carronades for the frigates. Only half of the guns produced passed proofing tests. The technology of casting carronades found its way from Europe to Henry Foxall's Eagle Furnace in Philadelphia, but by the spring of 1798 not a single carronade had been produced to line the spar decks of the American frigates. With plans for army and fortification expansion afoot, with the demands for cannon and naval stores to outfit the warships built for the Dey of Algiers, with ten revenue cutters building for the Treasury Department, with purchased vessels such as the *Ganges* and *Delaware* outfitting, and with new naval construction planned, American military manufacturers were unable to produce sufficient quantities of acceptable ordnance.[3]

Nevertheless, there were many cannon about the country, old guns from the Revolution, new American cannon, and recent imports. Effective administration could have managed the shortage. There were certainly enough cannon in the United States to have armed the few ships actually ready to sail in the late spring of 1798. But McHenry's almost total lack of coordination worsened the situation. There ensued a mad scramble for guns in which captains were left to their own devices. Twelve 24-pounders that passed proofing at Samuel Hughes's Cecil Furnace in Maryland were quickly grabbed by Truxtun, who decided to fit-out his frigate with the larger cannon. Whether this was due to a lack of available 18-pounders or a desire to up-gun his ship remains unclear. The 18-pounders were dearer than 24-pounders in the spring of 1798. For his upper deck battery, the War Department advised Truxtun that he was on his own and had best look for 12-pounders on the Baltimore market.[4]

Barry's search for cannon proved more difficult. Beaten to the draw by Truxtun, Barry found the next batch of 24-pounders totally unacceptable and in his search for substitutes no help was forthcoming from McHenry. The ailing captain was put on the trail of cannon when his convalescent surgeon, Dr. George Gillasspy of New York City, discovered twenty-six 24-pounders on Governor's Island in November 1797. Unfortunately, four months passed before Barry's repeated pleas for help moved McHenry to write Governor John Jay requesting their use. Barry had already gone to New York and tested the guns, new cannon cast by a Connecticut foundry, before McHenry and Jay finally agreed on the terms of a loan. The guns were at last delivered to the *United States* on 18 May 1798, six months after Gillasspy located them.[5]

The War Department proved of some help in finding 12-pounders for Barry's frigate, in lieu of carronades. Early in April 1798 McHenry informed Barry that a number of the smaller guns were at the fort at Point Whetstone in Baltimore harbor, but McHenry did little to expedite their movement to the Delaware. When Stoddert began his duties as secretary, he found Barry's 12-pounders still at Whetstone and made their delivery his first object. Within a week the guns were on board the frigate at New Castle.[6]

On assuming responsibility for the nation's naval affairs, Stoddert found that cannon were but one of several items—copper, canvas, hemp, gun-powder, muskets, and edged weapons—in short supply. Importation, par-ticularly from Great Britain, substantially supplemented domestic production. The policy of the War Department under Knox, Pickering, and McHenry had been to foster the development of American arms manufacturers. The foundries, however, failed to meet the government's expectations, necessitating importation. Despite these failures, Congress, the administration, and Stoddert decided to continue the War Depart-ment's policy, hoping that in the long run the United States would possess its own source of weapons, In the meantime, the administration looked abroad.[7]

The extent of American reliance on Britain for ordnance is difficult to determine with accuracy. Other than a June 1798 acknowledgment by McHenry to Congress that guns had entered the United States "from different countries," there is little documentation of importation before the establishment of the Department of the Navy. In July 1798, however, Secretary of the Treasury Oliver Wolcott, Jr., deposited £45,686 with Messrs. Baring & Company and instructed Rufus King, American minister to the Court of St. James, to spend £6,000 on "equal numbers of 24, 18, 12, 9, 6, & 4:pounders" for the navy, and £4,000 on cannon for the army. King ultimately purchased 370 cannon from Woolwich arsenal, of which about 225 were for the naval service. Additional guns, however, were imported privately, for resale to the government. The majority of the carronades that entered the navy during the Quasi-War were British ordnance imported in this manner. Probably between 300 and 400 cannon and carronades were imported for the United States Navy from Great Britain between 1797 and 1801. Considering that the navy at its peak strength in 1800 carried 900 guns, at least one-third, and perhaps as many as one-half of the naval guns in use were British.[8]

Yet as early as 1800 Stoddert felt confident enough to report to Con-gress: "The manufacture of cannon, and indeed of all kinds of arms, and military stores, is now so well established in the United States, that no want of them can be experienced in future, nor does it appear essential that large supplies of them should be laid up in store for the navy service." Jeremiah Yellott, the navy agent at Baltimore, found himself stuck with imported muskets and swords "inferior to those made in the United States." Since the navy no longer had need for the foreign-made weapons, Stoddert suggested that the laws be waived to permit Yellott to re-export them.[9]

What began as a wartime shortage became an arms surplus for three reasons. First, Stoddert more effectively administered existing resources. Second, the war provided an incentive of its own for arms manufacturers to produce more weapons. Third, Stoddert continued the policy of supporting American suppliers. Their performance between 1794 and 1798 had been poor, and high proportions of cannon failed to pass proofing tests; obligations were not met. But Stoddert continued to offer contracts to cannon foundries in the hope that in time their expertise would improve and the country would possess its own, secure, and dependable arms industry. Stoddert's expectations were justified. By the end of the Quasi-War quality cannon and carronades were being cast in sufficient numbers at several locations.[10]

*   *   *

With the battery of the *United States* at last complete, Stoddert ordered Barry to cruise with Dale's *Ganges* between Cape Henry and Long Island. Barry boarded his frigate at New Castle amidst much fanfare on the 4th of July. For three days he hastened to ready his ship for sea, righting the myriad minor problems that had gone undetected because of his absence gun-hunting at the seat of government. Early on the morning of the 7th, the *United States* weighed anchor and began her descent of the Delaware.[11]

At noon, while tacking in the channel, the frigate's green crew missed stays and the ship grounded. They struggled for over three hours before freeing the frigate. Fortunately, only the pride of Barry and his men were damaged. Even the embarrassment could have been worse, for it was dawn of the next morning when Barry met Decatur coming up river with his prize.

Shortly afterwards, pilot boats carrying dispatches from the capital hailed both ships. Stoddert was making new plans based upon pending Congressional action that would extend the area open to American naval operations and he wished the *United States* and *Delaware* to remain close at hand. On Monday, 9 July 1798, Adams signed an act permitting American men of war and privateers to strike at French armed ships anywhere on the seas. With these new powers, fresh instructions were soon on their way from the Navy Department to all captains, and accompanying Barry's and Decatur's were detailed orders for a new operation.[12]

Even with only a handful of ships available, Stoddert was eager to display American force in the Caribbean. French privateers were most active there, and the corsairs off the American coast sailed from Antilles bases. While it was too early to hope to crush the privateers at their source, Stoddert believed it to be possible to let the French know that the United States possessed both the will and the ability to carry the war to the islands. Stoddert's sources of intelligence, essentially whatever informa- tion reached the Navy Department from insurers, merchants, seamen, and the British, indicated that French naval forces in the Caribbean were weak. There were only "three light frigates" in the Antilles, he assured Barry, and they were anxious only to escape the British blockade at Cap François and make a run for France. At large in the Caribbean were only small privateers, incapable of challenging the mighty *United States*. Stod- dert wrote Barry that "a small squadron, under the command of an officer of your intelligence, experience & bravery might render essential service, & animate your country to enterprise, by picking up a number of prizes in the short cruise to the islands."

Barry was first to sail to Nantasket Roads, Boston, with the *Delaware,* where he would rendezvous with the *Herald* 18, and the Newburyport cutter *Pickering* 14. The squadron was then to sail southeast, to a position three or four degrees windward of Barbados, then northwesterly, keeping to the windward of Martinique, Guadeloupe, and Antigua. Barry was also to "look into" San Juan and cruise for two or three days off the southern coast of Puerto Rico. In San Juan, Barry was informed, the American ship *New Jersey* and a number of seamen were being held by Spanish au- thorities. He was given a letter to deliver to the royal governor of the island in an effort to gain their release. Barry was even given advice on his tactical order. He was to keep his vessels spread out to better their chances of contacting enemy privateers, but to keep the ships, "within protecting distance of the whole." The squadron, Stoddert hoped, could complete its operations and return to the American coast two months after leaving Boston.

While Barry's instructions were fairly detailed, Stoddert was wise enough to realize that he could not direct operations within the Caribbean from Philadelphia. Barry was given the authority to act as he saw fit, in keeping with the main goals of the operation: "The object of the enterprise is, to do as much injury to the armed vessels . . . of France, & to make as many captures as possible, consistently with a due regard (& more than a due regard you will not suffer to be paid) to the security of our own—and you will use your best means to accomplish this object." Barry was free to depart from his instructions, if "expedient or necessary." Even the two months' time allotted the cruise was not rigid. Stoddert wrote that the length of the operation would "depend upon such a variety of circum-

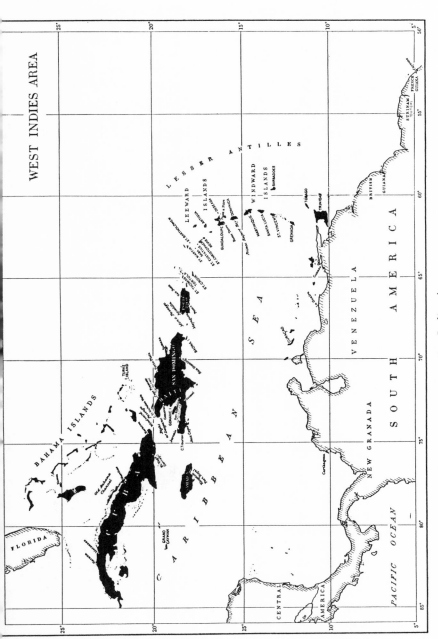

West Indies Area

stances, that no accurate judgment can be formed of the time of your return."[13]

Passing between Capes May and Henlopen on 13 July, Barry set out on the initial leg of the first sortie into the sea that would soon become the center of the American war effort. Sailing fast, Barry anchored at Nantasket Roads on 20 July, a journey somewhat slowed by the *Delaware,* which was unable to keep pace with the *United States* despite the latter's sprung foretopmast.[14]

Waiting for Barry at Boston were additional instructions from Stoddert and another letter to be delivered to the governor of Puerto Rico, this one from Secretary of State Pickering. Stoddert had written Barry to order him not to wait for the *Pickering* should she be delayed, but the word at Boston was that neither the cutter nor the *Herald* were prepared for the cruise. Barry decided that it served no purpose to delay longer than it took to repair his foretop, and prepared to sail for the Caribbean with only the *Delaware.* Barry was off to a good start with the secretary, who when he learned of the commodore's decision termed it "not to be regretted" and gave his approbation.[15]

On 26 July Barry and Decatur set sail for Barbados. Six days out of Boston near Bermuda, a sail was sighted shortly after noon bearing southsouthwest. Flying from the masthead was the tricolor flag of the French republic. Both the *United States* and *Delaware,* which took up a position on Barry's lee, cleared for action. Raising a French flag of his own, Barry adroitly maneuvered to gain the weather guage. Securing an advantageous position after several hours, he struck the French flag and ran up the American. Throughout the *United States* officers and men stood ready at their stations waiting only for Barry's order to fire, but no sooner had the American banner reached the top, than the other ship ran up British colors. Only by the narrowest margin had the British escaped their first taste of an American forty-four in action.[16]

The ship that Barry so nearly engaged was His Majesty's frigate *Thetis* 36, commanded by Captain Alexander Inglis Cochrane, who sixteen years later would command the forces that burned Washington. But the atmosphere that day in 1798 was quite different. Realizing their common error, Cochrane sent his boat for Barry. On board the *Thetis,* the American commodore told Cochrane of his mission. In order that future confrontation be avoided, Cochrane presented his American colleague with a copy of the British private signals for men-of-war in the West Indies. What began as a near prelude to the War of 1812, ended as a harmonious dinner gathering among quasi-allies as Cochrane, Decatur, and Barry supped on board the *United States* before parting.[17]

The remainder of the voyage south was uneventful, save for the continual efforts of Decatur to keep pace. At noon on 21 August the eastern end of Barbados was sighted. Barry sailed into Carlisle Bay, Bridgetown, where he spent only a few hours gathering the latest intelligence. Before darkness set in, the American squadron was out to sea on a course for Martinique.[18]

The following morning, Martinique bearing to the northwest, a ship was sighted. Barry ordered more sail set and signaled Decatur to join the pursuit. The chase lay eight miles ahead, running through the Martinique Passage between that island and Dominica. Not gaining quickly enough, Barry ordered the studding sails, royals, and the spanker set in an effort to run down the elusive sail before nightfall. Running before the wind, the *United States* had pulled to within range of her bow chase guns by dusk. A carefully loaded 12-pound shot was on its way, but the distance remained too great for accuracy. On raced Barry as darkness drew nearer, with the *Delaware* left far behind out of sight. About half an hour after the first attempt with the bow chaser, Barry ordered another. The range was now closer. The second shot missed, but not by much. The chase, discernible as a schooner, came to.

Out ran the boats from the frigate as Barry took possession of his first prize of the war, and the first French ship taken in the Caribbean. The captive schooner was the *Sans Pareil* 10, with eighty men on board. The Guadeloupe-based privateer had tried every trick to escape the American frigate; six of her ten guns had been thrown overboard. But as with Decatur, who found the *United States* three hours later marked by false fires, the French had been outsailed during the ten-hour chase.[19]

Only thirty-six hours after making landfall at Barbados, Barry had a prize, an auspicious start for his cruise. But he now made the first of a series of poor decisions that marred his initial operation of the Quasi-War. Having run through the Martinique Passage during the pursuit of the *Sans Pareil,* Barry and Decatur now found themselves leeward, rather then windward of the islands. A squally night and early morning made it impossible to regain any distance to windward. During the afternoon the weather cleared and Barry signaled Decatur to come to the flagship. There he informed his subordinate that he had decided to part company for four or five days. The *United States* would cruise to the windward, as ordered by Stoddert, and rejoin Decatur at St. Bartholomew (St. Barts). The *Delaware,* with the prize, would sail to the leeward of the islands on its way to the rendezvous. While Barry had the authority to act as he saw fit, his decision is questionable. Stoddert's instructions stated that the ships were to remain "within protecting distance of the whole," but Barry was now separating the two for an extended time in hostile waters. Of course, he had been informed by Stoddert that the French were weak in the

Antilles, and similar intelligence was probably gained during the brief stay at Carlisle Bay. If Barry was gambling that French action posed no threat even to the weaker *Delaware,* he was correct. Over the next five days neither ship sighted any save British and American sails. But it is also possible that Barry viewed the slower-sailing *Delaware* as a hindrance to his own operations, having left that vessel in his wake time and again. Had Stoddert wished the *United States* to sail alone, however, he would not have formed the squadron nor appointed Barry its commodore.

What makes Barry's behavior more puzzling is the track he followed after parting with Decatur. Instructed to cruise to the windward, and having told Decatur that the frigate would do just that, Barry cruised wholly to leeward of Martinique, Dominica, and Guadeloupe, essentially through the same waters traveled by Decatur. There is no mention in the journals kept on board the *United States* of any further efforts to beat to windward through either the Martinique or Dominica passages. Cruising to leeward, Barry was less likely to sight any privateers and poorly positioned to chase any he saw. Not surprisingly, he reached St. Barts on 29 August empty handed.[20]

Decatur reached St. Barts the following day. The reunited squadron sailed west for Saba, where it arrived at noon on the 30th, before being led on a chase eight miles downwind by a schooner that was brought to southwest of the island. She was a British privateer out of Tortola commanded by "an impertinent man." Barry next took the squadron to St. Croix which they reached on the morning of the 31st. Lookouts spotted a warship about 1:00 P.M. The Americans beat to quarters and spent three hours chasing His Majesty's *Perdrix* sloop of twenty-two guns.[21]

After exchanging information with the British commander, Barry had the American squadron on the move again, sailing separately for St. Thomas where they rendezvoused on the afternoon of 2 September. The Americans pressed on to Puerto Rico, sailing past San Juan during the evening. The squadron beat back to the harbor and "lay off and on" throughout the night of 3–4 September. At 6:00 A.M. Barry summoned Decatur to the flagship. Whatever the commodore had in mind was forgotten when word came from the top of another sighting. There followed a fruitless chase, but before Barry could resume the parley with his subordinate, yet another sail appeared. Barry signaled Decatur to remain off San Juan with the *Sans Pareil.* All sail was set on the frigate. Twelve hours later, Barry ran down his second prize, the French privateering sloop *la Jalouse.*[22]

Once again, however, an extended chase left Barry with a long beat to windward. In the face of contrary winds the *United States,* with the prize in tow, took two days to rejoin Decatur. Arriving off San Juan on 7

September, Barry once more summoned Decatur to the frigate. The squadron, Barry explained, would now return to Philadelphia. The provisions on board the *United States* were rotten, she needed ballast, and the hurricane season was approaching. The cruise thus far seemed unproductive, and having been advised by Stoddert to be off the American coast two months after leaving Boston, Barry considered it time to sail north. So homeward headed the squadron, the *United States* leading with *la Jalouse* in tow, followed by the *Delaware* and *Sans Pareil*.[23]

Barry passed Cape Henlopen on 18 September, anchored off Bombay Hook the following day, and made his way to the capital where he arrived on the 21st. Stoddert was aghast and wrote the president:

> Capt. Barry to my surprise made his appearance here at 1 oClock—
> His ship with about 100 Frenchmen & negros aboard he left at
> Chester. Decatur with 30 or 40 more, was following him in, with two
> prizes, a sloop & a schooner taken in the West Indies.
> Barry returned too soon—his reason, apprehensions from the hurricanes in the West Indies at this season.
> Upon the whole it is better than to have kept ships sleeping on our
> own shores. Tho' the result of the enterprise falls very far short of my
> hopes.
> [Captain Alexander] Murray, to whom I am sending orders this day,
> to proceed to the West Indies with the *Montezuma*, the brig *Norfolk*,
> and cutter *Eagle*, & the *Retaliation*, will return with more brilliancy. . . .

Stoddert was obviously disappointed, but he was also being unfair. No mention was made of Barry's rotting provisions, nor of Stoddert's own instructions regarding the length of the cruise. The secretary no doubt had forgotten a letter he had sent the president two months before in which he had written that he expected Barry to return at the end of August, by which time a second squadron would be on its way to take his place. That follow-up force, Murray's, had yet to sail, causing Stoddert a great deal of frustration and embarrassment. Although Barry had displayed less initiative than had been expected, taking two prizes in eighteen days, from the perspective of later operations during the war, was not a poor showing. Throughout the Quasi-War Stoddert harbored exaggerated expectations of the results of operations he ordered.[24]

Nevertheless, the secretary had some justification for his displeasure and the whole episode is indicative of Barry's declining powers. While he adhered to the general route and length of the cruise as outlined by Stoddert, Barry failed to follow the bulk of his instructions. He cruised to the leeward rather than the windward. Twice he divided his force. He

failed to carry out his orders relative to Puerto Rico. He neither cruised off
the south coast, nor did he attempt to gain the release of the *New Jersey*
and the American seamen being held in San Juan. Stoddert had gone to the
length of drafting the letter for Barry to deliver to the governor of the
island and had included it in the commodore's instructions. There was
Secretary of State Pickering's letter, also undelivered. Stoddert's interest in
the matter should have been evident, yet Barry made no effort to send the
messages ashore while off San Juan. Stoddert had even suggested the
possibility of detaching Decatur to San Juan to handle the business, and
during Barry's chase of *la Jalouse,* Decatur had had days to contact the
Spanish had he been so ordered.[25]

Barry's concern for the approaching hurricane season also failed to
impress Stoddert. Between June and October an average of seven hurricanes swept through the Caribbean. Great tropical cyclones with winds
of force 12 or greater on the Beaufort scale were of such danger to sailing
fleets that even the renowned Royal Navy curtailed its operations during
the stormy season. Often the great ships of the British navy sailed for
North American waters in May or June, returning to the West Indies in
October when the hurricane season was over and winter weather was
approaching in the North Atlantic.[26]

For this very reason Stoddert believed that the navy of the United States
could not operate in awe of hurricanes. He wrote:

> The hurricanes I understand are not dangerous, oftener than once in
> three or four years—and then the danger is very partial, and by no
> means extends over all the West India islands, nor even many of them.
> It is the custom of British cruisers to lie still and to come into our
> harbors during the hurricane season—at least in a great degree—
> knowing this, the French cruise with less caution during that sea-
> son—knowing too, that our force on our own coasts, is superior to any
> they can send,—they will employ their cruisers more about the is-
> lands. . . .

Stoddert viewed the protection of American commerce as the immediate
task of the navy. The greatest threat to trade lay in the Caribbean, posing
special problems. "The European vessels generally avoid the islands but
our own merchants are less influenced by the hurricane months, and go to
the islands in every month and every week of the year—they will therefore
require protection, at all seasons. . . ." Therefore, a protection of commerce
was a year-round requirement for the American navy and Stoddert
doubted "whether in making arrangements for the employment of . . .
ships, [he] ought at all to consider that there are hurricanes in the West

Indies?" He wrote Adams that "under such circumstances . . . the American navy should be taught to disregard problematical dangers."[27]

While it might appear foolish to consider tropical cyclones problematical dangers, Stoddert had little choice. Safeguarding American commerce was his responsibility, and he could not fear to send his ships of war where American merchantmen sailed. Clearly there were risks involved, but Stoddert thought them negligible. He was, after all, no stranger to speculation. And during the years of the Quasi-War, only five hurricanes were recorded. Two warships did vanish without a trace, however, the cause of their loss most likely weather related.[28]

Stoddert's expectation that French privateering activity would increase with the onset of the stormy season was also correct. While two American ships were taken in the Caribbean during July and five during August, eighteen were captured during September. A few extra days spent in the Caribbean by Barry might have yielded better results. As it was, he reached Cape Henlopen eight days short of two months. At least the time could have been used to complete Stoddert's instructions regarding Puerto Rico.[29]

Whatever one's judgment of Barry, in Stoddert's eyes he had accomplished less than expected from an officer of "intelligence, experience & bravery." Excepting his decision to leave Boston without the *Herald* as well as the *Pickering,* Barry displayed little initiative or activity. Given his eagerness to return home, perhaps the drive shown at Boston was nothing more than a wish to begin a cruise that it might be finished. Was this the spirit the senior captain in the United States Navy was to instill?

Following a long voyage to China, Barry had returned in 1789 to the life of a country gentleman at his estate, Strawberry Hill, a few miles north of Philadelphia. He expected to spend his remaining years at home with his ailing wife whose only wish was that her husband not return to sea. But when in 1794 President George Washington offered Barry the position of senior captain in the reconstituted navy, his affirmative reply was on its way within the hour. When Barry left the Delaware River early in July 1798, he was an old fifty-three, gout-ridden and asthmatic.[30]

Barry's appointment was not foolishly made. As James Fenimore Cooper writes, "of all the naval captains that remained [from the Revolution], he was the one who possessed the greatest reputation for experience, conduct and skill." Barry had outlasted his rivals to the claim of fathering the American navy. But over his remaining years, Barry's powers continually declined. He was frequently ill. Even an apologetic biographer admits that although only fifty-three, Barry was prematurely aged. "His was the same clear mind . . . it was physical deterioration only." But illnesses of the body, combined with a longing for a well deserved, comfortable retirement, cannot but affect the mind as well.[31]

Barry was simply past his peak. He was not up to the physical demands of command. He was rather old to be a frigate captain. In the Royal Navy, an officer of Barry's age and seniority would have been assigned a flag-captain to look after the commodore's ship and allow the latter to concentrate on the operations of the squadron. But capable captains were in short supply. During the Quasi-War American commodores would generally sail flying "ten shilling pendants"—meaning that for his added responsibility the commodore received nothing but the honor of being able to fly the broad pendant of command.

After receiving Barry's and Decatur's reports of their cruise, Stoddert began to doubt his senior captain's ability to meet the mental demands imposed by command and to handle competently more than a single ship. Barry's squadron had consisted of but two, yet he appears to have been at a loss as to how to make best use of the *Delaware*. He treated Decatur's ship more as a hindrance to his own operations than as an asset. Barry used the *Delaware* primarily to guard the first prize, the *Sans Pareil*, which could have been sent north with a prize crew. While Stoddert's criticism of Barry's initial cruise was too harsh, it was not undeserved. Given his present state of health, the responsibility of major command was too much for John Barry. His deficiencies would become ever more apparent as the war progressed.

2. *Rapacious Sam Nicholson*

Whatever his shortcomings, the nation owed a singular debt to John Barry and his conception of duty, for behind him as second ranking captain stood Samuel Nicholson. The brother of the famed Captain James Nicholson, "the Duke of Queen Anne County" Maryland, as Samuel was known, was the oldest of the American captains of the Quasi-War at fifty-five. But unlike Barry, Nicholson's faults were related more to his character than to his age.

Nicholson's career during the Revolution was one of long and wide service. Appointed captain in the Continental Navy on 10 December 1776, he commanded the cutter *Dolphin* 10, and the frigate *Deane* 32, during a career in which he captured scores of prizes in European and West Indian waters. But late in the war several episodes cast a shadow on Nicholson's character. In 1781, while in command of the *Deane* at Boston, he refused to turn over some of his crew to Barry's *Alliance* which Robert Morris, Congress's Agent of Marine, had ordered to transport the Marquis de Lafayette and his staff to France. Morris had instructed Barry, senior to Nicholson, to take men from the *Deane* to complete his crew, but Nicholson refused, even after being shown Morris's letter, so infuriating Barry that had a procedure for arrest and court-martial in such circumstances existed, he wrote, his fellow captain would surely have been brought to trial. In a second incident the following year, Nicholson was removed from command and subjected to a court of inquiry which found him guilty of, among other things, waste of public property, dishonorable and ungentlemenly conduct, and neglect of duty. An official court-martial, however, exonerated Nicholson.[32]

Despite the acquittal, Nicholson's conduct towards the end of the war was less than exemplary. He had problems with his junior officers and was occasionally unwilling to obey the orders of his seniors. There was surely something to the case against Samuel Nicholson, for during the Quasi-War similar charges arose.

George Washington appointed Samuel Nicholson second-ranking captain in the United States Navy in June 1794, to superintend and ultimately command the frigate to be built at Boston—the *Constitution* 44. Ironically, one of the first to congratulate Nicholson was John Barry who was pleased with the president's selections from "upwards of one hundred applications." "Powerful interest" went into each of the choices at a time when efforts were still being made to assuage sectional and political differences. Nicholson was a well-connected Marylander and a Republican. His niece was married to Albert Gallatin.[33]

By the spring of 1798, however, Samuel Nicholson was a man out of place in New England's major city. Party spirit had replaced nonpartisanship. Experienced naval veterans, such as Hoysteed Hacker and John Foster Williams, were refused commissions in the expanding navy for their democratic politics. Samuel Nicholson would never have been appointed in 1798; and his 1794 commission was itself at risk, for word made its way from Boston to Philadelphia that all was not well with the *Constitution*. She was the last of the frigates launched in 1797. Only on her third attempt did she reach the water after two perilous halts on the ways. Her outfitting and manning proceeded slowly. Pickering and Wolcott addressed confidential inquiries to Boston concerning the character and behavior of Captain Nicholson.[34]

Nicholson's most vehement critic in Boston was Stephen Higginson who became navy agent in 1798. The personal entity between the two men dated back at least to 1794 when Higginson had first sought the agency, and Nicholson had opposed him. Not surprisingly, the new navy agent was quite willing to answer queries concerning the *Constitution*'s commander. Higginson wrote Pickering on 6 June 1798:

> Capt. N[icholson] is in my estimation a rough blustering tar merely, he is a good seaman probably . . . but he wants points much more important as a commander in my view, prudence, judgement & reflection are no trait in his character . . . his noise and vanity is disgusting to the sailors. . . . [And on 12 June] Capt. N: is not intemperate [there apparently had been allegations that he was] . . . he has exerted himself all he could to man & get out the [*Constitution*]. His defects are more natural than acquired, they consist in want of natural talents rather than vicious habits; he is neither a gentleman, nor a popular man with the sailors, as some rough men are. . . .

In other words, Nicholson was disliked by both his officers and his men. But despite his low opinion of the *Constitution*'s commander, Higginson admitted that he knew of "no criminal conduct or neglect, nor such a gross incapacity as would justify perhaps dismissal . . . but I really wish he & some other of our old naval officers had never been appointed . . . our navy in the revolutionary war was a bad school to educate officers in."[35]

A similar view was held by James Lowell, who had known Nicholson since the Revolution. Lowell wrote Wolcott that he considered removal from command unjustified, but he noted: "if however [Nicholson] had not been appointed, I should think his unpopularity arising from his manners, his want of real dignity while he is pompous & his age would render his talents equivocal for command. . . ."[36]

By the time Stoddert assumed his duties as secretary of the navy, the manning crisis in Boston was passed, the *Constitution* was nearly ready for sea, and the movement to remove Samuel Nicholson from command was over. But the secretary learned of the allegations made against his second-ranking captain earlier in the spring. Pickering, the central figure in the effort to replace Nicholson, as acting secretary of war turned over responsibility for naval affairs to Stoddert. The secretary of state either showed his fellow cabinet officer the correspondence relative to the captain of the *Constitution*, or told him of the doubts held for Nicholson's capacity. Perhaps Stoddert, politically more moderate than Pickering and like Nicholson a Marylander, chose to attribute the attacks to partisanship and sectionalism. If so, the secretary of the navy would soon be disabused.[37]

* * *

Nicholson had his frigate ready for sea in July and she left Nantasket Roads soon after Barry's arrival. The *Constitution* patrolled for a month between Georges Bank and Long Island until 24 August when, off New-port, new orders were received from Stoddert instructing Nicholson to sail south to take up station between the St. Marys River and Cape Henry. Truxtun's *Constellation*, which had been deployed in that sector, was to be sent elsewhere on another mission.[38]

The swift-sailing *Constitution* was in southern waters off Cape Hatteras by 5 September. After two months at sea Nicholson had yet to sight a French sail, but then his old luck seemed suddenly to have returned. Early on the morning of 8 September a vessel "looking like a cruiser" was spotted ahead.[39]

Nicholson ordered all sail set as the *Constitution* answered her helm in pursuit. Drums beat to quarters as the guns were cleared for action and the divisions took their stations. For four hours Nicholson maneuvered until he had closed to within range. At his order the flag was run up and a cannon fired in signal for the ship to come to, but the chase ran up English colors and fired a gun to leeward, a sign of nonbelligerency. As the two ships rapidly closed to pistol-shot range, the English ship continued to maneuver in a manner that made it difficult for Nicholson to lay his frigate alongside. At short range the two ships stood cleared for action, each suspect of the other's intentions. Nicholson, well aware of his overwhelming superiority, put an end to this seaborne dance, hailing the vessel and warning whoever could hear that "if they offered to make sail or give . . . any further trouble . . . [he] would absolutely fire into them, sink them, and give them no quarter." The chase at last hove to.[40]

Despite her British banner, Nicholson was certain he had run down "pirates." "Never," he reported to Stoddert, had his eyes beheld "so impudent and daring a set of rascals." Many of the cosmopolitan crew were French, including the boatswain. A seaman in the *Constitution* claimed that he recognized this man from the crew of a privateering sloop that had plundered the merchant vessel the American had been serving in only seven months before. The captain of the "English" vessel, according to Nicholson, also proved unable to produce his papers or his vessel's log.

But Nicholson's report was less than frank. The ship was the *Niger* 24, and her captain, George DuPetit-Thouars, was a French Royalist. He had been in the English service for five years, now with commissions against the Spanish and French. On board were a cargo, the property of Phila-delphia merchants, an American gentlemen from Baltimore, and a number of Englishmen, three of whom were British officers. Such was hardly the portage of a privateer, especially one carrying twenty-four guns but only seventy-five men. It will be recalled that Barry's first prize, the *Sans Pareil* 10, had a crew of eighty.

To DuPetit, Nicholson and the Americans seemed the pirates. The

Niger's log, register, commissions, general clearance, bills of lading, and other pages had all been turned over to Nicholson, the French captain claimed, only to disappear. Nicholson, DuPetit reported, verbally abused him while an American lieutenant sat upon the British flag. Moreover, the American commander took the entire crew out of the *Niger* and put them in chains in the *Constitution.* The Frenchman feared for the safety of his crew and cargo.[41]

Having errantly made an English vessel his first prize of war, Nicholson followed with a more serious error of judgment. He decided to escort his "prize" to Hampton Roads, abandoning his station, and infuriating the secretary of the navy. With Nicholson's arrival off Norfolk, news of the incident traveled quickly to Philadelphia. Stoddert had both captains' reports in his hands, and it was evident to him that the *Niger* was more than likely an English ship, a deduction soon confirmed by Robert Liston, British minister in the American capital. Nicholson offered no proof for his assertion that the ship was guilty of attacking American merchantmen. Stoddert found it "remarkable" that he failed to mention in his report the presence of passengers, "passengers too, irritated by ill treatment they had received. . . ." Stoddert concluded, "I fear the truth has not been so much the object of [Nicholson's] enquiries, as might have been wished in an officer of his rank in the American navy." He found it difficult to believe that the *Niger,* with a crew of seventy-five, was a corsair. With such doubts, he began to suspect Nicholson's motives. He wrote Norfolk naval agent Will Pennock that proper care should be taken of the ship, the crew, "and attention should be paid to the money & goods. . . ." A similar concern about possible "plundering" was voiced by Adams when he learned of the capture.[42]

The more immediate problem for the secretary of the navy was to get Nicholson back out to sea. Stoddert's instructions clearly stated that prizes taken by American ships were to be sent to ports of the United States. The *Niger* with her prize crew on board should have been sent alone to Norfolk. Instead, Nicholson sailed with her to Hampton Roads and remained idly there for a month, leaving the southern coast, the sector most at risk, virtually undefended.

Nicholson was experienced enough to know that adjudication even in the case of a good prize, which he also knew the *Niger* was not, would take considerable time. Yet he remained in port, conduct that "mortified" Stoddert. The secretary at least vented his frustration in a letter to Nicholson after learning that the frigate, too long in port, was now racked by yellow fever. But Stoddert had second thoughts; he recalled his letter before it was delivered. In the meantime the fever had been contained, but not before sixteen-year-old Midshipman Samuel Nicholson, Jr., was claimed by the outbreak. Stoddert wrote that there seemed to be "no calculating the evils of [Nicholson's] first false step." Not until 7 October, almost a month to the day after the capture of the *Niger*, did the *Constitution* return to sea.[43]

For the time being, Stoddert had refrained from harsh treatment of Nicholson, being unwilling to send even a strongly worded letter to his second-ranking captain. But the shortcomings of the commander of the *Constitution* were fully apparent to him. The fears voiced during the spring about Nicholson's character were proving well-founded. Pickering, to whom fell the task of mollifying the offended British, was strongly critical of the man. He had been warned by his nephew, Timothy Williams, that Nicholson was "poor—it is his only living." "Poor" Nicholson no doubt was prize hungry. Pickering wrote: "Indeed the eagerness of Captain Nicholson to procure a condemnation savored of rapacity. And in the very letter in which he informed [me] of the death of his son (the consequence of this unfortunate capture) his thoughts seemed wholly engrossed with his prize and the means of ensuring, if possible, a condemnation."[44]

But there would be no "condemnation" of the *Niger*. Ultimately, the courts ordered the ship released and levied a $11,000 indemnity for the ship's owners. Since Nicholson's "circumstances were such that he would be unable to pay the sum in question" the administration had to go to Congress for the money which was voted in a supplemental appropriation on 2 April 1799.[45]

The early operations of the navy's two senior officers commanding its strongest ships served to alert Stoddert to potential problems. Doubts about the competence of Barry and Nicholson would influence the secretary's plans and affect the execution of operations. Stoddert, too, would come to share Higginson's wish that some of the nation's "old naval officers" had never been appointed to command.

4

"INCESSANT ATTACKS"

-----

1. Further Delays in Boston

When Barry sailed for Nantasket Roads in July, he expected to ren-dezvous with two ships, the *Herald* 18, Captain James Sever, at Boston, and the revenue cutter *Pickering* 14, Captain Jonathan Chapman from Newburyport. Stoddert had every expectation that the two vessels would be outfitted and manned in time to sail with Barry. But, as with Nicholson and the *Constitution,* New England-based ships were to prove the undoing of many a plan and the source of great irritation throughout 1798. Barry sailed for the Caribbean without either ship.[1]

While after reconsideration Stoddert was pleased that the two vessels missed sailing with Barry, he remained vexed in the face of reports on the constant delays that kept them in port. The government had purchased the *Herald* at Boston on 15 June 1798. As with the *Ganges* and *Delaware* it was expected that the sloop of war, a year-old Newburyport-built, ship-rigged vessel measuring 279 tons, could be outfitted with a few weeks.[2]

James Sever, born in Kingston, Massachusetts, was the sixth-ranking captain in the navy, originally named in July 1794 to command the *Constellation* when Joshua Barney refused his commission. In August 1794, however, Secretary of War Henry Knox ordered Sever to Ports-mouth, New Hampshire, to supervise the frigate *Congress* to be built there, while Truxtun was sent to Baltimore. This turned out to be unfortunate for Sever, for in 1796 work on the *Constellation* continued but work on the *Congress* was halted. Sever was left without a ship. With the French crisis in the spring of 1798, Sever, was recalled to service and ordered "to procure a ship to be commanded by you in the naval service, and to cause her to be equipped for sea with all practicable expedition."[3]

Despite his relative seniority, as Boston agent Higginson wrote, "Captain Sever [had] not had much experience in naval war, he [had] seen very little actual service. . . ." In fact, Sever appears to have had none. He was present on Dorchester Heights with General Thomas Kingston at the siege of Boston in 1775, but the fourteen-year-old gained little useful naval experience. He entered Harvard College in 1777, graduating four years later, and in October 1781 was commissioned an ensign, serving in the 4th and 7th Massachusetts Infantry of the Continental Line. Sever remained in the army after the Revolution, serving as a lieutenant in Henry Jackson's Continental Regiment until 20 June 1784.

In early 1785 Sever requested a certificate of service and recommendation from the War Department. His stated intention was to seek a career overseas in the Dutch service. According to biographical data from one of his descendants, Sever ended up in Russia as commander of the frigate *John Adams* where Catherine the Great offered the handsome New Englander an admiral's rank. The patriotic Sever refused, accepting only her royal portrait.

There are a number of inconsistencies in the tale of Sever's service. The *John Adams* was completed in 1799, but was never commanded by Sever. Catherine II died in 1796, before any American navy existed. Sever did spend the interwar years in command of merchantships on voyages that took him to Europe, and perhaps Russia. But when Knox informed the thirty-three-year-old Sever of his appointment to command a frigate in 1794, it was not due to the young captain's experience, but to his family and political connections. Sever's "friends" had "applied" on his behalf.[4]

Despite Sever's inexperience, Higginson considered him "to possess all the requisites to form a very good officer, such as spirit, judgment, prudence, firmness & sense of character which urges to great and brilliant actions. . . ." Unfortunately for Sever, he made a poor first impression on Benjamin Stoddert. With this initial disadvantage and later ill-fortune, Sever found himself the only one of the six captains appointed in 1794 not retained after the war.[5]

Having missed sailing with Barry because of delays in refitting the *Herald* that Stoddert considered unnecessary, Sever was ordered to cruise between Georges Bank and Long Island. Unable to recruit his full complement of marines, he remained at Boston until 22 August when, spurred on by Higginson's assurances, he realized that it would be better to sail short a few men than to remain in port. Word had reached Philadelphia of the delays in Boston. Three and a half months had passed since Wolcott had instructed Sever to find a ship and outfit her with "expedition." Stoddert sent Sever a harsh letter informing him that his dalliance for a "few marines" had left the New England coast unprotected, since the *Pickering,* which had dropped down to Boston from Newburyport, was under orders to wait for the *Herald* to sail. Stoddert wrote Higginson as well:

> I will not indulge a suspicion that Captain Sever wants zeal, activity or any other essential quality of an officer—but without any reference to him, I have always entertained an opinion that men who suffer trifling difficulties to interpose between them and their duty; are unfit for public service—It shall be my endeavor to rid our navy of such men—If our officers cannot be inspired with the true kind of zeal & spirit, which will enable us to make up for want of great force, by great activity, we had better burn our ships. . . . Has [Sever] not delayed too long on a most frivolous pretence? Does he deserve the high character given of him?[6]

By the time Stoddert wrote Higginson and Sever, the latter had already been at sea for a week. When the secretary learned of the *Herald*'s sailing, he wrote the Boston navy agent again, admitting that he had begun "to think unjustly of [Sever's] zeal & activity." Nevertheless, Sever had disappointed Stoddert. As with Barry and Nicholson, the secretary still harbored suspicions regarding "zeal & activity."[7]

2. The Treasury Navy

When the *Herald* finally sailed from Boston harbor, she was in company with the *Pickering* 14. In command was Jonathan Chapman, who had been "two years in the British navy, well versed in the practical parts of naval operations & [possessing] all the requisites to make an excellent officer."[8]

The command of the *Pickering* had been sought by an older Revenue Service master, John Foster Williams, whom the nephew of the cutter's namesake characterized as "old, without enterprise, & . . . not a little tainted in his politics." Treasury secretary Wolcott recognized before completion of the vessel that the *Pickering* would not serve "as a mere revenue cutter; she will be efficient for more important purposes." For that reason, Chapman, "a respectable, well-informed man, a thorough seaman & disciplinarian," who viewed the *Pickering* as a stepping-stone to a naval commission, was given command.[9]

The *Pickering* was one of several cutters available for use against France during 1798. Although the United States did not possess a navy at the beginning of the Quasi-War, the country was not without a maritime force. From the beginning of the federal experiment there were cutters controlled by the Department of the Treasury. Alexander Hamilton had asked Congress in April 1790 to create a force to assist the collectors of customs in carrying out their duties. Following Congressional action in August, ten ships were built between 1791 and 1793.[10]

The first maritime challenge to the United States fell on the Revenue Service. Even before the Franco-American crisis of 1798, the cutters were hard pressed to prevent violations of American commercial and neutrality regulations. French privateers, and some American, sought to arm, operate, and dispose of their prizes in American ports. The job of the cutters was to enforce the law in a dangerous wartime atmosphere. And as France and the United States moved towards open hostilities, the cutters suddenly became the first, and only line of national defense. While the naval act of 1 July 1797 empowered the president to man and employ the frigates *Constitution, United States,* and *Constellation,* a year passed before the three put to sea. Congress, in the meantime, gave Adams the authority to strengthen the crews of the cutters and use them to defend the coasts and commerce of the United States.[11]

Unfortunately, the already overworked cutters were ill-prepared for such duty. With crews of two masters and six mates, armed with only three small swivels, the cutters were outgunned, outsized, and outmanned by even small privateers. Increasing the crew size to thirty only worsened conditions on board small (thirty-five to fifty ton) worn-out ships.

At the end of 1797 only two cutters were judged fit for active service against the French, the *Virginia* and *General Greene,* the first of a second generation of Revenue Service vessels. The Quasi-War acted as a catalyst for the expansion of the Treasury navy as it did for the United States Navy. With the inadequacy of the ten original cutters obvious, Congress was forthcoming with funds to build bigger and better ships, capable of a dual role. Ten new vessels were built to replace the old: The *General Greene II* at Baltimore, the *Virginia II* at Norfolk, and the *Diligence II* at Philadelphia during 1797, the *Governor Jay* at New York, the *Pickering* at Newburyport, the *Eagle II* at Philadelphia, the *Scammel* and *Governor Gilman* at Portsmouth, New Hampshire, and the *Unanimity* and *South Carolina* at Charleston during 1798. The new cutters were mostly fine vessels, well designed by some of the best shipwrights of the day. With the exception of the sloop-rigged *General Greene,* 98 tons, 34 men, mounting ten 4-pounders, the others measured 187 tons, with crews of 70 men, armed with ten to sixteen 4 and 6-pounders. Their rigs varied, but most were "jackass brigs," double topsail schooners.[12]

As the new cutters became operational, Stoddert observed their early cruises with the intent of transferring to the navy not only the better ships, but also the best officers. He considered Chapman, for example, "a very meritorious man" and intended to offer him a captaincy and the command

of a larger ship. Another highly recommended Revenue Service master slated for a naval commission was Robert Cochran.[13]

Cochran was a prominent South Carolinian, known to George Washington himself. During the president's 1791 tour of the South, Cochran had the honor of serving as coxswain of the twelve-oared barge rowed by notables that carried Washington across the Cooper River from Haddrel's Point to Charleston. The president had first met Cochran in January 1776 when he came to Philadelphia to recruit seamen for his state. Before leaving Charleston, Washington named Cochran master of the cutter to be built there. Cochran commanded the first *South Carolina* until May 1798 when he took over one of the new cutters built in Charleston, the brig-rigged *Unanimity*.[14]

Cochran's prospects for a naval career came to an abrupt end on 29 July 1798, when he crossed paths with His Majesty's *Mosquito* schooner, sixteen guns, commanded by Lieutenant Thomas White. Cruising off the South Carolina coast on the prowl for French privateers, White sighted the *Unanimity* which he did not recognize as an American vessel. He beat his crew to quarters and closed with her. Seeing the brig run up an American flag, White fired a gun and ran up English colors, but rather than coming to and speaking the *Mosquito,* Cochran ran off on a south-westerly course along the coast towards Charleston.

Mistaking her for a French privateer, White pursued. Throughout the afternoon the faster sailing *Mosquito* gained on the *Unanimity,* caught between the shore and the British schooner. A shot across the brig's bow having failed to bring her to, White closed to short range and at 5 P.M., after a four-hour chase, loosed his broadside as the cannons bore. Cochran returned the fire, to no effect, then ran the *Unamimity* aground on the bar at Dewee's Inlet.

White was unfamiliar with the coast and was reluctant at first to pursue too close inshore. He ran out for deeper water. He reassessed the situation, however, and headed for the coast "with intention to stand in, destroy the brig, and if possible save the prisoners. . . ." His plans were cut short by the arrival of an American pilot boat and White discovered to his "utter astonishment" that his quarry was the United States Revenue brig *Unanimity.*

The incident did not have any serious diplomatic ramifications. The *Unanimity* suffered only minor damage. British minister Liston forwarded a copy of White's report to Pickering that convinced the American that the English commander had mistaken the brig for a French privateer. Moreover, it seemed to Pickering and Stoddert that Cochran's actions had contributed to the misidentification. Why had Cochran ran? Even if the schooner had been a French vessel flying false colors, she was of a similar size and strength to the *Unanimity*. Stoddert addressed confidential inquiries to Charleston seeking further details of the incident and appraisals of Cochran's character.

Responses and Cochran's own report reached Stoddert in early September. Even the latter did nothing to "place the transaction in a light more favorable. . . ." Nor did a mutiny of Cochran's men that followed the incident. Stoddert considered it a "disgraceful affair" and concluded that it would be incorrect "to trust a second time, an armed vessel & with it the honor of the country in the hands of a man, who had fled under such circumstances, from a vessel of force inferior to his own."[15]

Neither Cochran nor his brig were taken under the authority of the Navy Department, but most of the cutters and their commanders were. Stoddert formalized his control on 10 October 1798, officially notifying the collectors of customs of the appropriate ports that the *Pickering, Governor Jay, General Greene, Eagle, Diligence, Virginia,* and *Scammel* would henceforth sail under his orders. Stoddert's authority over the cutters was augmented in February 1799 when he was authorized to transfer the vessels into the naval service, providing equal pay and compensation were given to all men and officers so employed.[16]

In deploying the cutters, Stoddert remained cognizant of the main purpose of the Revenue Service. The fine sailing qualities of the cutters, designed to catch smugglers, made them equally suited for work against privateers. But Stoddert did his best to keep their dual roles harmonized, and as the newly built, small naval warships became operational, the secretary transferred most of the cutters back to the control of the Treasury Department. Only the *Eagle, Pickering,* and *Scammel* were retained in the naval service for the duration of the struggle with France.[17]

In the course of the Quasi-War the Revenue cutters performed yeoman service. The examples of Cochran and the *Unanimity* were not indicative of the qualities of the ships, officers, and men of the Revenue Service. During the early stages of the war when ships were few, their role was essential. Of the twenty-one ships operational at the end of 1798, nine were cutters, and between 1798 and 1801 they managed to capture twenty-six French ships and recapture ten American merchantmen. For the Revenue Service the Quasi-War was a formative experience, serving to establish precedent for its national role in wartime and to create an atmosphere conducive to qualitative and administrative expansion. By the end of the war the Revenue Service was a reputable organization with fine ships, equal pay and rank with the navy, and excellent experienced officers and men, all serving under a unique ensign proudly flown ever since.[18]

3. Carrying the War to the Caribbean

On 30 July 1798 Stoddert wrote Adams outlining his proposals for operations in the coming months. After six weeks as secretary, Stoddert at last had caught up with the affairs of his department. His letter to the president marks the beginning of his efforts to shape the operations of the navy and to take the initiative in the war with France. The ships of the navy at that date were deployed in the following manner: the *United States* and the *Delaware* were in the Caribbean under John Barry, the *Constellation* protected the southern coast, the *Ganges* the central, and the *Constitution* the northern. Stoddert expected several additional ships and cutters, some of which have already been mentioned above, to be ready to sail soon. With a growing force at his disposal, he believed that the best means of defending the American coast was to carry the war to the Caribbean. "By keeping up incessant attacks upon the French cruisers on their own ground," Stoddert wrote, "they will in a degree at least be prevented from coming on ours." He hoped to be able to send a frigate and another ship "on a cruise among the islands" some time late in August as a follow up to Barry's first foray. Events, however, would lead American operations in a different direction.[19]

On 28 July 1798, Truxtun in the *Constellation* had anchored off Charleston while patrolling the southern coast. He found the local merchants eager for him to go to Havana to escort homeward a convoy of merchant ships fearful of French privateers active off Cuba's north coast. Having no authority to leave his station, Truxtun declined to go, but suggested that the merchants apply to the government for the service of a public ship.[20]

Truxtun's recommendation was followed. Stoddert was contacted and formulated plans for such an operation before Truxtun next called at Norfolk. With new ships operational and a little juggling, Stoddert intended to send a frigate and a sloop of war to Cuba. The *Pickering* and *Herald*, expected to be ready for sea, would relieve Nicholson, who in turn would sail south to replace Truxtun. The newly outfitted *Baltimore* 20, would sail to Hampton Roads, rendezvous with the *Constellation*, and sail to Havana.

As usual, events failed to go according to plan. The delay of the *Herald* and *Pickering* nearly left the coast between Georges Bank and Long Island unprotected; but by the time Nicholson's orders of 13 August caught up with him off Block Island on the 24th, the two ships were at sea. Between Cape Henry and the St. Marys, Captain Francis Bright commanding the cutter *Virginia* 14, was already at sea when his orders to join Nicholson off the southern coast were drafted. But Nicholson, who received his orders late, failed to reach Cape Hatteras until 5 September, and then only for his unfortunate rendezvous with the *Niger*. So it was in the south that Stoddert's plan came undone, a victim of timing and Nicholson's "rapacity." For nearly a month, the more vulnerable southern coast remained protected by the weakest force, the little *Virginia*.[21]

Preparations for Truxtun's cruise to Cuba began on 9 August 1798. That day Stoddert sent orders to Captain Isaac Phillips of the *Baltimore* to sail for Hampton Roads. Truxtun's orders were sent the following day to Norfolk where he was expected next to anchor. The two warships were to sail with all haste to Havana, where they were to meet the convoy and escort it safely to the American coast. Truxtun was advised to avoid irritating the Spaniards with whom the United States was at peace, but also to "keep out of reach" of the guns of the harbor because of the variable directions Spanish policy might take under French pressure. Truxtun was also provided with, as were all American naval vessels from this point on, the mutual recognition signals developed for the use of the United States and Royal Navies.[22]

Arrangements thus far had been made without informing President Adams, summering at Quincy. Stoddert had asked for the president's approval of further operations in his letter of 30 July, but had yet to receive a reply. In that letter Stoddert had anticipated operations against the French islands, but he was now sending a force to Spanish Cuba, and possible diplomatic consequences had to be considered. Stoddert, however, was either confident of Adam's approval or intent on seeing the operation underway before it could be recalled, for he waited until 25 August to address the president again, by which time the squadron was ready to sail from Norfolk. Stoddert wrote that he assumed Adams approved the proposal, having heard nothing to the contrary. The secretary was sure the Havana plan would receive the president's "approbation." Stoddert was correct, for as he was writing the president, a week-old letter was on its way. Adams too had learned of the plight of the ships at Havana, and instructed Stoddert to organize just such an escort.[23]

* * *

The *Baltimore* joined Truxtun at Norfolk on 24 August. Phillips, eager to respond to Stoddert's plea for speed, sailed with bad water and a crew 35 men short of a full complement of 180. Truxtun was pleased by Phillips's energy, but was dismayed to learn that there were only 12 experienced seamen in the undermanned ship. Truxtun's mood was further troubled when a number of merchant captains, whose ships were beginning to congregate in the Roads, paid a call to the *Constellation*. He was astonished to learn that the merchantmen had come to Norfolk expecting to be escorted by the frigate to Havana. Truxtun's orders said nothing about an outward-bound convoy. He summoned Phillips to the *Constellation,* but his orders too were silent. He did, however, inform Truxtun that before leaving for Norfolk he had heard discussion of such a convoy. The topic had been common talk at the insurance houses and "other places" in Baltimore.[24]

As Truxtun looked from his cabin window at the ever-growing number of merchant vessels, he was perplexed. His orders called for speed, but how was he to sail quickly with a convoy? Had Stoddert drafted new orders that had yet to reach Norfolk? Was his destination common knowledge in the Caribbean as well as Baltimore? Truxtun took out pen and paper and wrote Stoddert "much embarrassed, by the daily assemblage of ships in these Roads." Why had the news of the convoy remained a secret to him alone? "Mischief," Truxtun advised the secretary of the navy, "tho' perhaps innocently, may rise from loose volatile habits."[25]

Truxtun's indignation was without foundation. Foreknowledge of the *Constellation*'s destination could not have been prevented. As Truxtun well knew, the initiative for the operation came not from the secretary of the navy, but from the merchants. When Adams and Stoddert assented to the requests, the merchants immediately knew of it. Their motivations were to safeguard their property and obtain lower insurance rates. To keep the news a secret from the insurance houses would have made no sense. The reason for the war was, after all, not only to protect American merchant vessels, but also the financial underpinnings of the entire commercial establishment. The war drove up insurance rates; news of a convoy would drive them down. As one authority on eighteenth-century convoys writes: "the employment of [escorted] convoys to protect merchant ships from attack is more than a matter of naval strategy and tactics . . . economic considerations at times had greater impact on the working of the convoy system than did the tactical and strategic requirements of the war."[26]

Nor was the episode an example of administrative collapse. Stoddert never intended to have a convoy escorted to Havana. In a letter of 31 August, a week after the slow merchant vessels had begun to gather at Hampton Roads, the secretary wrote Norfolk agent Will Pennock expressing disappointment that Truxtun remained in port as late as the 23rd. If Stoddert expected Truxtun to sail before that date, there certainly was no intention that the *Constellation* await the assembly of the convoy. Stoddert made no mention in his letter of any convoy. The merchants simply had taken matters into their own hands. Learning that Truxtun would be sailing for Havana, they assembled at Norfolk expecting an escort to Cuba.

Perhaps as the story of the convoy spread, the preposition used before "Havana" became subverted. Insurance rates were high; a great deal of money was at stake.[27]

A good naval officer, Truxtun set about organizing the convoy despite his lack of orders. Sailing instructions and signals were issued. Still troubled by the wording of his directive from Stoddert, Truxtun informed the masters of the merchant vessels accompanying him to Havana that he would not "make delay for any vessel."[28]

On 1 September Truxtun's two-ship squadron left Hampton Roads with sixteen sail under escort, and the *Baltimore* still thirty-four men understrength. The convoy arrived off Havana in good order twenty days later. Truxtun wrote American officials ashore that his only needs were "a few barrels of limes, and oranges . . . [and] about twenty boxes of the very best segars. . . ." By this time his concern about loosely kept information had obviously lessened, for he also wrote that he intended to leave Havana on 27 September and asked that "public notice of my determination" be given. As it was, bad weather delayed his departure until the 30th, when the *Constellation, Baltimore,* and forty-three sail headed east for the Straits of Florida.[29]

The return voyage was marred by more foul weather, and a single incident. Late in the evening of 30 September the small British privateer *Nancy,* operating from New Providence in the Bahamas, infiltrated the convoy and managed to get alongside the *Baltimore,* both vessels apparently mistaking each other for merchant ships in the dark. Captain George Broadwater, an American from Virginia's Eastern Shore, was prepared to board the American sloop of war when he discovered his error. Captain Phillips and his men were quick to respond and promptly boarded and seized the *Nancy.* Broadwater was held as a prisoner until the following morning when he was sent to Truxtun on board the *Constellation.* With the expatriate came a request from Phillips whose examination of the crew of the *Nancy* had revealed several other American crewmen. Phillips wished to enter the men into the short-handed *Baltimore.* Truxtun gave his "consent to take them out, provided you can ascertain beyond all doubt, that they are citizens of the United States, & that they are willing to enter with you, but not otherwise. . . ." He added: "our government wishes to be on good terms with Great Britain, and we must not counteract, what it desires." After volunteers were transferred, Truxtun dismissed Broadwater and his ship, ordering them away from the convoy.[30]

Confident of the ability of the *Constellation* to protect the convoy as it neared the American coast, about a hundred miles east of St. Augustine, Florida, Truxtun detached the *Baltimore.* He ordered Phillips to proceed to the coast off Charleston to cruise for four days before heading north to rejoin the *Constellation,* escorting the slower sailing convoy, at Hampton Roads. As the two ships parted, Truxtun noted that he was "perfectly well satisfied with the conduct and attention of Captain Phillips." But ahead lay stiffer trials for Truxtun's eager subordinate, and, unfortunately, another disgraceful showing on the part of a commander of an American ship of war.[31]

4. Incident Off the Havana

On 16 October, sailing north along the Georgia coast, Phillips had the misfortune to cross paths with the *Constitution,* accompanied by the *Virginia* cutter. Captain Nicholson signaled Phillips to come to the frigate and there ordered him to sail in his company. It is uncertain, but probable, that Phillips protested, citing Stoddert's and Truxtun's orders, but Nicholson was the second-ranking captain in the navy, senior to Truxtun, and on his way to Charleston as well.[32]

On 19 October they came off Charleston bar and remained there at anchor until the 24th. That day, Nicholson, with the *Baltimore* in company, headed south with eleven sail in convoy for Havana. An apprehensive Phillips left a letter for Commodore Truxtun with Captain Francis Bright of the *Virginia,* explaining the run-in with Nicholson. When Truxtun learned of the fate of his subordinate he was infuriated, considering "Nicholson's conduct highly reprehensible." He clearly had the authority to order Phillips about, Truxtun admitted, but he feared that "every plan of government may be frustrated by such proceedings, as those of Nicholson's, and the ships sent Lord knows where at the whim of an officer."[33]

Nicholson's reasons for sailing to Havana remain unknown. Leaving Norfolk after the *Niger* affair, the *Constitution* had been patrolling the southern coastal sector between Cape Henry and the St. Marys, as ordered by Stoddert. One author has claimed that while off Charleston Nicholson received new instructions, since lost, from the Navy Department. In fact, new orders were issued on 8 October, but they instructed Nicholson to remain on the southern coast and then return to Boston by 20 November to refit for another operation. Stoddert's 8 October orders, sent to Norfolk, did not reach Nicholson before he sailed on 19 October. They clearly demonstrate, however, that Stoddert had no intention of sending the *Constitution* on a cruise to Havana from which a timely return to Boston would have been impossible.[34]

Why did Nicholson go to Havana? He may have judged such service to be of more value to the government than cruising along a coast on which he had yet to sight a French vessel. But Truxtun, who had anchored off Charleston a few months before, suggested another explanation. He wrote: "I had every attention shown me by the merchants . . . they delicately hinted to me a wish, that I go to Havana." At the time, Truxtun referred them to Stoddert, and their official requests were the reason for the dispatch of the *Constellation* and *Baltimore* to Havana in September. In their correspondence with Stoddert, however, the Charleston merchants also expressed a desire that "a good deal of money" which lay at Havana be brought north in a frigate. Stoddert sent the information to Truxtun, but too late to reach him before he sailed from Hampton Roads. Transporting specie in a public ship, the custom of freight, was permitted. The Navy Department provided guidelines—a .5 percent charge on the first $10,000, .25 percent on the remainder—but a commander was at liberty to charge whatever he chose if the rate was agreed upon by both parties before the ship sailed. Truxtun made no mention in his log, journal, or correspondence of picking up the money. As late as 1800, $300,000 remained at Havana awaiting shipment north. Had "poor" Sam Nicholson been informed while at Charleston of the "freight" awaiting some fortunate commander and decided to go after it himself, taking the *Baltimore* along as insurance? Captains transported money at their own risk. What can be said with certainty is that whatever his reason for sailing for Havana, Nicholson's cruise was unordered.[35]

Four days out of Charleston, mishap struck the *Constitution*. On the morning of 28 October the frigate sprung her bowsprit. Nicholson decided to turn back, and the signal was made for Phillips to take charge of the fleet and continue on to Havana.[36]

The convoy, reduced to nine sail, was approaching Havana about 8:00 A.M. on 16 November when five warships flying Spanish colors were sighted to the northwest, standing on a course towards the southeast, Havana, and the American ships. By 8:30 English colors had replaced the Spanish and the lead frigate fired a gun to leeward, a sign of non-belligerency. Phillips, flying the American flag, answered with a leeward cannon of his own. The squadron was from Vice Admiral Sir Hyde Parker's Jamaica station and included the signaling frigate *Maidstone* 32, Captain Ross Donnelly, the *Greyhound* 32, Captain Temple Hardy, the *Carnatic* 74, Captain John Loring, the *Thunderer* 74, Captain John Cochet, and the *Queen* 98, Captain Mann Dobson. The second-rate *Queen* was Sir Hyde's flagship for the Jamaica station, but the aging admiral was not on board that November day. In fact, Sir Hyde rarely went to sea anymore. His forte had become administration, and the amassing of immense wealth in charge of the most lucrative command in the Royal Navy. Parker and his favored captains were growing rich, as the thirty-one ships of his command, comprising less than 5 percent of the strength of the navy, made one-third of all British captures. Sir Hyde received his share, one-eighth. Prize hunger was a spirit that permeated the station. And as Cuba was a colony of Spain, allied to France and at war with Great Britain, ships carrying contraband to Havana were good prizes.[37]

In Sir Hyde's absence, John Loring was the senior captain and flew a commodore's broad red pendant from the main topgallant masthead of the *Carnatic*. The Lorings were émigrés, former Tories during the American Revolution, from Massachusetts. Joshua Loring, Sr., John's father, had been a captain in the Royal Navy before the Revolution. John's brother, Joshua Loring, Jr., served the King during the rebellion in Boston, Halifax, and Philadelphia, where his wife became renowned as Sir William Howe's mistress. John Loring followed his father into the navy and as a sixteen-year-old midshipman was captured by the Americans early in the war and thrown into "Concord Gale." Young Loring was anxious to be released and petitioned his captors, assuring the "good people" of the United States that he had been "under the influence of my father, but I am now convinced I have been badly instructed. . . ." His only wish was to be "delivered from this place that I may work for my living and not any longer be a charge to the public. . . ." Paroled, Loring found employment in a respectable trade, the Royal Navy. He resumed his career and was promoted to lieutenant in 1779, and captain in 1794. President John Adams in a remark to Robert Liston spoke of the effect John Loring's personal and family background had on his subsequent actions: "Captain Loring . . . who is a native of America, was a Loyalist . . . and is supposed to return an emnity to [the United States], which is not unnatural to persons in that gentleman's situation."[38]

At 8:45 the *Carnatic* fired a lee cannon and Phillips noted the broad red pendant. He bore first towards the *Maidstone,* nearest to him, but observing the flagship lying to as well, Phillips "made the best of [his] way to speak" the commodore. It was nearly 10:00 when the *Baltimore* neared the *Carnatic* and Phillips found himself hailed by Loring, not from the quarter-deck, but from the commodore's cabin window. According to Phillips's own report, Loring "ordered" that the signal be hoisted to halt the convoy. The American captain "immediately obeyed," three of the nine American ships came to, aided in their decision by shots fired across their bows by the *Maidstone.*[39]

Loring sent his boat to the *Baltimore.* Two officers came on board and informed Phillips that the commodore wished to speak with him. Phillips agreed to go and was rowed to the *Carnatic* where he was "politely" received. Loring examined Phillip's papers. Having expedited his sailing in

August, Phillips had no commissions for either his own captaincy or his ship. The *Baltimore*, ex-*Adriana*, was a former merchant vessel and her captain a former merchant master. To prove that his command was, in fact, a ship of war of the United States, Phillips had had the foresight to bring with him to the *Carnatic* his orders from Stoddert and a copy of the Anglo-American private signals for men-of-war. These documents should have convinced Loring that the *Baltimore* and Phillips were duly commissioned. But Loring was not impressed. "Who is Ben Stoddert?" he asked. At last Loring came to the point of the interview. "His ship was distressed for men," Phillips reported (*see* appendix B), and Loring intended to take any sailors he considered Englishmen from the *Baltimore*. He then asked Phillips whether he would dine with him in the *Carnatic* or prefer to return to the *Baltimore*.[40]

A British crew rowed Phillips back to his ship which he found virtually in the control of the British officers he had left on board. Loring, choosing to consider the *Baltimore* a private rather than a public ship, sent a second boat to the American vessel carrying another officer who delivered a "verbal message from Captain Loring, to take all the men who had not protections. . . ." Phillips wrote: "Mr. Wright the second lieutenant of the *Carnatic* at this time requested I would have all hands called, and give him a list of their names, which I accordingly did. . . ." The men of the *Baltimore* were assembled and a British officer, muster roll in hand, walked the ranks and picked fifty-five "Englishmen," one-third of the crew, for transfer to the *Carnatic*. Fifty were returned later in the day. It was nightfall before the entire affair had come to an end.[41]

* * *

The initial report of the incident off Havana, that of the American consul, reached Philadelphia late in December and contained only the barest details of what had occurred. The impressment of Americans from a ship of war, however, outraged both the administration and its opponents. The former was particularly embarrassed, for Loring's actions called into question Adam's foreign and naval policies. The president, through Stoddert, issued a circular for the commanders of American naval vessels.

It is the positive command of the president, that on no pretence whatever, you permit the public vessel of war under your command, to be detained, or searched, nor any of the officers or men belonging to her, to be taken from her, by the ships or vessels of any foreign nation, so long as you are in a capacity to repel such outrage on the honor of the American flag;—If force should be exerted to compel your submission, you are to resist that force to the utmost of your power—and when overpowered by superior force, you are to strike your flag and thus yield your vessel as well as your men—but never your men without your vessel. . . .[42]

The anglophile Pickering was so outraged that he threatened to allow United States' warships to search British men-of-war for Americans, if Loring's actions were repeated. The secretary of state sent a New Year's Eve protest to Liston, enclosing the president's circular, and instructed Rufus King, American minister to the Court of St. James, to "make a representation of the affair" in London.[43] Liston viewed the incident as a serious threat to Anglo-American relations and sought clarification from London and Jamaica of his government's policy on impressment. The first response came from Vice Admiral Parker who forwarded a copy of Loring's report to Philadelphia (see Appendix B). The commodore provided ample justification for halting the American convoy and seizing one of the three ships searched. Several of the vessels were, in fact, loaded with contraband. The point in question with the Adams administration, however, was not the right of search, but the impressment of men from an American warship. Here, Loring stood on a technicality: Phillips's lack of a commission. But this defense, drawn up three months after the incident, was belied by an enclosure dated 17 November 1798, signed by Loring and addressed to "Captain Isaac Phillips American States Ship *Baltimore.*" Loring's report troubled the British minister, as did the uncooperative attitude of Parker, who refused to issue additional instructions to his commanders to prevent a recurrence of the affair. Nevertheless, with the Americans Liston took the line that the absence of a commission had given Loring "a right to look upon [the *Baltimore*] as a private trading vessel. . . ." But in his dispatches to Lord Grenville, the British foreign secretary, Liston voiced his concerns about the affair, and more generally about Sir Hyde Parker.[44]

A more positive response came from London. Evan Nepean, secretary of the admiralty, conducted a review of the relevant laws and practices which revealed that impressment of British subjects from foreign ships of war had "not recently prevailed." While Grenville refused to renounce future recourse to such practices, he assured the United States that Britain considered it inexpedient to press men from American warships given the friendly relations existing between the two nations. The king, Grenville wrote, would view a repetition of Loring's conduct with "displeasure."[45]

But by the time British diplomatic reassurances reached Philadelphia, most of the administration's ire had dissipated, the government's protests undercut by the conduct of the American captain. The extent to which Phillips had contributed to his own victimization remained unclear until he arrived in Philadelphia on 9 January 1799 bearing his lengthy report addressed to Stoddert.[46]

In an interview with the secretary on the 9th, Phillips confirmed the early reports of the incident. He mentioned also his lack of a commission, and before he left Stoddert's office, the secretary instructed a clerk to draw up another for his signature. Stoddert personally handed Phillips the new commission, the first had been lost in the mail between Philadelphia and Norfolk, and the *Baltimore*'s captain took his leave. Only then was Stoddert able carefully to read Phillips's ten-page report, and immediately, the captain's errors became evident to the secretary.[47]

Later that day, or the next, Stoddert met with Adams and Pickering to review Phillip's conduct. Stoddert advised immediate dismissal without a court-martial. Pickering, who believed that if Phillips "had manifested any sense of spirit, Loring wd. [would] have desisted from his attempt," agreed. Adams, who later admitted to Liston that Phillips's conduct lacked "spirit & dignity," kept the report to read it over more closely. After consideration, he returned it to Stoddert, "observing, that what was advised, must be done."[48]

Phillips had already left the capital on a journey to his home in Baltimore. Stoddert addressed his letter of dismissal there, dated 10 January 1799. The captain was dismissed under the special executive authority of the president; there was no court-martial. Phillips was condemned by his own report. A trial would have only tied up three captains at a time when their services were needed elsewhere, and caused the administration and the navy further political embarrassment. Stoddert had a large naval bill before Congress. What good were ships if commanders such as Cochran and Phillips would not fight them?[49]

For Stoddert, there were two major reasons for dismissing Isaac Phillips. Halting the convoy at Loring's command was Phillips's first mistake. He later sought defense for his actions in Stoddert's own instructions, which read in part: "I wish particularly to impress on your mind, that should you even see an American vessel captured by the armed ship of any nation at war with whom we are at peace, you can not lawfully interfere to prevent the capture. . . ." Indeed, Stoddert answered, that was the government's policy. "But it was not your duty," Stoddert retorted, "to obey the order of the British officer, to hoist your signal to stop your convoy. . . . Though you had not right to protect them . . . it did not follow that it would be proper to aid their capture. . . ." Phillips's most serious error, however, occurred on the deck of his ship after his return from the *Carnatic*. Stoddert considered his captain guilty of "tame submission to the orders of a British lieutenant. . . .":

If you could not have resisted the assumption of the command of your ship by the officer: a point not to be admitted, surely you might have contented yourself with passive submission—but you descended fur-ther and actually obeyed his orders, to have all hands called, and to give him a list of their names, under circumstances so degrading, it is ["impossible" *canceled*] improper that you should hold a commission in the navy service of the United States—and I am commanded by the president, to inform you, that your services are no longer required.[50]

Isaac Phillips's naval career was at an end. He might have considered himself fortunate to have escaped as the first captain in the United States Navy to be dismissed, rather than the first to be hanged. But Isaac Phillips attempted to regain his commission and mobilized his political friends in the effort. Stoddert refused to reconsider his decision. Phillips refused to yield; he last petitioned the Navy Department in 1825 for reinstatement, believing that his incriminating report had been consumed when the Washington Navy Yard was burned on the approach of the British in 1814. The document was not rediscovered until 1985, when Isaac Phi-llips's pleas for sympathy were finally put to rest.[51]

Captain John Loring was recalled early in 1800. After the end of Franco-American hostilities, he was returned to service and late in 1801 com-manded the *Prince* 98, in the Channel Fleet under Admiral Sir William Cornwallis. Two years later he regained squadron command on the Jamaica station, in the *Bellerophon* 74, in which he received the final French surrender at Cap François in December 1803, ending Napoleon's ill-fated attempt to reconquer St. Domingo.[52]

5. The Navy's First Defeat

Stoddert had hoped to be able to send a squadron built around a fifth-rate to the Caribbean in the later summer of 1798. In his correspondence, he never indicated which of the three frigates he intended to use for the operation. But with Barry expected to remain in the Antilles until Sep-tember and with Truxtun ordered to Havana in August, only the *Constitu-tion* remained. If Stoddert had intended to dispatch Nicholson to the West Indies, the *Niger* incident put an end to such ideas. As the summer ended, there were no frigates available for operations in the islands.

Nonetheless, Stoddert still intended to send a force south as soon as possible. Whatever doubts the secretary had concerning the dispatch of a frigateless squadron were overcome when Barry made, for Stoddert, a "surprise" appearance in the capital. The untimely return disappointed and embarrassed the secretary of the navy. His seeming inability to coordinate operations bred frustration that was vented on his senior captain. The ship *Montezuma* 20, originally intended to accompany a frigate to the south, was now designated to lead the squadron to the West Indies. Stoddert wrote Adams, on the day of Barry's arrival in Philadelphia, that he was going to send "the *Montezuma,* the brig *Norfolk,* the cutter *Eagle,* & the *Retaliation*" to the Caribbean. Stoddert was certain that this force would "return with more brilliance" than Barry's. Of risks he wrote: "there may danger of one or more of the vessels being taken, but the chance I think greatly in favor of [American successes]."[53]

Stoddert sent orders later that day to Baltimore to Captain Alexander Murray of the *Montezuma.* Murray's command would include the *Norfolk* 18, Captain Thomas Williams, the cutter *Eagle* 14, Captain Hugh G. Campbell, and the schooner *Retaliation* 14, commanded by Lieutenant William Bainbridge. The four ships were to rendezvous at Norfolk about 5 October and sail for the Caribbean.[54]

Murray was to take on stores for three months, carrying whatever extra supplies he could in the *Montezuma* and *Norfolk* to provision the smaller *Eagle* and *Retaliation,* unable to stow more than two. Murray's was a rather wide commission—to seek and capture French armed vessels where he saw fit throughout the Lesser Antilles.

As usual, delays set back the operation. Both the *Eagle* and *Norfolk* outfitted slowly. Manning proved to be a particular problem. Stoddert asked Murray to recruit forty extra men in Baltimore and proceed to the rendezvous with them to help man the other ships of his squadron. But by early October, the *Eagle,* outfitting in the capital, was still not prepared and Stoddert advised Murray to wait only a few more days before sailing. He also instructed Murray to return to the United States at the end of his cruise by way of Havana, where American ships would be awaiting a escort. The squadron left Hampton Roads on 24 October, without the *Eagle* which reached Norfolk on the 26th. Stoddert was disappointed, believing that Campbell, a thirty-eight-year-old South Carolinian, wanted "energy" and that his "shameful delay" had kept a fine ship from sailing. Having missed his rendezvous with Murray, Campbell would proceed to the southern coast and patrol.[55]

Command of the squadron was a singular honor for Alexander Murray. At sea for the first time as captain of a ship of war, this recently commissioned officer was already in charge of a multiship command on a distant station. The forty-three-year-old Marylander had extensive military and naval experience. He commanded his first merchant ship at eighteen, and fought with Smallwood's Maryland Regiment attaining the rank of captain in the Continental Army before resigning in June 1777. Murray then

returned to sea, commanding privateers before gaining a lieutenant's commission in the Continental frigate *Trumbull* in 1781. After the Revolution,
Murray remained with the Continental Navy, serving in the *Alliance*,
commanded by John Barry, until she was sold off in 1785. Murray then
began a successful career as a merchant in Philadelphia.[56]

Captain Thomas Williams commanded the other converted merchant
vessel in the squadron. The Virginian should have been the senior captain
and commodore. His commission bore the date 17 July, Murray's 3 August
1798. As Stoddert had first shaped the squadron around a frigate, the
relative ranking of the two men made little difference. But with no fifth-
rate available for the cruise, Stoddert faced a dilemma, "having confidence
in Murray, and not knowing William's true character, indeed being afraid
to trust him with a command of so much importance to the honor of the
navy. . . ." The secretary wrote Murray at Baltimore, instructing him to
mail his commission back to the Navy Department for an alteration that
would make the *Montezuma's* captain the senior officer. "You will see the
propriety of keeping the contents of this letter to yourself," Stoddert
advised. When the document reached Philadelphia, Stoddert wrote in
above the original date: "To take rank from the 1st. July 1798." The
commission was returned to Murray with the proviso that should Adams
object, the insertion would have to be "erased." But Stoddert delayed a
month, and four letters, before he informed the president. Had Adams
disapproved, which he did not, he was powerless to act before the squadron sailed for the West Indies. Stoddert's concerns about Williams were
well-founded, for in the course of the winter he gained the antipathy of his
seniors for "conduct . . . shameful to himself as a man, and disgraceful to
our country as an officer." Williams resigned to avoid dismissal or a court-
martial.[57]

Lieutenant William Bainbridge, a twenty-four-year-old New Jerseyite,
commanded the former *la Croyable,* renamed the *Retaliation.* Bainbridge
already had ten years' experience in merchant traders, the last six in
dangerous wartime European and West Indian waters. On one cruise in
the Caribbean, he beat off an attack by a British privateer and would have
taken her prize had the law allowed. On another occasion, a British frigate
sent a boat to board his ship and impressed one of Bainbridge's men. He
swore revenge, seized the first British ship he ran across, and took out of
her his compensation. Such verve, and political connections, earned
Bainbridge a position of command.[58]

* * *

Murray's squadron made landfall east of St. Thomas in mid-November.
For several days the three ships cruised to the windward of Antigua and

Guadeloupe. "Every day meeting British frigates," Murray wrote, "we concluded no other vessels were in these seas, and we were uniformly assured that the French had nothing larger than schooner privateers, except one ship of 18 guns."[59]

Stoddert had ordered the cruise on the same assumption, but the Americans were operating under the cloud of Britain's policy of distant blockade in Europe. Forty years earlier, Sir Edward Hawke had adopted a strategy of close blockade of Brest and other French ports in time of war. This forward policy placed severe strains on the ships and men of the Royal Navy, but had the advantage that it made less likely French forays onto the seas with squadrons of any size. The British had discontinued the policy during the war of 1778–1783. In bad weather the Western Squadron, responsible for watching Brest, retired to English ports, while even in good weather the fleet stood eight leagues west of Ushant. Admiral Richard Lord Howe deemed the good condition of his men and ships more important than close blockade. Howe's policy was continued between 1783 and 1800, and had a great impact on operations in the Caribbean, both British and American. There was little danger of the entire French fleet running into the Caribbean without the Western Squadron following close behind. But fast frigates, individually or in groups, could escape from France's Biscay ports, only distantly blockaded, and run into the Caribbean bringing reinforcements and supplies.[60]

Just such a squadron had cost the British control of the entire Lesser Antilles. Nine ships carrying 1,500 men for the reinforcement of Guadeloupe had sailed undetected from Rochefort in the spring of 1794. Britain had already captured the island, eliminating French power from the entire Windward and Leeward Island chains. But this minuscule French detachment, embarked in ignorance of Guadeloupe's fall and in the face of the dominance of the Royal Navy, carried Civil-Commissioner Victor Hugues to the West Indies and turned the tide against Britain, to the ultimate detriment of the United States. Hugues force landed on Guadeloupe and retook the island reopening the eastern Caribbean to French political machinations and privateering. By 1798, the Directory had decided to replace Hugues, and in the fall General Edme-Étienne Borne Desfourneaux left France in a squadron consisting of two frigates that eluded the British and descended upon the Caribbean.[61]

On 22 November, the American squadron sighted a small sail in the distance. Murray set out in pursuit and soon the chase came to. She was a American brig, in the possession of French privateers. The Yankees still in the brig told Murray that there were two French corsairs about, which had taken their brig and another prize. The information was accurate, for two sails were soon sighted. Murray left Bainbridge with the recaptured brig while the *Montezuma* and *Norfolk* set sail in chase. The privateers sought refuge in shallow water along the coast. Nightfall soon hid them from view.

Murray was not a man to give up easily, and throughout the night he and Williams stood offshore, their crews at quarters should the French attempt to sneak past in the dark. With the dawn came two sightings in rapid succession. First, lookouts sighted the *Retaliation* and the prize brig followed at a distance by two frigates. Murray sailed for Bainbridge and hailed him, but the commander of the *Retaliation* replied that the two sail were a pair of British frigates that had cruised in company with the Americans the previous day. Then, suddenly, in the opposite direction, the two French corsairs made their break. Murray pursued, leaving Bainbridge with the American brig. Disturbed by the appearance of the frigates, which were under full press of sail, Murray ran up the British private signals. There was no reply. They continued to press on; he presumed to join the chase.

As the frigates came abreast of the *Retaliation,* cannon fire reverberated across the water. Murray watched from his quarterdeck as the *Retaliation*'s flag came down. Unbelievably, but fortunately, he was still convinced that the frigates were English, supposing that they had demanded of Bainbridge some sign of deference. Murray continued the chase, the swifter *Norfolk* running down the sternmost sail, a second captured American brig. Joining Williams and the new prize, Murray was informed by the liberated Americans that the frigates were not English, but French. This information "at once marred our hopes of ever being joined by consort, and much valued officer Bainbridge, who," Murray wrote, "as well as our [first] prize brig, fell into [French] hands."

The French had evened the score, retaking their *la Croyable,* a loss more ironic than important. For the cost to the Americans could, and should have been greater; the frigates might well have run down all three unsuspecting Americans. Murray himself pondered his good fortune at escape, writing, "how they came to suffer us to take off the prize schooner, is incomprehensible, unless they were satisfied with their first booty." The French even lost the prize brig when the Americans left in the ship seized her and sailed to Antigua where they rejoined Murray.[62]

Bainbridge's report of 25 November detailing the loss of the *Retaliation* and his subsequent actions has eluded historians. How he came to mistake two French for British frigates is a mystery. He had copies of the private British signals which he, apparently, failed to use. To be fair, Murray did signal, but chose to believe the frigates British even when they failed to respond. Charles W. Goldsborough, a clerk in the Navy Department at the time, while silent on this question, did claim for Bainbridge the honor of saving the other ships of the squadron. Eager to please surviving officers when he wrote the *Naval Chronicle* in 1824, many of Goldsborough's accounts are inaccurate. What follows may be apochryphal.

According to Goldsborough, Bainbridge, like Murray, was surprised when one of the frigates fired into the *Retaliation,* hoisted the Tricolor, and ordered him to strike. The frigate *l'Insurgente* 36, in company with *le Volontaire* 40, was overwhelmingly superior to the American schooner. Bainbridge had no choice but to surrender. The American commander was ordered to come to the flagship *le Volontaire,* while the swifter *l'Insurgente* continued in pursuit of the other Americans. When Bainbridge reached the deck of the French frigate, he found her officers engrossed in the chase. He moved towards the rail to watch, borrowing a glass from a French lieutenant. Bainbridge saw the fast French frigate gaining steadily on the slower American ships, both former merchant vessels. As he watched, his presence on deck was finally noticed. The commodore of the French squadron came towards him, and standing by Bainbridge asked: "Pray, sir, what is the force of those vessels?" Without hesitation Bainbridge replied, "the ship carries twenty-eight twelve pounders, and the brig twenty nine pounders." This was a gross exaggeration of the strength of the Americans, but even so armed the two vessels stood little chance against the French frigate. The *Montezuma* actually mounted twenty 9-pounders, and the *Norfolk* eighteen 6-pounders, for a total broadside of 288 pounds. Bainbridge's ruse put the total of 516 pounds, but *l'Insurgente's* totaled 791 pounds, still significantly superior. But the combination of the malaise that gripped the French navy after 1789 and the fear of suffering damage in British-dominated waters was enough to bring the pursuit to an end. The signal for recall was made. The French passed up their only opportunity of the war to inflict a defeat on American naval forces. Stoddert's gamble on French weakness had failed, but the cost of the failure was small. Had Murray's entire squadron been captured, the blow to the United States Navy would have been severe.[63]

Despite his near demise, Murray remained undeterred by the presence of two French frigates at nearby Guadeloupe. He continued his work, windward of that island and Antigua, organizing convoys and escorting them clear of French cruising areas. Stoddert's orders were for a voyage of three months; Murray had no intention of returning early. He had seen how the secretary of the navy had greeted the esteemed John Barry. And Murray had taken his measure of the French. He remained in the islands on a cruise that would last longer than either he or Stoddert expected. For the secretary was organizing a new operation, and Alexander Murray was going to make himself part of it.[64]

5

WINTER IN THE CARIBBEAN:
1798–1799

───────

1. *"Service in a Warmer Climate"*

Thus far, American operations in the Quasi-War had been haphazard, hastily organized affairs, attempts primarily to show the flag and let American merchants know that support for the navy was worth their while. Only a few months old, the navy and its administration could not be expected to do much more.

Early in the fall, however, Stoddert began to prepare for what would be the largest American operation of the war. With the number of ships ready for sea increasing weekly, the exact configuration of the operation had yet to be decided, but Stoddert had every intention of making a strong show of force. The first signs of preparation appeared in Stoddert's orders to his commanders, instructing them to repair to port by mid-November to refit. Barry and Decatur, for example, were ordered back to sea on their return from the Caribbean in September, but only for a brief interval of coastal patrolling. Other captains received similar instructions.[1]

Stoddert had in mind a grand operation, by American standards, in the Caribbean. For on the day Decatur's orders to cruise the coast were drawn up, the secretary wrote Adams that arrangements were being made to prepare "three frigates and six or seven 20 to 24 gun ships, and some vessels of smaller size" for deployment by December in "the West Indies, or wherever ordered." There was, however, no suitable theater but the West Indies. Stoddert had from the first shown a willingness to gamble with the safety of the American coast in an effort to throw a few ships into the Antilles. As the war wore on, the ships patrolling the coast reported rare sightings of French privateers and saw no action. After much cruising between Cape Henry and Havana between July and October, Truxtun wrote Stoddert: "With respect to French privateers being on the coasts of the United States, it is folly to suppose it; besides the innumerable angles I have made, the number of vessels I have spoke (without one single exception) report, that they have neither seen or heard of any French cruisers, they are therefore all to the southward (what there is of them) you may depend." One merchant, about to dispatch a trading schooner from New York, felt secure enough that he decided not even to insure his vessel, "believing that our coasts are clear of French pickaroons. . . ."[2]

The evident dearth of French privateering activity off the American coast during the Caribbean hurricane season convinced Stoddert that there would be even less danger from privateers with the Atlantic's stormy season approaching. The winter months off the American coast would be hard on American ships as well. The rivers would freeze while the ships off shore would be battered by high seas, and to no purpose. Just as the British wintered their North American forces in more southerly waters, transferring them from Halifax to Bermuda, Stoddert believed of the American navy that during the winter "it may be desirable, that the whole should be sent into service in a warmer climate."[3]

Throughout September and October Stoddert made arrangements for the move south. He ordered ships to port by mid-November, and the naval agents "to make preparation as to provisions & ce." Soon ships' bread, beef, pork, fish, rum and other sundry supplies were being purchased up and down the coast. Work on still unfinished ships was hastened. Despite the youth of the navy and the lack of experience on the secretary's part, the effort was remarkable. Having taken over the Navy Department in June with but a single ship off the American coast, by the end of 1798 Stoddert would see twenty vessels in, on their way, or under orders to the Caribbean. All would be taking part in a well-planned and coordinated effort in a distant, foreign sea.[4]

* * *

Throughout the fall of 1798, Stoddert gathered intelligence on the dispositions of European forces—Spanish, French, and British—in the Caribbean. It is evident from the secretary's correspondence that he was well informed. As the war progressed and more United States naval vessels cruised the Antilles, commanders' reports contained valuable information. At this early stage of the Quasi-War, however, few men of war had gone south. Stoddert relied on civilian-supplied information. Traders and merchants passed on what they knew to the secretary, meeting Stoddert frequently in Philadelphia. Insurers were a particularly valuable source, for they made it their business to learn the extent of privateering activity to determine accurately risks and rates.

Thomas Fitzsimons, a prominent Philadelphian active in politics, commerce, and interested in naval affairs, was one of several valuable sources of intelligence for Stoddert. Fitzsimons had served in the House of Representatives from 1789 to 1795 and had been on the committee that drew up the naval act of March 1794. He was a founder and director of the Insurance Company of North America (INA) and during the Quasi-War was president of the Philadelphia Chamber of Commerce. Fitzsimons had been one of Forrest & Stoddert's early commercial contacts in the capital of 1784, and it is likely that Stoddert knew him from the Revolution. Robert Morris's financial collapse had ruined Fitzsimons, as it had Stoddert, and he would be forced to declare bankruptcy in 1805. During Stoddert's first week as secretary of the navy, he turned to Fitzsimons to organize the merchants of the capital to construct a frigate by subscription for the government. Fitzsimons eventually chaired the frigate committee that built the *Philadelphia* 36. He met frequently with Stoddert, but while Philadelphia remained the capital, few letters passed between the two men. Not until the government relocated to Washington did a sudden and regular correspondence develop. Between June and November 1800, Stoddert addressed ten letters to Fitzsimons, giving him accurate and timely information on planned naval deployments. Unfortunately, Fitzsimon's letters to the secretary of the navy do not appear in the navy's files. What they contained and what type of information Fitzsimons had been supplying to the navy is suggested by Stoddert who wrote: "communicate to me such ideas and information as might be useful to me in making such a disposition of our little navy . . .," and on another occasion: "wishing to hear from you frequently, and whenever you think it necessary to suggest any thing respecting the navy." Fitzsimons continued to supply the government with intelligence after the Quasi-War. In June 1801 he forwarded a Tripolitan order of battle to the Navy Department.[5]

Despite close Anglo-American ties, Great Britain and the United States did not establish any governmental agreement respecting intelligence sharing. The official correspondence in the State and Navy Department files, and Liston's and Grenville's dispatches, contain no hints of the British supplying the Americans with information. Royal Navy commanders and officials in the West Indies did share what they knew of French forces with American naval officers (and vice versa), and that information was passed to Stoddert in his captains' reports.[6]

From his American sources, Stoddert developed an accurate picture of a fluid and complex situation in the Caribbean. During 1797, America's commerce had suffered its heaviest losses to the French *guerre de course* in the Greater Antilles—Cuba, Hispaniola, and Puerto Rico—where trade was funneled through the Windward Passage. Of the more than 280 merchant vessels seized in the Caribbean that year, over 200 were taken by privateers based around the approaches to the straits between Cuba and Hispaniola. Over 60 were seized in the Lesser Antilles, virtually all by corsairs operating from Guadeloupe. Late in 1797, however, this pattern began to change. Losses in the Greater Antilles declined rapidly, while French activity around Guadeloupe increased. From 1797 to 1798, American ships captured by French privateers fell from over 300 to 150 world-wide, from about 280 to 105 in the Caribbean, while they rose from 58 to 89 at Guadeloupe.[7]

There were many reasons for the decline in the number of American merchant ships seized by French corsairs in the Windward Passage. The French were losing control of Hispaniola to rebellious forces that even-tually would lead St. Domingo to independence. Extensive British military activity, on the part of both the army and navy, suppressed privateering activity which, of course, posed a threat to Great Britain's commerce as well as that of the United States. American trading patterns with Euro-pean Caribbean colonies, especially French Hispaniola, also underwent major changes. Because of the turmoil of war, and the breakup of the plantation system, St. Domingo's sugar production dropped precipitously. Spanish Cuba replaced the French colony in the American market. Exports to Cuba from the United States rose from $2,800,000 in 1797, to $5,000,000 in 1798, and to $9,000,000 in 1799. Moreover, the very scale of French successes in the Windward Passage during 1797, led to prohibitive insurance rates, adoption of safer, if less direct routes, and ultimately to the embargo on trade with French colonies in June 1798. American exports to the French West Indies, principally St. Domingo, fell from $8,000,000 in 1797, to $2,700,000 in 1799.[8]

French privateering successes in the Lesser Antilles were primarily the work of the *commissair civil* on Guadeloupe, Victor Hugues. After recap-turing the island from British forces in June 1794, and repelling a coun-terattack, Hugues established a regime on Guadeloupe that mirrored that of revolutionary Paris in both its activity and its extremes. A Jacobin stalwart before his dispatch to the Caribbean, Hugues soon earned the name "the Colonial Robespierre" for his methods. Captured Royalists were butchered in mass executions. The corpse of the short-lived British governor was exhumed and thrown into a sewer. Hugues mobilized the newly freed black population and attempted to spread servile revolt to neighboring islands as a means to strike at Great Britain. While the British had too few troops on hand in the West Indies to eliminate Hugues as a threat, the Royal Navy was strong enough to interdict his island-hopping strategy. Frustrated by Britain's navy, in mid-1796 Hugues decided to attack English commerce through the *guerre de course*. Anything that could float was granted a commission, loaded with men, and sent out to sea. The number of prizes brought to the island for adjudication increased by over 400 percent.[9]

There were several aspects particular to Victor Hugues's brand of the *guerre de course*. As violence and anarchy born of social revolution spilled onto the Caribbean, privateering "degenerated rapidly into piracy, towards which that mode of warfare naturally tends." Hugues, a "demon of republicanism," proved to be the biggest pirate of all, collecting fees for the granting of commissions, gaining partial financial control of many corsairs, and manipulating court decisions to his own benefit. He dispatched cruisers to other ports controlled by France or her European allies— Holland and Spain—with blank commissions, spreading the campaign well beyond the immediate area around Guadeloupe. Increasingly antagonistic towards the Americans, who were guilty in his mind of supplying British forces in the West Indies and trading with French colonies now conquered by Britain, Hugues struck at the United States. The Directory's decrees of 1797 and 1798 permitted a full-scale assault on American Caribbean commerce and in the latter year the nearly 100 Yankee ships seized represented about half of Hugues's haul.[10]

That the Colonial Robespierre had gone too far, was a French as well as an American judgment. The Directors reported on 31 July 1798:

> . . . that information received from the French colonies and the continent of America leave [sic] no room to doubt that French cruisers, or such as call themselves French, have infringed the laws of the republic relative to cruising and prizes . . . [and] that foreigners and pirates have abused the latitude allowed at Cayenne, and in the West Indian islands, to vessels fitted out for cruising, or for war or commerce, in order to cover with the French flag their extortions, and the violation of the respect due to the law of nations, and to the persons and property of allies and neutrals. . . .

The French tightened up the regulations governing privateering. As part of this effort Desfourneaux was dispatched to Guadeloupe to replace Hugues. The general discovered on his arrival "a system of piracy almost general, sustained by a commercial tribunal which condemns without reserve and without exception neutral and allied ships on the most frivolous pretexts. . . ." Desfourneaux arrested Hugues and returned him to France a prisoner.[11]

Word of the Directory's effort to rein in Hugues and the Guadeloupean corsairs did not reach Philadelphia until early 1799. As Stoddert planned his winter offensive in the fall of 1798, however, his understanding that the island posed the most serious threat to American commerce, rather than the Windward Passage, was accurate. Even after the arrival of

Desfourneaux, while privateering activity never again matched the intensity it had under Hugues, Guadeloupe remained the major base for French corsairs in the Caribbean.[12]

* * *

In planning West Indian operations, Stoddert had also to consider Great Britain's policy towards the United States and her naval dispositions in American waters. The Americans were, after all, latecomers to a European conflict already in its seventh year. The same corsairs that preyed on Yankee traders attacked British merchantmen. Throughout the Quasi-War, the Royal Navy's Caribbean effort overshadowed that of the Americans in size, if not in effectiveness. Information relative to British deployments, plans, and prospective cooperation with the United States was almost as valuable as intelligence on the French.

When Stoddert reached Philadelphia in June 1798, a formal Anglo-American alliance seemed a distinct possibility. Britain allowed the American government to purchase badly needed "naval and warlike stores," especially cannon and copper. Lord Grenville instructed Liston to inform the Adams administration that Great Britain was prepared to loan the United States warships and would permit half-pay officers to serve in an American navy. The prize for this assistance—recruiting American seamen for service in the Royal Navy—was, however, a political and practical impossibility. So, too, were plans for combined operations against Spanish and French New World colonial possessions. Grenville came to realize that President Adams was determined to limit both the war with France, and entanglement with Britain. There would be no Franco-American declared war, nor a Anglo-American alliance.[13]

Accordingly, naval cooperation between the two English-speaking countries never fully developed. In July 1798, Stoddert and Vice Admiral George Vandeput, commanding the Royal Navy's North America station, devised simultaneously mutual recognition signals for use at sea. Stoddert accepted Vandeput's more practical system. By August, the Navy Department was issuing copies of the signals to its warships. Their use prevented many wasteful chases and mistaken clashes such as those that had occurred in July between the *Unanimity* and *Mosquito,* and the *United States* and *Thetis.* American merchant ships had been permitted to join convoys escorted by British warships as early as the spring of 1798. In September, Vandeput made the practice official, through Liston, on the trans-Atlantic routes. The privilege was soon extended to the Caribbean and as American naval vessels became operational, they reciprocated. By the late fall of 1798, however, the momentum towards further understandings dissipated.[14]

Winter in the Caribbean

Despite the fact that Britain and the United States were fighting a common enemy, a division of labor was never formalized, nor operational cooperation established during the Quasi-War. While Liston was kept abreast of American intentions, the minister did not possess comparable information to share with Adams, Pickering, and Stoddert. Major British operations in the Caribbean, for example the August 1799 attack on Dutch Surinam, came as complete surprises to Stoddert. The United States Navy was forced to rely on local British officials in the West Indies for cooperation, especially the senior naval commanders, Vice Admiral Sir Hyde Parker commanding at Jamaica, and Rear Admiral Henry Harvey commanding the Leeward Islands station. Given Loring's treatment of Phillips off Havana, respect, not to mention cooperation, was not always to be expected.[15]

That the British were not coordinating their efforts with the Americans is apparent from Stoddert's correspondence. He wrote Adams on 25 August 1798.

> I know not how the British employ the immense force they have in the islands—certainly not to afford much protection to our trade, nor to annoy much the cruisers from any island but that of St. Domingo, where they have views of conquest.—They some times indeed convoy a few of our vessels; I hope not merely that it may be talked about; yet I suspect we have ourselves alone to depend upon for the effectual protection of our commerce.—

The secretary was, however, being unfair to both the British and himself. The Royal Navy captured two French ships of war and seventy-eight privateers in the Caribbean during 1798. Between May and July, of the ninety ships in the Caribbean, seventy were concentrated under Harvey's command. American losses in the vicinity of Guadeloupe dropped sharply. By August, however, the British were shifting their forces from the Lesser Antilles to Jamaica, a pattern that continued until 1801. By the summer of 1799, the Jamaica station outnumbered the Leeward Islands command. The British redeployment had nothing to do with the arrival of American ships in the islands. The diminution of privateering activity at Guadeloupe and, primarily, a deteriorating situation on Hispaniola, dictated the shift of forces. The effect on American commerce, however, was marked. While four traders were captured by Guadeloupean corsairs in August, eighteen were taken in September.[16]

From his sources, Benjamin Stoddert was aware of the movement of British strength from the Lesser to the Greater Antilles. In his orders for Murray drawn up in late September, the secretary wrote that he "presumed that the British will attend sufficiently to the island of St. Domingo. . . ." Murray's squadron was to cruise in the Leeward and Windward Islands. Stoddert's accurate presumption shaped his plans for operations during the first winter of the war and into the spring of 1799.

$$* \quad * \quad *$$

Having surveyed the strategic situation in the Caribbean, or simply put, listening to the cries of American merchants and insurers, Stoddert drew up his plans for carrying the war to the French in the West Indies.

In forming a squadron for Cuba, Stoddert relied on Truxtun's advice on conditions off the Spanish colony. Ten French privateers were active off the north coast. Their impact on American trade was mostly psychological. The largest of the privateers mounted fourteen guns, but the rest were small vessels carrying one or two, sheltering along the coastal shoals for protection. Truxtun recommended the use of small ships off Havana, a small vessel with sweeps backed by a "smart brig equipped in like manner . . . will knock up the privateering system altogether. . . ." Small warships would have "ten times the chance of a frigate, or any other large ship in making captures." So advised, Stoddert saw no need to post a strong squadron to Havana. Command of a weak force was given to Stephen Decatur, Sr., in the *Delaware* 20. He was ordered to escort a convoy from Philadelphia to Havana in December and to remain there, to be joined later by a few small ships as soon as Stoddert could get them to sea. Eventually the cutters *General Greene* 10, Captain George Price, and *Governor Jay* 14, Captain John Leonard, were sent to join Decatur in January 1799.[18]

A second small squadron for the Windward Passage was to be built around the *Ganges* 24. Here, too, the presence of a frigate was deemed unnecessary because of the lessening importance of the Passage for American trade, and the activity of British naval forces off the coast of St. Domingo.

Having been rushed out to sea in May 1798, the *Ganges* returned to Philadelphia in August to refit. Captain Dale was less than enthusiastic about the sailing qualities of his old command as a warship. He found his cannon inferior and his crew disappointing. Stoddert was prepared to do what he could to improve the *Ganges,* but the secretary knew that the problem with Dale was related not to his ship, but to his rank.[19]

Dale had been the fourth-ranking captain appointed in 1794, but when work on three of the frigates stopped in 1796, he, Silas Talbot, and James Sever were left without commands. Did Truxtun, who had retained command since 1794, now rank ahead of Talbot and Dale? The question perplexed Stoddert. As Talbot and Dale argued, the intent of the act of 1796 had not been to place Truxtun before them in rank. Both Talbot and

Dale had been officers in the Continental Navy, while Truxtun had been a privateer; that had been the reason for the ranking in 1794. But Truxtun argued that, whatever the reasons for Congress's action in 1796, Talbot's and Dale's commissions had lapsed with the end of work on their ships. They had received no pay, nor served the government, and had been renominated and appointed a second time by the Senate. Stoddert leaned towards support for Truxtun and wrote Adams: "Truxtun is in possession—his commission, I understand is No. three." But the secretary feared that if the case were decided in Truxtun's favor, Talbot and Dale would resign, but if for the latter, Truxtun would quit.[20]

Talbot had yet to assume a seagoing command, and a judgment in his case lay in the future. Dale's situation demanded more immediate attention, but Stoddert hoped to put off any final decision. He appealed to Dale to remain in the service until a verdict could be reached. All three captains, Stoddert believed, were too valuable to be lost.[21]

Having put off Dale for the moment, Stoddert appears to have tried a ruse that would relieve him of the necessity of making a decision that would probably cost him the services of at least one commander. His intention was to bring the captains together, hoping that the gentlemen would work the matter out themselves. At the end of November, with Truxtun in the capital, Barry, Dale, Decatur, and Thomas Tingey were assembled, ostensibly to work out "regulations, or articles of war" for the navy. It is probable that Stoddert hoped that Dale and Truxtun, face to face, would settle their differences amicably.[22]

The scheme, if such it was, proved a partial success. After the Philadelphia meeting Dale decided to take a leave of absence and resume his career as a merchant, retaining rank without pay or emoluments. At a later date he would return to the naval service to command a frigate, when one became available. Stoddert was confident enough to write Alexander Hamilton, who had taken an interest in the matter, that Dale was "reconciled to what he conceived unavoidable, to rank after Truxtun." Talbot, Stoddert hoped, would also acquiesce in this regard, only Barry, Nicholson, and Truxtun ranking ahead of him. "Nicholson," Stoddert wrote, "cannot long be in his way—Barry is old and infirm. . . ." The matter seemed settled, but, in fact, it had yet to run its course.[23]

As for Dale's leave of absence, it was certainly untimely. Even Truxtun, his rival for rank, was appalled. "I have a very good opinion of Dale," Truxtun wrote, "but surely this is not time for a captain of a man of war to expect an indulgence of this sort. . . ." Stoddert was less forthright in stating his private opinion, but there was a hint of sarcasm in his letter to Dale informing him of Adams's approval of the leave, "not wishing to deprive any valuable officer in the service of the navy of an opportunity of bettering his fortune. . . ." The secretary might have been less satisfied with himself if he knew at the time that Dale's services were in fact lost for the duration of the war.[24]

While unsure about Dale's future service, Stoddert was certain that the Virginian would not return to sea again until he could have one of the frigates being built. Thomas Tingey was named as the new commander of the *Ganges*.[25]

Tingey was a forty-eight-year-old, London-born, ex-British warrant officer. He had met the daughter of a Philadelphia merchant before the American Revolution in St. Croix, and later settled in Pennsylvania and married her. Tingey was well known in the capital where he was considered a "gentleman of reputation, to be highly qualified for a command in the navy." He had served as a director of the Insurance Company of North America in 1794, and, like Dale, was familiar with the *Ganges*, having commanded her on a voyage to the East Indies.[26]

Ordered to the Windward Passage, Tingey was told to expect two or three smaller vessels to join him in the course of the winter. Subsequently, the brig *Pinckney* 18, Captain Samuel Heyward, and the cutter *South Carolina* 12, Captain James Payne, were ordered to join the *Ganges*.[27]

Historians of the Quasi-War have invariably placed these two ships with Tingey in the Windward Passage during the winter of 1798–99, but they actually never sailed with him. A letter written by a marine lieutenant in the *South Carolina* places both vessels still in Charleston at the end of February 1799. Stoddert wrote Charleston in March, mentioning the letter which he had seen, expecting to find the ships in port. The two were instead ordered to cruise between Cape Hatteras and the St. Marys River. The *South Carolina* had, in the meantime, at last sailed, being met by Murray in the *Montezuma* off Hispaniola in April. By that time Tingey had already returned to the United States. The *Pinckney* remained in port at the end of April. Tingey's was to be a one-ship squadron.[28]

* * *

With small forces of weak vessels off Havana and the Windward Passage, the remaining ships of the navy, including all three frigates, were available for operations in the Lesser Antilles. Here, the area to be covered was geographically dispersed, unlike the restricted waters of the Straits of Florida and the Windward Passage. With such a wide area to patrol, Stoddert, "pursuing European ideas," chose to divide American forces operating south of Puerto Rico into two commands, one to cover the Leeward Islands facing northeast, and the other the Windward Islands facing east and south.[29]

Initially, Stoddert planned to use three squadrons in the south, with the third force cruising off the northern coast of South America between Cartagena and Guiana. Each squadron would have been built around one of the frigates. But if such a course were followed, one of the squadrons would fall under the command of Samuel Nicholson, in whom Stoddert had "no confidence."

Instead, Stoddert was forced to adopt a two-squadron plan, and to build up the southernmost force to sufficient strength that detachments from it might cruise to the Spanish Main. Even in this arrangement, however, Nicholson's incompetence complicated the plan. Since any grouping of three frigates in two squadrons would be asymetrical, it would make the most sense to place one of the two forty-four-gun frigates at the head of each force, with the *Constellation* joining the southern, stronger, squadron. But then Nicholson would have command of one of the groups. Stoddert was forced to give command of the two squadrons to Barry and Truxtun and to place Nicholson, who was senior to Truxtun, under the authority of Barry. As a result the squadron with two frigates had both forty-fours, while Truxtun's weaker frigate, thirty-six guns, was left alone. This scheme of deployment so dissatisfied Stoddert that he wrote:

> I am afraid to trust [Nicholson] with a separate command—and to keep such a frigate as his under the command of Barry, in the present state of our affairs, when we have no force equal to either, to apprehend, is to make of her no more use or importance than a ship of 20 guns.
> I have long determined therefore, to prevent his going out in her again. . . . Had there been confidence in Nicholson, another division of our vessels might have been advantageously made in the West Indies—Barry has too many crowded together—and has not mind enough for their employment.

Unless Nicholson redeemed himself during the winter, his command of the *Constitution* would end.[30]

With the complications in planning caused by Nicholson's lack of ability, the most powerful command in the West Indies fell to John Barry, whose large squadron was to protect American commerce and capture and destroy French privateers from St. Christopher (St. Kitts) to Tobago. Stoddert placed a heavy burden of responsibility on Barry's shoulders, expecting that the coming American effort in the Caribbean would give "little short of perfect security . . . to our commerce in those seas; and that the inhabitants of the hostile islands, may be taught respect, and to fear the power of the United States." In his capacity as commodore, Barry was also to protect the trade along the Spanish Main that Stoddert would have liked to have had secured by a third squadron. As he had the previous July,

Stoddert gave Barry additional instructions that permitted him great latitude in his operations: "It is presumed your force will permit you to pay
considerable attention to Cayenne, Curaçao, and even . . . to La Guaira
and the Spanish Main. But above all, your efforts must be directed to
relieve our commerce, from the picaroons, and pirates, continually issuing
from the island of Guadeloupe." With such discretionary instructions,
Barry was being asked to act with judgment commensurate with his
rank.[31]

Stoddert was convinced that the French lacked the strength to challenge
Barry's force, and hoped that he would be able "to rid those seas" of
whatever French ships appeared. Stoddert was still unaware of the loss of
the *Retaliation* and the presence in the Caribbean of two French frigates.
In the event that powerful French forces did reach the Caribbean, however, Stoddert issued each of the squadron commanders—Barry, Truxtun,
Tingey, and Decatur—instructions outlining the entirety of American
dispositions in the West Indies. Here, too, a heavy burden fell to Barry. As
the senior officer controlling the most powerful squadron, if he learned of
threats to any of the dispersed American commands, he was either to
reinforce the threatened commodore, regroup with him, or if necessary,
withdraw all American naval forces to the United States.

Barry's squadron was to use Prince Rupert Bay on British Dominica as a
rendezvous where the ships joining him later in the winter would be sent.
As to the length of the operation, Stoddert wrote that he expected it to last
until April or perhaps May.

In the course of the winter, Barry's own *United States* 44, would be
joined by the frigate *Constitution* 44, the ships *George Washington* 24,
Captain Patrick Fletcher, *Portsmouth* 24, Captain Daniel McNeill, *Merrimack* 24, Captain Moses Brown, *Herald* 18, now commanded by Lieutenant Charles C. Russell, and the cutters *Pickering* 14, now commanded by
Lieutenant Edward Preble, *Eagle* 14, Captain Hugh C. Campbell, *Scammel*
14, Captain John Adams, and the *Diligence* 12, Captain John Brown.[32]

* * *

At the head of the remaining American squadron was Thomas Truxtun
in the *Constellation* 36. Truxtun's command would eventually include the
Baltimore 20, now commanded by Lieutenant Josias M. Speake; the brig
Richmond 18, Captain Samuel Barron; and the cutter *Virginia* 14, Captain
Francis Bright. Truxtun was also to take charge of the ships already in the
Caribbean under Murray: the *Norfolk* 18, and the *Retaliation* 14, which,
unknown to Stoddert, had been recaptured by the French. Truxtun was to
cruise throughout the islands extending from Puerto Rico to St.
Christopher (St. Kitts), the latter island serving as the place of rendezvous

for the squadron. Truxtun, too, was expected to do his part to teach the French respect. He was to deal harshly with pirates, Stoddert writing: "Nothing is said in your instructions respecting pirates, you know how to treat them."[33]

2. War Without Bases

In planning an extensive campaign in the West Indies, with the intent of maintaining forces in the islands beyond the spring of 1799, Stoddert had to overcome serious logistical problems. The geographical scale of operations was enormous for a navy only six-months-old. The rendezvous for the squadrons—Havana, the Windward Passage, St. Kitts, and Prince Rupert Bay—were respectively 1,136, 1,246, 1,537, and 1,674 miles from Philadelphia. Cayenne and Curaçao, to which Barry was to attend, were 2,470 and 1,760 miles. Even within the Caribbean, the distances that would separate the American forces were substantial. Decatur, cruising off Havana, would be closer to his home in Philadelphia than to Barry at Dominica.

In the age of sail the relevant distances were expressed in sailing days rather than miles. Speed and course would vary with the directions of winds and currents. The trade winds perpetually blew into the Caribbean from the east. Other prevailing winds blew northwards along the American coast. Ships sailing for the West Indies from North America would generally sail a southeasterly course into the Atlantic, often as far east as 60° west longitude if their destination was in the Lesser Antilles, before turning west to be carried by the trades into the Caribbean. Sailing with the wind on one of its quarters, a fast frigate could achieve speeds of eight to eleven knots. Sailing against the wind, the same vessel would have to follow a zigzag course, tacking, at speeds of two or four knots per hour. As an example, Barry's leeward chase of the French privateer off San Juan in September 1798, lasted twelve hours. To recover the same distance to windward took two days. On the same cruise, which lasted three months, only eighteen days were actually spent in the islands. Barry's first foray demonstrated that ships could not operate effectively within the Caribbean based from American ports.[34]

If the United States Navy was to carry the war to the heart of the French *guerre de course*, bases and supply would be needed in the Caribbean. America's nominal neutrality gave Stoddert an advantage here, for he could expect that his men-of-war would be permitted to anchor in the harbors of the belligerents. The French, of course, were not about to allow the *Constellation* to shelter within the anchorage at Basse-Terre, Guadeloupe, but the other warring powers—Spain, Holland, and Great Britain—controlled the entire Caribbean basin, except for the few islands still controlled from Paris. The British could be expected to welcome the assistance of the United States. The Spanish and Dutch despite their alliances with France were often eager to see American warships because their colonies needed American foodstuffs to survive.[35]

Provisioning ships in the Antilles was another matter. Stoddert had no agreement with the British to provide either provisions or stores for American ships in the West Indies. He assumed that water could be drawn locally, but neither Britain or France's allies were expected to yield their stores, sent at great expense from Europe, to American squadrons. Provisions, too, might be available from local merchants, but American operations dependent on European suppliers for victualing would be at risk. Provisions and stores, to the greatest extent possible, would have to come from the United States.

The goods consumed by the infant American navy were, by modern standards, insignificant. At its peak strength during the Quasi-War, the navy contained fewer than 6,000 men. Today, a full complement for a single *Nimitz*-class carrier is 6,286 officers and men. To provide for its personnel during the undeclared naval war with France, the Navy Department had to procure annually about 5,000 tons of provisions. About half of this amount had to be supplied to ships on station in the Caribbean.

Nevertheless, the provisions needed for a single ship, examined in components, appear somewhat more substantial. Six-months' supplies for a forty-four-gun frigate included 361 barrels of beef, pork, flour, and meal; 485 bushels of beans and potatoes; 33.5 tons of rice, bread, fish, butter, cheese, candles and soap; 1,547 gallons of molasses, vinegar, and lamp oil; and 4,325 gallons of rum.[36]

Stores were less of a problem because of the nature of the Quasi-War. Few "battles" occurred and expenditures of powder and shot remained low. Spars, cordage, and canvas, however, were always needed owing to damage caused by normal wear and tear, and the elements. Ships sailing from the United States generally loaded their decks with extra stores that would be off-loaded, whenever possible, on arrival in the Caribbean. In the face of extensive damage (the loss of a mast, for example) American warships had to return to their home ports for repairs.[37]

Stoddert directed his initial efforts to supply men-of-war on station in the Caribbean to the small, three-ship squadron off Havana commanded by Decatur. A merchant ship was chartered at New York, loaded with ten tons of ships' bread and 100 barrels of meat, and sent to Cuba in January 1799. Stoddert hoped the ship would fall in with Decatur, who would take charge of the provisions and disperse them among his ships. If Decatur could not be found, the master of the storeship was ordered to land his supplies to be warehoused by the American consul at Havana, Daniel Hawley. Once ashore, the provisions could be drawn upon by Decatur's ships whenever they were in port.[38]

Surprisingly, while Stoddert was confident that the Spanish, allies of the French, would permit the United States to operate a squadron from Havana, he was uncertain of the response of the British to such an arrangement. Stoddert's fears are another indication of the absence of governmental coordination between the two countries during their war with France. Stoddert arranged through Gabriel Wood & Co. of Baltimore, for Frazier Urquhart & Co. on Dominica, and Denniston & McLaughlan on St. Kitts, to store the provisions if British officials allowed them to be landed. Truxtun and Barry would draw on the supplies as needed. In the event that Britain refused permission for the supplies to be brought ashore, the contracts of the ships chartered contained clauses for their retention on station as squadron tenders.[39]

In his use of American merchants and diplomats in the West Indies, Stoddert gravitated toward the extension of the navy agent system to the Caribbean. Later that winter when a new consul was sent to Havana, Joseph d'Yznardi, he was instructed by the State Department to act as navy agent, although Spain's alliance with France necessitated that the position remain unofficial. But the agency went along with the consulship at Havana, for d'Yznardi's replacement, John Morton of Philadelphia, was given similar orders. These same procedures were eventually followed in the Dutch colonies of Curaçao (Benjamin Hammel Phillips), and Guiana (Turell Tufts). In St. Domingo, after reaching an agreement with the de facto ruler of much of the colony, Toussaint L'Ouverture, the first official Caribbean navy agent (Nathan Levy) operated from Cap François. On British St. Kitts, an agent (David Matthew Clarkson) was appointed in April 1799.[40]

Service as a navy agent was not viewed as a burden, but as a source of income by consuls who were, after all, merchants. The close relationship between the State and Navy Departments, and between Pickering and Stoddert, has been mentioned. That between consuls and commodores developed during the Quasi-War, but it had been symbolized as early as February 1798 when Pickering issued instructions that stated that "the consuls and vice-consuls of the United States are free to wear the uniform of the navy, if they choose to do so . . . [with] small swords."[41]

The logistical system developed during the winter of 1798–99 enabled Stoddert to maintain significant forces in the West Indies throughout the Quasi-War. The lessons learned and the techniques developed were applied in the Indian Ocean in 1799, and the Mediterranean during the Barbary Wars. In fact, the Quasi-War system served the navy until the end of the nineteenth century. Commodore George Dewey, coaled and provisioned at British Hong Kong, sailed for battle with the Spanish in 1898 much as Commodore Thomas Truxtun sailed from St. Kitts against the French a century earlier.[42]

3. A Winter Short Only on Glory

American men-of-war fought few battles of note during the winter, though they were far from inactive. Of the twenty-two warships available between December 1798 and April 1799, an average twenty were operational, and nineteen sailed the Caribbean. Commanders organized convoys and escorted them to, within, and from the West Indies. They sought French corsairs, capturing nine, and recapturing five of the twenty American merchant vessels taken by French privateers.

On the Havana station, many sails but few privateers were sighted. Decatur recognized that his ships could be more profitably employed protecting convoys than trying to run down elusive corsairs. While the cutters *General Greene* and *Governor Jay* escorted merchant ships between Havana and the Straits of Florida, the *Delaware* cruised between Havana and Matanzas, on the lookout for a large French privateer mounting "26 to 28 guns." If the rumors concerning such a powerful privateer were true, Decatur never located the ship.

The only victory scored by Decatur's squadron came on the night of 5 March 1799. The *Delaware* was in company with the *General Greene* escorting a convoy of twenty sail clear of Havana when, shortly after midnight, a lookout on the *Delaware*'s deck spied "a sail standing atho't us." Decatur gave the vessel four guns and she quickly hove to. She was *le Marsouin* out of Cape François armed with one 9-pounder and ten swivels, with a crew of twenty-six. Loaded in the ship were seventy barrels of provisions from Havana. The French master protested that the little ship was merchantman, not a privateer.

After examining his prize, Decatur concluded that *le Marsouin* was subject to capture under Stoddert's instructions. While the French ship was undoubtedly moonlighting as a cargo carrier, attesting to Decatur's success in making the north coast of Cuba unprofitable for privateers, the fact that *le Marsouin* was armed made her a good prize. Just to make sure, in his report to Stoddert Decatur included "ten muskets, thirty cutlasses" along with the single cannon and the swivels in the list of *le Marsouin*'s armament.

Winter in the Caribbean

With French privateering activity off Cuba minimal, the Spanish authorities at Havana accommodating, it was left to the Royal Navy to threaten the operations of Decatur's squadron. On 8 February 1799, the *Delaware* fell in with an American convoy consisting of four merchantships, the storeship *America* loaded with the squadron's provisions, and the cutters *General Greene* and *Governor Jay*. "Under easy sail" Decatur joined the convoy, observing a large vessel that had been trailing him for several hours. This ship came up and fired several shots among the American ships. She was the *Solebay* frigate, 32 guns, from Sir Hyde Parker's Jamaica station. Her captain was under standing orders to search for contraband all vessels bound for Havana.

In response, Decatur ran up his colors and beat his crew to quarters, a wise step that would both demonstrate his determination, and help maintain control of his crew in a crisis. He had probably learned from the American consul in Havana of Phillips's meeting with Loring in November. News of the fate of the captain of the *Baltimore,* however, had not yet reached the Caribbean. Decatur went alongside the British frigate, whose commander informed him of his desire to search the American ships. Decatur pointed out the public ships among the convoy adding: "I told him if I was of equal force he should not, examine one of them." His opinion of the "right" of the British to search American merchantmen made clear, Decatur bore away, "hurt at seeing the flag over my head insulted. . . ." The other American ships followed. The *Solebay*, which had attempted to overhaul two of the convoy's vessels, desisted when it became evident the Yankees were not going to halt.

When an extract of Decatur's letter mentioning his meeting with the *Solebay* appeared in the Philadelphia press in March, Robert Liston, newspaper in hand, marched to Stoddert's office to wait upon the secretary of the navy. Nothing illegal had occurred off Cuba. Decatur had not refused the British the right of search, although he had most certainly done nothing to assist them. The King's minister was concerned, however. What would Decatur have done had his force been superior to the *Solebay*'s? What would other American commanders do? Liston represented to Stoddert "the necessity of his giving the commanders of the American vessels of war such instructions as might prevent the bad consequences of their attempting to resist British men of war, in the exercise of a right which His Majesty could not possibly give up in favour of any neutral nation." He "was glad to find" that Stoddert agreed, and had, in fact, issued a circular on 16 January 1799 meant to clarify confusion evident in that of 29 December 1798 drawn up as a response to the Havana incident. Apparently, some had considered the command not to permit "public vessels" to be detained or searched, to extend to merchant ships under convoy. Stoddert considered himself responsible, not "having been long enough in office to be master of all the questions of the law of nations which have a relation to maritime affairs.."[44]

If the secretary was troubled by Decatur's conduct, he made no mention of it in his official correspondence. On his return to Philadelphia in May 1799, the *Delaware*'s captain received only praise for a job well done, and promotion to the command of a frigate of his choice. Perhaps Stoddert asked himself, what would have become of his plans for operations off the Cuban coast had the British seized the squadron's storeship, the *America?* Decatur's spirit had prevented that, and Stoddert found zeal refreshing in the wake of the dismissal of Isaac Phillips.[45]

* * *

Captain Thomas Tingey's *Ganges,* ordered by Stoddert to the Windward Passage, reached Cap François on 2 January 1799, where he fell in with a strong British squadron of blockade under the command of Commodore Edward Smith. Smith invited Tingey to the flagship, the *Hannibal* 74, where the American captain received "the most friendly and marked attention—withal informing of it being the particular order of Admiral Sir Hyde Parker, for a like regard to our ships public or private, to every captain in his fleet." Tingey should have had reservations, for Parker's treatment of private American ships was far from friendly. The admiral and his captains were notorious for their ill-treatment and impressment of American seamen.[46]

After conferring with Smith, Tingey wrote Stoddert that the British blockade and the activity of the black revolutionary Toussaint L'Ouverture had brought about "an almost total stagnation to the French privateering . . . from this I could presage little business for the *Ganges.*" Tingey nevertheless cruised for a few days to leeward, making his way into the Windward Passage. Here he found nothing but the British flag. "In short," Tingey wrote, "during my stay here, scarce an hour passed, but one, two, or more British cruisers were in sight."[47]

It was in the Windward Passage on 8 January that Tingey fell in with the sixth-rate *Surprise* 24, commanded by Captain Edward Hamilton (who later in the year would earn fame and a knighthood cutting out the *Hermione* in Puerto Cabello harbor). Having met with nothing but goodwill thus far from the British, Tingey hove to when hailed by Hamilton.[48] A boat from the *Surprise* pulled for the *Ganges* and a Royal navy lieutenant was soon on the deck of the American warship asking an astonished Tingey "whether any Englishmen were in my crew; observing that my assurance would be sufficient to prevent an officer being sent to examine their protections, I did not hesitate to say I considered all my crew

Americans by birth or adoption—but I also observed to the officer, that there were no protections on board to my knowledge—the only one we carried in our public ships being our flag." The British lieutenant accepted Tingey's reply and returned to the *Surprise*. Tingey gathered his officers on the quarterdeck to discuss the situation. Soon, a second boat was pulling for the *Ganges*. Tingey turned to his assembled officers: "I declared to them my determination to fall sooner there than suffer an investigation or permit any man's name to be called over."

Coming on board this time, however, was not a commissioned officer, but the surgeon with a request for some medical supplies. Perhaps the second visit was just that, or perhaps it was an attempt on Hamilton's part to measure the American reaction to his initial request. The *Surprise's* surgeon, John M'Mullen, longed for action. (He volunteered to lead, and led, a division of Hamilton's men in the night attack on the *Hermione*.) In any event, some token supplies were turned over to the British, and M'Mullen departed. There would be no repetition of the Havana incident. Tingey ordered the crew mustered, however, just in case. He knew many of his men were of British birth, as was their captain. "[I] did pledge myself to them that not a man should be taken from me, by any force whatever, while I am able to stand at my quarters—which declaration they received with three cheers, and high spirits."[49]

Tingey's handling of the encounter with Hamilton was resolute, the type of response Stoddert expected from the men entrusted with the warships of the new American navy. And Tingey's behavior was born of his own spirit and zeal for the service. At the time, he knew nothing of Phillips's run in with Loring, nor the dismissal of the *Baltimore's* commander. Captain Tingey learned of that from old newspapers he read at St. Thomas later in the month. Tingey's determination to make the British show their hand if they were serious about taking men out of his ship, proved sufficient to deter Hamilton.

Tingey's actions deserved praise, but stories do have a way of growing. News of the incident reached the United States on the heels of the dismissal of Isaac Phillips and took on herculean form. Newspapers published the following extract from an officer in the *Ganges*:

An officer of the *Surprise,* an English frigate of 44 guns, boarded us off Cape Nichola Mole, and demanded all the Englishmen on board, also to examine the protections of the American seamen. Captain Tingey's answer was manly and noble.—'A PUBLIC SHIP CARRIES NO PROTECTION BUT HER FLAG, I DO NOT EXPECT TO SUCCEED IN A CONTEST WITH YOU; BUT I WILL DIE AT MY QUARTERS BEFORE A MAN SHALL BE TAKEN FROM THE SHIP'—The crew gave him three cheers, ran to quarters, and called for Yankee Doodle. The *Surprise* upon hearing our determination, chose rather to leave us than to fight for dead men!

In response to such stories, Tingey wrote the *Norfolk Herald* trying to set the record straight. He did not want the incident to sour American relations. Perhaps, of English parentage and Royal Navy service himself, he better understood the costs of a war with Britain. If he did not, those costs were driven home to him by Alexander Cochrane in 1814. For it was Thomas Tingey who commanded the Washington Navy Yard that year when the British came to town.[50]

After the encounter with the *Surprise,* if Tingey doubted the wisdom of remaining longer in the Windward Passage, a strong northwest wind saved him the problem of departing his instructions by blowing his tender ship to San Juan, Puerto Rico. At last escaping the grip of this rather extraordinary breeze, Tingey cruised off the north coast of the island, but found privateers just as scarce there. Merchants with ships at St. Thomas, however, approached Tingey requesting a convoy north.

By this time the *Ganges* was nearly out of water and in need of ballast. To solve the latter problem, Tingey had complicated the former. He had tried to fill bags with sand for ballast while off Hispaniola, but gave up the attempts for fear of losing his shore parties on hostile beaches. As a recourse, he had filled his empty water casks with seawater, contaminating them. Short of water, Tingey decided that he had best escort the convoy from St. Thomas north, and return to the United States for new water casks, ballast, and instructions.

Tingey departed St. Thomas on 2 February with ten sail. After seeing the convoy clear of privateer-infested waters, he returned for a final sweep of the Hispaniolan coast. Working his way along the shore, he looked into several ports, but concluded that he was "only wasting the time for which the ships was fitted to sea."[51]

When Stoddert learned of Tingey's arrival at Norfolk in late February, the secretary was not in the least displeased by the unordered return of the only ship cruising in the Windward Passage. Negotiations had been underway with the British regarding Hispaniola, and Adams and Pickering had decided to send an American consul to Cap François. The new appointee, Edward Stevens, was on his way to Norfolk in the ship *Kingston;* Tingey's timely arrival made it possible to provide the vessel with an armed escort. The *Ganges* was soon retracing her wake towards the Caribbean.[52]

*   *   *

John Barry's second command in the West Indies proved more elaborate than his first, but similarly disappointing. In company with the *George Washington,* Barry entered Prince Rupert Bay, Dominica, on 30 December, exchanging a thirteen-gun salute with the British fort. Over the next two weeks, Barry was content to exchange several other salutes with British garrisons and to dine with officials such as Rear Admiral Harvey.[53]

Prince Rupert Bay was the best anchorage on Dominica. American men-of-war could moor in eight fathoms of water, in a bay three miles wide and one mile deep, using the tall spire of the Roman Catholic church in Portsmouth, a small town in the northeast, as a landmark. Every Saturday the townspeople held a market where provisions could be obtained. Just south of the church, the Americans could draw water from the Indian River. The bay was convenient for operations against Guadeloupe, the next major island to the north. In fact, Prince Rupert Bay was best approached from that direction, either along the lee of Guadeloupe, or through the Dominica Passage. The highlands to the south of the bay, especially Morne au Diable, 4,747 feet above sea level, caused variable winds. A ship sailing north along the lee shore of Dominica was as likely to find itself becalmed as struck by a sudden, dangerous squall.[54]

Barry spent most of his time near this rendezvous, considering it important for him to remain there to meet the vessels sent out to join his command. This routine, however, virtually immobilized the *United States*.

The *Constitution* arrived on 19 January. Stoddert had written Barry that he hoped that Nicholson would "not justify by his conduct under your command, the predictions of his enemies. . . ." Nicholson's litany of failure throughout the summer and fall of 1798 had done little but injure an already doddering reputation. The present cruise would be Nicholson's last chance to save his command, for Stoddert was himself becoming one of the "enemies" of his second-ranking captain.[55]

But Nicholson was ever consistent in his behavior. His orders, dated 5 December 1798, were sent to Boston where the *Constitution* had been moored since 10 November. But Christmas Day found the frigate still riding in Nantasket Roads, and Stoddert wrote Higginson that Nicholson "should not loiter his time away in port." If the frigate was not soon at sea, he would have to answer not to Stoddert, but to the president, who would "expect that a better reason than can at present be conceived, will be given for the delay." The *Constitution* was soon plying the North Atlantic for the Caribbean.[56]

Heading south on 16 January, Nicholson sighted two sails near Bermuda. one of the vessels was rather large, apparently a ship of war. Nicholson prepared for action, raising both British and American signals. Receiving no reply, the overloaded and badly trimmed *Constitution* set out in pursuit, but before she could overtake her quarry a squall enveloped all three ships. Contact was lost. When the *Constitution* emerged from the tempest, ahead lay the smaller of the two ships. After a futile attempt at escape, a few shots from the *Constitution* brought her to. She was an English mer-chantman, the *Spencer,* prize to the French fifth-rate *l'Insurgente.* Nic-holson had just missed his chance to revenge the loss of the *Retaliation,* for the larger ship he had sighted had been the French frigate. But at least Nicholson had his first prize of the war; he put a crew of ten men into her and continued on his way.[57]

The *Niger* affair, however, weighed heavily on his mind. He knew that his career could not afford another mistake. Was the *Spencer* an English or a French ship? Once again poor Sam Nicholson made the wrong decision. He concluded that his instructions did not permit him to capture English merchant vessels; hence the ship had to be released. But to whom? After twelve hours, Nicholson pulled his men out of the ship, returning control to *l'Insurgente's* prize crew. The *Spencer* soon arrived at Guadeloupe to the chagrin of American and British merchants in the Caribbean.[58]

Reports of Nicholson's release of the *Spencer* reached Philadelphia in March 1799, confounding both Stoddert and Liston. Lest such behavior be repeated, the secretary of the navy issued a circular on 12 March, embar-rassingly mentioning Nicholson by name, and clarifying what should have been obvious to the *Constitution's* commander. "A vessel captured by the cruisers of France," Stoddert wrote, "must be considered as sailing under the authority of France. . . ." As such, the *Spencer* was subject to capture. Liston reported the incident to Lord Grenville, noting that after this latest miscue, the Adams administration appeared "determined that as soon as [Nicholson] returns from his present cruise he shall be dismissed from the public service."[59]

After rendezvousing with Barry in Prince Rupert Bay, Nicholson sailed for a few days in company with the *United States.* A sudden squall struck the frigates, carrying away the main topmast crosstrees, stays, and top-gallant yards of the *Constitution.* "Very much disabled," Nicholson limped back to Dominica for repairs.[60]

After mending the damage, he returned to sea on 2 February, patrolling near Guadeloupe and Montserrat. Nicholson then took up a position windward of la Désirade, a small island notable principally because it served as the divide between the Leeward and Windward Islands. La Désirade was also a major landfall for ships coming from Europe, especially those sailing for Guadeloupe. Nicholson's cruise off the little island demon-strated his understanding of the West Indies, the product of years of experience. He was well placed to intercept any French men-of-war bound for Basse-Terre from France. Even *l'Insurgente,* should she return to Guadeloupe after her cruise near Bermuda, might be expected to sail out into the Atlantic in order to approach Basse-Terre from the windward, rather than attempt to wind her way through the Leeward Islands. But

Nicholson was to be given no chance to redeem himself. After two weeks, he moved on having made not a single capture.[61]

The other ships of Barry's squadron also saw little action. Barry dispersed his ships among the islands, organized convoys, and escorted them clear of the West Indian danger zone. His activity in this regard was reputable, and it is no wonder that the commodore's busy ships made so few captures. L'Amour de la Patrie, a small privateer that foolishly attempted to escape Barry's frigate by running under her battery, was sunk on 4 February when a 24-pound shot fired at close range passed through the little ship. Another small privateer, le Tartuffe, was captured during March 1799 by the United States and was used as a tender to carry spare provisions and stores for the squadron.[62]

Despite his activity, Barry's conduct did not satisfy Stoddert. The commodore again failed to carry out subsidiary sections of his instructions, and he did not act in a manner befitting his relative rank and command of the major American squadron—making virtually no attempt to coordinate his actions with Truxtun's.

Stoddert expected Barry, with his large force built up for that purpose, "to pay considerable attention to Cayenne, and Curaçao, and even . . . to La Guaira and the Spanish Main." Privateers were known to be active to the south of Barry, especially off the Dutch colonies of Curaçao and Guiana where American trade was booming. Yet Barry considered himself unable to detach a single ship. Well aware of Stoddert's intentions, Barry wrote Truxtun demanding that he send a vessel south. The message angered and hurt Truxtun, who viewed it as a snub from his superior. He wrote in reply.

> I have taken great pains to communicate with you, since I have been on this station, and to nourish and cherish a good understanding with you, not only as an officer, but as a private gentleman, for no difference has ever existed between us, in an acquaintance of upwards of twenty years . . . but since I came out here, I have only received a single letter from you, and that merely demanding one of my vessels from this station . . . the good of the service, the protection of commerce in addition to our former good understanding, induces me to write you freely: and I expect you will do the same. . . .[63]

* * *

Truxtun had reached his squadron's rendezvous, Basseterre Roads, St. Kitts, late in the afternoon of 16 January. He knew the island well, having lost a ship, the Charming Polly, there in 1776. There were no proper harbors on St. Kitts, only several roadsteads, considered by the British "indifferent" and unsafe in poor weather. Basseterre Roads was one of these, a small, semicircular indentation on the island's southeastern coast, a mile and a half long, but only a half-mile deep. Despite these shortcomings, Basseterre was a convenient site from which a small American squadron could keep watch on Guadeloupe, just to the south. Truxtun sailed into the roadstead, moored in ten fathoms, then veered out a half-cable, leaving the *Constellation* riding on the edge of the anchorage a full half-mile from shore. He had no intention of going into the town, "a very small disagreeable place," that night, for he knew the bar, 300 feet out, caused a heavy surf to pound the black, volcanic beach. In fact, American ships throughout the war watered not in Basseterre, but five miles up the coast at the Old Road where the surf was less dangerous and a rivulet provided ample excellent water.[64]

Early the following morning Truxtun officially announced his arrival, saluting the town with thirteen guns and receiving the same in reply. He spent the next few hours seeing to minor repairs for his frigate, and receiving British officials on board. In the afternoon he went ashore, meeting with Governor Robert Thomson, who assured Truxtun he would have the fullest support from the British. Truxtun also met with David Matthew Clarkson, a former Philadelphian, now a "respectable" businessman on St. Kitts, eager to serve his ex-countrymen.[65]

Truxtun directed his purser to work through Clarkson, making his yard the base of operations for the squadron. The extra spars and stores that encumbered the *Constellation's* decks were sent ashore. As Truxtun's other ships arrived, they did the same. Clarkson eventually procured provisions for the squadron, handled French prisoners, and recruited seamen to fill out the ranks of the American ships. Truxtun left his correspondence for his squadron with Clarkson, and instructed his commanders to do the same. Even John Barry was informed to direct his letters, the few he wrote, to Truxtun, care of David Clarkson, Esquire, St. Kitts. This rather simple procedure freed the *Constellation* for productive cruising, while Barry kept the *United States* tethered to Prince Rupert Bay. Truxtun used Clarkson as a de facto navy agent and pleased with his initiative, informed Stoddert of the man's willingness to serve as such, stating his intention to continue to work with him "until I hear advice of your appointing a public agent." If Stoddert had not yet decided to extend the agency system to the Caribbean, or to St. Christopher, his hand was forced. Truxtun's recommendations were accepted and Clarkson was named as the United States' navy agent on the island. Henceforth, St. Kitts would serve as the American navy's major base in the Lesser Antilles.[66]

Truxtun also displayed his administrative abilities by establishing a sensible routine for his squadron's most frequent activity—convoying. Merchantmen wishing to be escorted clear of the Leeward Islands gathered at St. Kitts. Truxtun's ships escorted these vessels from the various islands to this rendezvous, and from there the convoys sailed north protected by ships of war until they were clear of the Virgin Islands.[67]

Barry operated along similar lines on his station, but Truxtun recognized that there was a great amount of redundancy in their efforts since both were busily escorting separate convoys northward. Truxtun suggested to Barry that the latter's ships, instead of escorting the convoys clear of the islands, escort them to St. Kitts, only 143 miles from Dominica. There, twice a month, convoys from the whole of the Lesser Antilles could be combined, and escorted by Truxtun's ships to the north.[68]

The proposal made perfect sense and would have freed a number of Barry's ships for other duties, including cruises to the Spanish Main, but Barry never bothered to reply. The first Truxtun heard from Barry was the demand for a ship. Truxtun had a copy of Barry's instructions from Stoddert and was aware that Barry was placing on him responsibility for carrying out the secretary's orders. Barry was passing the buck, leaving it to Truxtun with his five-ship squadron operating to the north to cover an area far to the south that Stoddert had assigned to Barry's much larger squadron.

Barry's failure to communicate on a regular basis with Truxtun did more than just hinder the coordination of the two squadrons; it endangered American operations in the Leeward Islands. Soon after reaching Dominica, Barry fell in with the *Montezuma* and *Norfolk* and Alexander Murray informed him of the presence of the French frigates that had captured the *Retaliation* in November. Yet Barry made little effort to locate the French. It is possible that he ordered Nicholson to lie off la Désirade to catch the frigates should they approach Guadeloupe from the windward. But for one of the pair of French cruisers, Barry need not have looked very far, for while *l'Insurgente* was out at sea, *le Volontaire* lay anchored at Guadeloupe, the only French base in the Lesser Antilles. Barry sailed along the coast of Guadeloupe on 13 January, but withdrew when a French battery at Deshaies fired on him. He did not return to the island until 17 February, attempting to exchange some captured privateersmen. Barry sent Lieutenant John Mullowny towards Basse-Terre under a flag of truce. The French fired on the American boat which returned to the *United States*. Barry withdrew once more.[69]

Having failed to locate the French himself, Barry should have warned Truxtun of the possibility that enemy frigates were at large. According to the latter's 21 February letter, however, no word of any kind had been received from Barry before that date.

Nevertheless, intelligence regarding French naval forces in the Caribbean did find its way to Truxtun. When he made landfall at Antigua on 13 January, warnings were on their way from Stoddert in Philadelphia. The secretary advised Truxtun that if neither Barry nor the British had Guadeloupe under blockade, his squadron's position would be hazardous. Stoddert advised Truxtun to take no chances and to join Barry at Dominica.[70]

The British also came forward with information about the French. At St. Kitts Truxtun learned that two frigates had been at Guadeloupe, but *l'Insurgente* had departed for France about the first of the year, while the other remained at Basse-Terre preparing to make a run for Cayenne.[71]

Unconcerned by the reported presence of a lone French frigate, Truxtun went about his work organizing convoys and coordinating the efforts of his squadron. But with his affairs in order, he headed south towards Guadeloupe, within Barry's sector, for a personal reconnaissance. On 29 January Truxtun worked the *Constellation* to within gunshot range of the fort at Basse-Terre and could see in the harbor a frigate and a twenty-gun corvette. Even though outgunned, Truxtun sailed close off the French base for three days inviting a fight. The French refused the challenge.

Truxtun reported his activities off Guadeloupe to Stoddert, noting that he had not sighted a single British or American warship those three days. As the only French base in the islands, the British might well have found it profitable to have detached a frigate or two to blockade Basse-Terre, but they had not. Guadeloupe was also the focal point of Barry's operations and he should have paid more attention to the French forces there. Had Barry proved more resolute in his mid-January cruise off Guadeloupe, he would have discovered the presence of *le Volontaire*. His only excuse for not properly reconnoitering the anchorage would have been if he had already been informed of the frigate being there, not unlikely. But then Barry should have sent an immediate warning to Truxtun, or blockaded the base. Had Nicholson been cruising off Basse-Terre instead of la Désirade, he would have intercepted *l'Insurgente* which returned from her Bahamian cruise in early February. Stoddert expected that in such a circumstance Barry would have blockaded the French port, for had they chosen to strike at American vessels operating around Guadeloupe, the frigates could have wreaked havoc among Barry's and Truxtun's dispersed squadrons. Even the twenty-gun corvette could have challenged most of the American ships cruising alone in the West Indies. The loss of the *Retaliation* could have been repeated many times over.

With *le Volontaire* contentedly riding at anchor in Basse-Terre harbor, Truxtun sailed north to resume work on his proper station. After cruising to the leeward of Barbuda, he brought the *Constellation* about and headed south intending to pass between Nevis and Redonda. Then on 9 February, Truxtun noted in his log: "At noon saw a sail standing to westward, gave chase. I take her for a ship of war."[72]

4. A Plume for Young John Truxtun

The chase was l'Insurgente 36. She had not returned to France as the British had asserted. She had cruised as far north as the Bahamas, where she had been sighted by Nicholson, and returned to Basse-Terre in early February, having taken five British merchantmen. She sortied again on 8 February.[73]

With Nevis five leagues distant, bearing west southwest, Truxtun set out in pursuit. About one o'clock he ran up the private British signals. There was no answer from the chase, which ran up an American flag. Truxtun next tried American signals, but no further reply was forthcoming, and he "had no doubts respecting the chase being a French frigate."[74]

Truxtun ordered the drummer to beat to quarters and the Constellation was instantly a flurry of activity. The topmen took their stations aloft; the crews formed their divisions on the gun deck, and the marines on the quarterdeck and forecastle. The gunports swung open; the tampions were jerked from the muzzles; cartridges, wads, shot, and more wads were rammed down the eight-foot-long barrels. The fifteen-man gun crews bowsed-out the cannon, each of which weighed nearly three tons.

From the quarterdeck of the Constellation, Truxtun saw l'Insurgente lower the American flag, and the Tricolor replaced it as a cannon boomed to windward (leeward according to the French captain).

While Truxtun had no doubt respecting the identity of his opponent, Captain Michel Pierre Barreaut was unsure of both the strength and nationality of his pursuer. His initial response to the sighting was to run, but not from cowardice. His quarry was merchant ships, not warships. He hauled off the wind, blowing from the east, and stood on a northwesterly course in an attempt to escape between St. Kitts and Saba. But as he observed the Constellation, still some distance off, her strange new lines confused him. He decided his pursuer was but an English corvette. To run from such a ship would be both foolish and dishonorable. L'Insurgente abruptly hauled her wind in an attempt to take the weather gauge and join combat.[75]

Both frigates were sailing on the same tack when they were suddenly challenged by a squall. The wind quickly reached gale force as the crews of the ships struggled in the tops. On the heeling *Constellation,* Truxtun decided that there was no time to shorten sail set full in pursuit. He ordered the lee guns housed and the weather guns run out. As the wind struck there was "such a cracking and snapping I never heard before," wrote seaman John Hoxse. All eyes looked aloft, but only a single studding sail boom dangled from a yard. Truxtun's well-trimmed frigate, "like a race horse," sailed on under press of full canvas.[76]

On *l'Insurgente* Barreaut ordered the topgallants taken in, but the wind struck in the middle of the endeavor, and in a crash the main-topmast fell to the deck. Men with axes and cutlasses were soon at work cutting away the wreckage. Barreaut decided that he ought to run, taking once more a northwesterly course, hoping to be able to reach St. Eustatius in his injured condition. He realized now that the frigate was American, closing the range fast. Recognizing that battle could not be avoided, Barreaut changed course for the third time. He hauled and stood on a starboard tack eight points off the wind.[77]

At 3:15 P.M., the wind was blowing strong. Truxtun held the weather gauge, but as he closed with the French frigate his lee guns were still housed, the *Constellation* heeling badly. As the distance between the frigates narrowed to a cable's length, Truxtun decided to surrender the wind. "The ship being rather crank," First Lieutenant John Rodgers wrote, "we ran close under the enemy's lee, for the sake of working our guns with more facility." The *Constellation* passed behind *l'Insurgente* and pulled abreast her larboard side. Barreaut hailed the American frigate several times, hoping to avoid combat. The Americans drew nearer. The range was less than fifty yards. From the quarterdeck of the *Constellation* came but one reply: "Fire!"[78]

At his order, the fourteen starboard 24-pounders spoke for Truxtun. Each eructed smoke and death in a rolling broadside aimed in the English fashion—into the hull. From *l'Insurgente* came a broadside in return, French style, shot crashing through the rigging, yards, and masts of the *Constellation.* The effect of the American fire was immediate, creating "terrible havoc" on *l'Insurgente*'s quarterdeck and confusion throughout the ship. Unlike Truxtun, Barreaut had failed to instill confidence and spirit in his crew. Before the smoke of the first broadside had cleared, the French captain had lost control of his men, his ship, and the battle. With the frigates so close, Barreaut's crew took up their small arms, "invading" the captain's cabin itself, leaving their guns and rushing to the quarterdeck, gangway, and forecastle shouting to board. His decisions made for him by the mob, Barreaut gave the appropriate orders. He had to rush himself to the helm to luff *l'Insurgente* in order to run aboard the passing American frigate. Missing her main topmast, *l'Insurgente* failed to respond and momentarily lost way. The *Constellation* ran across her bow firing a double-shotted raking fusilade along the length of the frigate's crowded deck.[79]

As the *Constellation* passed ahead of *l'Insurgente* and took up a new position on her starboard side, the gun decks of both frigates were full of activity. The French raced to man their starboard battery, while the Americans, running closer to the wind, were able to work their lee guns that were now run out. Truxtun worked his sails to slow his ship and allow the French to come up. Side by side, the frigates exchanged three broadsides until *Constellation* reached ahead again, once more raking *l'Insurgente* to deadly effect.

The action continued in this fashion until 4:15 P.M. when Truxtun maneuvered to rake a third time. The *Constellation,* Rodgers wrote, stood "directly athwart [*l'Insurgente's*] stern and should certainly have sent her to the infernal regions had we fired whilst in that position." Barreaut knew that his situation was hopeless. The fire from his own batteries slackened. The mizzen-topmast had fallen to the deck; the spanker was shot away; and the braces, forebowlines, and fore-topsails were all cut through. Barreaut could neither match Truxtun's firepower nor maneuverability. There was nothing left to do but strike and avoid further bloodshed.[80]

Barreaut's mind was set on capitulation, but he sought to avoid some of the odium of surrender. He left the quarterdeck (in battle, a station a captain should quit only on a litter) and approached his first lieutenant along the gangway. Other officers gathered about their commander, and they were told that the frigate, now identifiably American, had no right to take a French ship. Barreaut intended to end the battle and explain these facts to his adversary. Barreaut's lieutenants would later report that they believed the battle not yet lost, but the action had been all too one-sided to credit such an assertion. They remained silent, except for the first lieutenant who gave a response befitting his relative rank: "Do as you please." At Barreaut's order, the Tricolor was hauled down.[81]

Seeing *l'Insurgente* strike, Truxtun summoned Lieutenant John Rodgers to the quarterdeck and instructed him to take Midshipman David Porter and eleven men to effect the capture of the French frigate and send her captain and first lieutenant to the *Constellation.* A boat was quickly away and Rodgers rowed towards his first command. Climbing on board he surveyed first-hand the effect of the *Constellation's* 24-pounders: "Although I would not have you think me bloody minded, yet I must confess the most gratifying sight my eyes ever beheld was seventy French pirates (you know I have just cause to call them such) wallowing in their gore, twenty-nine of whom were killed and forty-one wounded."[82]

Barreaut and his second in command were soon on their way to the

American frigate. They had no time to gather their kit and carried with them only what they wore and their sidearms. As far as Barreaut knew, France and the United States were not at war. He himself was under orders from General Desfourneaux not to fire on the American flag. Without such restrictions, Barreaut would have used his stern 18-pounder chase guns to punish the American frigate during the long pursuit of the afternoon. But Barreaut also knew that he had shared in the capture of the American naval schooner *Retaliation* only two and a half months before, and knew from that incident that the Americans, despite their lack of a declaration of war, had sent ships into the Antilles authorized to take any French armed ship, public or private, on the high seas. Barreaut was aware that every captain, in war or peace, was responsible for the defense of his ship. In the age of sail there always existed the possibility that the first announcement of a declared war would come from the mouth of a hostile cannon. And at the opening of the chase, the American frigate had fired a gun to windward, the universally recognized sign of belligerent intentions. According to a French naval historian, Barreaut had deceived himself; Truxtun would relieve him of those illusions.[83]

Behind him Barreaut left a ship so "dismantled" that it was "like a hulk." Damage to the *Constellation* was confined to the rigging, heavy, but reparable. Only five Americans were casualties and they, by this time, had probably been removed from sight. The American crew seemed most intent on getting boats away to begin the transfer of French prisoners from *l'Insurgente* to the *Constellation*.

On deck, Barreaut saw the American captain approaching. Barreaut spoke first.

"Why have you fired on our national flag? Our two nations are not at war."

Truxtun had little time for conversation. With the wind still at gale force and night approaching, he faced difficult problems. Two damaged frigates had to be readied to beat back to St. Kitts. To best secure his prize, the bulk of the French crew, 409 men, would have to be brought in boats through rough seas to the *Constellation*. Truxtun had no time to argue the legality of his actions. He had, however, a few questions of his own.

"Your name sir, and that of your ship?"

"I am Capitaine de Frégate-Citizen Michel-Pierre Barreaut, commanding the French national frigate *l'Insurgente* of forty guns."

"You, sir, are my prisoner."

With that curt response, Barreaut and his first lieutenant were relieved of their weapons and led below.

The following morning, with the *Constellation* and her prize safely on a course for St. Kitts, Truxtun paid a call on his prisoner. From the start of the conversation, Barreaut repeated his surprise and indignation at being taken by an American ship.

"Why was our national flag fired on? I am surprised that America has declared war."

Truxtun must have been puzzled: "America has not declared war against France!"

"Pardon me," Barreaut replied, "your taking me with a ship of the French nation is a declaration of war."

"If a capture of a national vessel is a declaration of war," retorted Truxtun, "your taking the *Retaliation* commanded by Lieutenant Bainbridge, which belonged to the United States and regularly placed in our navy, was certainly a declaration of war on the part of France against the United States."

To this Barreaut apparently had no response. Truxtun continued.

"Whether be it war or be it peace, I will certainly take every French frigate I meet, and other French armed vessels as well, and you can tell that to General Desfourneaux."

The conversation ended.[84]

Later that same day, Truxtun sat at his desk to write his official report of the battle for the secretary of the navy. Truxtun wrote of the clash of the frigates and his conversations with the French captain. Having finished, he paused, and thought back to what Barreaut had said about the capture of *l'Insurgente* being "a declaration of war." Truxtun added a brief postscript: "The French captain tells me, I have caused a war with France, if so I am glad of it, for I detest things being done by halves."[85]

* * *

After a difficult journey, Truxtun reached St. Kitts in company with his prize on 13 February. He returned to a hero's welcome, received amidst great "joy demonstrated by the inhabitants on this occasion." It was the high point of his naval career. Even the vanquished Barreaut, paroled on the 14th, took his leave calling the American commander a "man of honor, courage, and humanity." As a gesture, Barreaut plucked a feather from his chapeau and gave it to Truxtun, who had admired the French captain's fashionable uniform. The "beautiful plume" became Truxtun's second trophy. Carefully packed, it was sent north as a present for godson John Williams Truxtun.[86]

Truxtun remained at Basseterre Roads for five weeks, directing the operations of his squadron while he saw to the disposition of several hundred prisoners and the repair of two frigates.

The victory over *l'Insurgente* netted Truxtun 380 prisoners, too many to be kept and fed on board two frigates cruising in the islands. Rather than immediately return the prize with the Frenchmen to an American port, Truxtun hoped to refit the frigate for operations and keep her on station. He looked to the British to relieve him of his prisoners. Governor Thomson was willing to help, agreeing to keep the French in the Basseterre jail until cartels could carry them to Guadeloupe. Clarkson handled the payments for the use of facilities on St. Kitts, and helped arrange for the exchange and the cartels with General Desfourneaux. The arrival of *l'Insurgente's* crew in Basseterre marked the beginning of a development that kept the island's jail overcrowded throughout the Quasi-War.[87]

Repairing the two damaged frigates took time and absorbed much of the stores sent from the United States and warehoused with Clarkson. The material damage to *l'Insurgente* had been as heavy as the human cost. The main top had been lost in the squall; the mizzen-top and spanker in the battle. The rigging was badly shot up as well, and the sails well holed. Damage to the *Constellation* was also heavy. Because of the French tactic of firing into the top, Truxtun's frigate was "much injured in spars, rigging, and sails." But French practices spared the crew, and American casualties were light, two wounded (one mortally), while a midshipman had his foot shot off. The only American to die during the battle was Neal Harvey, one of the gun crew from Third Lieutenant Andrew Sterett's division. Sterett wrote: "One fellow I was obliged to run through the body with my sword, and so put an end to a *coward.* You must not think this strange, for we would put a man to death for even looking pale on board *this* ship." Sterett's post-battle bluster was apparently not shared by Captain Truxtun. Harvey's death was recorded as "killed in action."[88]

Truxtun spent the remainder of February and early March refitting at St. Kitts. His most pressing problem was finding enough men among his small squadron to man the *l'Insurgente.* With the help of his fellow captains and Clarkson's assistance in recruiting some Spaniards locally, Truxtun was ready to resume operations.[89]

Not long out to sea, he spotted a sail six leagues from Redonda. The *Constellation* quickly overhauled the little chase. After two shots she struck and Truxtun had his second prize, a private schooner *l'Union 6,* with thirty-two men. Like *la Marsouin,* captured by Decatur off Havana, Truxtun's prize was full of cargo. In the Leeward Islands, too, commerce was becoming more profitable than privateering.[90]

5. To the Spanish Main

While Truxtun was clashing with *l'Insurgente,* Barry was wrestling with his instructions, trying to decide what force, if any, he should send south. He had received intelligence that a considerable number of American merchant ships were at Paramaribo in Dutch Guiana (Surinam), virtually blockaded there by French privateers operating from Cayenne. These latest reports convinced Barry that Stoddert's full instructions ought to be carried out. So he turned to Truxtun demanding one of his ships for the mission. Despite Truxtun's own difficulties following his victory over *l'Insurgente,* he ordered the *Richmond* brig to sail for Prince Rupert Bay to join Barry.[91]

On 21 February, however, Barry sailed into the bay at Dominica to find two ships fresh from the United States, the *Portsmouth* 24, and *Scammel* 14. Learning also of the temporary loss of the *Constellation,* Barry decided he better send part of his own force to Surinam. The *Portsmouth* and *Scammel* were sent on their way. Unfortunately, the *Scammel* sprung her bowsprit and was forced to return to Dominica, but Captain Daniel McNeill's *Portsmouth* reached Paramaribo and found nearly sixty American sail waiting there for deliverance. He convoyed them as far north as the latitude of Cuba before returning to Surinam to resume operations there for the remainder of the winter and into the spring.[92]

The dispatch of the *Portsmouth* to Paramaribo was certainly worth the effort. Stoddert had included the north coast of South America within Barry's area of responsibility because the secretary was aware of the growth of American commerce with that region. Foremost in Stoddert's mind were the Dutch colonies of Surinam and Curaçao. Barry never managed to send any of his ships to the latter colony, conduct that "mortified" Stoddert. American trade with the island, however, did not go unprotected.[93]

* * *

During December 1798 and January 1799, every ship in the American navy, save one, received orders for the Caribbean. The small force under the command of Alexander Murray in the *Montezuma* was already in the West Indies having sailed from Norfolk in November. Truxtun's orders instructed him to take command of Murray's other ships—the *Norfolk* and *Retaliation*—but made no mention of the *Montezuma.*

Murray was in a quandary. He saw his squadron usurped by Truxtun, but he received no orders himself. His first reaction was fear that his own conduct had been somehow unsatisfactory. He penned a poignant letter that caused Stoddert "real pain" when he received it. For what Murray took as a condemnation of his conduct had a very simple explanation. He had received no new orders because Stoddert expected him to follow his old ones. Murray had been sent to the Caribbean in November for a cruise of three months, and Stoddert assumed that the *Constellation* would reach the Leeward Islands shortly before the end of that period. Truxtun was to keep Murray's small ships in the West Indies, but the *Montezuma* was to return, as ordered, to the United States. Murray had failed to consider such a straightforward explanation. Undoubtedly, the loss of the *Retaliation* weighed heavily on his conscience. He should have realized that the loss could have had no impact on Stoddert's opinion of him, for the secretary's orders to Truxtun to take command of the *Retaliation* made evident that Stoddert was as yet unaware of the schooner's capture.[94]

Murray fell in with Truxtun on 16 January, learning of the transfer of the *Norfolk* to the latter's squadron. Although stung by what he mistakenly saw as a rebuke, Murray immediately offered to place himself under Truxtun's command as well. But Truxtun had no orders regarding the *Montezuma* and left Murray on his own.

With three months' cruise at an end, Murray should have sailed for home. But with the whole of the navy now joining him in the West Indies, the thought seems never to have crossed his mind. Instead, he stayed on, offering his service to Truxtun and Barry, escorting convoys, carrying messages, and doing whatever needed to be done. When he met Truxtun after his engagement with *l'Insurgente,* and found the latter in need of men, Murray gave up fourteen of his own.[95]

During one of his meetings with either Barry or Truxtun, Murray learned of the content of Stoddert's instructions relative to the northern coast of South America. Since Barry had not sent any of his ships to Curaçao, Murray took it upon himself to fulfill Stoddert's wishes. On the way south, Murray took his first prize of the war.

Reaching Curaçao in early March, Murray found the Dutch willing to supply him with water and provisions "upon better terms, than almost any island in the West Indies." French privateers were active off Curaçao, but their strength was weak and Murray believed that a frigate and a smaller ship would suffice to "destroy this nest of pirates." The Dutch officials were anxious to see American trade increase. They needed Yankee goods, especially food, to replace those lost because of the Royal Navy's control of the Caribbean. Since the French corsairs threatened American trade, the Dutch were eager to see the privateers driven off, but lacked the naval strength to do the job themselves. Though allied to France, the Dutch longed for an American naval presence off Curaçao as strongly as did the American merchants.[96]

Murray sailed north with a convoy in late March, but he had initiative yet to display. After clearing the Mona Passage he parted with the convoy and cruised for a few days off the northern coast of Hispaniola. Falling in with the *South Carolina* cutter, at last at sea and searching for Thomas Tingey, Murray took the ship under his own command and scoured the north and west coasts of St. Domingo. He next sailed to Kingston, Jamaica, where he took another fold of merchantmen under his protection, sending the *South Carolina* ahead to Havana to organize yet another convoy. Rounding the western end of Cuba, Murray stopped briefly at Havana before sailing for home in late April with fifty-seven sail.[97]

Murray wrote Stoddert on reaching the United States in May, "after a longer cruise than either you or myself contemplated, having left Baltimore on the 20th of September." Murray's was one of the longer cruises of the Quasi-War. At one time or another he sailed on each of the four stations of the navy in the West Indian theater. He convoyed over 100 ships clear of privateer-infested waters. Most importantly, his most fruitful operations were carried out on his own initiative. Murray's actions would not go unnoticed or unrewarded.

6

DERANGED OPERATIONS

---

1. Operational Collapse: Spring 1799

In the spring of 1799 several new ships and a number of new frigates were preparing for sea. As the navy's strength increased, Stoddert looked towards renewed operations in the West Indies and contemplated some new undertaking in a more distant sea. He expected that the performance of the navy in the Caribbean could be bettered.

Nevertheless, the very scale of that deployment made difficult a smooth transition to the next phase of operations. Literally the entire naval force of the United States was in the Caribbean and would have to return soon to American ports to refit. Ideally, the ships would be recalled a few at a time. A well-coordinated withdrawal would avert a situation wherein a large number of ships would be refitting simultaneously in the same port, allowing pressure to be maintained on the French in the West Indies. For Stoddert, the synchronization of the return of his ships to the United States would be much more difficult than their dispatch to the Caribbean the previous December.

Stoddert was well aware of the problems he faced. The winter of 1798–99 had been a hard one. The construction and outfitting of new vessels fell behind schedule. As late as 12 May snow fell in Boston. Plans to relieve ships in the islands with newly outfitted vessels were thus undermined, but Stoddert's intention remained to have the men-of-war in the Antilles return home a few at a time.[1]

In March the secretary of the navy began the rotation of ships out of the West Indies. The *Ganges* refitted at Norfolk and returned to Hispaniola only briefly to carry Edward Stevens to Cap François. Tingey then sailed on to Guadeloupe. On 15 March Stoddert instructed Barry to send the *Constitution* and *George Washington* to Boston and Newport, respectively.

Deranged Operations

About 27 March, the *Norfolk* arrived in Philadelphia, having been sent there by Truxtun so that Captain Williams could answer charges of misconduct. Refitted and placed under the command of William Bainbridge, who had been released by General Desfourneaux, the brig returned to St. Kitts in mid-April. The new frigate *General Greene* 28, Captain Christopher Raymond Perry, was ordered on 7 May to sail for Havana to relieve Decatur in the *Delaware*. Perry was to keep the cutters *General Greene* and *Governor Jay* on that station.[2]

Stoddert's plans, however, were already going awry. The two cutters were on their way home, and as the secretary was writing out Decatur's orders, the *Delaware* herself was leaving Havana for Philadelphia. On 10 May Barry made another surprise appearance in the Delaware River, and over the next few days Stoddert learned that the *Merrimack, Herald, General Greene* cutter, *Scammel,* and *Montezuma* were all in American ports. More bad news followed—the *South Carolina, Constitution, Governor Jay,* and *Delaware* had also arrived.[3]

Other than the *Montezuma* and *Constitution*, none of the vessels had been ordered or expected to return so soon. Moreover, Stoddert discovered that the other warships in the islands also intended to sail for the American coast. He drew up general orders instructing all commanders of American men-of-war in the West Indies to remain on station until they received orders to the contrary. The circular was sent out in any ship leaving Philadelphia for the Caribbean, but it was too late. Stoddert learned that the *Diligence* and *Virginia* had returned, and that the *Portsmouth, Constellation, l'Insurgente, George Washington* and *Pickering* were close behind. Stoddert wrote the president: "It was never intended that so many vessels should be in port, in the United States at the same time, as there are at present.—Barry came too soon, and ordered the return of those under his command too soon—Truxtun too if he has returned has come sooner than I intended."[4]

The only American force remaining in the Caribbean consisted of five ships: the *Ganges* 24, *Baltimore* 20, *Norfolk* 18; *Richmond* 18, and *Eagle* 14. In addition, the frigate *General Greene* was on its way to Havana, with the *Pinckney* and *South Carolina* under similar orders. Where more than twenty warships had cruised as late as March, by June only five remained.[5]

Stoddert was both disappointed and embarrassed. Over a dozen American naval vessels were in port at the same time—competing with one another and the new ships, for men, naval stores, and provisions. A smooth transition from one operation to the next was impossible. Refitting in crowded ports would be retarded; few ships remained in the islands to protect trade. "The plan of operations for the W[est] I[ndies]," Stoddert admitted to Adams, "will be somewhat deranged, and I wish our commerce may not feel the effect." Adams was aware of what had occurred; to the president the problem was clear and the solution simple. "There are too many ships in our ports and . . . every exertion ought to be made to get them to sea as soon as possible." Adams, too, was disappointed.[6]

Responsibility for the fiasco rested with the secretary of the navy and his senior captains. Stoddert's orders of December 1798 ambiguously gave the period April–June as the end of the operation. What would follow the winter in the Caribbean was unclear. Whatever course Stoddert determined to pursue in the spring, his main considerations should have been the end of the terms of enlistment of his seamen—recruited during the Quasi-War for twelve months "from the time the [ship] weighs."—and the time lag in sending instructions to warships cruising over 1,000 miles from the capital.

In the case of Decatur's unordered return, the fault was primarily Stoddert's. He waited until 7 May to send new instructions for the *Delaware* with Perry, but the *General Greene* did not leave Newport until 2 June. Admittedly, it made little difference, Decatur having left Havana in early May. But Stoddert should have considered delay probable in outfitting Perry's frigate, and he should also have considered that come May, Decatur might return on his own. The *Delaware* had been one of the first ships operational in the spring of 1798.[7]

Responsibility for the collapse of operations around Guadeloupe must be more evenly apportioned. Stoddert sent orders to Barry quite early—15 March—but the *United States* began its journey homeward on 19 April, before the new instructions reached the commodore. Barry had written Stoddert on 16 March informing the secretary of his intent to sail for Philadelphia during mid-April. As reasons, he offered the expiration of his crew's enlistments and his own declining health. What was most unfortunate was that Barry ordered his entire squadron, save the cutter *Eagle,* north as well. While the return of the *United States* was excusable, the other ships in the squadron were under no immediate pressure to sail for home and could have remained in the Caribbean a few more months.[8]

Only Truxtun remained near Guadeloupe, with his small squadron and *l'Insurgente.* The terms of his men were also due to expire, stores were running short, and no word had been received from Stoddert since early February. Truxtun could have followed Barry homeward, but he stayed on waiting for orders or relief. By mid-May, time was running out. His crew began to grow disgruntled, and Truxtun addressed the men informing them of his intention to sail for home. With their enlistments expiring, he considered it a matter of "good faith."[9]

Truxtun left the West Indies, with *l'Insurgente,* on 21 May, a full month later than Barry. Yet the *Constellation* had put to sea earlier in 1798 than the *United States,* and it seems that Barry could have remained in the Caribbean another month had he been so disposed. The keys to his early return were ill-health and declining will.

Stoddert was now disappointed and worried that not a single frigate remained near Guadeloupe. He considered the presence of at least one indispensable "to protect the other vessels from [French] frigates." The loss of the *Retaliation* had taught the secretary a lesson; but the fault was primarily his own. He should have kept his commodores informed of his intentions. His plans were unrealistic. He expected the *Constitution,* the first frigate to return from the Caribbean, to reach Boston by 10 May, refit, recruit a new crew, and sail for the West Indies by 1 June. Even Stoddert admitted that "to accomplish this very great exertion . . . prudent management seems necessary."[10]

The *Constitution* did not sail from Boston until 23 July, nearly two months later than Stoddert anticipated. Neither Barry nor Truxtun, no matter how determined, could have remained in the Caribbean long enough to have been relieved by the *Constitution.* Stoddert should have realized that refitting a frigate at Boston within twenty days was improbable.

The most sensible procedure would have been to bring Truxtun north first. The *Constellation* had been the first of the frigates to sail. Truxtun was more likely to refit in a short time; his victory over *l'Insurgente* would speed recruiting. And the turnaround between Norfolk and St. Kitts would have been quicker than between Boston and Dominica. But here again, Stoddert's plans were complicated by the Nicholson factor.

2. Exit Sam Nicholson: "Out of Harm's Way"

By the spring of 1799, Stoddert was becoming increasingly dissatisfied with his two senior captains. The summer and fall of 1798 had been full of disappointments, but reports from the Caribbean during the winter did nothing to raise the stature of either Barry or Nicholson in the secretary's eyes. Writing to Alexander Hamilton in February 1799 Stoddert pronounced Barry "old and infirm" and hinted that Nicholson's command of the *Constitution* would not last much longer. By the spring, as Barry and Nicholson were sailing north, Stoddert directed his opinions to the president himself: "I fear these gentlemen will return without an increase of reputation. Barry no doubt is brave, and well qualified to fight a single ship—poor Nicholson is not allowed to rank so high in the public estimation—Our navy at this time when its character is to form, ought to be commanded by men who, not satisfied with escaping censure, will be unhappy if they do not receive, and merit praise."[11]

In Stoddert's mind, Barry had become "Barry the brave," a captain who commanded a great number of ships but possessed "not mind enough for their employment." Letters complaining of poor health only confirmed Barry's inability to act as an aggressive senior commander. The secretary wished that Barry would ask for a job ashore or retirement. But John Barry was not ready to end his career and was too powerful a figure for Stoddert to relieve.[12]

Despite Barry's shortcomings, he was at least brave, honest, and responsible, traits missing from the character of Samuel Nicholson. In his reports, Barry, somewhat surprisingly, stood by his subordinate, praising Nicholson. But the latter's performance spoke for itself: no prizes, the *Spencer* incident, and lack of aggressiveness, on the heels of the $11,000 liable against the government from the mistaken capture of the *Niger.* Stoddert at one point considered arresting the captain of the *Constitution,* but hesitated being uncertain of his political ground and his own sense of vindictiveness. Despite his conviction that Nicholson was not suited to command, Stoddert wished to avoid injuring a man who had served his country for a quarter-century and whose personal finances left the navy his sole source of income. "I wish this poor man was richer," Stoddert wrote, noting on another occasion that if Nicholson were "not a poor man, with a large respectable family, I should very much doubt, whether some parts of his conduct, with respect to the *Niger,* ought to be passed over."[13]

Nicholson's connections, familial and political, were another consideration. Brothers James and John were heroes of the Revolution, and James was a Republican power in New York. The secretary's friend James Wilkinson would later intercede on Nicholson's behalf, as would Joseph Hopper Nicholson, a nephew and House Republican from Maryland. In the spring of 1799, the Maryland faction led by Samuel and Robert Smith was as yet not fully committed to the candidacy of Thomas Jefferson. It was through Stoddert that Adams remained in contact with these men hoping to have their support until late in 1800. Considering the probably serious political repercussions if Nicholson were to be dismissed and disgraced, Stoddert decided to appoint Nicholson to superintend the construction of a seventy-four-gun ship of the line, conveniently authorized by Congress in May 1799. On paper, the new command was a promotion, and a gesture meant to allow Nicholson to spend more time with his family. But to Stoddert it was "an expedient merely to get him out of harm's way for the present. . . ." The secretary expected some political clamor, but after clearing the move with Adams, Stoddert was determined to send

Nicholson ashore where "he will certainly remain as long as I am in office." He considered the officer fortunate to have escaped so lightly.[14]

And Nicholson remained ashore in Boston for the remainder of the war despite the efforts of his supporters. Stoddert probably hoped that Nicholson's appointment to oversee the construction of a seventy-four-gun ship in the most Federalist of cities, where he would have to work closely with old nemesis Stephen Higginson, would induce a resignation. But Nicholson was so poor that he could not afford to resign. He drew his pay and rations and followed the advice of James Wilkinson to "be patient, be prudent," and await a political change. It came in 1801, but his age, health, and record kept Sam Nicholson on land—and in Boston—until his death in 1811.[15]

Command of the *Constitution* was turned over to Silas Talbot, a tall, fearless, forty-eight-year-old who would earn for the frigate the fine reputation it had long deserved. Talbot's career during the Revolution had been illustrious: a captain in a Rhode Island regiment to a lieutenant-colonelcy by 1778. As an army officer, Talbot found himself in command of ships, and in reward for his service was awarded a Continental Navy captaincy in 1779. Unable to get a ship to command, Talbot took to privateering, but was captured by the British in 1780.

After the war Talbot settled in New York, became involved in politics, and served in the Congress that passed the naval act of 1794. Washington appointed him third-ranking captain that year, but he lost command in 1796 when Congress halted construction of the frigate building in New York. Talbot was then sent to the West Indies as an agent for the United States in an effort to secure the release of American seamen impressed into the Royal Navy. His strenuous endeavors met with moderate success, but left him on bad terms with several British officials, most notably Hyde Parker.[16]

With his varied military experience, the knowledge of the British and the Caribbean, Talbot had much to offer the new navy and he was employed initially as captain of the New York frigate he had begun to oversee in 1794, the *President* 44. By the spring of 1799, however, Stoddert began to view Talbot as the logical replacement for Nicholson, and he was given that appointment on 28 May 1799.[17]

*   *   *

In solving one problem, Stoddert found that he had complicated another. The question of the ranking of Talbot, Dale, and Truxtun had risen late in the summer of 1798. Stoddert favored Truxtun's position, but deferred to Adams. With Dale in the East Indies and Talbot's frigate still building at

New York, a strategy of delay had been adequate, but with Talbot now in command of the *Constitution* preparing for sea, a judgment on seniority could no longer be postponed. Despite the passage of a year, however, Adams had yet to reach a final decision.

Stoddert and the president were to be disappointed if they hoped that Talbot would allow the question to be ignored. As talk of his appointment spread, Talbot raised his demands anew, enlisting the support of Alexander Hamilton in New York. Once again, Stoddert responded that Truxtun was the senior of the three as of 1796. Talbot continued to press his argument, nevertheless. With Barry ailing, and Nicholson ashore, the senior command of the navy at sea was at stake.

Stoddert continued to procrastinate, promising not to employ Talbot under Truxtun and to refer the matter again to President Adams. The secretary's main concern was that the sailing of the *Constitution* not be delayed. In the meantime, Stoddert turned to his fellow cabinet officers— Attorney General Charles Lee, McHenry, and Wolcott—and a number of Senators who had considered the question of rank when Adams sent Talbot's nomination for command to the Congress in 1798. All advised that Truxtun was now the senior. Furthermore, Truxtun's commission of 1796, signed by George Washington, bore the notation "No. 3," making the case clear enough to the secretary of the navy. In an effort to pry Talbot out of Boston harbor, Stoddert sent him a commission ranking behind Truxtun, but leaving the ultimate decision to the future and Adams. The secretary asked Talbot to sail for the good of the service.[18]

Talbot refused to budge. With his frigate outfitted, he offered to surrender his commission rather than force his point any longer. A distraught Adams wrote Stoddert who remained unmoved by the veiled threat and continued to support Truxtun. Stoddert believed that an impasse had been reached; either Truxtun or Talbot was bound to resign. Stoddert suggested that James Sever, superintending a frigate at Portsmouth, New Hampshire, take command of the *Constitution* if Talbot refused to sail.[19]

Adams was at last moved to a decision. The frigate was ready for sea, awaiting only her commander. The president decided in Talbot's favor, perhaps on the merits of the case, perhaps out of favoritism to Talbot, perhaps as an attempt to mollify the Hamiltonians. Adams wrote Stoddert a long letter citing the retention of the Catholic Dukes of Norfolk of their titles, despite the suspension of their functions. There followed a lengthy history of Talbot's career, ending with the admonition that he had done more for the country before 1798 than had Truxtun. The *Constitution*, coincidentally, sailed that same day, 23 July.[20]

Whether he recognized it or not, and despite the use of a rather strange example, Adams's support of Talbot set an important and progressive precedent for the establishment of a professional officer corps for the United States Navy. In ruling that Talbot's commission as a captain was unrelated to his command of a ship, Adams was establishing the concept of rank, that is holding a commission to grade issued by the government, rather than post, an appointment (or posting) to a position in a ship. In making this step, Adams set the navy ahead of Britain's marine in form, if not in practice. During the Quasi-War, American officers received general commissions for rank, while the Royal Navy continued to issue commissions for each ship to which an officer was posted until 9 June 1860.[21]

With Talbot the third-ranking captain, and Richard Dale the fourth, Adams and Stoddert could only hope that Truxtun would not resign. Stoddert advised him of the president's decision, asking Truxtun to place himself in Talbot's position. And when Truxtun learned of Adams's choice, he acted much like Talbot, refusing to serve—certainly not what the secretary had in mind. Truxtun considered himself "much injured and much mortified." He wrote bitterly to Stoddert on 1 August, enclosing his commission. On the 9th, Truxtun informed the officers of the *Constellation* that he had "quit."[22]

For Stoddert, the whole affair had been long and troublesome. For over a year the arguments had ranged back and fourth, with Dale, Talbot, Truxtun, Adams, and Stoddert each arguing his point. In the end, the navy had lost the services of Dale for the war, the *Constitution* was delayed, Truxtun resigned, and the *Constellation* left leaderless. Stoddert, foreseeing the problems caused by rank, had summarized his feelings on the subject and outlined a procedure he would have liked to follow in a letter written to Hamilton shortly before Adams's decision.

> This avarice of rank in the infancy of our service is the devil—What think you of an early introduction of this principle in the navy service—I presume not to meddle with the land—that the president may appoint if he pleases a lieut. to command the oldest captains on any particular enterprise—I ask not this in levity but for your serious opinion—I have thought for some time of getting Truxtun & some other capt. of most understanding to go on a cruise under the command of a younger officer—Something like this must be adopted—or the best concerted plans will be ruined in the execution.

Indeed, Nicholson's seniority had upset Stoddert's plans for the winter of 1798–99. But if the secretary of the navy had hoped that he could enlist Hamilton's support, he had been disappointed.[23]

3. Posts of Danger—Posts of Honor

Despite the operational fiasco of the spring, the war in the Caribbean continued and Stoddert had to make do with the limited number of ships available to him. The *Ganges,* after depositing Edward Stevens at Cap François, was under orders to sail for Guadeloupe to join either Barry or Truxtun. On arrival, Tingey discovered neither commodore present, himself the senior captain, and his sloop of war the most powerful American ship on station. He found the *Baltimore, Pickering, Richmond, Norfolk,* and *Eagle* at St. Kitts shortly after making landfall there, but learned that the latter three ships had been ordered by Truxtun to return to the United States. Without orders, Tingey proposed to let Truxtun's directions stand.[24]

Thomas Tingey found himself suddenly thrust into the command of the largest American squadron in the Caribbean. With the hurricane season approaching, a French frigate still at large, and with "severe pain in the small of [his] back & intestines," he eagerly awaited additional instructions from the Navy Department.

In Philadelphia, Stoddert anticipated Tingey's quandary. New orders were sent out instructing the commander of the *Ganges* to remain at St. Kitts as commodore. Any dispatches addressed to Barry or Truxtun were to be opened, and all warships Tingey met were to be retained under his command. The ships *Delaware* and *Merrimack* were hurried south as reinforcements.

Stoddert implored Tingey to remain in the Caribbean until relieved. The presence of *le Volontaire* the secretary dismissed as an insignificant threat, the French frigate not being a "fast sailing vessel." Cruising in the lumbering *Ganges,* Tingey must have been amused. The hurricane season had to be weathered, American commerce had to be protected, and Stoddert was gambling, with Tingey's command, that stronger ships and the forces of nature would not pose serious challenges. And Stoddert, the speculator, was correct in his judgments. He was, in fact, so confident of Tingey's capability that he instructed the impressed commodore to prevent French privateers at Guadeloupe from transfering their activities to Hispaniola, where the American embargo was about to be lifted. Stoddert knew that he was demanding much, but he offered to Tingey both moral and material recognition. "The post of danger," the secretary wrote, "is the post of honor—when you return you shall have a frigate."[25]

Despite the return of the *Baltimore, Richmond, Eagle,* and *Pickering* to the United States, Tingey carried on off Guadeloupe with only the *Norfolk* until joined by the *Merrimack* in June and the *Delaware* in early August. Convoying took up the majority of the little squadron's time, but Tingey's ships also accounted for three captures between May and July. The most notable was the privateer *la Magicienne* 12, with 163 men, after a three-and-one-half hour chase during which the *Merrimack* fired twenty-three shot, climaxed by a full broadside that forced the French to strike. *La Magicienne* was an old hand at being captured, being known previously as the *Retaliation*, *la Croyable*, and whatever name she first bore after being built in Baltimore. She would not change hands again.[26]

Tingey found himself operating on a shoestring because heavier demands were being made on an overstretched naval establishment. Stoddert's first move of the spring had been to send the frigate *General Greene*, the brig *Pinckney*, and the cutter *South Carolina* to Havana. A stronger Cuban deployment reflected a new emphasis in American operations in the Antilles. Just as the face of West Indian privateering had changed between 1797 and 1798, so did it change again in 1799. Activity increased off Puerto Rico and near Spanish and Dutch colonies on the periphery of the Caribbean.

The French made an attempt to limit privateering from Guadeloupe, but their efforts were not wholly responsible for this shift. After General Desfourneaux reached Basse-Terre in November 1798, he tried to regularize the *guerre de course*, not to halt privateering, but to end the abuses permitted by Hugues. Desfourneaux's policy was in part dictated from Paris, where the Directory adopted a conciliatory stance towards the United States. But Desfourneaux was also acting in response to the needs of Guadeloupe. The island desperately needed the American trade ended by the embargo. The general launched a minor diplomatic offensive timed to coincide with the leashing of the corsairs. He released Bainbridge, the commander of the captured *Retaliation*, had offered to halt all privateering from Guadeloupe against American commerce if the embargo were lifted, but his maneuver failed. He was unable to control completely the privateers' operations against Yankee shipping, and as a response to his plea for the neutrality of Guadeloupe in the struggle between France and the United States came the *Constellation*'s capture of *l'Insurgente*. Convinced of American resolve, Desfourneaux renewed the *guerre de course* on 14 March 1799. His three-month-old policy of reconciliation was at an end. It had been so short-lived, that few Americans were aware that it had begun.[27]

Nevertheless, Desfourneaux's efforts to curb the corsairs, the work of the British, and the activity of the Untied States Navy in the Lesser Antilles, resulted in fewer captures by Guadeloupe-based privateers. Losses around Guadeloupe dropped from eighty-nine in 1798, to thirty-eight in 1799. Many American merchant ships were escorted in convoys, while warships cruised defiantly off the French colony and other islands on the lookout for privateers. Some of the latter began to carry cargo, while others capable of a wider range moved away in search of less dangerous hunting. Once beyond the reach of French law, which had at least licensed the corsairs even though it had not hindered their plundering, the *guerre de course* degenerated further into piracy.[28]

Stoddert was aware of the changing pattern of war in the Caribbean. As early as the winter of 1798–99 he had instructed Barry to protect the trade of the United States with Dutch Curaçao and Surinam, and the Spanish Main. Reports from captains who cruised off those areas confirmed the necessity of an American naval presence. The reports were supplemented by others from American consuls who wrote of the vitality of commerce, the strength of the privateers, the availability of provisions, and the desire of colonial governments to see the United States supply the power to halt the activity of the French corsairs. Isolated from Europe by the Royal Navy, the Caribbean colonies of Holland and Spain were more dependent than ever on American supplies to survive, but they lacked the means, and frequently the will, to combat the French with whom they were allied. Britain controlled the seas, making it impossible for the Spanish or Dutch to use their own ships to stop the privateers. The French, to keep their West Indian "allies" in line, threatened to revolutionize their black slave population should they break rank.[29]

As a response to the changing situation in the West Indies, early in the summer of 1799 Stoddert decided to refit Daniel McNeill's *Portsmouth* and the cutter *Scammel* (now officially taken into the naval service under the command of Lieutenant Mark Fernald) and send them to Surinam as soon as possible.[30]

On the Havana station, Stoddert considered the presence of a frigate a necessity. During the winter small ships were deemed sufficient to contain the activity of the tiny French privateers off Cuba. In the spring of 1799, however, Stoddert received reports that indicated a much altered situation. Four good-sized corsairs were operating from a key fifteen miles east of Matanzas. These pirates had fortified the key with two-dozen cannon, including several 24-pounders. A number of American ships had been taken. A New York ship put up a spirited defense, killing ten of the attacking pirates, but as a reward, the captain and crew were executed when the merchantman finally struck. Captured goods were sold and some ships burned, but no attempt was made to seek legal condemnations. These men were pirates and their sole objective was booty.[31]

The American consul at Havana, Joseph d'Yznardi, reported the outrages committed by the Matanzas pirates suggesting that a "frigate and two sloops of war with red hot balls" would suffice to end the local reign of seaborne terror. The consul's report, forwarded as usual by Pickering to Stoddert, had its effect. The navy secretary and the president had feared the degenerating nature of the war.

Sending d'Yznardi's letter to Adams, Stoddert wrote that "it shows that a state of things which you have long foreseen, is commencing in the West Indies: and forebodes that the American commerce may have more to apprehend from unauthorized piracy, than any other."[32] Entrenched east of Matanzas "these fellows" were well placed to annoy the whole of American trade with Spanish America. Stoddert wanted not only to eliminate the pirates, but also to make an example of them.

Captain Perry, commanding the squadron consisting of his own frigate the *General Greene,* the *Pinckney,* and the *South Carolina,* would carry a letter from Pickering demanding that the Spanish governor of Cuba remove the Matanzas cutthroats. If the Spanish failed to act, Stoddert wished to be allowed to take care of the matter himself. He wrote Adams that "a land force of 300 men would probably be sufficient to inflict such exemplary punishment as might for a long time check attempts at similar establishments." An operation on Cuban soil was, of course, beyond the scope of the war powers granted by Congress thus far to the executive. It would have raised serious diplomatic problems as well. Stoddert's Cuban amphibious undertaking would never be mounted. Even the operations Stoddert had planned for the Havana station fell short of expectations.

* * *

The frigate *General Greene* was one of eight ships built by the government during 1798–99. Constructed under the act of 27 April 1798, the frigate's design was more akin to the small standard British models of the late eighteenth century, than the super-frigates *Constellation* and *United States.* Built at Warren, Rhode Island, the 654-ton frigate carried twenty-four 12-pounders and eight 9-pounders, with a crew of 220. Her commander, Captain Christopher Raymond Perry, was a thirty-eight-year-old Rhode Islander whose youth was spent in the service of the nation on land and sea. Perry fought with the Kingston Reds under John Sullivan, in privateers, and in the Continental ships *Queen of France* and *Trumbull.* Between wars he served as a merchant master on voyages to Asia, South America, and Europe. Perry remains, however, more noted for his sons Oliver Hazard and Matthew Calbraith than for his Quasi-War exploits.[33]

Stoddert ordered Perry south on 7 May, instructing him to do what he considered best to protect American commerce from the Matanzas freebooters. Any that were unfortunate enough to be taken alive were not to be exchanged as prisoners, but to be sent to the United States to be proceeded against as pirates. Perry was also warned to stay out of Havana harbor, that place being "very sickly." The health of the crew, Stoddert noted, could best be preserved by remaining at sea cruising. Unfortunately, the secretary's advice regarding the necessity of keeping out of port was habitually ignored by captains sent to the Havana station.[34]

Complications, like those so evident during 1798, continued to plague Stoddert's operations. The *Pinckney* and *South Carolina* did not leave Charleston until mid-July. Delays in outfitting and recruiting, attributed to Perry by the navy agents at Newport, kept the *General Greene* in port until early June. On the journey south to Havana, Perry's crew suffered from a minor outbreak of fever. Worse yet, upon reaching Havana the ship was found to be taking water and the frigate's officers concluded that proper repairs could only be performed in port. Perry entered Havana harbor, made the repairs, and sailed north with a convoy. Yellow fever swept through the ship; Perry decided that he had best return to healthier northern climes. He arrived at Newport on 27 July having buried twenty of his men at sea and with twenty more in need of hospitalization.[35]

Perry was fortunate to escape with only twenty dead. His crew, freshly recruited in a new ship, were still healthy. Had the frigate been at sea for months before the outbreak of fever, the men would have been weakened by exertion and poor living conditions and would have succumbed much more easily. Perry's prompt return north probably saved many of his men, but it ruined Stoddert's plans for the Havana station. With Perry at Newport, and the two Charleston ships still in port, the end of July saw no American warships off the northern coast of Cuba. Even after the arrival of the *Pinckney* and *South Carolina,* Stoddert was left with a weak force at Havana, as at Guadeloupe.

Hispaniola had been all-important during 1797 and virtually ignored during 1798. By the spring of 1799 this rebellious French colony was once again becoming the focal point of the American struggle with France. Closed by the embargo to American commerce in mid-1798, St. Domingo was now to be reopened to American merchants. The intricate diplomatic maneuvering that brought about this volte-face will be discussed later in this work, but the problem for naval operations was immediate.[36]

The suspension of the embargo on trade to Hispaniola surprised Stoddert. Adams had asked his cabinet officers for their opinions and Stoddert advised, and supposed, that trade would not be renewed. Nevertheless, Stoddert expected that an American rejection of the overtures from the island's leaders would spark "greater enterprise than heretofore" from Hispaniolan privateers. Accordingly, he began to plan for a larger American naval presence in the Windward Passage. What Stoddert did not expect was that Adams would lift the embargo relative to St. Domingo as

Deranged Operations

suddenly as he did. The decision, kept secret, was made on 26 June, with commerce to resume as of 1 August. Toussaint L'Ouverture committed himself to do his best to halt privateering, but his forces controlled only part of the colony and corsairs could also operate from southeastern Cuba and the Spanish half of Hispaniola. Renewed trade would require an American naval effort that Stoddert was now pressed to provide on short notice.[37]

The American consul at Santiago attested to the danger to trade from corsairs based in southeastern Cuba athwart the Windward Passage. Pickering had sent Josiah Blakely to the port in the spring of 1799. He made the journey in a merchant ship carrying cargo partly the new consul's property. "When within two leagues of the [Santiago] Moro," Blakely wrote, "a French privateer was between us & the entrance to the harbor," The consul had no intention of allowing himself to be captured. He gathered his papers, had a small boat swung out, and "rowed for the castle." The ship was taken as a prize, but Blakely made it safely ashore.[38]

The consul reported the harbor at Santiago excellent, water and fresh provisions plentiful and cheap, and American merchants welcome. He deplored the fact that thus far no American warships had visited Santiago and recommended that they be sent in the near future.

Stoddert knew that ships were needed to watch the Windward Passage. The British, their troops withdrawn from Hispaniola, would no longer be controlling important stretches of the coast, which would be open to French corsairs. Expecting that ultimately American ships would be deployed off St. Domingo, Stoddert had already laid the logistical foundation for the build up of the squadron. On 30 March 1799 he appointed an old friend, Nathan Levy, navy agent to Cap François. With trade to be resumed on 1 August, Adams believed that Stoddert would have American warships on station ahead of the arriving merchantmen. Commerce had to be protected, and a show of strength to Toussaint was necessary. The British, too, would have their eyes on the Americans.

Stoddert was eager to comply and send a ship to Cap François before August, but which one? By the time the secretary was aware of the decision to renew trade, only two ships were nearby ready for sea and still uncommitted, the *George Washington* and the newly built frigate *Boston*. Captain Patrick Fletcher in the *George Washington* had been ordered to cruise off the southern coast, but was now instructed to sail south, "just showing" himself off Charleston to calm jittery southern nerves, before proceeding to Cap François. Bad weather delayed his sailing until 2 July, and he failed to reach St. Domingo until mid-August.[39]

To head the squadron Stoddert planned to concentrate off Hispaniola was the frigate *Boston* 28, measuring 530 tons, mounting twenty-four 12-

pounders and eight 9-pounders. She was, like the *General Greene,* a smaller frigate, most notable because she was the first American-built ship of war whose copper bolts and spikes were manufactured domestically, by Paul Revere.[40]

It had become European practice by the 1790s to sheathe the hulls of warships with copper to prevent the formation of barnacles, which slowed sailing, and the destructive boring of the shipworm—*Teredo navalis.* There were problems, however, with the process. The copper sheets corroded the iron bolts that held together the ship's hull. Use of copper, or copper-headed bolts covered by a preservative (in the United States a layer of flannel soaked in tar) proved to be the solution. To sheathe the frigates planned in 1794, Americans had turned to the British for both sheets and bolts. The first shipments had arrived in 1795 and continued to reach the United States until 1799 when the deliveries were halted. As he had with ordnance manufacturers, desiring to be "out of leading strings," Stoddert had begun a program of advancing money to domestic producers of copper, such as Revere. Ultimately, the secretary pumped $76,000 into the industry, and his efforts were successful. Revere, who had produced the first copper spikes in early 1799, successfully rolled sheets late in 1801. The long-term interests of the United States Navy were well served. But throughout the undeclared war with France, American warships were sheathed with English copper. British assistance was of critical importance because uncoppered warships would have been nearly useless. French warships and even many privateers were sheathed. And even though Britain halted the supply in 1799, sufficient stocks had been accumulated to carry the American navy through 1801.[41]

Command of the *Boston* was first offered to Jonathan Chapman, who had served as captain of the cutter *Pickering,* but he refused a navy commission over a question of his relative ranking. The Boston committee responsible for the construction of the frigate next suggested the appointment of George Little, a forty-five-year-old scion of the state whose Revolutionary service was wholly in the Massachusetts navy. Little's "laudable ambition" was to command the United States Navy; and Stoddert, apparently considering such a desire to be indicative of "a man of spirit & enterprise," ordered a commission drawn up on 16 April 1799, backdated to 4 March. On 2 July the secretary dispatched orders with sealed instructions to Little, expecting him to be prepared to sail by the 10th.[42]

Little was ordered to sail on a general course for Puerto Rico, and to open the sealed packet only on the third day after leaving Boston. The secret enclosures instructed him to proceed to St. Domingo where he was to protect American ships that would be "flocking in great numbers" to Cap François and Port Républicain. On 3 July, however, Stoddert received his second shock in connection with the reopening of trade with His-paniola. He learned that Adams's proclamation lifting the embargo would soon be made public. New orders were dispatched that same day to Little, instructing him to sail direct for Cap François, taking with him any merchantmen prepared to sail. The *Boston* was to be delayed no longer than two extra days, however, for if she sailed later than 12 July, with the removal of the embargo public, there was a good chance that eager mer-chantmen would reach the French colony before Stoddert's ships arrived to protect them.[43]

Boston was once again a pitfall in Stoddert's plans. Recruiting simul-taneously with the *Constitution,* Little had a difficult time completing his crew. Delay followed delay; Stoddert feared that the holdups would expose American ships heading for St. Domingo "to unnecessary hazard." Cap-tains had to learn that they could not always expect to sail with full crews. Little was finally pried out of port on 24 July, too late to reach Cap François before 1 August; too late to fulfill Stoddert's and Adams's expecta-tions. Only the "dull" *George Washington,* a ship judged by Stoddert "not fit to chase a French privateer," had a slim chance to reach Cap François in time.[44]

4. To Be Seen in Europe

Conspicuous by their absence during the early summer of 1799 were the mighty frigates *United States* and *Constitution.* Both had returned to American ports by early May and should have seen useful service in July.

Whatever his other shortcomings, on his arrival from the Caribbean Barry's refit was expeditious. The *United States* was back at sea by 2 July. Barry found himself patrolling the southern coast after transporting an artillery company to Charleston. He was under orders to return to Hampton Roads by 15 July for further instructions.[45]

Stoddert did not believe that the defense of the southern coast necessi-tated the presence of the *United States,* but his retention of Barry's frigate in coastal waters was part of a larger plan, the misfire of which kept both ships tied up during July. In the meantime, southern apprehensions would be quieted.[46]

As the navy grew—so did the demands made of it. Federalist con-gressmen, reflecting the desires of their constituents, made increasing numbers of requests for a naval presence in the corners of the world. Thus far, only the Caribbean trade had received protection, but all the mer-chants were providing the revenue and political support for the navy, as well as building new ships for it. Every merchant believed that his trade needed the navy's attention. What they generally wanted were naval escorts for their convoys, and as 1799 wore on, demands for such from Europe mounted. Stoddert disliked the idea of running convoys from the Old World on both tactical and strategic grounds. Tactically, he believed that American warships had been "employed too much in convoying instead of being kept entirely for cruising." Stoddert advocated offensive patrolling. Strategically, Stoddert held that more important objectives lay closer to home and ought to receive the navy's attention.

> Our first care certainly ought to be, the security of our own coast—the next to avail ourselves of the commercial and perhaps political advantages which the present state of the West Indies & Spanish America, is calculated to afford us. By attending to these objects it may be possible to produce such strong conviction of dependence on the United States, that it may be difficult thereafter to arm those countries against us. It would be a great point gained in a war with France, that they should be obliged to make their attacks from Europe. At any rate, it seems to be in the power of France to shut us out from almost the whole of Europe—and perhaps our only means of compensation are to be found nearer home.[47]

Nevertheless, Stoddert was eager to do something for the merchants whose political support the navy needed. He was also not adverse to making a show of force in European waters. In the end, these latter considerations overcame his strategic good sense. The result was another minor fiasco.

A request received at the Navy Department in April for a convoy from Elsinore (Helsingør), Denmark, due to head home in July, was the first to intrigue Stoddert, but the notice was so short that no force could be mustered in time. Only days later another request was received for an escort for a convoy from Bilbao, Spain. Initially, Stoddert was not receptive to the scheme. Word of a convoy from Bilbao would certainly reach the French, and the small force Stoddert could send to Europe would be at great risk so close to France. But the secretary saw the need for some gesture to the merchants, and Congress, and while he would not countenance a convoy escort, he was ready to show the flag. He wrote Adams discussing the requests, offering instead to send a few fast ships to cruise off the coasts of France and Spain.[48]

Over the next month Stoddert refined his plan. The frigates *United States* and *Constitution* were to sail from Norfolk with the trade winds to a landfall at Cape Clear, on the southwest coast of Ireland. This cape was the landfall for much of the traffic plying the Atlantic between North

America and Europe. He expected that French privateers would be active in the area. The frigates would then sail south, again with the prevailing winds, across the English Channel, through the Bay of Biscay along the French, Spanish, and Portugese coasts. Following the northeast trades, the frigates would be carried through the Madeira and Canary Islands—the "Western Islands"—thence across the Atlantic to Cayenne. From there, the *United States* would return home, whereas the *Constitution* would join the American squadron off Hispaniola. Stoddert's plan was well thought out, making the best use of the winds around the North Atlantic basin to strike hard and fast into European waters. At the same time, the whole operation remained connected to the main theater of the war, the Antilles. Stoddert expected the expedition to yield results,

> but if no other good is produced, our officers & men will learn that they are not always to be nursed at home—our very fine ships will be seen in Europe—it will be seen there too, that we are not afraid of provoking the French nation, when they give us cause—but what is more important, that will be seen at home also—and if our vessels do not capture French privateers or frigates, which ought however to be expected, they will at least produce the impression, that a little more caution in their depredations on our commerce, may become necessary.[49]

Barry had been held at the ready off the southern coast; it now fell to Talbot to prepare the *Constitution* for sea. Unfortunately, the *Constitution* was in sorry shape on her return from the Caribbean. Nicholson's officers were ranged against one another and their captain. Even the usually steady marines were found to be ill-disciplined and untrained. Stoddert saw no recourse but to break up the frigate's wardroom. The lieutenants were transferred to other ships. One was court-martialed. To assist Talbot, who was not noted as a "thorough bred seaman," Stoddert assigned Isaac Hull to serve as first lieutenant.[50]

With delays in working in new officers, in recruiting a new crew, and with Talbot's attention diverted to his quest for seniority over Truxtun, the days passed with the *Constitution* still in port. On 29 July Stoddert wrote Adams informing the president that the season had grown too late for the European operation. The secretary's focus returned once again to the Caribbean.[51]

5. Retrospect: The First Year

The mid-year collapse of American naval operations in the Caribbean provides a convenient opportunity, and reason, to review the first-year's performance of the reborn United States Navy, the administration that served it, and Benjamin Stoddert, who as secretary directed both.

By the summer of 1799, Stoddert had settled into the life of the capital. He had journeyed to Georgetown in mid-October to bring his wife and children north. Returning to Philadelphia a month later, he moved his family into a rented house on Chestnut Street, between Ninth and Tenth, convenient to the navy offices. He resumed his duties on 15 November, thanking Timothy Pickering who had served as acting secretary during Stoddert's absence. Rebecca Stoddert had come to enjoy her life as a cabinet officer's wife, as best she could managing seven children. By July, however, the stifling humidity in the city was becoming unbearable, especially for a woman five-months pregnant. She, like her husband, looked forward to the move of the government to Trenton to escape the heat and fevers prevalent in Philadelphia during the season.[52]

Stoddert was beginning to master the duties of his office. He pursued his conceptions for an American navy with a single-minded determination that at times exceeded Congressional intent and presidential design. But this drive, motivated by zeal for his charge rather than duplicity, aroused feelings of respect and trust from fellow cabinet members and John Adams. In other areas of executive concerns, domestic policy, diplomacy, and especially the intraparty struggle between Adams and the Hamiltonians, Stoddert steered clear of involvement, humbly citing ignorance of such matters as his excuse. He had learned in York in 1778 the dangers of bureaucratic and political machinations. He kept his opinions to himself, and while he enjoyed the attention the Hamiltonians paid him, Stoddert remained loyal not to Pickering, to whom he had been connected for twenty years, but to the president. Oliver Wolcott wrote late in 1799:

> Mr. Stoddert is a man of great sagacity, and conducts the business of department with success and energy: he means to be popular; he has more of the confidence of the president than any officer of the government. He professes to know less than he really knows, and to be unequal to the task of forming or understanding a political system; he will have much influence in the government, and avoid taking his share of the responsibility.[53]

In his official role as secretary of the navy, Stoddert shouldered an enormous burden of administration and direction. The scope of his wartime correspondence is broad. While he shaped policies to serve the nation for generations, he worked as his own chief of naval operations deploying squadrons far from the capital. He made decisions regarding timber, anchors, the number of clout nails needed to construct a frigate, cordage, cables, canvas, cannon, shot, powder, provisions, reworking copper spikes, etc. Every item that went into every ship came to the attention of the overworked administrator. Stoddert had to write much of the early correspondence himself, even addressing the envelopes. He advised Congress in 1801: "I will take the liberty of observing that the business of the Navy Department embraces too many objects for the superintendence of one person, however gifted. . . ."[54]

Only a staff of six assisted Stoddert, including chief clerk Garrett Cottringer, another financial victim of Robert Morris's bankruptcy, and Charles Washington Goldsborough, a nineteen-year-old son of a prominent Maryland family who would serve the Navy Department for decades. An office keeper and messenger was also employed. In the summer of 1799 the secretary named a new chief clerk, Colonel Abishai Thomas, a former deputy quartermaster general in the Continental Army, who would ultimately direct the work of Goldsborough, Joseph Parrot, John Lockwood, and John M. O'Connor. In July 1798, Congress had established an Office of the Accountant of the Navy, an appointment Stoddert filled with William Winder, another Marylander, whose staff ultimately grew to include seven clerks. Including the Navy Storekeeper, Robert Gill, and two constructors, Joshua Humphreys and Josiah Fox, the entire naval bureaucracy consisted of eighteen men drawing a total salary of just over $22,000.[55]

Despite the enormity of the immediate tasks facing him in building a naval force virtually from scratch in the midst of war and controlling operations over a thousand miles distant, Stoddert made time to consider the nation's long-term naval policy. He had always believed "that a navy was the only national system of defence" for the United States. On 23 November 1798 Stoddert proposed to Adams "to lay the foundations *now*, for an increase of the navy . . . [to include] twelve ships of the line, as many frigates, and twenty ships not exceeding 24 guns on the gun deck. . . ." The secretary's plans were not in accord with Adams's conception of the nature of sea power and the needs of the United States. Adams later wrote: "I never was fond of the plan to build line of battle ships." But Stoddert had his way, presented the plan to Congress in December, and in February 1799, the legislature voted to construct six liners.[56]

Stoddert's proposals are of indirect and direct importance to this study. Obviously he and not Adams was the driving force behind American naval policy, as well as administration and operations. In his message to Congress, Stoddert used the phrase "to command our own coast," demonstrating not only his desire to possess such instruments of national policy, but also his understanding of their use. Concentration on the navy's long-term needs, although important to the nation's maritime future, proved to be a distraction for Stoddert. While he busied himself with the details of naval expansion for the future, Decatur, Truxtun, and Barry were left cruising the West Indies, unsure of when, or if, they were to be relieved. As a result, American operations in the Caribbean suffered.[57]

Despite early support, by the end of the war Stoddert was aware that his plans for a battle fleet were doomed. After 1801 work on the seventy-fours stopped, and the assembled timber was left to rot. The secretary's vision, however, survived his tenure. Of the $700,000 appropriated to construct six liners, Stoddert had spent $135,000 to purchase a half-dozen navy yards—Portsmouth, New Hampshire, Boston, Brooklyn, Philadelphia, Washington, and Gosport, Virginia—despite the fact that Congress had consistently voted against the acquisition of public sites in 1794, 1797, 1798, and February 1799. Of the $200,000 authorized to buy timber for the ships, Stoddert bought two wooded islands—Grover and Blackbeard off the Georgia coast—for $22,000. An 1802 Congressional investigation, headed by Joseph Hopper Nicholson, concluded "that no authority was given, by law, nor any appropriation made . . ." for Stoddert's actions. But what the government had come to hold, it chose to keep. Stoddert's yards and timber islands well served the navy of the nineteenth century, even if the Marylander's seventy-fours were never built. Yet, here too, Stoddert's ideas lived on in the Navy Department files.

In the fall of 1811, as the crisis with Great Britain worsened, Congress looked to Secretary of the Navy Paul Hamilton to propose appropriate naval augmentation. Hamilton was an inebriate, who would be forced to resign the following year. He was no naval philosopher. The secretary turned to his chief clerk, responsible for preparing exhibits and estimates for Congress, for assistance. Charles W. Goldsborough, who had begun his career under Stoddert, rewrote the December 1798 proposal that had been drawn up by the navy's first secretary. Again, a call for twelve liners, frigates, and supporting facilities and industries was sent to the House. Though no immediate action was taken, the following fall (after the war had begun), Congress turned to Hamilton once again, and the secretary referred them to his 1811 message. On 9 January 1813 Congress passed a naval act authorizing the construction of the Federal navy's first four line of battleships.[58]

While Stoddert believed that the United States could best trust its long-term defense to a squadron of capital ships, seventy-fours would be of little service combatting a *guerre de course*. To wage the Quasi-War, the navy needed the smaller ships that had fought the French thus far in the conflict. Their record by the summer of 1799 was mixed. Truxtun's victory had demonstrated the power of the thirty-six-gun American frigates. While another decade would pass before the forty-fours would have a similar opportunity, doubts about the designs of the new Yankee fifth-rates were

Deranged Operations

disappearing. The navy's sloops of war and brigs, at this point all converted merchantmen, had proven at best serviceable, while many were "dull." Several of the Revenue cutters were already earning reputations for smartness, but many had to be returned to the Treasury Department.[59]

Within the strictures imposed by the budget, recruiting difficulties, and occasional scarcity of ordnance and stores, Stoddert sought to limit the expansion in the navy to a fair number of vessels suited for operations against small, fast corsairs. Eleven additional frigates, seven ships, and two schooners were outfitting or under construction in 1799, all designed and built for war. In the spring, he began to pare the navy of the "dull" sailers and managed to reduce its strength from twenty-two to nineteen by July, despite the addition of a few new ships to the rolls, and in the face of shortages of vessels in the West Indies. In October, Stoddert advised Adams that he doubted "whether in the present state of our affairs, any more small vessels should be added. . . ." As a result, while forty-two men-of-war answered the secretary's orders in the course of the Quasi-War, the maximum strength of the navy was thirty-two ships, operational in June 1800.[60]

From the beginning of his tenure as secretary, Stoddert had believed that quality officers were of greater importance to the service than mighty men-of-war. Unless commanders with "zeal & spirit" were found to command its ships, the United States "had better burn its vessels."[61]

By the summer of 1799, few of Stoddert's captains had gained his approbation, many his opprobrium. Of the six senior officers, only Truxtun had demonstrated possession of the requisite traits of command, and he was about to resign. The navy's first-ranked captain was a proud man who wore at his side the sword once carried by John Paul Jones, but the John Barry of the late 1790s showed little interest in sailing "in harm's way." Dale had taken a leave of absence, his second since 1794. Nicholson had narrowly escaped dismissal, if not arrest. Of the more recent appointees, Murray, Preble, and the elder Decatur had impressed Stoddert. Isaac Phillips had been summarily dismissed; Thomas Williams forced to resign. Hugh G. Campbell had dallied at Philadelphia in the fall of 1798, and Christopher Raymond Perry had dawdled in Newport the following spring.[62]

After a year as secretary, Stoddert was wholly dissatisfied with his corps of officers. Their quality as seamen and commanders was uneven. Many were triflers. They were concerned too much with rank and prestige, at the expense of the interests of the navy. When they failed to have their way, they transferred to the merchant service from whence they had come. Stoddert was not about to "burn" his ships in response, but he was determined to reshape the American naval officer corps by flooding the service with twice the number of midshipmen authorized by Congress:

> Young men of good education—parts & connections—we have never objected to such young men, although they had never been at sea—the more midshipmen of this description, the better the chance of good officers some years hence—those who leave the merchant's service to enter into the navy, especially from the eastward, often wish to return to their first employment, and at times most inconvenient. . . .[63]

Over the course of the Quasi-War, Stoddert improved the pay and emoluments of officers, established a half-pay fund for times of unemployment, and pensions for those invalided from the service. He sought to have six admirals appointed "that the brave & experienced officers should be rewarded, & the young stimulated, by conferring on long & extraordinary skill & valor, the usual naval honors. . . ." The plan doubled as a scheme to send the navy's "Barrys" ashore in honorific retirement. These latter proposals failed to attract sufficient Congressional support. Nonetheless, Stoddert made the navy a career institution, a proto-professional force, attractive enough to keep Isaac Hull, James Lawrence, William Bainbridge, Charles Stewart, Stephen Decatur, Jr., and other excellent young officers in the service. For "Stoddert's Boys" the United States Navy became their life, their profession, their means of earning a living. Charles Stewart, who entered the navy as a lieutenant in March 1798, would live long enough to see the nation promote its first admirals.[64]

Stoddert's strategic direction of the Quasi-War during its first year was nearly flawless. He correctly assessed patterns of French privateering activity and American losses, identifying the Caribbean as the major theater of war. After insuring the security of the American coast from invasion and interruption of trade (security of base), Stoddert concentrated all his available resources in the West Indies. He resisted attempts to disperse his limited forces, refusing to maintain ships in northern waters or send men-of-war to the Old World. By mid-1799, however, the secretary began to yield to political pressures and plan deployments that would stretch the navy's strength. The proposed foray of the *United States* and *Constitution* to Europe was a strategic mistake. Politically, however, such diversions were inevitable. Throughout the war, Stoddert managed to avoid most deployments to subsidiary theaters.[65]

American naval operations during the first year of the war with France were based upon well-conceived plans that took into consideration the major points of French activity, British deployments, geography, patterns of trade, prevailing winds, and logistics. Stoddert demonstrated, as he had expected in May 1798, that he could manage ships in time of war, as he had those in time of peace. Yet, the secretary's operational conceptions were marred by a major flaw. Time and again he ignored what Carl von Clausewitz would come to term "friction." Stoddert's plans were usually a bit too neat, based upon assumptions concerning outfits and refits of ships that were overoptimistic. Stoddert was not responsible for the primitiveness of the navy's shore-based administration, nor the many unzealous officers who commanded his ships, but he was at fault for not factoring into his plans probable, if inexcusable, delays.

One questionable operational decision Stoddert made involved captured French privateersmen. Early in the war, Adams had written the secretary: "We must sweep the West India seas, and get as many French seamen . . . whether they are Italians, Spaniards, Germans, or negroes [sic], as we can." The president believed that "seamen are so scarce that they cannot send out large privateers." Through the attrition of French manpower in the Caribbean, Adams held that corsair activity could be halted. Whether the president knew it or not, Vice Admiral Henry Harvey, commanding the Royal Navy's forces in the Lesser Antilles, was pursuing just such a policy, with some success.[66]

Stoddert, however, chose to authorize exchanges with the French in the islands. His reasons were practical. For one, carting captives about the Antilles consumed a squadron's stores, and transporting them to the United States tied down ships, always in short supply. Second, one of the greatest administrative headaches of Stoddert's service as secretary of the Board of War during the Revolution had been the maintenance of British prisoners of war. He was less than anxious to find himself charged with a similar burden twenty years later.[67]

In July 1799, Adams was outraged to discover that his navy secretary had authorized prisoner exchanges within the Caribbean, calling it "one big mistake." If all captives were sent north, Adams reiterated, "we shall soon exhaust [Guadeloupe] of seamen. . . ." Despite Adams's insistence, and a clear annunciation of the administration's policy on the part of Stoddert, American commanders remained eager to unload captives as soon as possible. Of the 6,500 prisoners taken during the war, less than 1,000 ever reached the United States.[68]

Whatever the shortcomings of American naval operations as directed by Benjamin Stoddert, they were effective. During 1799 the number of merchant ships lost in the Caribbean fell by almost two-thirds. Captures around Guadeloupe declined from eighty-nine to thirty-eight. Rates charged by Philadelphia marine insurers for ships and cargos sailing to and from the West Indies fell from 17.5 to 12.5 percent. As early as January 1799 a Congressional committee had estimated that the navy had saved the nation $9,500,000. The improved situation was not solely the work of the United States Navy. The British had taken over seventy privateers in the Antilles during 1798, and on Guadeloupe General Desfourneaux's arrival marked the end of Hugues's *guerre de course.* Considering these factors, it is easy to discount the effectiveness of the Americans. Yet, throughout 1799, the Royal Navy, with an average of eighty-one ships in the Caribbean, captured nine French privateers, while Stoddert's men-of-war, with an average of fourteen vessels in the islands, took twenty-eight.[69]

* * *

During the first year of the French war, the United States Navy demon-strated both strengths and weaknesses. It was a force undergoing a metamorphosis in the midst of war. Already evident was the spirit of the early nineteenth-century navy, marked by zeal, enterprise, and the stirrings of professionalism. Present as well, however, was the ghost of the Conti-nental Navy, represented by infighting, anarchy, maladministration, and amateurism. The ultimate shape the navy would take would be decided by Stoddert, who by the summer of 1799 was coming to grips with the administration that served him, had recognized the long- and short-term problems facing the service, but had yet to grapple seriously with the senior captains who commanded his ships. For all his commercial and administrative experience, Benjamin Stoddert lacked one attribute pos-sessed by Adams's first choice for secretary. Unlike George Cabot, the Marylander had never commanded a ship at sea. Truxtun noted the deficiency to Charles Biddle, writing: "Stoddert directs his business very well in most matters—but for want of sea information, he is deceived. . . ." Only time would tell if the navy secretary was a man able to learn from his mistakes and take full charge of the navy as a good captain takes charge of his ship, or whether Stoddert was liable to the very criticism he levied against Barry—brave and honest, but lacking the attributes of higher command.[70]

7

OPERATIONS RESUMED

---

1. "To Hoist Our Flag in European Seas"

By the end of July 1799, the worst of the miscarriages of the spring had passed. American naval forces in the Caribbean were weak, but their numbers were increasing as autumn approached. One advantage of having so many ships in port, Stoddert discovered, was that the bulk of the navy was momentarily within dispatch distance of the capital. The crisis in deployment seemed temporary.

Stoddert looked towards the fall with special confidence primarily because the shortage of frigates appeared at an end. During his first year in office, the secretary had juggled three fifth-rates in an effort to maintain sufficient strength in the West Indies and on the American coast. The newly constructed frigates *General Greene* and *Boston* and the captured *l'Insurgente* were expected to be outfitted by the end of July. In the fall, two other frigates bearing the name of the president—the *Adams* built at New York, and the *John Adams* 28, built at Charleston—were to become operational.

With eight frigates available, Stoddert believed that he could protect American commerce in the Caribbean and still be able to send Barry and Talbot to Europe. The *General Greene* would cruise the Havana station, the *Boston* the Windward Passage, the *Constellation* the Guadeloupe station, and the *Insurgent,* as she was to be called in the United States Navy, would join McNeill's *Portsmouth* off Surinam. The powerful *United States* and *Constitution* would show the flag in European waters. To give the latter expedition an added touch, Captain James Barron was appointed second-in-command to Barry in the *United States.* The navy's senior captain would now be an established commodore, having a flag captain to look after the affairs of the frigate.[1]

Stoddert's plans turned out to be unrealistic, and the European sortie

132

was not practicable. It was too late in the year. Stoddert wrote: "my impression of the vast importance of securing the West India trade now and laying a good foundation for it in the future is so strong, that I almost consider it treason to employ a vessel elsewhere which can be employed in the West Indies while a single French privateer remains to infest those seas."[2]

Nevertheless, Stoddert still intended to send Barry and Talbot as far as the Madeiras and Canaries for a short cruise. The frigates would then make for Cayenne, from where Talbot would sail north to take command of the squadron off Hispaniola, while Barry returned to the American coast. Within two days the secretary had come to consider even the latter plan no longer feasible. "After having obtained your approbation of an enter-prise [to Europe] . . . ," Stoddert wrote Adams, "it is painful for me to propose a different arrangement. . . ." Barry and Talbot would make direct for Cayenne.[3]

But Stoddert had not given up on the application of naval power beyond American waters. Since the *Constitution* and *United States* would be sailing directly to Cayenne, the *Insurgent* could be spared for a short cruise to the Western Islands. Stoddert had already sent the appropriate instruc-tions to Norfolk on 27 July for the new captain of the *Insurgent* 36, Alexander Murray.[4]

* * *

Murray continued to display the initiative he had demonstrated during the winter in the *Montezuma*. He had fully recovered from yellow fever contracted at Havana in April and from the doubts that had plagued him in January when he thought himself reproached by Stoddert's dispositions off Guadeloupe. On his own authority, Murray ordered Captain Samuel Barron to halt his recruiting for the *Baltimore*, since it interfered with the *Insurgent*'s. Barron only reluctantly obeyed his senior. If Murray was in the least apprehensive about his action, his self-confidence was bolstered when instructions arrived from Stoddert not only to halt Barron's recruiting, but also to take from the *Baltimore* the men already enlisted. It was a vindi-cated Murray who made his way to Barron's ship with the orders of the secretary of the navy in hand.[5]

With nearly a full crew, thanks to Barron's efforts, Murray was ready to sail as soon as orders arrived, yet he was not completely satisfied with his new command. The former French frigate had been hastily refitted. Her spars were of poor quality, and her copper bottom "in a bad state." But what most surprised Murray was the *Insurgent*'s actual size and strength.

Captured by Truxtun in February 1799, the *l'Insurgente* had been con-demned by an Admiralty court in Norfolk, judged a vessel of superior strength to the *Constellation*, and turned over to Truxtun and his crew.

Operations Resumed

The ship was valued at $120,000 and purchased by the government for the United States Navy.[6]

Murray expected to be taking command of a frigate stronger than the *Constellation*, but his first tour of the *Insurgent* told him otherwise. Murray had sailed with the *Constellation*; he was familiar with her dimensions and armament. He recognized at once that his frigate was shorter, narrower, less deep, and, most importantly, more weakly armed. The cannon still mounted in her numbered four more than the thirty-six the *Constellation* had carried into battle, but Truxtun's main battery consisted of 24-pounders, the *Insurgent*'s 12-pounders. The nominal difference in weight of metal, the standard determination of superiority, favored Truxtun by 40 percent.[7]

The court's ruling had not deceived Stoddert. He was unhappy with the $120,000 valuation of the prize and with the judgment that cost the government its half-share of the prize money meant to provide half-pay for officers not employed. The secretary wrote Truxtun making his opinions known, and making the captain of the *Constellation* an offer. Truxtun and his crew could have $84,000 in prize money; or, Stoddert would hand over $60,000, order a revaluation of the French frigate by "competent persons," and appeal the decision in Truxtun's favor to a superior court.[8]

Truxtun was after every penny he could earn in prize money. He denied the Norfolk naval agent—William Pennock—a commission on the prize, even though Pennock was a friend and had been instrumental in over-assessing the frigate at $120,000. Truxtun's letter to Pennock reflects the low regard in which the agents were often held. "Not one dollar of commission will you or anyone else receive on that prize. . . . you are capital fellows for commissions at Norfolk; let me ask you, if you don't dream of commissions every night . . . but no commission, no, no. . . ." Such ingratitude, but if navy agents could be bullied, the secretary of the navy could not. Truxtun knew that Stoddert was incensed at the court's ruling. He accepted the $84,000 offer.[9]

Not long after his arrival at Norfolk, Murray had looked into the court's proceedings. John Rodgers, Truxtun's first lieutenant, had been called by the court to testify regarding the strengths of the two frigates. He replied only in bare numbers: forty cannon for the French; thirty-six for the American. The judges pressed Rodgers no further. In explaining the affair to Stoddert, Murray wrote of the atmosphere at Norfolk. "There is one thing certain, that his [Truxtun's] word is law here, which may not be his fault, as mankind will sometimes be blinded in the radiance of glory."[10]

In early August Murray received Stoddert's instructions of 27 July:

> The *Insurgent* being intended for a cruising ship is to be stationed at no particular place, nor subject to the command of any officer older in commission than her commander, except in cases strongly warranting

the interference. . . . In the West India islands the Western Isles, Madeira, the Canary Islands and the coast of South America as far south as Cayenne French cruisers are to be found and you may direct your course . . . in such manner you shall judge will afford you the greatest chance of falling in with & capturing the greatest number of them, and of giving the most protection in your power to our com-merce.

Talbot would be at Cayenne until about 20 September, and Stoddert expected that Murray would arrive in time to relieve him. But the secre-tary repeated, "consider yourself unfettered by instructions as to the points where you should operate." As if his orders were not ambiguous enough, Stoddert added a postscript: "You may conclude that I have a strong desire for you to go to the Western Islands—the fact is not so, as already observed—I want you to go where you please."[11]

Murray could interpret his orders in one of two ways. He could assume that Stoddert intended him to sail anywhere within the area mentioned in the letter of the 27th—the West Indies, Cayenne, and the Western Is-lands—or he could construe his orders to have given him the latitude literally to go wherever he pleased. Murray "seriously weighed" what line of action he ought to pursue, and on 5 August he wrote Stoddert informing the secretary of his destination—Gibraltar.[12]

Murray knew that he was interpreting his instructions in the widest possible fashion. On 11 August a second letter from Stoddert arrived by dispatch boat: "I know not where you can do better than off Cayenne a little while, still I do not mean to dictate." Stoddert's preference should have been clear, but he had given Murray the right to use his own judgment, and Murray was determined to sail for Gibraltar. "I feel an ambition to hoist our flag in the European seas, upon a French staff, and our commerce in that quarter, certainly suffers heavy grievances. . . ."[13]

The key word in Murray's explanation for his planned European cruise was "ambition." Norfolk had been the rendezvous where Talbot and Barry were to take on their final stores before departing for Europe. In con-versations with Barry and Pennock, Murray learned of the now defunct plan. A similar situation had presented itself to him during the winter when Barry had failed to send one of his ships to Curaçao, and Murray, operating on his own, had undertaken the task himself. His initiative had earned him the secretary's trust and the command of a frigate. Seeing another of Stoddert's plans undone, Murray decided to sail for the Old World and recoup the secretary's scheme.

* * *

The *Insurgent* cleared Cape Henry on 14 August, following the Gulf Stream on an easterly course a few degrees south of latitude forty. Murray passed through the Azores the first week of September before making landfall off the continent on the 13th. He estimated that of the four-week passage, a quarter had been spent pursuing American, British, or neutral sails. There were no French to be captured.[14]

On 13 September Murray anchored in the Tagus. He needed freshwater and some minor repairs, but he could have reached Gibraltar had he so chosen. Murray had friends in Lisbon, John and Thomas Bulkeley, former business associates from Philadelphia, and Thomas was the American consul in Lisbon. Murray spent four days there, filling his water casks, purchasing needed stores (from the Bulkeleys, of course), exchanging visits with captains of British warships, and throwing a gala breakfast on board the *Insurgent*. On the 16th, the frigate was ready to sail for Cadiz.[15]

Also moored in the Tagus was the British frigate *Phaeton* 38, carrying Lord and Lady Elgin to his new post as minister to Constantinople. At a reception for the Elgins at the home of the American minister to Portugal, William Smith, Lord Elgin "expressed a wish" to the Bulkeleys that the American frigate in the harbor accompany the *Phaeton* to Gibraltar "as a greater security." The Bulkeleys relayed the request to Murray, who considered it an honor to assent.[16]

On the 17th, the *Insurgent* and the *Phaeton* sailed together, reaching Gibraltar on the 21st. Murray then cruised for a few days between there and Cadiz, but only British and Spanish ships were sighted. The *Insurgent* sailed on, reaching Madeira on 5 October. Murray anchored in the roadstead only long enough to send one of his lieutenants ashore to purchase a hogshead "of the best Madeira wine." Still no French sails were sighted. A week later the American frigate was off Teneriffe, where she remained a few days. Murray had yet to see a French flag. On 13 October, he caught the northeast trade, on a course for Cayenne.[17]

2. *The Frigate Situation Improves*

Murray's intention to sail for Europe disquieted neither Adams nor Stoddert. The secretary had given Murray such leeway in his instructions that he had no cause to censure the decision. Stoddert wished to show the flag in European waters, and he may have been enthusiastic about the venture. President Adams, too, longed to strike a blow across the Atlantic. Learning of the cancellation of Barry's cruise, he had written: "I am very solicitous to strike some strokes in Europe." With both men disappointed by the impracticality of sending two forty-fours to Europe, Murray's action drew no reproach. Though Stoddert correctly assumed that Murray would prove unable to reach Cayenne by 20 September to relieve Talbot, there seemed to be a frigate to spare. The new *John Adams*, outfitting in Charleston, would be ready to sail by early September and could reach Cayenne by the end of the month.[18]

But one by one, Stoddert saw his frigate strength decline, his operations upset. Chief Justice Oliver Ellsworth and North Carolina Governor William Richardson Davie were to be sent as envoys to France seeking peace. Adams required of the navy a ship to transport them to Europe, and Stoddert offered the services of Barry's *United States*. The secretary probably had in mind a short cruise to Europe for the frigate, but having made the offer, he was surprised to learn that Barry was expected not only to carry the envoys across the Atlantic, but also to wait until the following spring to bring them home. The thought of losing one of his two most powerful frigates for so long a time took Stoddert aback. He feared as well that the crew, if kept so long idle in port, might mutiny.[19]

Barry reached Newport on 12 September to await the arrival of the diplomats. But Stoddert had not given up the fight to save Barry's services for the navy. He offered instead to use the *George Washington*, expected to return from Hispaniola during October, to take the ministers to France. Adams, however, had decided that the envoys must depart by 1 November at the latest, and it would be impossible to refit the *George Washington* in time.[20]

Stoddert then offered to send the refitted *George Washington* to France to await the return of the envoys, freeing Barry to sail after they had been safely landed. Adams accepted this offer.[21]

On 3 November, Barry sailed from Newport for France. To his disappointment, the *United States* made the journey as a flag-of-truce ship and could not take any prizes. Stoddert had offered his senior captain a prospect of reward: "I hope to salute you an admiral on arrival at Philadelphia." Nevertheless, Stoddert would be without the services of Barry's frigate for seven months.[22]

* * *

Frigates remained the root of all Stoddert's operational problems. Each of the Caribbean stations deserved one, but only the *Boston* was as yet cruising in the West Indies. The *General Greene*'s return to Newport upset plans for Havana. Stoddert accepted Perry's explanation for the outbreak of fever, but Adams did not, blaming the captain for remaining too long in Havana harbor. Still, it was important that the frigate be refitted and dispatched back to Cuba. Stoddert spared no effort to pry Perry out of Newport, despite a continued shortage of men; yet, as August came to an end, the *General Greene* remained at anchor.[23]

Operations Resumed

For once, it appeared that a captain's delay had worked to Stoddert's advantage. American relations with Spain suddenly cooled, and there was serious talk that the Spanish would halt Yankee trade with Cuba. There had also been less privateering activity off the island than expected. The *Pinckney* and *South Carolina* were due to return to Charleston in September. Thus far, they had captured only a single prize, an unarmed schooner later released by the courts. There appeared to be no need for a frigate or a squadron off Cuba. With Talbot delayed at Norfolk and the *George Washington* scheduled to return from Hispaniola, Stoddert ordered Perry to Cap François to join the *Boston* and take command of the American squadron.[24]

The Guadeloupe station needed a frigate as well. The *Merrimack* and *Delaware* had reinforced Tingey during July, but the *Norfolk*, her crew's enlistments expiring, had returned to New York, leaving the commodore with only four ships. During August, Stoddert further built up the squadron. The *Montezuma* was ordered to St. Kitts, but only to transport prisoners held in the Basseterre jail. She returned to Baltimore where she was sold off on 13 September. The *Eagle* left Philadelphia on 8 August for the Antilles. Eager to strengthen Tingey's force, Stoddert ordered the *Baltimore*, Lieutenant William Cowper, out to sea with only 100 men in a ship authorized to carry a crew of 180.[25]

Recruiting full crews was a difficult task during the Quasi-War. Operations were never threatened by any widespread inability to recruit for the fleet such as occurred during the Revolution and the War of 1812. Slow manning, however, did cause frequent delays in the refitting and outfitting of ships of all sizes. Truxtun took two months to recruit 300 men for the *Constellation* in the spring of 1798. The *Herald, Baltimore, Eagle, Norfolk, Governor Jay,* and *General Greene* cutter were either delayed in sailing or left port short-handed on their first cruises. With the frigates *Boston* and *Constitution* recruiting simultaneously during June and July 1799, neither vessel could enlist a full crew. Stoddert had to halt recruiting for the *Boston* to allow Talbot's frigate to fill her complement.[26]

Throughout the war, Stoddert found many of his captains still in port unable to complete their crews weeks after they had been ordered to sea. By the middle of 1799 Stoddert had developed a standard rejoinder for dilatory commanders. He wrote Perry at Newport that the *General Greene*'s complement of "220 men . . . would be a very full crew—perhaps more than necessary. You might with propriety sail 20 or 30 short that number. British ships of the same size, have seldom as many as 200." Even after Perry's losses to yellow fever, Stoddert had forced him back out to sea. "The *General Greene* must not be delayed a single moment for any additional supply of men," Stoddert wrote, for "the ship has as many men on board as nine out of ten of the British navy of the same force." Stoddert expected his captains to sail 10 or 15 percent undermanned. In the case of Lieutenant Cowper, even two-thirds of a full crew was sufficient for a secretary concerned about American strength in the Caribbean.[27]

To relieve Tingey's *Ganges* and add a frigate to the Guadeloupe squadron, Stoddert had expected to send Truxtun's *Constellation* back to St. Kitts after her refit at New York. Truxtun's resignation ruled out the ship's early return to the Leeward Islands. To replace Truxtun, both Adams and Stoddert favored the elder Decatur but he preferred the captaincy of the *Philadelphia* being built by his hometown merchants. Truxtun recommended Captain Samuel Barron, a thirty-six-year-old Virginian then commanding the *Baltimore*; Stoddert acquiesced. The appointment would please Truxtun, who was a friend of Barron, but disliked Decatur, a man "fit for nothing above a boatswain or master. . . ." Decatur, eager to move up a notch in seniority himself, would have been difficult to remove had he been given command of the *Constellation*; Barron would not be.[28]

Technically, Stoddert had yet to accept the resignation of Thomas Truxtun. "Your commission still lays [*sic*] on my table," Stoddert wrote, urging the captain to reconsider his action. To coax the obstinate man, Stoddert tried a ruse. A French frigate was rumored off the American coast in mid-August. The secretary sent orders to New York for Barron, who had not yet reached New York, to take the *Constellation* to sea in hot pursuit. Stoddert enclosed the instructions in a letter addressed to Truxtun, who had agreed to remain with the frigate until his replacement arrived from Norfolk. Stoddert wrote that Barron's orders were "open for your perusal," imploringly adding, "I wish you would add one more laurel to your brow by taking the ship under your command & proceeding after the French frigate." Who could doubt that once at sea on the quarterdeck of the *Constellation,* in hot pursuit of the enemy, thoughts of resignation would disappear? While Truxtun pondered his reply, Barron arrived. Truxtun retired to his home in Perth Amboy, New Jersey.[29]

The effort to convince Truxtun to return to the service continued. In September, George Washington invited him to Mount Vernon, and the two men spoke of duty. Not long afterwards, Truxtun began to display a readiness to rethink his resignation. In Philadelphia, two of Truxtun's friends, Charles Biddle and James Wilkinson, disturbed by his action, decided to intercede on his behalf. They went to Trenton, where the government had relocated to escape the fevers in the capital. Biddle wrote of the meeting with the secretary of the navy:

> Mr. Stoddert made some difficulty on account of the other captains, who he thought would resign. I told him it was not probable they would, that although most of them were brave men, as a naval officer

none of them were equal to Truxtun. Wilkinson and myself after some time persuaded the secretary to send Truxtun his commission, and it was understood that Talbot and he were not to be on the same station.[30]

Just as everything seemed settled, Truxtun became ill. Perhaps he was still having doubts; perhaps his sickness was genuine, for after the winter of 1799–1800 his powers steadily declined. Whatever the cause, Stoddert soon had Truxtun up and on his feet. The secretary offered him the choice of command of the frigate *President* 44, (Talbot's old ship) in the spring or the immediate captaincy of the *Constellation*. Stoddert advised Truxtun, however, "I believe (this is my private opinion) that before [the *President*] will be ready for sea we shall have peace with France and that the present winter is the only season we shall have to gather laurels." Truxtun caught the first ship for Norfolk, reclaiming his command in late November. On Christmas Day, 1799, Truxtun sailed past the lighthouse at Cape Henry, bound for St. Kitts.[31]

* * *

With the *Constellation* patrolling the coast, the rapid outfitting of the *Adams* and *John Adams* grew in import. Both Captain Richard Valentine Morris of the *Adams* and Captain George Cross of the *John Adams* were urged by Stoddert to make all possible haste in their preparations: "Our ships of war are very much wanted in the West Indies—pray lose not a moment in preparing . . . for sea."[32]

The more forward in fitting out was the *Adams* 28, at New York. Morris was the thirty-one-year-old son of a Federalist shipbuilder and signer of the Declaration of Independence, Lewis Morris (half-brother of Gouverneur Morris). Stoddert ordered the captain to take command of the American squadron off Guadeloupe on his first cruise in a man-of-war. The secretary did his best to infuse him with the spirit he would need as commodore. Stoddert suggested that Morris attempt to cut out French vessels, "privateers and others," from the Basse-Terre anchorage on Guadeloupe. A moonless night would render the guns of the fort ineffective, Stoddert advised, and the success of such an operation "would cover with laurels the officers under whose auspices it was conducted."[33]

As 1799 drew to a close, Stoddert was becoming desperate to see the navy gain some "laurels." The mission to France, the secretary incorrectly supposed, would soon lead to peace. Thus far, only Truxtun's victory over *l'Insurgente* had caught the public's attention. Fewer American ships were being captured, thanks to the numerous convoys provided by the navy, but Stoddert needed obvious victories, not just steady accomplishments that were noticed only by the insurance houses. Since the French navy rarely appeared for battle, victories could only be won against the privateers— little ships that were difficult for the frigates and converted merchantmen of the navy to catch. Only one French corsair had been captured in May 1799, two in June, not one in July.

Stoddert ordered more cruising and less convoying, probably an opera- tional mistake. He considered daring strokes—not even the Royal Navy had tried to cut out French ships moored in their major Caribbean base. Moreover, such an attack was beyond the scope of his authority. Congress had limited actions against French armed ships to the "high seas," but the secretary was willing to stretch the law. He had advocated the small invasion of the pirate key at Matanzas. In October 1799, when asked to define an "armed ship," Stoddert replied: "I have always supposed French vessels with muskets pistols, or any small arms on board so as to be rendered formidable to an American vessel entirely without arms would be considered armed vessels."[34]

Stoddert intended to deploy the *John Adams* 28 off Surinam. The citizens of Charleston built the frigate by subscription. After Robert Cochran's run in with the British schooner *Mosquito,* George Cross be- came the city's candidate for command. A prominent citizen, with political and business connections in Philadelphia, Cross received his commission dated 10 September 1798. Stoddert now ordered Cross to join the *Ports- mouth* off Surinam with all haste and to place himself under the command of Daniel McNeill. On 1 October, however, the secretary sent Cross new orders to sail instead for St. Kitts to join Morris. Stoddert had "received information from Cayenne" that rendered the presence of the Charleston frigate unnecessary.[35]

3. Operations Off Guiana

In September 1799 word reached Stoddert at Trenton of the arrival in New York of the *Scammel* from McNeill's squadron off Surinam and of the British capture of that colony.[36]

The commander of the little American squadron off Surinam was Daniel McNeill, an eccentric fifty-one-year-old veteran privateersman from Mas- sachusetts. Detached from John Barry's squadron, McNeill had cruised off the Surinam coast and Cayenne the previous winter and was ordered to return to that station in June 1799. The cutter *Scammel,* sent out in July, was the first of a number of ships Stoddert intended for McNeill's com- mand.[37]

Operations Resumed

Arriving on his station, McNeill found French privateers very active from both Cayenne, French Guiana, and from the inlets and river near Paramaribo, Surinam. With his two ships, he could not possibly watch both points, separated by 321 miles of sea. Several of the corsairs were large, and the *Scammel* was too small to operate independently. McNeill was fortunate enough to take the small French schooner *la Friponne* shortly after his arrival. Not long afterwards he trapped the French corvette *l'Hussard* 20, at anchor in the Surinam River and proceeded to blockade her there.[38]

Keeping the *Portsmouth* immobile for two months proved to be a mistake. The Surinam River was infested with sawfish, making swimming or bathing hazardous. Even on board the men were at risk because poisonous aquatic snakes would wind their way up the cables into the ship. Furthermore, while the *Portsmouth* lay at anchor, the French had the run of the coast. Privateers and men of war—a frigate cruised the waters for a short time—were free to attack American shipping. Eventually, McNeill himself was blockaded by a superior French force. Only the presence of an American frigate seemed likely to give the initiative back to the American squadron; accordingly, Stoddert had ordered the *John Adams* to Surinam.[39]

French activity and the lure of colonial conquests also attracted British attention. On 31 July a Royal Navy squadron of two ships of the line, four frigates, a brig, a sloop, and troop transports under the command of Vice Admiral Lord Hugh Seymour, sailed from Port Royal, Martinique. On 12 August this force arrived off Paramaribo, demanding the surrender of the colony. The Dutch complied, and a peaceful occupation followed.[40]

The capitulation left McNeill in an awkward position. He had unloaded his spare spars and stores and prepared the *Portsmouth* for battle with the blockaded *l'Hussard*. He had heard that the corvette carried a "considerable sum of money" and that it intended to sail for France. The slow-sailing *Portsmouth* would have little chance of catching the French ship at sea, assuming McNeill himself could leave the river. Cutting her out in the river would be dangerous—and illegal. *L'Hussard* was too rich a prize to let slip away, so McNeill had continued his blockade awaiting an opportunity to strike. His patience seemed rewarded when the Dutch surrendered to Lord Seymour and the commander of *l'Hussard* chose to strike to McNeill.[41]

McNeill placed a lieutenant and 100 men from the *Portsmouth* and *Scammel* into his prize, removing the French prisoners to the American ships. Not long afterwards, two British fifth-rates approached in the river. Concerned by their presence, McNeill decided to go himself to *l'Hussard* to issue the prize master instructions. A boat's crew from the *Portsmouth* was rowing McNeill to the French ship when the captain of one of the British frigates ordered the Americans to stand clear. Standing in the boat in his captain's uniform, McNeill ignored three such demands, to which the Royal Navy captain had one of his men discharge a musket at the *Portsmouth*'s commander, who "took no further notice of, further than turning his head round, told the British captain to fire again, which he did twice, but neither ball did any injury." McNeill reached *l'Hussard* where he told his men to stand firm until his return. He then set out to confer with Seymour and report to him the actions of his subordinate. No sooner had he reached shore than the British frigate sent men in boats towards the French corvette, but American fire drove them off.[42]

At the meeting ashore, Seymour apologized for the conduct of his captain, but he pressed McNeill for the surrender of *l'Hussard* and the release of the French prisoners. She was by right a British prize, having been in inland waters at the time of the surrender. McNeill acquiesced.[43]

The episode in the Surinam River had minor diplomatic ramifications, but nearly terminated McNeill's career. The British lodged an official protest, Lord Grenville terming the capture of *l'Hussard* "pretended," forwarding Seymour's correspondence on the matter to Liston in Philadelphia. McNeill's own report of the affair failed to place his behavior in a more favorable light. Stoddert not only considered the American commander largely at fault, but also suspected that he had struck a "pecuniary" deal with the French captain. Had he been more certain, the secretary would have dismissed McNeill.[44]

The captain's troubles, however, continued. McNeill ordered the *Scammel* to sail immediately to New York with the news of the British landing. The *Portsmouth* cruised alone until she was joined by the *Maryland 20*. Returning to Paramaribo in November, McNeill was greeted with a cannon shot from the fort guarding the entrance to the river, meant to bring to an unwelcome visitor. The American commodore rightly considered the gesture an insult. Then several of the *Portsmouth*'s men deserted. McNeill formed a party commanded by one of his officers and sent it ashore to reclaim his people. Two of the seamen were seized and returned to the American ship by force. The British protested the "infringement of the territorial rights of the colony" and demanded an apology, which McNeill refused. The governor responded by promptly ordering the *Portsmouth* to sail, and not to return. McNeill sailed for New York where he arrived in January 1800.[45]

* * *

The British occupation and the increased presence of the Royal Navy greatly simplified the American task off Guiana. Only Cayenne remained as a French base, much easier for a small squadron to cover. In fact, after the return of the *Portsmouth* to the United States, only the sloop of war *Maryland* remained on the station.[46]

Her commander was John Rodgers, formerly Truxtun's first lieutenant in the *Constellation*. Rodgers's conduct in that post had earned him Truxtun's esteem and advocacy and he had been given command of *l'Insurgente* after her capture in 1799.[47]

According to an undocumented account, Rodgers, with Midshipman David Porter and eleven seamen, sailed the battered prize frigate in gale force winds for three nights and two days following the battle while they held 173 French prisoners at bay. Without shackles, handcuffs, or gratings, the French were kept below by constant vigilance of men armed to the teeth with cutlasses, pistols, and blunderbusses. There are several factual inaccuracies in the tale, for Truxtun's journal mentions the frigates sailing in company. Truxtun recommended his first for promotion to captain and the command of the *Insurgent*. Stoddert agreed to the former, but was unwilling to give the frigate to so junior an officer.[48]

The secretary had no reason to regret his decision not to give a frigate to Rodgers. Before the *Maryland* had even left the Chesapeake, information reached Philadelphia that Rodgers was having some difficulty in his new role. Pickering received a letter from James Buchanan, a Baltimore merchant, that included a postscript concerning an early September visit to the *Maryland*. "The order on board was *great*, & *probably* too much *all a mode L'Truxtun*—& too distant, for officer to officer—& more than I ever saw in any ship of war before, of any *rate*, or any nation! & I rather fear, that favorite systems may be carried too far. I will however hope for the best!!!" Buchanan had once employed Rodgers as master of the ship *Hope*, a tobacco trader seized by a French privateer and condemned at Lorient in February 1797. Buchanan apparently held Rodgers partly responsible for the *Hope*'s capture, which cost the merchant and his partner $20,000. Whether Buchanan's opinions of Rodgers were objective or not, from Pickering they undoubtedly found their way to Stoddert. And more importantly, for Rodgers, Buchanan shared a business association with Samuel Smith, who would replace Stoddert at the Navy Department in April 1801 as acting secretary until July when brother Robert became secretary of the navy in Thomas Jefferson's cabinet. The Smiths' would recommend the dismissal of Rodgers late in 1801. In 1799, however, Buchanan's warnings served to put Stoddert on notice concerning Rodgers. The secretary would closely observe the performance of the *Maryland* off Surinam. Unfortunately for Rodgers, on arrival at his station he found "the coast . . . perfectly clear of French privateers."[49]

Other ships ordered to Guiana before news of the British occupation reached Philadelphia also met with little success. Talbot, in the ship

Constitution, swept through the area between 24 September and 3 October before sailing north for Hispaniola. He recaptured a Hamburg brig in the possession of a French prize crew. Murray in the *Insurgent,* reached Cayenne on 30 October from Teneriffe. He fell in with Rodgers and sailed along the coast four days. With the British now occupying Surinam, and having yet to sight a French sail, he considered any further effort "time lost" and sailed north for Barbados.[50]

4. Recovery in the Lesser Antilles

The operations of the British in Dutch Guiana, and the expected Spanish closing of Cuba to American trade, seemed to secure the flanks of the American campaign in the Caribbean. (Commerce with Cuba would continue, however, to the administration's surprise, forcing a redeployment of ships from the Cap François station.) Stoddert was able to concentrate his ships in the center, off Hispaniola and around Guadeloupe.[51]

The secretary was particularly concerned about Tingey and his squadron based at St. Kitts. Without a frigate to cover their operations, Tingey's ships were dong their best to protect American trade in the whole of the Lesser Antilles.

Tingey was spurred to greater activity when he realized that his concerns for his health and the dangers posed by hurricanes voiced in the spring, had drawn not only a mild rebuke from Stoddert, but had also given "opportunity" to his "animadverting *seniors,* to decant so much" on the good commodore's fears. Truxtun noted that "prejudices" had developed against Tingey, "a clever fellow & a worthy man in every respect . . . [whose] feelings must be hurt. . . ." Tingey himself assured Stoddert of his energy and determination:

> What I intimated on the subject of the hurricanes, was only meant as a general observation—It being determined to keep a force here during these months: of which I daily see the absolute necessity—No ship in the service (I speak from experience) will be found better able to sustain their violence than the *Ganges*—nor a crew that can with more alacrity, bring a ship to a state of preparation to bear heavy weather. . . .[52]

Taking the elements into consideration, Tingey made St. Kitts the major base for operations in the Lesser Antilles. Truxtun had begun the process in early 1799 when he made Clarkson defacto navy agent at Basseterre. While Stoddert ultimately endorsed the appointment, he continued to consider Prince Rupert Bay the superior anchorage, which it was. Tingey reasoned, however, that since the secretary of the navy wished American ships to spend as little time as possible riding at anchor, the comforts of Dominica were offset by the calms that frequently preceded the gales, trapping ships at their moorings. From St. Kitts, warships could "more easily put to sea at the appearance of bad weather."[53]

Between July and September Tingey's command—the *Ganges, Merrimack,* and *Pickering*—operated from Basseterre, mostly between St. Thomas and Dominica. The little squadron cruised and convoyed, trying to satisfy the demands of the local merchants for protection, and patrolling the major routes from Guadeloupe to Hispaniola in the hope of interdicting and intercepting privateers. But Tingey's force was too weak. "I find it impracticable," he wrote Stoddert, "with our small squadron to check the progress of the French privateers of Guadeloupe, equal to my wishes—but our endeavor shall not slacken." In addition, Tingey's physical strength was failing; he awaited relief, exhausted.[54]

Nevertheless, Tingey's efforts met with moderate success. American losses to Guadeloupe-based privateers, after the year's high of nine in June, fell to four in July, two in August, and none in September. It is impossible to measure his success at interdicting the movement of corsairs. The small number of American losses could be indicative of a high level of redeployment. Tingey's squadron captured three French privateers and recaptured two brigs, one British and one American.[55]

In early September, Tingey at last received reinforcements, the *Delaware* and *Eagle.* With their arrival, however, came new instructions depriving the squadron of another ship. French privateers operating from the Spanish Main were harassing American commerce in the Gulf of Mexico. Stoddert ordered Tingey to send one of his ships "to cruise along the south side of Santo Domingo and Cuba & to scour the coast between Cape Catouche [Yucatan Peninsula] to Vera Cruz & operate between these two places until 15 November. . . ." Stoddert recommended Captain Moses Brown of the *Merrimack,* an experienced fifty-seven-year-old Massachusetts seaman who was "well acquainted" with the Gulf.[56]

Tingey and Brown met at St. Barts on 18 September. Intending to make the most of the required detachment, Tingey ordered Brown to proceed first to St. Kitts to escort a convoy from there through the Anegada Passage, clear of the corsairs' cruising grounds. After leaving the convoy to sail north alone, the *Merrimack* was to cruise along the northern coast of Puerto Rico, an island Tingey had been unable to cover. From Puerto Rico, Brown as to sail south through the Mona Passage, along the southern coasts of Hispaniola and Cuba, through the Yucatan Channel, and then on to Vera Cruz before returning to Boston.[57]

Brown left Basseterre with the convoy on 20 September. Recapturing a

Commodore Richard Dale, by John Ford.

Commodore Thomas Truxtun, by Bass Otis. (Courtesy of the Long Island Historical Society)

USS Constellation *(1797–1854), by Rear Admiral John W. Schmidt, USN (Ret).* (Courtesy of Mr. & Mrs. Samuel M. Jemison)

Stephen Decatur, Sr., by St. Memin.
(Collection of Mrs. William F.
Machold)

John Barry, by S. Zveg.

Captain Samuel Nicholson.

Commodore Alexander Murray.

USS Delaware *seizing* la Croyable, 7 *July 1798.* (Courtesy of The Mariners' Museum, Newport News, Va., Bailey Collection)

USS Constitution.

USS Baltimore II, *1798–1801*. (Courtesy of Arthur N. Disney, Sr.)

Commodore Thomas Tingey, by Captain T. T. Craven after Gilbert Stuart. (Courtesy of Mr. Oakley)

William Bainbridge, as a lieutenant. (Collection of Mrs. Theodore Frothingham)

British brig on the way, he reached Vera Cruz on 19 October. The Americans received a warm official reception from the authorities. Dragging her anchors during a strong gale, only the assistance of a Spanish frigate prevented the *Merrimack* from being driven ashore and wrecked. After leaving Vera Cruz, Brown spent a few days of desultory cruising along the coast before sailing for Havana. There, he met another convoy and headed for home, sighting Cape Ann on 7 December.[58]

* * *

In early October, Captain Richard Valentine Morris in the *Adams* relieved Tingey. The *Ganges* sailed, by way of Havana, for Philadelphia, berthing at the Catherine Street wharf in mid-November. Morris soon found his already hard-pressed squadron further weakened by detachments. He carried with him to St. Kitts orders from the secretary of the navy to do what could be done to protect American trade with Curaçao. Stoddert left to Morris's discretion how much help, if any, might be rendered that commerce. The secretary recognized that the squadron was small and advised Morris "you cannot well be too adventurous" in that quarter.[59]

The situation on Curaçao was steadily deteriorating. Pirates, flying "a dark [flag], with a skull & cross bones painted on it," were operating from the island against American ships. One pirate vessel, *le Trois Amis*, captured a New York brig, murdering the master and five of the crew. Benjamin Hammell Phillips, the American consul, noted that the Dutch frigate *Ceres* fired salutes whenever the corsair entered the harbor at Willemstad.[60]

In September, conditions on the island worsened. Piracy and privateering increased, while the Dutch cowered, unable to act against the French. Rumors spread of an impending insurrection led by the French aimed at social revolution and the elimination of the white, English-speaking merchants. Phillips wrote Pickering, fearful for the lives and property of Americans, requesting that two warships be sent "immediately" to Curaçao.[61]

Pickering forwarded the letter to Stoddert, who that same day drew up instructions for Morris to dispatch two ships to the island. Phillips, in turn, was advised by the secretary of state that "if the aid of our armed vessels can be of a/c [account?] to the government of the island in checking the machinations of the French, and they desire to avail themselves of it, it may be given to them." Pickering's letter for Phillips, and Stoddert's for Morris, were rushed to New York for the cutter *Scammel*, recently returned from McNeill's squadron off Surinam. Lieutenant Fernald was ordered to sail with all haste to join Morris.[62]

Fernald fell in with Morris off St. Kitts and the commodore received his orders to detach the two ships to Curaçao. Stoddert had recommended that at least one "strong" vessel be included, preferably the *Baltimore* or *Delaware*. Morris chose the latter, commanded by Captain Thomas Baker.[63]

Baker was a forty-year-old veteran seaman and privateer. Born in Leicestershire, England, he came to America about 1770 with an older brother to make a new life for himself. During the Revolution Baker apprenticed himself to Gustavus Conyngham and later served in a privateer under Stephen Decatur, Sr. When Decatur received command of the *Delaware* in the spring of 1798, he brought his comrade, friend, and fellow-Philadelphian on board as his first lieutenant. When the captain left to take command of the frigate *Philadelphia*, Stoddert promoted Baker to the captaincy.[64]

Accompanied by the *Scammel*, Baker sailed for Curaçao, reaching the island on 10 November, capturing in route the privateer *l'Océan* 10. His first independent command appeared to be off to a fortunate start. Conditions ashore at the Dutch colony, however, proved so alarming, that both Consul Phillips and Baker agreed, at the governor's request, that the American men-of-war "remain in port for some time." A call for further reinforcements sailed for the capital. Baker, his ships moored, would have little opportunity to cruise.[65]

After detaching the *Delaware* and *Scammel*, only the *Adams*, *Baltimore*, *Pickering*, and *Eagle* remained with Morris. Operations continued, the commodore doing his best to meet the seemingly limitless demands made upon his limited resources. In the late fall, rumors swept the Caribbean that a force of frigates and troops had sailed from France. American commanders off Cap François, Cayenne, and Guadeloupe searched the horizon each morning for their arrival. Fortunately for Morris, Murray in the *Insurgent* made a timely appearance off Guadeloupe in early November. Informed of the expected French reinforcement, Murray decided that he had better cruise with Morris.[66]

French men-of-war were, indeed, on their way to the Caribbean. In the fall, the Directory planned to dispatch forces to Hispaniola, Guadeloupe, and Cayenne, each transporting new governors, supplies, and in one case troops. *L'Aréthuse* corvette sailed from Lorient for Cayenne, as did a small squadron commanded by Commodore Jean Marie Reneaud consisting of his own frigate *la Sirène* 36, and the corvette *la Bergère* 18. Leaving La Rochelle, Reneaud's ships carried 450 troops and the new governor of Cayenne—Victor Hugues. Cleared of charges related to his administration at Guadeloupe, "the Colonial Robespierre" was sent to energize the *guerre de course* at Cayenne. In December 1799 two British frigates, the *Glenmore* 36, Captain George Duff, and the *Aimable* 32, Captain Henry Raper, intercepted, but failed to destroy Reneaud's force. Hugues reached Cayenne and in 1800 American commercial losses to the colony's corsairs tripled.[67]

The corvette *la Diligente* 12, reached St. Domingo in September 1799. Although she had captured an American merchant ship on her passage from Rochefort, because her captain placed the vessel at the service of Toussaint L'Ouverture, her subsequent operations around Hispaniola were not molested by the American squadron. On 3 December Captain Little in the *Boston* chased down *la Diligente* but released her when Captain Dubois presented the American with a passport signed by Edward Stevens. On 7 December the French corvette lay at anchor in Môle St. Nicolas with the *Constitution*. Three French frigates were to have joined *la Diligente* off Hispaniola after delivering representatives from the Directory to Cap François, but the coup of 9 November 1799, led to the cancellation of the mission. In April 1800 the frigate *l'Africaine* reached Cap François with agents from the Consulate.[68]

On 15 November 1799 the frigate *la Vengeance* 40, Captain F. M. Pitot, and the corvette *le Berceau* 24, Commander Louis André Senes, left France for Guadeloupe bearing three of the Directory's agents to relieve General Desfourneaux. On 10 December they made landfall at la Désirade and anchored off Grande Terre the following day.[69]

The arrival of a half-dozen French warships in the Antilles late in 1799 complicated American naval operations. The French commanders displayed little aggressiveness towards American men-of-war or merchant ships. Their principal concern was to deliver passengers, refit, and return to France with other civil and military personnel, and the latest intelligence. But Stoddert and his commodores had to base their plans on French capabilities, not intentions. The presence of the ships posed a threat, and it became apparent as the new year began that the agents fresh from Paris brought with them instructions meant to accelerate the *guerre de course*.

Since *la Vengeance* and *le Berceau* reached Guadeloupe so late in the year, Morris's operations were little disrupted. The frigate *John Adams* 28, Captain George Cross, the ship *Connecticut* 24, Captain Moses Tryon, and the new schooner *Enterprize* 12, Lieutenant John Shaw joined the squadron off Guadeloupe. With three frigates on hand to meet the French if they sought combat, Morris directed his command with greater confidence and success. Nine merchant ships were recaptured and six French privateers were taken.[70]

The most notable victory was the capture of the corsair schooner *l'Egypte Conquise* 18. Reputedly one of the "best vessels belonging to the French in the West Indies," the privateer had been fitted out and double-manned, mounting fourteen 9-pounders and four 6-pounders, with a crew of 250. Her quarry was the American brig *Pickering* 14, commanded by Lieutenant Benjamin Hillar. About 18 November, off Pointe-à-Pitre, Guadeloupe, hunter found intended prey. Carrying only fourteen 4-pounders, with a crew of seventy, twenty shy of full complement, Hillar wisely chose to fight a running battle with the French. The lieutenant demonstrated his seamanship, patience, and ability, denying the over-manned corsair the opportunity to board, and forcing a ship with a three-to-one advantage in weight of metal to strike after a nine-hour engagement.[71]

8

"PROBLEMATICAL AND PRECARIOUS"

---

1. The St. Domingo Game

A major cause of Stoddert's inability to concentrate greater strength at St. Kitts was the growing demand for a naval presence off Hispaniola. The station served by Tingey's *Ganges* during the winter of 1798–99 began to rival in importance the entire Lesser Antilles.

The roots of American involvement on Hispaniola lay in the decade and a half following the peace of 1783. Searching for open markets, Yankee traders found the largest cracks in the reestablished European mercantilist structure in the French Antilles. By 1791 nearly 20 percent of all American exports were carried to French Caribbean ports, representing over 56 percent of all the trade with the islands. Most of this commerce centered on Hispaniola. In August 1791, the pressures of the French Revolution brought permanent change to the island. The nonwhite population revolted, throwing off the bonds of slavery. The white colonists tried to suppress the growing revolt. Rallying under the royalist banner, they sought trade (mostly foodstuffs) from the United States and military assistance from Great Britain. The Americans were eager to trade with the island, freed from French commercial restrictions. British planters, merchants, and imperialists were just as eager to aid the royalists, reestablish a slavocracy, and win the colony for their empire.[1]

Early in 1793 the British cabinet authorized operations against Hispaniola in the event of hostilities, and France's declaration of war in February set the plans in motion. Commodore John Ford's weak Jamaica squadron, with a handful of British and colonial troops, launched a series of amphibious moves in support of the French royalists. By the end of the year the British flag flew at Jérémie, Môle St. Nicolas, Jean Rabel, St. Marc, Arcahais, Boucassin, and Léogâne. The following year, after conquering all

151

"Problematical and Precarious"

French possessions in the Lesser Antilles, reinforcements were shifted to St. Domingo and operations accelerated. On 4 June 1794 Port-au-Prince, the colonial capital, fell. The British were on the verge of totally eliminating the French from the Caribbean basin.[2]

Victory, however, slipped from England's grasp. As the British flag was raised at Port-au-Prince, the squadron bearing Victor Hugues's relief expedition appeared off Guadeloupe. His reconquest of the island, and its effect on American commerce, has been mentioned. More immediate, however, was its impact on British operations to leeward. Troops were recalled from Hispaniola to counter Hugues's threat in the Windward Islands. Operations faltered. The seven battalions remaining on St. Domingo were reduced by yellow fever to 3,700 men, of whom only half were effectives.[3]

Throughout 1795 and 1796 the continued activity of Hugues, and the shift in allegiance of Spain and Holland to France, diverted British attention from St. Domingo. Rather than fight for a colony torn by social unrest and ravaged by war, London chose to gather up the richer islands of ex-allies. On Hispaniola British operations stagnated. Except for a few coastal points on the northern and southern peninsulas, control was limited to the central, western district along the Bight of Léogâne. In the north opposition consolidated under the control of the black François Domingue—Toussaint L'Ouverture. In the south the British faced the mulatto André Rigaud. Both generals, nominally under the authority of the Directory in Paris, continually pressured the outnumbered redcoats and their royalist supporters.[4]

By 1797 the monetary and personnel costs of campaigning on Hispaniola had forced a reassessment of British policy. Over 40,000 soldiers were dead and as many again lost to the service, their health destroyed on a service that was often considered a sentence of death. Great Britain lost more men to disease alone on St. Domingo than Wellington would lose "from death, discharge, desertion and all causes from the beginning to the end of the Peninsular War [1808–1814]." Expenditures were just as enormous. Operations ashore drained the treasury of £300,000 in 1794 but escalated dramatically thereafter, totaling £700,000 for the month of January 1797 alone. The new British policy sought to reduce these costs. No reinforcements would be sent to the colony and expenditures would be cut to £300,000 per annum. Operations would be curtailed, with reliance placed on the royalists, while British troops concentrated on the defense of key strategic coastal positions such as Jérémie and Môle St. Nicolas. To implement the decision, the cabinet named Major General John Graves Simcoe to command.[5]

Simcoe reached Hispaniola early in 1797. He was soon disillusioned. With their subsidies cut, the French royalists and their local forces gave up the fight. The burdens placed on the British troops increased. Simcoe held on as best he could to isolated coastal positions, keeping most of his forces in the western plains, relying on the Royal Navy to maintain communications between dispersed units. From the uncontrolled expanses of the northern and southern peninsulas, scores of privateers struck at British (and American) commerce in the Windward Passage. The strain on the Jamaica squadron increased. Hyde Parker's command grew from fourteen ships in January 1797 to thirty-two by August. Nevertheless, the situation continued to deteriorate and in July 1797 Simcoe returned to London with his aide, Lieutenant Colonel Thomas Maitland. Major General John Whyte was left in command.[6]

The cabinet decided not to return Simcoe to Hispaniola and replaced him with Major General Nesbitt. Nesbitt, seconded by Maitland, was instructed to hold on to three strategic points—Môle St. Nicolas in the north, Port-au-Prince in the west, and Jérémie in the south. The primary objective remained, however, to reduce expenditures. There would be no reinforcements and outlays were to be kept under £300,000 a year. Maitland was ordered to return to Hispaniola immediately to be followed by Nesbitt, but the commanding general fell ill at Madeiras, and the delay in his arrival at Port-au-Prince led to the assumption that he had been lost at sea.[7]

Although he carried the authority of a brigadier general, Thomas Maitland was but an eccentric thirty-eight-year-old lieutenant colonel whose character was marked by self-esteem and a dislike of Americans and French royalists. He was known as "a rough old despot" in his later years. Despite his junior ranking, "King Tom" was eager to assume gigantic responsibilities on his arrival in St. Domingo. His decisions were to have enormous consequences for Britain, and especially for the United States.[8]

Returning to Hispaniola in March 1798, Maitland found that conditions had worsened. Given the manpower and financial restrictions imposed from London, he came to favor near complete evacuation as soon as possible, holding only three strategic positions. Maitland carried with him the cabinet's confidential instructions for Nesbitt's command that authorized just such a pullback if necessary. He refused, however, to communicate the contents of his orders to either Admiral Parker or General Whyte. Frustrated, Whyte returned to England leaving Maitland in charge.[9]

There followed months of offensive/defensive operations designed to cover the orderly withdrawal of British troops, equipment, and supporters. To facilitate the exodus, Maitland reached agreements with both Rigaud and Toussaint. By July, with Port-au-Prince already abandoned, Maitland decided that neither Jérémie nor Môle St. Nicolas could be defended with the forces and funds available. He determined to withdraw from the former, and at the latter, met with Toussaint on 31 August. The two men signed a secret convention, Maitland agreeing to evacuate all British forces from Hispaniola, refrain from future intervention, and permit trade with Toussaint's territory. The black general agreed not to attack Jamaica, to halt the *guerre de course* against the British, and to open one of his ports to English ships.[10]

Maitland's decision to withdraw from Hispaniola was based on his understanding of the colony's affairs drawn from two years' experience. He recognized that the British were not being opposed by the French, but by armies of blacks and mulattos resisting Britain's attempt to reestablish a slavocracy. In the absence of this threat, Maitland expected these same forces both to oppose French efforts to reconstitute colonial control and fall once again into civil war. In a colony with fewer than 30,000 whites and 25,000 mulattos, but with 500,000 blacks, it made sense to back Toussaint. Beyond the simple demographics, however, Maitland had come to respect and trust the black general.[11]

While Maitland's policy had at last rid Britain of "the hateful incubus" of involvement on Hispaniola, its wisdom escaped Sir Hyde Parker, a factor that helped shape American naval operations off St. Domingo. Parker remained convinced that Toussaint was a tool of the French, bent on invading Jamaica. He was completely taken aback by Maitland's decision to evacuate even Môle St. Nicolas, which the admiral viewed as a virtual *sine qua non* for his squadron's operations.[12]

The Môle was known as the "Gibraltar of the West Indies" and was strategically located opposite the Windward Passage. The enclosed harbor was expansive and deep. Even the largest of Parker's ships could moor in the anchorage, which offered protection from an enemy fleet and conve- nient watering. The Môle was the forward base of the Jamaica station where Parker's own *Queen* 98, frequently lay at anchor. From there the admiral could direct operations in the Passage or the Bight of Léogâne. Deprived of this anchorage, the Jamaica squadron's ships would have to operate from Kingston, almost 300 miles to leeward.[13]

What Parker failed to recognize was that the Môle, although its natural and man-made defenses were formidable to attack from the sea, was not blessed with Gibraltar-like impediments to a land assault. A series of hills dominated the harbor, and with only a few thousand troops, Maitland did not believe he could long resist the combined forces of Rigaud and Tous- saint, who alone had 50,000 men under arms. It would be better to withdraw and allow the warlords to fall upon each other, supporting Toussaint in the hope that he would in return honor his agreements with respect to Jamaica and deny the colony to France as well as Britain.[14]

Having entered into a convention, both the British and Toussaint looked to the United States, whereas the Americans, aware of the agreement but not its terms, sought information and inclusion.

In late 1798, Lord Grenville still hoped to lure the United States into closer cooperation in the struggle with France. Having approved Maitland's decisions, the foreign minister sent him to Philadelphia with copies of the secret agreement and draft proposals for Anglo-American cooperation. Toussaint would be denied the right to outfit his own ships in order to prevent an attack on Jamaica, the American south, or privateering against commerce around Hispaniola. In return Great Britain and the United States would resume trade, limited to Port-au-Prince, monopolized by a joint Anglo-American company and restricted to British manufactures and American foodstuffs and livestock.[15]

The Americans disappointed Maitland. He disliked their national character, although he respected their self-interest and hard bargaining. Pickering rejected a number of the proposals, refusing to join in a three-way *de jure* agreement and the restriction of commerce to a single port. Because the British were anxious to involve the United States and realized that Toussaint's forces needed American food if they were to prevail over Rigaud's, the American qualifications were mostly accepted. By 20 April 1799 Liston, Maitland, and Pickering had worked out an agreement that could be taken to Toussaint. Pickering refused, however, to sign anything; for the Americans the convention would have to remain verbal. It was not politically feasible to sign a pact with both Great Britain and a black revolutionary.[16]

In the meantime, Toussaint had contacted the Americans on his own. Writing directly to Adams on 6 November 1798, he offered to accept any reasonable terms if the United States would lift the embargo and open trade to ports under his control. He held no illusions about the nature of American society; he simply needed food to feed his people and his army. A relationship with the United States would also be a useful counterweight in his struggle for independence from both Britain and France.[17]

As for the American leaders, their motivations varied. Some Federalists saw cooperation with Toussaint as a means to foment the dissolution of the French colonial empire in the Caribbean and as a way to prevent the establishment of a British commercial monopoly. Others harbored hopes that the United Sates might draw closer to Britain by joining her in the affairs of Hispaniola. Underlying all such geopolitical conceptions, however, was the lure of renewed trade with St. Domingo. In March 1799, Doctor Edward Stevens, boyhood friend of Alexander Hamilton, sailed as consul general for Cap François.[18]

"Problematical and Precarious"

The American diplomacy towards St. Domingo was largely the work of Secretary of State Timothy Pickering. The negotiations with the British took place in the capital while Adams was off at Quincy. The major burdens of the policy, however, fell on the United States Navy. The two men responsible for the direction of American naval forces, Adams and Stoddert, had grave doubts about involvement in Hispaniolan affairs.

Adams feared that American ties with Toussaint might wreck his plans for a peaceful settlement with France. Support for a colonial revolution against the Directory would be viewed in Paris as an escalation of the struggle. He was also afraid that Anglo-American cooperation with a revolutionary slave leader would be viewed by the colonial governors of the other European powers as a threat to their rule. Thus far in the war, despite the power alignment in Europe, the Caribbean colonies of Spain, Holland, and even France (to some extent) had looked towards the United States and Great Britain for protection against the spread of Jacobinism from Paris. The economic and social threat posed by hundreds of thousands of freed slaves put fear into the hearts of white colonial officials. Association with the British and Toussaint might force these colonies closer to France. Overriding these other concerns, however, was a more important factor. Adams wrote Pickering:

Harmony with the English, in all this business of St. Domingo is the thing I have most at heart. The result of the whole is in my mind problematical and precarious. Toussaint has evidently puzzled himself, the French government, the English cabinet and the administration of the United States. All the rest of the world knows as little what to do with him as he knows what to do with himself. . . . [19]

Stoddert shared many of Adams's concerns and probably had doubts of his own. Slavery was legal in Maryland, and the secretary of the navy, unlike the president or the secretary of state, was a slave owner. But Stoddert was most troubled by the practical problems the relationship with Toussaint would place on his department. A concentration of forces in the Lesser Antilles would become impossible. Off Hispaniola the navy would be the agent for the government's policy of de facto recognition of, and cooperation with, a revolutionary ex-slave running half of a colony nominally controlled by the European power with which the United States was in a state of undeclared, limited war. Faced with such a complex situation, Stoddert could not fail to voice his concern to Adams: "I wish it may not turn out that we are not match for the French in the kind of game that seems now playing at San Domingo."[20]

2. "Allied Cooperation"

The Americans were quickly initiated, disappointed, and disillusioned in Hispaniola. No one in Philadelphia in the spring of 1799 had foreseen the complications inherent in the United States' involvement with Toussaint and Great Britain. Reaching a three-way agreement was simple enough, but its implementation in the Caribbean was charged with confusion and danger. Adams sought harmony with the English, and, if there was one place in the West Indies where the British and the Americans should have cooperated during the Quasi-War, it was on and around St. Domingo. The president, Pickering, and Stoddert discovered, however, that their "ally" Toussaint was in dire straits, while the British officials charged with carrying out the terms of the diplomatic agreement, primarily Lord Balcarres, Governor of Jamaica, and Sir Hyde Parker, commanding the Royal Navy forces in the Greater Antilles, disagreed with the policy of their own government. Rather than cooperating with the Americans, Balcarres and Parker worked to undermine the accord.

* * *

The ship *Kingston* carrying Consul General Edward Stevens reached Cap François on 18 April 1799, and Toussaint hurried back to the city to meet with him. By 14 May, when Maitland arrived off Hispaniola from Philadelphia, Stevens had used the time to gain Toussaint's trust. In negotiations, Toussaint usually took the American position, and in the draft agreement reached on 22 May, he agreed to open two ports to trade. This was the American proposal. The British wished to restrict commerce to Port-au-Prince, convenient to Jamaica, whereas Pickering argued for also opening Cap François, more accessible to ships sailing from the United States. On 13 June, Maitland and Toussaint signed their second secret convention. Stevens observed, verbally guaranteeing the adherence of the United States.[21]

Toussaint had been such an amenable negotiator partly because of his increasingly desperate situation. Years of warfare, isolation from France, and the American embargo of 1798 had left Toussaint's forces poorly equipped and fed. In his early contacts with the Americans in the winter of 1798–99, he had made known his plight. Adams, anxious to make some gesture of support, had asked the cabinet if some loophole could be found that would permit a shipment of provisions for Toussaint despite the embargo. McHenry, Wolcott, Pickering, and Stoddert found such an opening in the act of 9 February 1799 that allowed the president to selectively lift the embargo against French possessions. Vessels "as shall be solely employed in any purposes of political or national intercourse" were exempt from the restrictions of the embargo. Over the objections of Attorney General Charles Lee, Adams ordered the *Kingston* loaded with provisions to be sold at Cap François, ostensibly to help pay for the costs of the diplomatic mission. Despite dissatisfaction of merchants who learned of the secret cargo and suspected administration figures of seeking personal profit, the *Kingston* sailed from Philadelphia. Adams was happy to have Tingey's *Ganges* provide an armed escort for the ship, a move that demonstrated the importance the president attached to the shipment. And it had its intended effect. Stevens reported on his arrival at the Cap that Toussaint "seemed particularly pleased with the president's humane permission to afford a temporary supply to the colony, at a moment when it was reduced to the extremest distress by a total want of all articles usually imported from America." The *Kingston* shipment was, however, only the first of a series of instances in which the Americans found themselves compelled to bend, if not break the legal bounds within which war and diplomacy were carried out during the Quasi-War.[22]

During the course of their final negotiations with Toussaint during May and June 1799, Maitland and Stevens recognized that their ally was in trouble, needing far more than a gesture of support. His army, four times the size of Rigaud's, was ill-clothed, ill-equipped, unfed, and unpaid. In June the civil war began in earnest. Rigaud's forces seized the initiative and rolled back Toussaint's armies. Rigaud's troops were well armed and provisioned by an "uninterrupted trade he has carried on from the south with St. Thomas, the continent of America, and the island of Jamaica. . . ." Given a similar supply, Stevens believed, Toussaint would overwhelm his rival. He advised Pickering that the United States would have to assist its ally "by every legal measure" and that naval vessels "cruise on the south side of the island" to cooperate with the British in "cutting off" Rigaud's supplies. Maitland sent similar advice to Lord Balcarres and Hyde Parker at Jamaica.[23]

Faced with the possible collapse of his Hispaniolan policy, Pickering was willing to go beyond "legal measures." Aware of the difficulties imposed by American law, he had made clear to Stevens that for any regular supply of arms Toussaint would have to rely on Britain. The secretary of state approved Stevens's action taken in June to purchase arms for Toussaint in Jamaica. Alarmed by the consul general's report, Pickering wanted to send 4,000 Prussian-made muskets and several thousand cartridges to Cap François. Stephen Higginson, the navy agent at Boston and a good friend of Pickering, had imported the arms but had been unable to sell them domestically. Pickering planned to load the *Herald* with the arms while the warship's provisions were carried in an accompanying storeship. Though Higginson was anxious to unload the weapons and worked out the details of the plan for the secretary of state, he was unwilling to act without the secretary of the navy's authorization. Stoddert, however, considered the scheme illegal. He was willing to allow the portage of lead to the Cap, "as ballast." Toussaint would have to be satisfied with provisions from the United States when trade resumed in August.[24]

The resumption of trade, however, also proved a disappointment to the Americans. Despite the confusion about the 1 August lifting of the em- bargo, and the departure of the merchant ships before the *George Wash- ington* and *Boston* reached Cap François, American traders arrived off St. Domingo without incident. They discovered that Hispaniola was no longer the market of old. The ravages of war and the collapse of the slave system had drastically reduced output. There were fewer commodities to be sold to the Americans who had been so eager to reach the colony that a flood of ships arrived simultaneously. The commercial effect was marked. The cost of a barrel of American flour fell from $40 to $10 in one month, while the island's coffee rose from 7¢ to 21¢ a pound. Trade fell off, as rapidly as it had begun. The navy agent at Cap François, Nathan Levy, wrote Captain George Little of the *Boston*: ". . . if you know of any particular port in hell where trade is brisk—do let me know." What commerce continued was handicapped by the demands of corrupt local officials for "l'argent."[25]

As Little and other American naval commanders joined the squadron off Hispaniola, they faced special problems rooted in the confused political situation. Identification of the "enemy" was no simple matter. As part of the Anglo-American agreement with Toussaint, he was not allowed a naval force of his own, a restriction meant to safeguard commerce and to prevent the launching of an expedition against Jamaica. It was also ex- pected that in the event of civil war with Rigaud, Toussaint's ties with France would be broken; thus, any ship flying a French flag would be fair game.

Internal communications on Hispaniola, however, were virtually nonex- istent. Troops could march overland with difficulty, but supplies and guns could best be moved by sea, and Toussaint was permitted to employ unarmed transports. These, however, were soon preyed upon by small privateering barges outfitted by Rigaud. Stevens and the resident British officials on St. Domingo considered it necessary to have Toussaint outfit some small ships of his own.

Moreover, Toussaint's French connections were not severed. While favoring Rigaud, Paris was unwilling to gamble everything on his success, and Toussaint chose not to burn his bridges with France. As a result, French merchant ships, privateers, and warships anchored in Toussaint's ports bringing him provisions, carrying off the trade of the colony, and occasionally offering him armed assistance against Rigaud.

Since all of these vessels flew the same flag, distinguishing friend from foe was difficult. Stoddert's initial instructions allowed his captains to seize any ship coming from or going to France beyond "the reach of a cannon ball from the shore." Following a number of such captures, however, French merchants at Cap François, and Toussaint himself protested to Stevens. As a result, Stoddert found himself forced to draw up new directives that forbade his captains from ambushing French ships outside the ports of St. Domingo. Additionally, Toussaint's ships, and the French vessels operating in his service, received passports from Stevens that would protect them as long as they remained within five leagues of the coast. Through such measures, by early 1800 the confusion off Hispaniola had been lessened, but certainly not eliminated.[26]

Another dilemma many captains faced was to what extent they ought to support Toussaint. By December 1799 he had wrested the initiative from Rigaud. Toussaint sent over 10,000 troops south to lay siege to Jacmel. The struggle would be the decisive battle of the war, for both sides soon found themselves short of supplies—facing starvation and destruction.

Both Rigaud and Toussaint looked towards the sea for aid, but the waters at first favored the former. As early as June 1799, Stevens and Maitland had reported that Rigaud's forces in the south were receiving supplies by sea, primarily through the port of Jacmel. A fleet of barges and small privateers protected this lifeline, and at the same time struck at Anglo-American commerce. Maitland had requested that Hyde Parker deploy ships off the southern coast to blockade Rigaud's ports. Despite the continual reinforcement of his squadron, which had grown to forty-three ships by October, the admiral had chosen not to comply. Ships cruised off the southern coast, but Rigaud's provisions continued to arrive, often from Jamaica.[27]

Toussaint appealed to his allies for assistance. It was imperative that artillery and supplies for the army around Jacmel be shipped by sea. Toussaint had at his disposal a squadron of seven armed French ships and he asked Stevens and the British agent at Port-au-Prince, Hugh Cathcart, for passports. The Anglo-American representatives acquiesced and Toussaint expectantly waited for the arrival of his train that would allow him to seal off Jacmel from both land and sea.[28]

Off Cape Tiberon on 24 November, Captain Stephen Poyntz commanding the thirty-two-gun *Solebay* frigate intercepted and captured four of Toussaint's ships, carrying the lot to Kingston. Toussaint sent a representative to Jamaica to demand their release, but Lords Balcarres and Parker supported Poyntz's action. A vice admiralty court condemned the ships "on pretence that they were of a larger size than was permitted by the convention entered into between General Toussaint and General Maitland."[29]

In his report on the affair to Spencer, first lord of the admiralty, Sir Hyde detailed his own thinking on the seizures and British policy towards Toussaint. On Jamaica the authorities had captured two of Rigaud's agents, sent to foment rebellion on the island. Under interrogation they admitted that Toussaint had, according to Parker, consented to furnish four thousand troops for an invasion of Jamaica. The ships sent around Cape Tiberon were, in fact, "a part of a plan" against the British, and not Rigaud with whom Toussaint was in concert. Yet the admiral contradicted his own presumption of cooperation between the two rebels in the next breath. Parker was certain that Toussaint could not be trusted. "It therefore becomes politic," Sir Hyde wrote, "for the further security of this island that that contest should be prolonged; for as long as Rigaud and Toussaint are carrying on the contest, no great danger can be apprehended from either, as to the projected plan against Jamaica. . . ."[30]

Despite these inconsistencies, and the incongruity of Poyntz's and Parker's actions with the spirit if not the letter of the Toussaint-Maitland convention, Lord Spencer backed up his subordinate. He wrote Parker that the precautions he had taken appeared fully justified. In the same letter, however, the first lord informed Parker of his imminent recall. No gazette-letters heralding the "victory" were published, despite the fact that Poyntz's attack had been daring. Before the winter was out there was talk of an indemnity, and Toussaint would ultimately receive 1.5 million francs. The key to the Admiralty's rather peculiar behavior perhaps lay in the fact that Captain Poyntz was Lord Spencer's nephew.[31]

The American reaction to the British seizures was marked. Stevens considered it a grave derangement of Toussaint's operations that would "inevitably prolong the war." Pickering expected "a rupture" between his two allies. "Assurances of *indemnity*" were not what Toussaint needed, but artillery and stores at Jacmel. The secretary of state wrote Rufus King in London: "this bad policy of the British (ascribed to individual rapacity—perhaps to insidious views, that the two chiefs may destroy each other,) I fear may prove injurious to the commerce of the United States."[32]

Toussaint, of course, was the most directly affected. Robert Ritchie, American consul at Port Republicain, was with Toussaint when he learned of the loss. "I found his vexation & disappointment great, he could not avoid plainly discerning his chagrin & expressing himself warmly on the subject." Toussaint was in a predicament and he turned to Doctor Stevens for help. From Cap François the American consul sailed in the *Experiment* 12, commanded by Lieutenant William Maley, for a meeting at

Léogâne. There he learned that while supplies continued to reach Rigaud, unimpeded by Parker, Toussaint's army at Jacmel had neither the artillery to support an assault, nor the provisions to maintain a siege. From the Americans Toussaint wanted assistance moving stores to the southern coast and naval support to blockade Rigaud's ports.[33]

Conveniently, while Toussaint and Stevens were conferring at Léogâne, Commodore Silas Talbot, who by this time had arrived from Cayenne and assumed command at Cap François, was setting in motion an operation that would lead to Rigaud's defeat. Because of "unpromising" opportunities for captures off the northern coast of Hispaniola, Talbot ordered Captain Christopher Raymond Perry to sail on a counterclockwise circumvention of the island in the frigate *General Greene*. Talbot's decision was based primarily on threats to American commerce from Rigaud's privateers and barges operating in the Bight of Léogâne and off the southern coast, not on any desire to provide Toussaint with direct American assistance.[34]

The *General Greene* made a timely appearance off the southern coast just as Toussaint's forces around Jacmel were growing desperate. Perry, cruising near Jacmel on the lookout for privateers and American merchantmen trading illegally with embargoed ports, met with Toussaint who requested the assistance of the frigate. Offering to do what he could, Perry at last established the blockade of the town that Toussaint had long desired. The garrison began to weaken. Toussaint, his own forces near exhaustion, decided to take full advantage of Perry's presence. He planned an assault in conjunction with the American captain who would provide the missing artillery support. As the troops stormed Jacmel, Perry sailed close offshore. An American officer in the *General Greene* wrote: "We engaged three of Rigaud's forts warmly for 30 or 40 minutes; in which time we obliged the enemy to evacuate the town and two of the forts, and repair to their strongest hold; this fort however, soon hauled down its colors. We . . . got our boats out ready to take possession of the place, and a number of Rigaud's cruising vessels and barges in the harbor. . . ."

Perry's bombardment of Jacmel and its forts, and his intention to cut out Rigaud's vessels at anchor as the town fell, exceeded the limits of the authority under which he operated from either the president or Congress. In any event, the latter expedition was cut short when a British frigate, mistaken at first for a French warship, appeared on the scene. Technicalities of American law, however, were not Toussaint's concern. That night Rigaud's surviving troops broke out and the next day—11 March 1800—the entire town and its forts were in Toussaint's hands. He knew whom to thank. An American officer wrote: "it is impossible for me to describe to you the manner in which Toussaint expressed his gratitude to Captain Perry on the occasion."[35]

Perry received 10,000 pounds of coffee "for the use of the crew," for to do otherwise would have broken section thirty-nine of the naval regulations of 2 March 1799. But 10,000 pounds for a crew of less than 200 men—over fifty pounds per man—appears to be an unusual amount of coffee. Toussaint was lavish in his treatment of those captains who assisted him. When Alexander Murray relieved Talbot in mid-1800, he found that the majority of American commanders had "generally degraded themselves by receiving presents for their services." What form these other gifts took has gone unrecorded, but it is little wonder that after the fall of Jacmel American officers were eager to aid Toussaint.[36]

The importance of the service rendered by Perry was evident in the continued pleas that came from Toussaint for provisions. Despite the capture of Jacmel, his armies in the south were starving, unable to follow up their success against Rigaud's routed forces. Troops so exhausted could not have long maintained the siege had Perry not arrived to blockade Jacmel and support the assault with his guns. But Toussaint needed more American help in the form of protection from the British as he shipped provisions southward. He also hoped that his newly captured ports would be opened by the Adams administration to direct American trade.[37]

Writing Stevens and Talbot, Toussaint suggested that a brig be purchased at the Cap, loaded with provisions, and sent to Jacmel under the American flag. If the British intercepted the ship, they would be told that the supplies were for the *Augusta,* then cruising off the southern coast. Unsure about the legality of the scheme, Stevens left a final decision to the commodore, but Talbot opposed the plan on practical grounds. He was certain that the British would never accept the explanation. The quantity and type of the provisions belied a resupply of the *Augusta.* Instead, Talbot proposed that provisioning vessels sail under Toussaint's authority, without passports. The *Constitution* would wait offshore, make prizes of the ships, and then escort them to Jacmel where the commodore would return them to Toussaint. Talbot's plan was not executed, however. He remained too concerned about the rumored arrival of a squadron of frigates from France to spare the *Constitution* for such duty. Toussaint was left with no immediate recourse but to send the ships south protected only by an American passport and hope that there was no repetition of Poyntz's seizures. Subsequently, however, provisions were transported from Cap François to the southern coast in American ships of war.[38]

Resupplied, Toussaint resumed the offensive, breaking the opposition by August. Rigaud fled. In September, Adams declared the whole of French Hispaniola opened to American trade. The United States was charting its own diplomatic course on the island, breaking the restrictions of the June 1799 convention. Shortly thereafter, Toussaint overran the remainder of

St. Domingo on the pretext of ending the slave trade in the adjoining Spanish colony, and under the terms of the Franco-Spanish 1795 treaty of Bâsel in which the latter had agreed at some future date to surrender their share of the island to France.[39]

American participation is significant in three respects. For Toussaint, in the words of Rayford Logan, an eminent historian of Haitian-American relations, "it was decisive." The support of Perry's frigate sufficed to break the resistance of Rigaud; later assistance enabled Toussaint to overrun the whole of Hispaniola. For the British, American commercial and naval cooperation made a success of the strategy devised by Maitland and pursued by Grenville. Policies adopted in London and Philadelphia were better served by the ten-ship American squadron at Cap François, than by Hyde Parker's forty-ship Jamaican command. The bombardment of Jacmel by the *General Greene* best exemplified the United States Navy's support of the three-way diplomatic accord undermined by the *Solebay's* seizure of Toussaint's flotilla off Cape Tiberon. Lastly, for the Americans, involvement in the affairs of St. Domingo marked the beginning of an era of Caribbean interventionism. Gunboat diplomacy was born.[40]

3. The Cap François Station: Operations

While providing support for Toussaint, the squadron off Hispaniola attended to its regular duties. Stoddert had been caught off guard when Adams lifted the embargo against trade with the French colony and had not been able to deploy ships on the station before 1 August. The *George Washington* reached the Cap on 13 August, followed by the *Boston* in September. Fortunately, American commerce was not affected. Silas Talbot, who arrived off Cap François in October and assumed command from George Little, saw his squadron grow to include his own *Constitution*, the *Boston*, *General Greene*, *Herald*, *Augusta*, *Experiment*, *Richmond*, *Patapsco*, *Trumbull*, and *Norfolk*. At times, Talbot also saw his area of responsibility broaden to include both Cuba and Puerto Rico. The *Norfolk*, commanded by Master Commandant William Bainbridge who was already gaining a reputation as a brutal martinet, was lost to Talbot, deployed off Havana as the nucleus for another squadron. It became apparent in September 1799 that trade with Cuba would not be halted.[41]

With a half-dozen or so ships under his command at any one time, Talbot faced difficult operational problems. The larger French corsairs stayed clear of Hispaniola, cruising between latitudes 22° and 26° north and east of the Bahamas, positioned to intercept American merchant vessels sailing the

Atlantic routes to Puerto Rico and the Lesser Antilles. Scores of barges and small privateers, outfitted by Rigaud, operated in the Bight of Léogâne and off the southern coast. Other privateers and pirates sailed from Span-ish territory, some from eastern Cuba fronting the Windward Passage, and others from the eastern two-thirds of St. Domingo. With nearly 400 miles of sea separating the two main zones of activity, Talbot was hard pressed to find sufficient forces to contain simultaneously the privateers and Rigaud, and to support Toussaint.[42]

Also, as did Morris and McNeill, Talbot scanned the horizon for the French frigates rumored on their way to the Cap. The commodore elected to keep two frigates—usually the *Constitution* and *Boston*—within sup-porting distance of Cap François to combat the French should they arrive. Stoddert, who possessed similar intelligence in Philadelphia, supported Talbot's decision. There was a need to concentrate, despite the restrictions imposed upon the squadron's operations against corsairs.[43]

Nevertheless, between August 1799 and July 1800 the ships on the Cape station took twenty French privateers and recaptured numerous American, British, and neutral ships. The capture of so many vessels attests to the skill of Talbot's commanders and to the increasing activity of French corsairs in the Greater Antilles.[44]

* * *

Although the operations of Talbot's squadron did not lead to clashes with the French navy, a few actions of note occurred.[45]

In December 1799, Stevens sailed south for his meeting with Toussaint after Poyntz's action off Cape Tiberon. The consul took passage in the *Experiment* schooner, twelve guns, commanded by Lieutenant William Maley. The *Experiment* was escorting four American merchant ships as well, when the little convoy was becalmed in the Bight south of St. Marc, opposite the Île de la Gonâve. After dawn on New Year's Day 1800, Edward Stevens learned the desperate nature of the pirates who had been plundering America's commerce.[46]

About 6:00 A.M., Maley saw eleven barges "making" for his convoy. They mounted a few light cannon and swivels, the bulk of the 400 to 500 pirates manning the craft being armed with muskets, sabres, and boarding pikes. From the manner of their approach it appeared to Maley that they had not yet discovered that the *Experiment* was a warship. Maley, his guns readied but run in with the ports closed, positioned himself with his sweeps so that two of the merchantmen were on either side of the schooner. The barges, also under oars, made for all five Americans in separate groups. Maley waited until the pirates had reached musket range before opening fire. The musket-armed crews of the merchant vessels,

"Problematical and Precarious"

Maley's marines, and the grape-loaded 6-pounders of the *Experiment* unleashed a hail of death on the surprised bargemen. With many killed and two barges sunk, the pirates withdrew towards Gonâve.

Over the next ninety minutes three more barges joined the remaining nine. Dividing into three groups of four, they made their way directly for the *Experiment*. Still becalmed, Maley prepared for the renewed onslaught. He divided his fourteen marines between the quarterdeck and forecastle. His men raised the boarding nettings. The twelve 6-pounders were loaded with grapeshot. Sufficient men were stationed at each oar to bring the schooner around so that both broadsides could be used. For three hours the second attack raged, the guns firing, the marines loading as quickly as they could to keep up a stiff musketry, the men at the sweeps bringing the guns to bear protecting the unarmed bow and stern of the *Experiment*. Two more barges were sunk and the rest were driven off again.

While Maley was occupied in the midst of the second attack, two of the barges made their way between a pair of merchant ships, where they were safe from Maley's guns. Having driven off the remaining barges, Maley now swept to save the threatened Americans. One of the barges was sunk with a well-placed 6-pounder shot, but the other managed to board the *Mary*. Captain William Chipman, master of the *Mary*, fell wounded to the deck in the assault. Surviving crewmen either hid in the hold or jumped overboard. Some forty pirates stormed onto the deck of the stricken ship, "inhumanly" murdering the wounded Chipman, leaving his body "mangled in a dreadful manner." The savage band then set about plundering the *Mary*, breaking into the captain's trunks and carrying away clothes, treasure, and whatever else they could lay their hands on. So occupied, they failed to notice Maley, who had by this time positioned the *Experiment* to sweep clear the *Mary*'s deck with a rake of grape. The survivors beat a hasty retreat in the remaining barge.

Unfortunately, two of the merchantmen caught a current and drifted away from the others. Maley could no longer cover all four ships. At 4:00 P.M. the pirates resumed their attack, this time concentrating on the isolated pair of Americans. The ships were lost when their crews sensibly refused to fight and abandoned their vessels.

With night came the land breeze. The *Experiment* escaped with her two wards. In an engagement that had lasted ten hours, Maley had fired nearly his entire supply of grape. On the *Experiment* not a single man had been lost and only three were wounded. Edward Stevens was surprised that any of the ships had survived.

* * *

The 1 January 1800 defense of the *Experiment* and her convoy was the only bright spot in Lieutenant William Maley's short-lived naval career.

By February some of his own officers began to doubt their commander's competence. In the spring Commodore Talbot considered replacing Maley. By the end of the year the lieutenant had been dismissed from the service. His travail, however, had yet to end. In 1876 the dead Maley was denied his one moment of glory when Admiral David Dixon Porter claimed for his father the honor of the victory over the pirates in the Bight. The admiral wrote that Maley had wanted to surrender, but that Lieutenant David Porter, with the support of his fellow officers, took the command upon himself and fought off the barges. In support, Dixon Porter cited a communication from one of his father's former shipmates, then Midshipman Joshua Blake. According to this account, the whole affair was common knowledge in the West Indies. From it, David Porter earned the sobriquet "Logan," derived from Léogâne. Admiral Porter's version of the 1 January 1800 engagement continues to find its way into accounts of the Quasi-War.[47]

But documentary evidence contradicts this tale. Early histories of the war make no mention of it. Edward Stevens's report of the engagement speaks only of Maley's skill and bravery. The *Experiment* was too small a vessel for a cowering commander to have escaped the consul general's notice. Besides, the barges were filled not with privateers but pirates; the butchers from Gonâve did not take prisoners. Talbot, who by June 1800 had been "wearied" by reports of Maley's "improprieties of conduct," ordered the *Experiment* to Philadelphia in order that an enquiry be held. Yet Talbot made no mention of any assumption of command in battle by Porter, having previously referred to Maley's "gallant defense." Nor did the long list of charges made against the *Experiment*'s captain include an abdication of authority in battle to "Logan" Porter.[48]

Talbot had attempted to enforce a truce among the lieutenants and midshipmen in the *Experiment*. His ships were too few to send the schooner north before her crew's enlistments expired. He was moved to action, however, on 12 June when the *Constitution* anchored in Môle St. Nicolas, now an American forward base of operations in the Windward Passage. The *Experiment* was also moored in the harbor, and Midshipman John Roche had quickly drafted a letter for the commodore when he saw the flagship drop anchor. Roche had served in the *Constitution* under both Samuel Nicholson and Talbot, but had been detached to the schooner in the spring, perhaps for the express purpose of observing Maley's conduct. Talbot considered Roche "a midshipman of great decency, and in whom full confidence may be given to his assertions."[49]

Roche's charges against Maley were voluminous. They included intoxication at sea and ashore, challenging and fighting with his commissioned and warrant officers, auctioning plundered goods, ransoming a captured neutral vessel for $300 while flying British colors and identifying the

Experiment as His Majesty's schooner *Lark,* and giving a prize worth $25,000 to a known English privateer of bad reputation, who promptly absconded with the ship. (This prize, the Danish vessel *Mercator* was captured in turn by a British corsair and carried to Jamaica where she was condemned.) Having joined the *Experiment* in March, Roche had nothing to report concerning Maley's conduct on the first of the year, although if the commander's abject cowardice was such common knowledge, Roche might have been expected to have passed such a report to Talbot, for the young mid was serving as the mouthpiece for Maley's wardroom opposition. In fact, in his attack on Maley, Roche's charges involved ungentlemanly and unofficerlike, rather than unmanly conduct.[50]

But there was another attack upon Maley, although its substance and author can be determined only by implication. In Maley's Court of Enquiry record are five depositions attesting to his courage during an engagement with an unidentified vessel during the night of 4 February off the south coast of Hispaniola. The *Experiment* had taken two prizes earlier in the day and several of her crew were detached under the commands of Lieutenant Porter and Sailing Master Shubael Downes. Maley found himself so shorthanded that he was unable to work all of his guns. He turned from his attacker and sailed, or fled, to rejoin Porter and Downes. Reinforced, the better-manned schooner turned in pursuit but, according to the depositions, missed stays and lost track of the ship.[51]

Recriminations followed the February action and were still being heard in Philadelphia in July, prompting Maley to elicit the depositions in support of his conduct. The principal points addressed in the documents were that Maley had acted bravely (he had been badly wounded in the hand) and had only failed to pursue his opponent because the *Experiment* had missed stays. This implies that the charges against the lieutenant were that he had acted cowardly during the action and had failed to follow the unidentified ship when it reversed course, while other officers wished to continue the hunt. It is probable that the tale of Porter's heroics sprang from the 4 February engagement. Another feature of the depositions makes it more likely, for three of the documents point out that Joshua Blake rode out the action belly-down on the deck. There was a personal emnity between Maley and Blake, who, of course, was David Dixon Porter's source for the story of his father's assumption of command. Blake's own career ended in 1805 with a dismissal for cowardice.[52]

While such behavior may have been a characteristic of Blake, it was not one of William Maley's. He owed his commission not to Stoddert, who considered the *Experiment*'s commander "a very ignorant illiterate man," but to Pickering. In 1798 the secretary of state gave Maley, a tough skilled seaman familiar with the Mediterranean, command of the armed schooner *Lelah Eisha.* The vessel was one of five storeships sent to Algiers in 1798 under the terms of the treaty made with the Dey two years earlier. Pickering's nephew, Timothy Newman who had been a prisoner in Barbary, commanded the sixth of the State Department's fleet, the *Crescent* frigate of thirty-six guns. On their return from the Mediterranean four of the six men received naval commissions. Master Commandant Newman commanded the ship *Warren* 20. William Penrose held a lieutenancy in the sloop of war *Patapsco* 20, commanded by another of Pickering's men, Captain Henry Geddes. Maley took the *Experiment* out on her first cruise.[53]

But by July 1800 Pickering was no longer secretary of state, having been dismissed on 12 May by Adams. Maley's future lay in the hands of Stoddert, who was directing the navy's affairs from Washington to where the capital had at last moved. The secretary of the navy considered Maley's defense, lengthy but frequently lame, "sufficient to condemn him." Yet Stoddert had doubts. Maley had been an active commander. In seven months he had captured fourteen ships, chased ninety, and spoken "one hundred & eleven sail." As Maley had pleaded, "Sir . . ., if I had been that *coward—drunkard—and ignoramus,* which Mr. Roche and the boys (men, some of them are not) . . . represent me to be . . . the services above stated could possibly have been performed by the *Experiment* with me as her commander?" Stoddert forwarded all the relevant material to Captain Richard Dale, now back from the East Indies, for review. The secretary wrote: "I will not be precipitate in my judgment—I may not understand Lt. Maley."[54]

Dale conducted the review, personally interviewing Maley who remained in Philadelphia. The captain found that the accused "acknowledges to most of the charges . . . except being a coward and a drunkard. . . ." Maley blamed his problems on bad officers, which even Talbot had admitted as a contributing factor. But it was still a commander's responsibility to gain and hold the respect of his subordinates. This Maley had failed to do. Respect was not gained by beating up officers in the wardroom. Dale wrote Stoddert:

> It is my opinion from his own statement in his answer to the charges brought against him and from what I have heard from himself that he is a very unfit person to command a vessel of any description in the navy of the United States. A man may be a very good seaman, and be qualified to command a merchant vessel, but at the same time very unfit to command in the navy. If I am not misinformed there are several of that description in the navy. . . .[55]

By the fall, Maley's faults and guilt were obvious to Stoddert. Even the lieutenant's activity had become a liability. Of his fourteen captures, only four were good prizes. In June Talbot had warned the secretary of the possible complications that might arise from Maley's practices. In fact, Maley would find himself before American judges until 1806 when he lost a case before the Supreme Court. Stoddert decided to dismiss Maley, "principally for his conduct towards neutral vessels." Like Isaac Phillips, William Maley would have no court-martial.[56]

* * *

While Maley's difficulties were rooted in his own shortcomings as an officer, they were exacerbated by the confused situation off Hispaniola. Maley's worst offenses, to Stoddert, were his seizures of neutral merchantmen that were trading with ports controlled by Rigaud. Talbot had instructed Maley to assist Toussaint in the south, and halting and capturing neutrals certainly did that. This is not to say, however, that a desire to help Toussaint motivated Maley, for the misfit was most interested in filling his own purse. Nevertheless, the atmosphere around St. Domingo served to corrupt American naval commanders and blurred the lines between legal operations and extralegal assistance for Toussaint. Even Silas Talbot lost sight of the limitations of his instructions, and the actions of Captain Christopher Raymond Perry off Jacmel have already been discussed. Further involvement with Toussaint brought the Rhode Islander's career to an abrupt end.

After cruising off the southern coast assisting Toussaint, Perry completed his instructions by circumnavigating St. Domingo. On 5 April he fell in with Talbot off the northern point of Montecristi. The following day, the commodore conveyed to Perry instructions received from Stoddert for the *General Greene* to sail for New Orleans to pick up Major General James Wilkinson and his family. Perry was to return to Newport via Havana, where he could expect to find a convoy awaiting escort.[57]

Perry reached Cap François on 8 April, where he was to unload stores and provisions not required for the voyage home with the navy agent, take on water, and ship some of the *Constitution*'s invalids before sailing north. The last provision troubled Perry, who feared the men might infect his crew. He addressed a letter to the commodore, dispatching it with Lieutenant David Porter, commanding the armed tender *l'Amphitheatre*. Porter, unfortunately, mislaid the message, finding it seven days later in his berth under the bed. Cruising between Montecristi and Puerto Plata, Talbot received the note on 24 April and was disturbed to think that the *General Greene* might still remain at the Cap. What would Stoddert think? And as for the invalids, as Perry would have realized had he bothered to examine the men, their maladies were hardly communicable, related to "old age, broken bones, & long debility." Talbot hastened to the Cape, finding Perry still at anchor. The commodore ordered the *General Green* to "leave port immediately."[58]

Perry continued to prevaricate. He had sent Talbot's invalids home in the prize ship *Juno,* but had discovered new restraints on his leaving port. Perry was unable to secure a passport or a pilot. But most importantly, Toussaint had requested that the *General Greene* delay forty-eight hours to transport two of the general's envoys to the United States. "I am at a loss how to act," Perry wrote Talbot, "I wish to oblige and accommodate General Toussaint . . . and I also wish to be on my way to America. . . ." Receiving Perry's letter, Talbot ran in for Cap François once again, arriving on the afternoon of the 25th. He found there the *General Greene, Boston,* and *Herald* "all dressed with colors, firing a federal salute." "The occasion of this parade and waste of powder I know not," Talbot wrote Stoddert. The "occasion" was not a surprise reception for the commodore, but a greeting for Toussaint who had come on board Perry's frigate with full panoply. The fete continued into the following day.[59]

Talbot sent Porter into the harbor again, with orders for Perry to sail again. Talbot warned Perry that he would have to answer for his conduct to the secretary of the navy, a task the commodore considered impossible. The *General Greene* should have sailed one, or two days after reaching Cap François, yet eighteen days later she still rode at anchor. Perry had waited for a passport, while Porter and others, as Talbot had himself observed, came and went at their own pleasure. Most importantly, Perry, by his own admission, had been "at a loss" whether he should accommodate Toussaint or follow his superior's orders, in fact the direct orders of the secretary of the navy. That, to Talbot, was simple insubordination.[60]

Perry reached Newport on 21 July, his frigate racked again by yellow fever contracted during an unnecessarily long four-day stay in Havana harbor. Many of his officers were disaffected. By September, numerous complaints had reached Stoddert's desk, among them Talbot's letters. Stoddert ordered Captains Richard Dale, Richard Derby, John Mullowny, and Thomas Robinson to assemble a court of enquiry at Newport. Perry was charged with disobedience of an order from a superior officer, detaining a neutral vessel until one of Toussaint's ships could come up and make the capture, "oppression and cruelty" to his midshipmen, and "bringing in the *General Greene* a large number of swine for the use of his father's farm and thereby producing so much filth as to endanger the lives of the crew."[61]

The court considered the difficulties inherent in balancing governmental and command priorities with regard to the charge of disobedience. Not only Toussaint, but also Consul General Stevens had requested the *General Greene's* delay. The judges concluded that Perry was guilty "in some measure." On the second charge, the captain was found not guilty. The third and fourth counts were the most damaging, calling into question Perry's competence to command. He had pilloried his mids as punishment, and on one occasion when a midshipman had passed out drunk on the deck, Perry had a subordinate "piss" in the youth's mouth. The captain's defense was unusual; he stated that urine was a noted emetic, applied to prevent the inebriate from succumbing to alcohol poisoning. Perry could also have sent for a surgeon's mate who could just as conveniently made use of the ipecac carried in American warships. His willingness to trans- port pigs on board the *General Greene,* after refusing to porter the navy's own invalids, did little to aid Perry's defense. The court found that while the frigate's mids were no doubt "very ungovernable and bad young men," Perry had been "very much remiss & highly blameable in suffering the midshipmen to be punished in the manner that has appeared before the court. . . ." "Captain Perry has been very much wanting," the judges concluded, "in not having proper discipline and good order kept on board his ship. . . ."[62]

Stoddert and Adams reviewed the findings in Washington. For the secretary it must have been a singular embarrassment. He had never thought when he offered the services of a frigate for the transportation of his old friend James Wilkinson that the general and his family would have to share the ship with a herd of swine! Nevertheless, "believing you to be a brave man & a skillful officer—and qualified to render important services to your country," Stoddert wrote Perry, "the president has determined to pass over the irregular & improper conduct. . . ." Perry was suspended for three months without pay. He was not recalled to duty, however, before the end of the war and was one of the first captains to be dismissed by the Republicans under the Peace Establishment Act.[63]

* * *

Another captain guilty of irregularities off Hispaniola was the com- modore himself. The appointment to command at Cap François pleased Silas Talbot. The strength of the squadron rivaled the American force based at St. Kitts. His area of responsibility included the whole of the Greater Antilles. Actually, Talbot's was the most difficult command in the navy, for in addition to regular operational chores, he had to cope with a complex diplomatic situation. The squadron had to support Toussaint and the commodore had to cooperate with his Royal Navy counterpart at Jamaica—Hyde Parker. The two men disliked each other. Talbot had been agent for impressed American seamen in the West Indies. Parker's captains were the worst offenders, and the admiral was the most recalcitrant British officer with whom Talbot worked. Parker's complaints about, and inability to work with Talbot, had led to the appointment of another agent. Now Sir

Hyde, who had earned his knighthood fighting the "rebels" in 1776, was forced to serve with his American quasi-ally and old nemesis.[64]

While he relished his role as commodore, Talbot remained frustrated. He proved more than able to cope with the problems he faced. He dispatched his subordinates to cruise in the Windward Passage, in the Bight, off Cape Tiberon and Jacmel. He sent ships to Havana and the Bahamas to search for corsairs. His operations were crowned with success. But as captain of the frigate *Constitution,* Talbot found himself forced to return to Cap François every few days to keep in touch with his squadron, the British, and Toussaint. There were privateers off the northern coast of St. Domingo, but the *Constitution* was ill-suited to chase barges into the countless bays and inlets. Talbot cruised between Capes St. Nicolas and Samana to no seeming effect.[65]

He was at Cap François on 13 February when the prize schooner *l'Amphitheatre* anchored in the harbor. Prize master David Porter had much to tell his commodore. Rigaud had organized a relief force at Les Cayes for Jacmel consisting of the schooner, a sloop, and a barge carrying a detachment of troops. Early on 4 February Maley's *Experiment* intercepted the squadron. The sloop was sunk; the schooner and barge captured. With less than seventy men of his own, Maley could neither feed nor guard the fifty prisoners he took. His only options were to leave his station and return to Cap François, or release the men. He chose the latter, disarming them and sending Rigaud's troops off in the barge. The following day he ordered Porter to sail for the Cape. On his arrival, Maley's able lieutenant also informed Talbot of the shortcomings of the *Experiment's* commander and charged him with cowardice in the action with the unidentified ship later on the 4th.[66]

The advent of *l'Amphitheatre* was to Talbot a blessing. He ordered the schooner's case to be brought before a Cap François prize tribunal, a move Stevens had assured him would result in a rapid condemnation. But the American consul remained unconvinced of the legality or wisdom of such a procedure. He wrote Pickering for advice.[67]

A similar situation had arisen the previous winter at St. Kitts. Truxtun refitted the prizes *l'Insurgente* and *l'Union* schooner taken in February and March respectively. The latter vessel he chose to make his tender and so informed Stoddert. The secretary was not pleased and considered it an effort "to increase improperly, our navy." Truxtun should have sent the prizes home for adjudication. By keeping them in the islands and outfitting them for his squadron, the commodore was adding ships to a naval service bound by Congressional acts that specified the number and strengths allowed. Such action could cause the administration difficulties, but Adams was little disturbed. "If you correct Truxtun's ardor a little, as you ought to do," the president wrote Stoddert, "I pray you do it very gently and with great delicacy. I would not have it damped in the world." But Stoddert had sent nothing more than a reminder to Truxtun to send ships home for condemnation, or if impossible, to keep them in British ports until his return.[68]

Receiving Stevens's request for guidance, Pickering conferred with Adams and Stoddert. The law governing American privateers permitted condemnation of prizes in British courts and one could make a case for a like procedure with a naval prize. But Great Britain was a belligerent power at war with France. Cap François remained technically a French port, and Toussaint a French agent. And Stoddert's instructions to his captains were clear on the matter: prizes were to be sent to the ports of the United States for condemnation. Adams recommended that Pickering advise Stevens to have the schooner sent north, but if a local condemnation had been achieved, which the secretary of state expected, to let the matter drop. To Stoddert fell the task of writing Talbot, but the navy secretary added his advice only as a weak afterthought: "Prizes should be sent in to the United States if practical."[69]

The executive advisories reached the Cap too late. Talbot already had his condemnation. "There are as I suppose many precedents of the kind in point in our service," Talbot wrote, "and thousands in the British service; Capt. Truxtun manned out the *Insurgent,* and kept her cruising for a considerable time. . . ." So *l'Amphitheatre,* a schooner captured from André Rigaud, nominally an agent of France, was condemned in a court of Toussaint L'Ouverture, nominally an agent of France as well. And as a result, Silas Talbot had a tender, well suited to inshore operations along the northern coast of Hispaniola.[70]

Talbot had only one hurdle to overcome: as a prize the schooner was the property of William Maley and his crew. On 27 February the *Constitution* fell in with the *Experiment* escorting two prizes that had been loaded with provisions at the Cap by navy agent Nathan Levy and had been sent under Maley's protection in search of the commodore. Talbot signaled Maley to come to the flagship. The lieutenant learned that he had been accused of "*cowardice & ill usage*" by his officers, and that Talbot wanted to use *l'Amphitheatre* as his tender. Not surprisingly, Maley acquiesced to the request. He yielded as well when Talbot asked for the services of Porter. In exchange Maley received the Edward Bosses, a father and son lieutenant and midshipman duo. The elder Boss was a quarrelsome alcoholic and apparent narcoleptic. He did little to improve Maley's chances of gaining a grip on his crew. He also caused his commander his greatest embarrass-ment. Boss had charge of the deck, and its use as a berth, at 1:00 A.M. on 18 May when the *Experiment* collided with the *Boston.*[71]

Talbot gave command of *l'Amphitheatre* to Lieutenant David Porter. When in company with the *Constitution* the tender was to remain in-shore, able to cut off or force out any ships attempting to escape the frigate in shallow water. With regard to prizes, Porter and his men were to be considered a part of Talbot's crew. For the moment, however, *l'Amphitheatre* would cruise alone off Montecristi, a safe night anchorage and a key point for small vessels piloting their way along the coast. In April, Porter rejoined Talbot at the Cap. To the tender fell the duty of ferrying messages between Captains Talbot and Perry during the former's attempt to get the *General Greene* on her way to Havana.[72]

While at Cap François, Talbot learned that a French privateer lay at Puerto Plata, about 100 miles to the east. "Boasting publications" proclaimed the ship a fast sailer and one of France's most successful corsairs. Formerly the British packet *Sandwich,* she was loaded with coffee and preparing for a run for France. Talbot decided to make the ship his prize.[73]

To take a ship out of an enemy harbor was no easy task in the age of sail, but for Talbot it was a form of combat with which he was familiar. He was no great seaman, like Truxtun. For that reason Stoddert had assigned to the *Constitution* as first and second lieutenants two skilled mariners—Isaac Hull and Robert W. Hamilton. (The latter was a relation of Alexander Hamilton and a former British merchant master.) Talbot had earned his commission in the Continental Navy by his success in boats operating against British ships in restricted waters. He gained notoriety in October 1777 cutting out the *Pigot* schooner, eight guns, off Rhode Island. The *Constitution*'s captain was more a soldier at sea, than a sailor.[74]

Leaving Porter off Montecristi, Talbot sailed eastward to see if the stories at the Cap about the privateer were true. About 6:00 P.M. on 1 May, the *Constitution* reached Puerto Plata. Talbot could see at anchor not one, but three ships. From the port, the tall American frigate was also visible as she stood off and on under easy sail until dark. At daybreak, Isaac Hull and another sea lieutenant left the *Constitution* in the small cutter to reconnoiter Puerto Plata, while Talbot continued sailing in full view of the shore. At 10:30 A.M. one of the three vessels ran out. Talbot pursued and in ninety minutes brought the chase to with a gun. She was a Danish ship bound for Cape Samana. Talbot detained the Dane and returned to his station to await the return of the cutter. At 7:00 P.M. Hull was back and made his report.[75]

Puerto Plata is a small, semicircular harbor a half-mile across. The channel is deep, fifteen to twenty fathoms, but shoals quickly to less than twelve feet a half-mile from the head of the bay. The approach is narrowed on either side by reefs, and on the west by Owen Rock. On the eastern point is a sixty-five foot hill, at the summit of which in 1800 was a small fort with three heavy cannon. South of the fort is the town itself. The *Sandwich* was moored in the harbor on an east-west axis with all of her cannon—four 6-pounders and two 9-pounders—facing seaward.[76]

Hull's report disappointed Talbot. He had intended to run into the harbor with the *Constitution* "and to have silenced the fort and ship." But the channel was too narrow, and the frigate drew too much water for such a direct approach. Nor was an attack mounted with the frigate's boats or the detained Danish ship likely to succeed. The element of surprise was already lost and the guns of the fort and the *Sandwich* would destroy an assaulting force. Talbot stood off during the night.[77]

While Talbot pondered his next move, a second ship left Puerto Plata. The French privateer *Ester* used her sweeps to move silently along the coast to the east. On the evening of 7 May she captured and plundered an American brig, the *Nymph* out of Newburyport. The following day the corsair and her prize rendezvoused with a barge in a bay near Old Cap François, Cabo Francés Viejo.[78]

After a fruitless chase to the west of a sail that proved to be an American merchant ship, Talbot fell in with George Little's *Boston* and *l'Amphitheatre*. Returning to Puerto Plata, the commodore discovered that a second ship had slipped out. The American flotilla cruised to windward until they were off the Old Cape. Talbot ordered Little off on a cruise to the southern coast in support of Toussaint. He ordered Porter to sail inshore. Late in the afternoon two sails were sighted—the *Ester* and *Nymph*—but it was too late in the day to cruise close to the coast. The Americans stood off and on throughout the night. Their vigilance was rewarded at 11:30 A.M. when another sail was sighted in the lee of Old Cap François.[79]

Talbot ordered Porter to reconnoiter with *l'Amphitheatre*. At 2:00 P.M. the tender ran out from the shore, coming within hail only long enough to inform the commodore that an American prize brig, a privateer, and a barge were in the bay. Talbot sent a detachment of marines to reinforce Porter's crew. Four of the frigate's boats were armed, manned, and swung out. The party headed for the bay and in a smart thirty-minute action recaptured the *Nymph* and drove the *Ester* ashore, her crew fleeing into the bush leaving behind three dead and sixteen prisoners. Only the barge, the lone sail that had been sighted in the morning, escaped along the coast to the west.[80]

After recovering his men, Talbot decided to pursue the barge. Two boats were again armed and manned, the barge commanded by Lieutenant Isaac Collins, and the large cutter by a midshipman. At 7:00 P.M., 8 May, Collins rowed off into the gathering darkness. Talbot, with the *Ester*, *Nymph*, and *l'Amphitheatre* stood off on a westward course hoping to regain contact with his boats after dawn. But with the sunrise came no sightings. Under easy sail the frigate cruised along the coast. About 1:00 P.M. a lookout sighted the large cutter. The mid in command reported that he had lost contact with Collins during the night. Talbot, who had a low regard for Collins, grew concerned. A lieutenant, twenty-five men, and a barge were missing. Porter was ordered to search inshore, but he returned in the evening empty handed. Early the following morning. Talbot fell in with the *Herald* and Lieutenant Charles Russell had good news for the commodore. Russell had spoken Collins the previous night and had briefly towed a sloop the *Constitution*'s barge had cut out. Two hours later the sloop was sighted. At 9:00 A.M. Talbot sent his small cutter to bring Collins and the sloop's master to the flagship.[81]

The prize was an American, the *Sally*. Her master was Thomas Sanford, a twenty-eight-year-old from Massachusetts. The *Sally* had anchored for the night in a bay near Port Santiago, thirty-miles from the Old Cape. At 2:00 A.M. on 9 May, Collins and his men pulled into the bay, spotted the sloop, and fell upon her. Sanford and his six-man crew were overwhelmed. The *Constitution* cut her cables and carried her off. Sanford protested to Collins, but an examination of the ship's papers and cargo convinced the lieutenant that the *Sally* was engaged in the contraband trade and subject to seizure.[82]

On board the *Constitution* the next day, Sanford repeated his appeals to Commodore Talbot. The *Sally* was an honest trader, her master argued, carrying cargo between the Bahamas and the Spanish ports on the northern coast of St. Domingo. She had left Puerto Plata only a few days before and was supposed to return there shortly. Sanford's protests sealed his ship's fate. Talbot supported his subordinate's detention of the sloop for violations of American law. (A decision upheld by the New York District Court on 4 September 1800.) But Talbot saw in the *Sally* more than another prize. To his mind she was "suitable for a disguise."[83]

Talbot devised a plan. the *Sally* would sail into Puerto Plata harbor in broad daylight with the morning sea breeze. Sanford would stand prominently on his quarterdeck, an American officer by his side, a half-dozen of Talbot's men working the ship. Concealed in the hold would be more men and marines. They would seize the *Sandwich*, storm the fort, and spike the guns. If possible, they would then sail both ships out of the harbor and rejoin the frigate. If not, the privateer would be burned or sunk. The risk was great, for during the day a steady wind generally blew into the harbor. There could be no retreat before the breeze came off the land after sunset.[84]

The afternoon and early evening of 10 May were spent preparing the *Sally* for her short voyage. To lead the attack Talbot named his first lieutenant, Isaac Hull with Marine Corps Captain Daniel Carmick and Second Lieutenant William Amory. Eighty tars and leathernecks would make up the force and all worked excitedly throughout the day. Carmick wrote: "it put me in mind of the wooden horse at Troy." Outfitted and provisioned, at 10:00 P.M. the *Sally* sailed into the darkness for Puerto Plata.[85]

At midnight Hull and his men were surprised by the report of two cannon and a hail in English followed by an order to come to. The ship was the British frigate *Alarm* 32, commanded by Captain Robert Rolles. He sent a boat to examine the *Sally,* and the English lieutenant who boarded the sloop "was much surprised . . . to find the hatch ways filled with American officers and seamen." Informed of the Americans' intention to cut out the *Sandwich,* Rolles's lieutenant suggested that the *Alarm* was off Puerto Plata for the same reason, to which "Lieutenant Hull replied that it must be effected before the next morning or the frigate would be too late, as he (Lt. Hull) should certainly take her out if he found [her] there in the morning, the British officer left the sloop wishing success to the expedition."[86]

About noon on Sunday, 11 May 1800, the *Sally* sailed into Puerto Plata harbor. The sight of the familiar sloop with Master Sanford standing on the quarterdeck provoked no alarm. That was fortunate, for throughout the approach Hull sailed directly into the *Sandwich*'s broadside within musket range of the fort to port. He stood by the stern ready to let go an anchor, directing the helmsman to lay the *Sally* aboard the corsair by the starboard bow. As the two ships came together, Hull let the anchor go and gave the order to board. The men, cooped up for twelve hours, sprang to life with a vengeance. They "went on board like devils," Carmick wrote, "and it was as much as [Hull] and myself could do to prevent blood being spilt." There was no resistance offered, the *Sandwich*'s crew having been completely surprised, but the Americans discharged their pistols into the air, as ordered, to create an illusion of battle and determination for those ashore. The prize secured, Carmick, Amory, and a boatload of marines stroked for the shore: their objective the fort atop the hill. As the boat neared the low, sandy shore, the eager marines lept over the gunwales. In water up to their necks, their muskets and cartridge boxes held over their heads, the leathernecks charged up the hill before the Spanish garrison had time to react. After spiking the guns, Carmick and his men returned to the *Sandwich.* Hull had had all of the corsair's cannons shifted from her larboard to her starboard side, facing the town. Twenty-two prisoners were confined below. The whole affair had taken only thirty minutes.

Throughout the afternoon, Carmick's marines held off irresolute Spanish probes. The Spanish seemed little interested in fighting to retrieve the

The Constellation *vs.* l'Insurgente. (Courtesy of Arthur N. Disney, Sr.)

USS Merrimack (1798–1801)

USS Experiment (1799–1801) *attacked by pirates, 1 January 1800.*

Commodore Silas Talbot, by Thomas Birch.
(Courtesy of Miss Frances K. Talbot)

Captain Isaac Hull, by Orlando S. Lagma

Commodore Edward Preble, by Rembrandt Peale.

Lieutenant Hull cuts-out the Sandwich, *Puerto Plata, 11 May 1800, by Robert Salmon.* (Collection of the Boston Athenaeum)

The Constellation *vs.* la Vengeance, *1 February 1800, by Arthur N. Disney, Sr.*

USS Essex, *by E. Tufnell.* (Compliments of Melvin Conant)

The Boston *vs.* le Berceau *(October 1800), attributed to Warren.* (Courtesy of The Mariners' Museum, Newport News, Va., Bailey Collection)

French privateer. Hull's men worked unhurriedly to rerig the ship. They had found the *Sandwich* wholly unprepared for sea with only her lower masts standing. Fortunately, the remaining spars, cordage, and canvas were stored below. "Before sunset," Talbot wrote, "Lieutenant Hull had her completely rigged, royal yards athwart, guns scaled, men quartered, and in every respect ready for service." The land breeze failed to blow that evening until midnight. With it sailed the *Sandwich* and *Sally*. Hull had his first victory. Not a man had been killed or wounded on either side.

*   *   *

Pleased with his success at Puerto Plata, Talbot planned other cutting out expeditions for Hispaniola's northern coast. After a return to the Cape, he received two separate reports of privateers to windward. In early June the *Constitution* and *l'Amphitheatre* sailed for Cape Samana.[87]

Silas Talbot had another plan, referred to as a "Secret Expedition" in his journal. There were reports of a privateering nest in a small bay in the lee of Cape Cabron. Talbot intended to land a small force east of the bay, for a surprise overland assault on the town timed to coincide with a seaborne attack by *l'Amphitheatre*. It was Lieutenant Hamilton's turn for glory and his force would consist of the barge, cutter, and pinnace manned with ninety-five seamen and marines, each armed with a musket, pistol, and cutlass. At dawn on 3 June *l'Amphitheatre* took the trio in tow while the *Constitution* sailed out to sea lest her presence off the coast alert the pirates. The following morning Talbot headed in towards the shore, about 10:00 A.M. sighting the tender with the boats. The gunpowder had gotten wet during a landing complicated by high surf. Both Porter and Hamilton had decided to abort the mission, greatly disappointed because in addition to one privateer at anchor, two more were building in the town. Talbot decided to risk an attack with the frigate. Sending the tender sounding ahead to find a place to anchor, the *Constitution* moored about 2:00 P.M. and began a bombardment of the corsair and the town. But the range was too great. Talbot gave up and sailed to leeward.[88]

Early in the evening of the 7th, the *Constitution* was four leagues east of Old Cap François, Talbot intending to check the veracity of his second report, of a privateer and a barge in a small bay to leeward. *L'Amphitheatre* with two boats manned with forty seamen and marines made their way inshore. At dawn came a series of sightings. The first was schooner sailing east, to windward, which Talbot pursued. He soon discerned his boats chasing as well. When they had closed to within musket range, they fired a volley of small arms, supplemented by three 18-pounders discharged form the *Constitution*. The vessel came to, a Dane from St. Thomas which Talbot left to his boats.[89]

During the chase, the commodore had seen his quarry, the French privateer, escape to leeward, pursued by Porter. The *Constitution* ran to the west and by noon had reached Puerto Plata with *l'Amphitheatre*. The corsair anchored in the harbor. About 3:00 P.M. Talbot's boats rejoined the frigate and were sent with the tender to sound for a suitable place for the *Constitution* to moor from which she could bombard the privateer. But none could be found. Talbot wore ship and stood to leeward.[90]

Talbot sailed for the Cape where he expected to meet the next com-modore for the squadron. His crew's enlistments would expire on 23 July, the day the frigate had weighed the previous year at Boston. Reaching Cap François on the 10th, he found no relief, but he remained at his post despite growing tension among the crew. Moored in the roads at the Cap on 20 July, eight men deserted. Where was his replacement?[91]

Talbot's final command decisions involved the dispatch of three vessels—the brig *Augusta* 14, commanded by Lieutenant Archibald McElroy, the ship *Herald* 18, Lieutenant Charles Russell, and the ship *Trumbull* 18, Master Commandant David Jewett—to the south coast. There instruc-tions were indicative of the extent to which American naval operations around Hispaniola had routinely become subordinated to the need to support Toussaint. All three commanders received similar orders. They were to protect Toussaint's small cruisers from Rigaud's privateers, seizing the latter, French ships, and Americans trading with the southern ports which were still subject to the embargo. Neutrals were not to be molested, but left for Toussaint's vessels. Talbot expected that these combined opera-tions would isolate Rigaud's forces from resupply and lead to his defeat. Russell and Jewett also received special instructions to appear off Jacmel flying a red pendant at the main, and a white at the foretop. The *Herald* carried provisions from the Cap for Toussaint's forces. The *Trumbull,* her own bread casks removed to make more room, bore a supply of gunpowder too large for her magazine.[92]

The *Constellation,* at this point commanded by Commodore Alexander Murray, reached the Cap on 17 July. But the *Constitution* lay moored in the road, in no shape to proceed north. Her foremast had sprung badly, requiring a fifty-one-foot-long fish to secure it. Finally, on the afternoon of the 22nd, Talbot weighed, but the fates had determined to keep him at the Cape a bit longer. Taken aback in the channel, the frigate ran aground. There was more shock than damage. Her cannon shifted forward, the *Constitution* was hove off on her bower anchors. The next day she at last sailed with a convoy for home.[93]

* * *

During his command of the Cap François station, Silas Talbot had shown himself to be a competent and aggressive captain *and* commodore.

Adams had no cause to regret his support of Talbot during the dispute over rank with Truxtun. The commodore and his commanders performed well against the French. They supported Toussaint and Anglo-American diplomatic objectives, while Hyde Parker's most significant contribution, Poyntz's seizures off Cape Tiberon, had nothing but a deleterious effect. After a fortnight off St. Domingo, Commodore Murray was already referring to the British as the "enemy."[94]

But there was another side to Talbot's command. The improprieties that led to the dismissal of Maley and the suspension of Perry have been mentioned. But all the captains on the station, excepting Talbot and Russell, were guilty of "receiving presents for their services," especially George Little. Stoddert was forced to dismiss the navy agent, Nathan Levy, who took his commissions on what he considered market value rather than the actual price (only when the latter was lower, of course).[95]

Talbot could not be, and was not, held responsible for the shortcomings of his subordinates and Stoddert's administrative appointees. The atmosphere at the Cap and off Hispaniola was conducive to such behavior. And the zealous commodore, too, caused problems for the department through his actions on the northern coast.

Trouble began with the arrival of *l'Amphitheatre* at Philadelphia. Porter tried to draw on the navy agent for supplies and provisions for his ship and crew, stuck in a fifteen-day quarantine in the Delaware. But Stoddert directed the Philadelphia agent—George Harrison, another victim of Robert Morris's bankruptcy—to meet demands for pay and food only. The tender was not a naval vessel, but a prize; and as such it had to be turned over to Maley's prize agent. Benjamin Hodgdon found a schooner that had been "totally dismantled," according to Talbot's own journal, before her sailing for the United States. She was "entirely worn" and sold for only $1,550. Maley and his agent sought compensation for "wear and tear" from Talbot. But the dispute was ultimately immaterial, for *l'Amphitheatre*'s owners appealed the condemnation and won. The court levied damages of $7,040.55 against William Maley.[96]

About the same time, Talbot received more bad news. In early July the Spanish had protested the seizure of the *Sandwich* in Puerto Plata, and Stoddert had halted the legal proceedings against the prize in New York. The Americans, the Spanish claimed, had had no right to take the ship from their territory. Since the Spanish had ceded the whole of Hispaniola to France in 1795, but the latter had yet to effect actual occupation, it was an arguable point. But for Stoddert, it mattered not. He knew that Talbot's capture would not hold up if challenged in court, for his instructions permitted seizures of French armed ships only on the "high seas," which the harbor of Puerto Plata certainly was not. In fact, all of Talbot's endeavors along the coast in May and June were extralegal. The administration determined that the return of the *Sandwich* to her owners would best serve American diplomacy if it came from the executive, rather than the judicial branch. Stoddert so informed Talbot, adding: "At the same time that I make this request, I cannot withhold my entire approbation of the spirit which dictated & the gallantry which achieved an enterprise which reflects honor on the American navy . . . no part of the merit of making the capture can be taken from you, by the relinquishment of the vessel." In fact, Talbot and his men were ultimately left with only "honor" to show for their entire cruise. The owners of the *Sandwich* sought and won damages that offset the prize money earned by the salvage for the recapture of the *Nymph* and the capture of the *Ester* and *Sally*.[97]

9

ENEMIES AND FRIENDS

---

1. A "Fair" but Reckless "Challenge"

On 19 January 1800, twenty-six days after leaving the Chesapeake with a storeship and a convoy, Captain Thomas Truxtun made landfall in the Caribbean, the outlines of Antigua visible to port and Barbuda to starboard. Both captain and crew were happy to be in the islands. The warmer weather was already curing the men's ills, except for a half-dozen "venereal complaints." The following evening the *Constellation* and the storeship anchored in Basseterre Roads, St. Kitts. Moored there Truxtun found the bulk of his squadron—the *Adams, John Adams, Baltimore, Pickering,* and *Eagle.* Only the *Connecticut* and *Enterprize* were out cruising, as was Alexander Murray's independent frigate *Insurgent.* Morris struck his broad pendant, and Commodore Truxtun was once more in command off Guadeloupe.[1]

Truxtun's responsibilities extended throughout the whole of the Lesser Antilles, and with Silas Talbot currently commanding in the Greater Antilles, a rivalry of sorts might well be expected. The dispute over rank left scars that never healed for Thomas Truxtun, so he was especially pleased to learn from Morris that a pair of French warships were at Guadeloupe. The commodore wrote a friend: "I have not time to say much at present, having arrived only two days ago, and have yet been on shore. A 44 gun ship and a corvette of 28 guns are at Guadeloupe. I shall give them a fair challenge to come out in a day or two, and I am hurrying to put all things in readiness for that purpose." All the spare stores and provisions were sent ashore to Clarkson's yard. The orlop deck was cleared, Truxtun ordering his crew "not to leave a rope yarn in the way, as in one week . . . he was determined to have five hundred prisoners on board."[2]

But before seeking battle with the French, Truxtun's first duty was to

183

disperse the ships he found in the Roads. Their presence was convenient for a newly arrived commodore. Truxtun knew Cowper and Campbell, but had yet to serve with Morris, Cross, or Hillar (or Shaw and Tryon out cruising). He could meet personally with his subordinates, size them up, and order them out to cruise alone. Stoddert had been emphatic on that point in his lengthy instructions to Truxtun. Warships were to be kept out of port, patrolling singly. A wider area could be covered with a greater chance of meeting the French, Stoddert trusting "to the superiority of *American valor & skill*" to do the rest.

> Although I have already said so much on this subject, I cannot help repeating my efforts to impress on your mind the disadvantages of suffering our vessels to cruise in company—Cruising in squadrons for small privateers seems of all means the best to avoid capturing them, it teaches commanders of the small vessels, a reliance on force, not their own for protection—it is enough to make them cowards—It prevents all means of knowing who are brave among them, because none are exposed to danger—I pray you not to fall into this error—It is better to have our vessels sometimes beat, than to let them cruise for months without meeting or beating an enemy. Even the smallest vessel we have should cruise by herself, at least this should be the practice until the enemy cruise more in squadrons than singly. . . . Nothing fills the president with more disgust than the paragraphs frequently seen in our papers, giving an account of three or four of our vessels having sailed from some port in the West Indies on a cruise—Three or four vessels sailing in company when there is no prospect of meeting an enemy equal to the smallest of them—[3]

In his orders, the secretary of the navy spoke of cruising for privateers. Truxtun intended to sail for Guadeloupe to "challenge" two men-of-war. A well-informed man with regard to the state of naval science, Truxtun knew that a French forty-four-gun-frigate, while not as powerful as the *Constitution* or *United States,* was much more heavily armed than the *Constellation.* And he hoped to engage a corvette of twenty-eight guns as well! He could have kept the *Adams* or *John Adams* with him, if not for an entire cruise, at least as far as the French base at Basse-Terre. Or if he meant to be "fair," the fast sailing *Connecticut,* which returned to St. Kitts on 25 January, could have been brought along. But Truxtun sailed south alone. Only a fool, which Truxtun was not, would have considered himself bound by Stoddert's instructions to purposefully seek battle with a vastly superior force. Since supporting ships were at hand, the commodore's intention must have been to secure for himself the glory and the prize money to be earned in action. Self-esteem bordered dangerously on over-confidence.[4]

Truxtun left St. Kitts on the afternoon of 30 January. The following morning lookouts sighted a frigate. Her lines were French, but it was the *Insurgent* escorting a convoy. The commodore delivered to Murray Stoddert's orders to return home by way of Jamaica. Not a word was spoken of any intention to sail to Guadeloupe to seek a battle with the French. Murray, under independent command, might have insisted on coming along.[5]

* * *

At 7:00 A.M. on 1 February, the *Constellation* was sailing a southerly course with Guadeloupe bearing east about five leagues. Truxtun was preparing for a look into Basse-Terre Roads when a large ship of war was sighted about two leagues distant to the southeast. He took the ship, on a larboard tack heading southwest, to be a British frigate, probably returning to Martinique after its own reconnaisance. Truxtun ran up English colors, hoping that the ship would come about to speak him. The *Constellation* was gaining rapidly on the frigate but she appeared uninterested in communicating, continuing on her course. Truxtun studied her through his glass, and as the distance closed it became clear "that she was a heavy French frigate mounting at least 54 guns."[6]

As she had the year before, the *Constellation* prepared for battle. The crew stowed their hammocks, cleared the gun deck of furniture, and removed the wooden bulkheads. Tarpaulins were spread over the hatchways. Men broke out water, wet the passages to the magazine, and filled the casks by the guns. There would be hot work ahead. The decks were wetted and sanded, to give the tars footing on bloody planks. Truxtun, his rigging shot up by *l'Insurgente* in 1799, took extra precautions, making sure that the sheets were stoppered and the yards "slung with chains." Drums beat the crew to quarters. Down came the British jack as the American frigate drew ever closer to her chase. Then, shortly before noon, the wind died. The distance separating the two ships remained steady. The pursuit continued to leeward.

From the quarterdeck of *la Vengeance* 40, Captain F. M. Pitot observed the man-of-war that pursued him. Pitot had left Guadeloupe the previous day, his intention being to sail to the leeward to exercise his crew before turning north for the Mona Passage and a return to France. Pitot had two generals, eighty passengers (many soldiers among them), a large sum of money, cargo, and thirty-six American prisoners on board his frigate. He had no desire to offer battle with any vessel approaching his own in strength. Damaged French frigates, even victorious ones, had short life spans in the British-dominated Caribbean. Sighting the *Constellation* about 7:45 A.M., Pitot decided to continue to run before the wind in an effort to escape. With the light breeze, it appeared that the approaching nightfall might end the chase. Nevertheless, he prepared for action should it be forced upon him.

After 1:00 P.M., the wind freshened and the *Constellation,* with "every inch of canvas being set . . . except the bag reefs . . . in the top sails," gradually clawed her way towards *la Vengeance.* Seven hours later, with darkness already fallen, Truxtun drew near his adversary. At his order the Stars and Stripes were run up and candles lit in the battle lanterns. Truxtun, in a supreme gesture of braggadocio, grabbed a speaking trumpet and made his way to the lee gangway "to speak him, and to demand the surrender of his ship to the United States of America."

Not surprisingly, Truxtun's speech was preempted by fire from chase guns hauled to the stern of *la Vengeance.* "No parley being then necessary," Truxtun issued his final instructions before commencing actions. Typically, the French were firing into the *Constellation's* rigging, but Truxtun ordered that fire be directed into the enemy's hull. And he had no intention of wasting his first broadside—the most carefully loaded and effective— and told his division commanders to hold their fire.

With the *Constellation* drawing ever closer, Pitot realized that battle could not be avoided. He hauled his wind, bringing the frigate onto a southeasterly course on a larboard tack, a maneuver that would neutralize to some extent the superior speed shown by the pursuing ship. As *la Vengeance* came about, her full broadside bore on the approaching *Constellation.* Absorbing the French fire, Truxtun hauled his own wind, gaining the weather-gauge and ranged along the larboard quarter of *la Vengeance,* pouring a double-shotted broadside into the frigate.

For two and one-half hours, the frigates hammered at each other. Several times Truxtun tried to pull ahead of the French to take up a raking position, but without success. At 10:45 P.M. the distance between the ships suddenly narrowed. Pitot gave the order to prepare to board and his men crowded the rigging, forecastle, and quarterdeck. At pistol-shot range Truxtun unleashed a deadly fire. Lieutenant John H. Dent's grape-loaded carronades rained death on the packed Frenchmen, while First Lieutenant Bartholomew Clinch's marines lobbed grenades and kept up a steady musketry. The frigates drew apart. The broadside-to-broadside encounter resumed. Red flashes illuminated the night. The light from the battle lanterns escaped through open gunports. For another two hours the savage pounding continued. Finally, about 1:00 A.M., the fire from the French frigate halted. She had struck, for the second time, an earlier attempt having gone unnoticed in the darkness. Only twenty-five yards separated the ships. "She is all our own," declared Truxtun as he prepared to take charge of his prize. Then suddenly the *Constellation's* mainmast collapsed.

All efforts made to clear the wreckage and get under way proved fruitless. For the next two hours Truxtun watched the glow of his opponent's gunports drift farther and farther away. By 3:00 A.M. they had disappeared.[7]

* * *

Pitot bore away and headed before the wind towards Curaçao. Nothing but his bowsprit and lower foremast and mizzenmast remained standing. Seven feet of water filled the hold. A dozen shot had holed the frigate below the waterline, 180 above. Officially, French casualties numbered 28 dead and 40 wounded, but reports from Curaçao put the figure more accurately at 160. Pitot considered it possible that his adversary, the American frigate"*Constellation, of 60 guns and . . . 500 men,*" mounting "*24's and 18 pounders,*" had sunk.[8]

Truxtun limped towards Jamaica. Surgeon Isaac Henry described his ship as "the most perfect wreck you ever saw." The horrific casualties, compared with those suffered in the engagement with *l'Insurgente,* also distressed the good doctor. Fifteen men lay dead, another twenty-five wounded. Henry had performed six amputations.[9]

Truxtun's drawn battle can be judged from two perspectives.

Operationally, the action of 1 February 1800 was a defeat for the United States. The services of the *Constellation* were lost for five months, while the crippled *la Vengeance,* which had been sailing for France, remained at Curaçao where her presence created problems for the Americans. Truxtun, of course, was not at fault, for he could not be expected to know the intentions of French naval captains. But the commodore could have brought to the action superior strength. Without a doubt, had the *Constellation* met the corvette in company with *la Vengeance,* as Truxtun had intended, the French would have won a victory. Had Truxtun ordered a second American warship to accompany him, and had that vessel kept pace during the long pursuit, *la Vengeance* would have been *Constellation's* second victim. While Truxtun may have acted in a fashion befitting a frigate captain in the age of sail, as commodore he had erred.

Tactically, despite the escape of *la Vengeance,* Truxtun demonstrated the superiority of his ship and complement over their French opponents. The two frigates were roughly equal in size. By British standards (for sake of comparison), the *Constellation* measured 1,225 tons; *la Vengeance* 1,180. But the latter carried a heavier battery than the American frigate. Rearmed in New York in June 1799, the *Constellation* mounted twenty-eight 18-pounders and ten 24-pounder carronades, for a one-side weight of metal of 372 pounds. When captured by the British frigate *Seine* 38, Captain David Milne, *la Vengeance* carried twenty-eight 18-pounders, sixteen 12-

pounders, and eight 42-pounder carronades, for a total of 516 pounds per side. Since the French pound was heavier than the American or British by 8.33 percent, the comparable figure was 559 pounds. Truxtun was outgunned by as much as 50 percent. Yet the French ship and her crew received the heavier battering. The Americans suffered 40 casualties, the French admitted to 68, but when captured by the *Seine* frigate in August, only 160 men remained of a crew that had numbered 320 on the morning of 1 February. The disparate casualties were caused by a number of factors. The French had been caught massed in preparation to board. They fired into the rigging while the Americans shot into the hull. But the training and discipline of the gun crews also differed greatly. By Pitot's own account, *la Vengeance*'s fifty-two guns discharged 742 rounds. Since only a single broadside was engaged throughout the entire action, twenty-six cannons fired on average twenty-eight times, or once every ten minutes over the course of a five-hour engagement. Truxtun's nineteen starboard guns fired 633 round shot, 106 bar-shot, and 490 cannisters, for a total of 1,229 rounds. The American guns were being worked twice as fast as the French, averaging over sixty-four firings, or one every four and one-half minutes.[10]

Truxtun's edge in crew quality enabled him to offset a significant French advantage in weight of metal. Given the comparative rates of fire, the *Constellation* might just as well have carried twice as many cannon as far as the French were concerned. No wonder Pitot thought the American frigate mounted fifty-five guns! But how many American crews were as well exercised as Thomas Truxtun's? And how many foreign frigates, including the British, were as poorly manned as *la Vengeance*? Looked at dispassionately, the engagement of 1 February 1800 demonstrated the vulnerability of the thirty-sixes to the larger class of European fifth-rates. The *Constellation* was a fine ship, but she owed her reputation and success neither to her bulk nor power, but to the men who sailed her. Neither she, nor the *Congress*, nor the odd-duck *Chesapeake* bestowed on a commander any quarantee of victory.[11]

* * *

Following the battle, Truxtun considered attempting to locate Morris. The commodore's intention was to retain the command, shifting his flag to the *Adams* and sending Morris on to Jamaica where Truxtun expected the British would provide the necessary assistance to refit the *Constellation*. Without a mainmast, however, Truxtun considered it impracticable to search out Morris to windward. There was no recourse but to sail on to leeward and Port Royal.[12]

On 3 February, the *Constellation* fell in with the schooner *Enterprize* 12.

Truxtun sent for Lieutenant John Shaw, her commander, and ordered him to Perth Amboy with the dispatches on the battle and the commodore's decision to make for Jamaica. Shaw provided an additional favor before departing, scouting out a large frigate that appeared in the afternoon. An exchange of signals showed her to be British, and Shaw fired a cannon to leeward, a predetermined sign that set Truxtun's mind at ease. The brief "scare" was the only show of concern on Truxtun's part during the entire war. The bloody action had shaken the *Constellation's* captain. The next morning another frigate was sighted. She was the *Insurgent*, Captain Murray, with whom Truxtun had spoken on 31 January. On his way home by way of Jamaica, Murray was happy to provide an escort for the *Constellation* and the two frigates sailed together to the west. But Truxtun's expectation that his ship would be repaired in the Caribbean probably diminished as he conferred with Murray, for the *Insurgent's* commander had experienced the Janus-like nature of British naval cooperation.[13]

2. *Made Masts . . .*

Murray had arrived off Guadeloupe late in 1799 a disappointed man. The display of initiative that took him to Gibraltar brought him off Cayenne a month later than Stoddert had intended and without a single prize to justify the effort. The self-confidence that came with posting to the *Insurgent* yielded to apprehension about how his European sortie would be viewed in the capital. As it had in the winter of 1798–99, Murray's state of mind bordered on mild paranoia. He remained in the Lesser Antilles with Morris making four recaptures while seeking a greater opportunity by which he could redeem the reputation of the *Insurgent* and its commander. Murray wrote apologetically to Stoddert: "we have not yet had it in our power to convince the public of our energy. You may remember an old adage of Julius Caesar in his ideas of an officer (tell me whether he is fortunate & I will determine whether he will suit my purposes) I confess I should not have been a favorite of his. . . ."[14]

And fate seemed determined to prevent Murray's redemption. He had sailed in August dissatisfied with the physical state of his "crazy" ship, and in early January his foremast sprung in many places from decay. In an effort to remain in the West Indies, Murray wrote Lord Hugh Seymour requesting the assistance of the British arsenal at Antigua. Reaching English Harbour on 6 January, Murray fully expected to receive the help of his quasi-allies. He found the island's officials solicitous and convinced of Seymour's eventual approval. To speed the refit they pulled out Murray's foremast in order that the new stick could be quickly fitted.[15]

By the 17th, word from Seymour having arrived, the *Insurgent*'s new mast was secured and the frigate ready for sea. Murray was effusive with praise for the British, writing Stoddert: "the attention, & polite deport-ment of his Majesty's officers to me & my officers has been genteel & civil to the greatest degree, & which I think it my duty to make known to you."[16]

But Murray's laudations were short-lived, for he found himself forced to return to Antigua. He had been deceived. He sent a letter ashore to Chester Fitch, the head of the arsenal.

> I . . . am sorry to say that I have had a great injustice done me with regard to my fore mast, we had not been to sea twelve hours before we discovered it open & shut in several places & to a dangerous degree. Upon close examination we found it full of large knots, that had been worked out & the vacancy plugged up & filled with putty so as to prevent the discovery of any outward defect . . . the master builder and mast maker, must have both been very conscious that the mast they gave me was not trustworthy & such a one as they would not have offered to one of their own ships when at the same time I am charged with the full value of a first rate mast. . . .

The American captain received no satisfaction at Antigua.[17]

Embarrassed, and with another defective mast, Murray lost his resolve to remain in the islands. In his letters he began to write of a longing for home and family. It was with relief that he learned from Truxtun on 31 January that the *Insurgent* had been ordered home by way of Jamaica, where a large sum of money awaited shipment north. The prospect of a freight enlivened Murray. Even though his frigate was "almost a wreck," Murray eagerly followed his orders, despite the diversion. Falling in with Truxtun on 4 February, the two battered ships sailed for Port Royal where they anchored on the 8th.[18]

Hyde Parker gave the Americans "a kind and friendly reception," but the admiral was unwilling or unable to spare a mainmast for the *Con-stellation*. Truxtun remained at Port Royal until 2 March, readying the frigate "in the best manner that was possible" for a return to the Chesapeake. He escorted nine merchantmen northwards. The British re-fusal to help had disappointed him, as it had Stoddert.[19]

Murray's short stay in Kingston was more rewarding. He picked up his freight, a perquisite allowed American officers rooted in the British naval tradition. Murray received a $14,000 shipment from one merchant, and $120,000 from Alexander Baring & Company, who requested that the *Insurgent* put in at Havana where another $300,000 awaited carriage north. For the Jamaica freight (assuming he charged only the minimum)

Murray would earn $385; a stop off the Morro would bring another $775. For a captain earning $60 a month, that was a year and half's pay. Advised by Truxtun to go, Murray sailed for Cuba. Unfortunately, the weather off the island's northern coast was so poor, and the *Insurgent* so disabled, that Murray's officers petitioned the captain to desist. Disappointed again, he sailed directly for Baltimore arriving on 13 March. [20]

* * *

The temporary loss of the *Constellation* and the recall of the *Insurgent* halved the number of American frigates deployed in the Lesser Antilles just as the French *guerre de course* showed signs of rejuvenation. Morris, who as senior officer resumed the command at St. Kitts, directed the operations of his own *Adams,* Cross's *John Adams,* and from five to ten smaller men-of-war. The squadron captured fourteen French privateers and recaptured twenty-four merchantmen before the arrival in late May 1800 of Morris's replacement, the elder Decatur in the frigate *Philadelphia* 36.[21]

Such a respectable number of captures were indicative of success, yet the merchants saw their losses grow. Frustrated, they questioned the effectiveness of Stoddert's navy. Too many ships, some claimed, had spent the winter in American ports, while in the islands, Commodore Morris lacked aggressiveness and allowed his warships to remain moored in Basseterre Roads. Stoddert declared the charge of winter idleness unfounded. He admitted to the administrative fiasco of the previous summer, "when from circumstances not necessary to detail," too few ships cruised off Guadeloupe. But there had been no derangements since. Of the twenty-seven ships available during the winter of 1799–1800, twenty-one had been operational in the Caribbean. In March 1800 all but three of the navy's twenty-nine vessels were at sea. In a service with one-year enlistments cruising in a sea where the United States had not a single base, there would always be a few ships in port. As for Morris, the secretary himself was dissatisfied, but for different reasons. Thirty-eight captures contradicted the charge of inactivity. The New Yorker only commanded a handful of ships, but he never sent a single report to the department during his time in command. The only letters from the squadron's officers were those that appeared in the press. And Morris's practices of rendezvous brought the ships of the squadron to Basseterre Roads for three, four, or more days every five to six weeks. Decatur, Stoddert assured the president of the Philadelphia Chamber of Commerce, would no longer bring the operations of his entire command to such regular halts.[22]

Higher American shipping losses were caused not by any deficiency on the part of the United States Navy, but by the policies of Great Britain and France.

Enemies and Friends

The spirit of reconciliation evident in the July 1798 pronouncements of the Directory had yet to bear fruit. Desfourneaux's failure to curb the privateers at Guadeloupe was obvious. Condemnations had continued "on the same grounds *as usual*" even before the loss of *l'Insurgente* and the agent's 14 March 1799 personal declaration of commercial war on the United States. Adams and Pickering had no reason to treat with the general as a "neutral." Such an effort would have complicated relations with both France and Britain. Desfourneaux was not Toussaint. A Franco-American agreement could result only from direct negotiations between the governments. But it was October 1799 before Adams's envoys finally sailed, by which time there had been another coup in Paris.[23]

Following the coup of 18 June 1799, Count Karl Friedrich Reinhard replaced Charles Maurice de Talleyrand-Périgord as Minister of Foreign Affairs. Reinhard sought peace with the United States, but the means by which he expected to reach a settlement differed substantially from his predecessor's. The new foreign minister intended to pressure the Americans and hold talks in Philadelphia rather than Paris. Fortunately, his tenure was short.[24]

On 9 November 1799, the Directors were at last swept from power by another coup (the famous 18 Brumaire in France) and replaced by the Consulate—Abbé Sièyes, Roger Ducos, and General Napoleon Bonaparte. The latter, was the real power in this triumvirate, and within twenty-four hours of the coup Talleyrand had the new First Consul's ear. Anxious to improve relations with neutrals, as a means to isolate Britain, Bonaparte agreed with Talleyrand that France should come to an agreement with the Americans. In December the offending decrees were repealed and replaced by the law of 26 July 1778. The French were in such haste that they did not bother to engrave new plates and the twenty-one-year-old originals were used still bearing the name of Louis XVI. Learning of the death of Washington, Bonaparte declared a ten-day period of mourning to begin on 7 February. France and the United States were on the path towards peace.[25]

While Reinhard's brief stint as foreign minister had no impact on the negotiations in France, it had a deleterious effect on American commerce in the Caribbean. The governors and agents who sailed for the Antilles in the fall of 1799 did so before the revocation of the decrees and before the shift in their government's American policy. This mattered little on Hispaniola where Toussaint and not the agents sent from Paris wielded real power. But at Cayenne Victor Hugues stepped up the pace of privateering, while at Guadeloupe Baco dela Chapelle, Laveaux, and General Jannet instituted more aggressive policies. Months passed before the effects of the

Consulate's rise to power were felt in the Antilles. By then the intensity of the *guerre de course* approached and perhaps surpassed the level it had reached in 1797–1798.[26]

With Desfourneaux replaced, privateering in the Lesser Antilles increased dramatically. By May an estimated 170 corsairs operated from Guadeloupe. Over one ten-week period in the spring of 1800, thirty-eight American ships were captured and twenty-four of the prizes found their way back to the island through the gauntlet of British and American cruisers. Official French records list only seven captures. The difference in the figures is in part attributable to gaps in documentation, but it is also indicative of what was probably simple piratical behavior on the part of some captains and officials. French successes, however, were not only the result of greater numbers, but also of new tactics. Captain Alexander Murray reported:

> the major part of the privateers, cruise far to windward from the longitd. of 50° to 59 degrees in the range from latitd. 17°. 13' to 14°. 30' & they seldom can be taken by our frigates unless by chance they are discover'd to leeward. They lie there generally with all sails handled, till they see their prey, & are readily decoy'd by brigs, or schooners latterly we have found the small fry of privateers take their stations under the lee of the islands, vizt. Martinico, Dominico & Guadeloupe, in fact their art & ingenuity puzzles the imagination, for one would suppose the vast number of our cruisers, as well as those of the British would discourage them, but the fact is not so, they bid us defiance & feed themselves very handsomely at our expence for they are like Hydra's heads & multiply daily. . . .

The positions given by Murray lie 500 to 600 miles to the east of Guadeloupe, where the trade routes of ships sailing to the Lesser Antilles, or from southern Europe and the East Indies converged. With never more than a dozen ships Morris could not be expected to give to American commerce complete protection throughout the entire Lesser Antilles and their approaches.[27]

British naval redeployment also contributed to the American problems in the Leeward and the Windward Islands. In July 1798 the Admiralty had concentrated seventy-one ships under Harvey to combat the corsairs of Victor Hugues at Guadeloupe. Eighteen months later, the *guerre de course* resurgent, only thirty-five remained. Could a dozen American men-of-war be expected to replace three-dozen British? Morris did his best, and while his squadron captured fourteen privateers, the Royal Navy took but ten during the same period.[28]

3. . . . And Unmade Alliances

With the squadrons of Talbot and Morris busily engaged off Hispaniola and Guadeloupe, Stoddert considered it a mistake to divert even small forces to Surinam, Curaçao, and the Spanish Main. When Decatur sailed from Philadelphia in April, he carried recall orders for the ships sent south the previous fall—the *Delaware* and *Scammel* at Curaçao, and the *Maryland* off Surinam. From the reports that reached the Navy Department it was evident that the vessels had made few captures. Diversions of even three men-of-war in a navy with less than thirty ships were significant.[29]

Privateering off the coast of Surinam declined for several reasons. Victor Hugues, arriving at Cayenne in December 1799, intensified the *guerre de course*, but he directed his corsairs to operate out in the Atlantic to the Northeast and to the south off the point of Brazil. Turell Tufts, consul at Paramaribo, reported that Hugues vessels were capturing Americans between latitude 13° and 18°, and longitude 51° and 58°. "Not a single Amn.—has been captured on this coast since the surrender of the colony [to the British]," Tufts wrote, "indeed it is to the windward of Guadeloupe that most of our vessels are taken." Tufts's coordinates are nearly identical to those given by Murray in his report on Guadeloupean corsairs. Obviously, the new French governors were instituting a concerted plan. Just as clearly, it had become too costly to operate off the coast of Surinam or among the islands of the Lesser Antilles.[30]

While there were fewer (if any) privateers to catch off Guiana, there were also fewer Americans to protect. So many restrictions were laid on American commerce by the British that trading opportunities collapsed. Ships carrying any cargo other than molasses were likely to be seized. Duties on imports were raised to 19.5 percent. The Dutch situation was so grave that Tufts expected that a French counterstroke would be welcomed. When word reached Paramaribo that Hugues had arrived at Cayenne with two frigates and several hundred men, Tufts believed that the expected French blow would better serve American interests than continued British rule. In any event, the consul recommended that the American squadron off Surinam be withdrawn. He also advised that "should no American [merchant vessels] arrive in the course of 2 or 3 months with provisions—*permission would be given to do as we please.*" Conditions in the colony were desperate, the need for American foodstuffs great, for despite the protection afforded British merchants, "but one English ship" had reached Paramaribo seven months after its capture.[31]

Stoddert had long since reached the same conclusion and chose not to replace the *Portsmouth* which sailed north in December 1799. As for the *Maryland,* the secretary expected that Captain John Rodgers would leave a barren coast on his own initiative. Stoddert instructed Talbot and Morris to take the *Maryland* under command should they fall in with her, an occurrence he considered "not improbable." But Rodgers remained off Surinam until August 1800 when he at last sailed for the United States with a convoy. After nine months of cruising, he had "the unexceptionable mortification to inform" the secretary of the navy that he had but one prize to show for the effort, a recaptured Portuguese brig. Even that minor success proved fleeting, for the British seized and condemned the vessel at St. Kitts.[32]

For Rodgers, the decision to remain off Surinam almost destroyed his career. His next cruise in the *Maryland,* had the French war not ended, would not have been a combat patrol, but a ferry service for another mission to France. This was the type of task the secretary assigned to the likes of Barry and McNeill, captains for whom he had lost respect. Under the Republicans in 1801, Rodgers was in fact discharged under the Peace Establishment Act but somehow managed to retain his commission. Even Thomas Truxtun, who had spoken so highly of his first lieutenant after the battle with *l'Insurgente,* came to recognize the man's limitations as a commander. Truxtun wrote Biddle in June 1811: "I have long since lost all opinion of Rodgers, *and he knows it*—he is a trifler and a sycophant—such men I despise *and I despise Rodgers*—have done much for him and made him what he is—and he has said—but for me—my discipline & counsel, he would never have risen above a master of a common merchantman." Rodgers's services during the War of 1812 paralleled closely his cruise off Surinam in 1800.[33]

* * *

At Curaçao the internal instability that led to the dispatch of the *Delaware* and *Scammel* continued. Consul Phillips believed it was in the American interest to send a frigate "immediately" to the island, a recommendation with which Captain Thomas Baker concurred. Their common concern kept the American ships in port as a show of force. They sailed infrequently, not so much to cruise as to call at ports along the Spanish Main for provisions which were exorbitantly priced at Willemstad. But as Stoddert so often warned, lying at anchor in West Indian ports was an invitation to disease. Both American ships were soon fever-ridden. Baker, who had barely survived imprisonment in the *Jersey* hulk during the American Revolution, became so ill that he had to be taken ashore. The *Delaware*'s incompetent surgeon plied the captain with liquor until he was reduced to a wreck.[34]

While Stoddert did not doubt the accuracy of Phillips's reports from Curaçao, the secretary considered the consul's demands on the navy impracticable. With a thirty-ship service, Stoddert could not allow men of war to be immobilized in every sickly Caribbean port where the banditti threatened American lives and property. The fate of the *Delaware* and *Scammel* bore out his fears. The secretary favored a policy of visiting Curaçao occasionally with warships detached from the Guadeloupe station. He ordered Decatur to look in on the island from time to time but to send Baker and Fernald home.[35]

The situation at Curaçao deteriorated with the arrival of the battered frigate *la Vengeance* in February. For months the victim of the *Constellation*'s cannon lay peacefully in the anchorage with the *Delaware* and *Scammel* while Pitot and the French officials ashore tried to squeeze assistance out of their Dutch allies to repair the damage caused by the Americans. But the local authorities offered little help and refused to accept bills drawn on Guadeloupe. In early June the frigate still lay moored, not having yet completed her repairs as the two Yankee men-of-war sailed for home.[36]

The presence of *la Vengeance* at Curaçao concerned the Americans at St. Kitts. Neither the *Philadelphia* nor the *John Adams* could hope to best a frigate that had fought the *Constellation* to a draw. Intelligence on her delayed preparation for sea was met with keen interest in the Leeward Islands. In late July reports circulated that the French had sent an expedition from Guadeloupe against Curaçao. At least two of the American commanders on the station were privy to the information, but if it found its way to Commodore Decatur, he chose to do nothing.[37]

On 23 July the French flotilla reached Curaçao. General Jannet, agent of the Consulate at Guadeloupe, intended to seize the island with his force of 5 armed ships and about 500 troops, supported by Pitot's frigate. But he kept his plans secret until the men and the supplies brought from Guadeloupe for *la Vengeance* were safely ashore. When all appeared ready, he took his demands to the Dutch: they would make a loan to the French, allow Jannet's troops to garrison the forts, and would seize American property ashore and afloat to compensate for the damage to *la Vengeance*.[38]

The Dutch were not taken entirely by surprise. The militia, about 400 strong, had been called out. Governor Johan Rudolph Lausser agreed to consider the ultimatum and called a meeting of the colony's council. But while the Dutch stalled, Jannet's scheme began to come unraveled. Captain Pitot wanted no part of the plan. He met with Phillips, inquiring if there was any truth to the rumors of a Franco-American peace, but the consul had received no official word from the United States. Pitot continued to prevaricate until Jannet threatened the recalcitrant captain with an enforced return to Guadeloupe under arrest. With that, Pitot cut his cables and sailed. The frigate gone, Lausser rejected Jannet's terms.[39]

With only 500 men Jannet could not hope to defeat the Dutch who were mobilized and controlled all the strong points. He tried a new tack, offering to depart if Lausser would provide a few ships and some supplies for the journey, promising compensation on return to Guadeloupe. The Dutch, anxious to rid themselves of the French, agreed, turning over a half-dozen ships and provisions to the general. With this assistance, the French prepared to sail, but slowly. On 2 September a second French force appeared off Willemstad, but found the channel into the harbor barred by a chain. Jannet protested, stating his intention to sail and take the entire force back to Guadeloupe. On the 3rd the French at last departed. The Dutch relaxed, the militia burgers returning to their homes.[40]

But Jannet had not given up. With both forces in hand, he doubled back to the island and landed on the 5th at a small bay a few miles west of Willemstad. The French, now 1,500 strong, overran the small fort at St. Michaels commanding the western approaches to the capital. Lausser attempted to block the advance, but his 400 militiamen, joined by many Americans, were defeated. As many as eighty of the latter were reported massacred. By the 6th Jannet's troops were in the Othrabande, the district of Willemstad on the western side of St. Ana harbor. Consul Phillips chartered a small vessel, the *Escape,* and sent American merchant William D. Robinson to St. Kitts with a request for assistance from the command-ing officer of the squadron. Phillips considered the situation critical. If a frigate and a ship of twenty guns did not reach the island within fourteen days, he wrote, *"we are lost."*[41]

On the 14th the *Escape* reached St. Kitts. Commodore Decatur was out cruising, but the frigate *John Adams* and the sloops of war *Merrimack* and *Patapsco* lay in the Old Roads. Robinson conferred with Cross, who recognized the necessity of quick action, but was unwilling to take his frigate, one of only two in the Lesser Antilles, to Curaçao. He offered no objections, however, to either or both of the other American ships going. Robinson reported that "Capts. Brown and Geddes, with a promptitude that evinced their zeal for the service, prepared for sea and sailed the next day."[42]

In the interim, assistance appeared to have reached Willemstad from a different source. On the 10th, Captain Frederick Watkins, commanding the British frigate *Néréid* 36, sighted two French privateers off the eastern point of Curaçao. Jannet had left the ships there to warn of the approach of an enemy force and to fall in with the ship bringing his train from Guadeloupe. At the sight of the British frigate the ships fled to leeward along the southern coast, pursued by Watkins who found about fifteen privateers moored in the small bay. Watkins returned to Willemstad where he noted the firing coming from the town. He joined the ruckus, engaging all parties, until he was hailed from an American ship, the *Sally*, that had run out of the harbor. Her master, William Hampton informed Watkins of the situation ashore. The Dutch were prepared to surrender to the British if Watkins could provide assistance against the French. Great Britain had long recognized the value of the island. Two years earlier Hyde Parker had advised Lord Spencer that its conquest "might be had at a very easy rate." Now it appeared that Watkins could effect it more cheaply than anyone had expected. He transferred twenty British marines to the *Sally* and sent her back to Willemstad, agreeing to the idea of a surrender. Three days later Watkins and Lausser signed a formal capitulation.[43]

Despite the presence of the British frigate, Jannet continued to press the Dutch. He delayed his main assault while he awaited the arrival of his train and provisions, bound to the island in a large American ship. The *Eagle* made landfall off Curaçao's east end but found no ships there and proceeded along the southern coast. Her master mistook the *Néréid* for *la Vengeance* and ran alongside Watkins's frigate as it lay off Willemstad. The British captain sent a party on board and they hauled up and opened several barrels from the *Eagle*'s hold. The *Néréid*'s master found grain on the top but thrusting his hand deeper discovered gunpowder below. A further examination turned up mortars, shot, more gunpowder, and several thousand muskets, all intended for Jannet's forces. Watkins seized the ship and sent her to Jamaica, minus some powder and arms sent ashore to the Dutch.[44]

General Jannet had no reason to delay longer. Lausser noted the French preparations for the final attack and turned to Watkins for further assistance. The governor wanted the frigate in the harbor to forestall the assault. This Watkins refused to do. The narrow channel could easily become a deathtrap for the *Néréid*, and her crew was already short-handed with many men detached in prize vessels. No more could be sent ashore. Watkins placed his faith in the Dutch defenses and the relief force he was certain would sail from Jamaica where he had sent word of the capitulation.[45]

Watkins had good reason for caution. The entrance to St. Ana harbor was only a half-cable's length across, running between two long projections of land. The town of Willemstad lay on the eastern tongue and Fort Amsterdam guarded the approach. The French held the western tongue—the Rif—and the sections of the town on that side of the harbor, known as the Othrabande. The harbor itself varied in width from a half, to a cable's length for three-quarters of a mile where it opened into the Schottegat, the main anchorage. To storm the Dutch position in Willemstad, the French had to cross St. Ana harbor. A ship of war in the harbor would make such an assault nearly impossible. But the French had established batteries on the Rif and in the Othrabande and a ship in the channel would be exposed even to musket fire. Watkins considered it too risky a venture.[46]

By 22 September the French were prepared to launch their amphibious attack in the evening, unless the Dutch capitulated. The situation appeared grim. Phillips had fled with his family to the *Néréid* but his countrymen, their ships trapped in the Schottegat or their property and families ashore, took up arms with the Dutch. Captain Hampton of the *Sally* erected a battery of two 18-pounders with some other Americans. For these men there would be no escape. Their's was a forlorn hope; that the Dutch would even fight, and if they did, that the French could be repulsed. But in

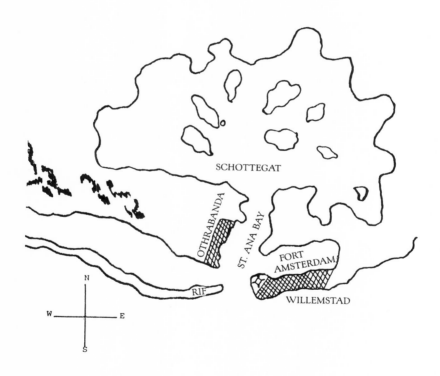

Willemstad Area, Curaçao

the afternoon the *Merrimack* and *Patapsco* appeared off the town. Jannet, unsure of what the unexpected arrival heralded, postponed the assault.[47]

Brown and Geddes met with Phillips and Watkins in the *Néréid*, while Robinson went ashore to confer with Lausser. The governor insisted on help, specifically a ship in the channel if he was to continue resisting. He remained unmoved by Robinson's recounting of the Congressional strictures binding the actions of the American navy. Joining the conclave on the British frigate, Robinson made his report, recommending that one of the ships enter St. Ana harbor. If not, he feared that the Dutch would surrender and the Americans ashore would be massacred. Phillips agreed. He had Pickering's instructions of 15 October 1799 that read in part: "if the aid of our armed vessels can be of a/c [account] to the government of [Curaçao] in checking the machinations of the French, and they desire to avail themselves of it, it may be given to them." For Moses Brown, the senior American captain, that was sufficient. Transferring twenty of his marines to the *Patapsco*, he ordered Geddes into the channel.[48]

At 5:00 P.M. on the 23rd, Geddes stood in, supported by the Dutch in Fort Amsterdam and Hampton's American battery. The *Patapsco* braved a stiff French fire from cannon along the harbor's edge and from troops in the windows and rooftops of the houses of the Othrabande. Geddes responded with grape from his larboard battery of ten 9-pounders and three 6-pounders and a steady musketry from his own and Brown's marines. The action continued for over two hours, the American ship within half-pistol-shot of the western shore. Finally, the French fire slackened. After another hour it all but ceased, the attackers withdrawing from the approaches to the harbor having suffered 150 casualties. Only two Americans were wounded.[49]

The following morning Geddes landed Brown's twenty marines and fifty of the *Patapsco*'s leathernecks and tars under the command of Second Lieutenant James Middleton, USMC. They took up positions in support of the Dutch in Fort Amsterdam as another attack was expected with the French maintaining a desultory fire from across the harbor. But the sniping was but a cover for withdrawal. On the 25th Brown took the *Merrimack* down the coast, discovering that the French had completely evacuated the island. At Willemstad, the *Néréid* finally entered St. Ana harbor.[50]

Phillips, Brown, and Geddes were busily organizing a convoy for the American merchantmen now freed from the Schottegat when Watkins asked if the two warships would not cruise for a few days to windward of the island. The British captain had information, or so he said, that another expedition was on its way from Guadeloupe. The *Néréid*, of course, had to remain at Willemstad to effect the actual surrender of the island. The request seemed reasonable, so the *Merrimack* and the *Patapsco* cruised for ten days. Brown took a single prize, but no invasion flotilla was sighted. But on their return to Willemstad, the Americans discovered a new threat to their merchants—Frederick Watkins! He had embargoed forty-one ships in the harbor, including all seven Americans. He had outfitted a half-dozen British ships to cruise, instructing them to take all American vessels they met. He gave the widest possible definition to contraband. He opened letters addressed to the American consul and discovering that Phillips had specie among his belongings in the *Néréid,* seized that as well. One American master who complained of Watkins's treatment, was threatened with a flogging and driven from the island.[51]

For the Americans, Watkins's behavior at Curaçao was another instance of perfidious conduct on the part of a commander from the Jamaica station. The captain had even lacked the decency to mention in his letters the contributions of the *Merrimack* and the *Patapsco.* The *Naval Chronicle* heralded "the only instance, perhaps, of the surrender of a whole island to a single frigate." Edward Thornton, the former secretary of legation who had replaced Robert Liston as minister in Washington, noted that the Americans had been slighted, and at the very least Brown and Geddes ought to receive a share of the prize money should the merchantmen be condemned by the vice admiralty court at Kingston.[52]

But Watkins's actions did not meet the approbation of his superiors. Lord Hugh Seymour had replaced Hyde Parker at Jamaica and the at-mosphere had changed markedly. In February 1801 the *Néréid* was ordered to return to England. On arrival Watkins found a new government in power. Pitt, Grenville, and Spencer had been replaced by Henry Ad-dington, Lord Hawkesbury, and Lord St. Vincent, all of whom took office with the intent of improving relations with the United States. Watkins was relieved of command and was not employed again until 1808.[53]

10

THE TRAIL OF THE *GRAND TURK*

---

1. *"A Quaker Squeeze"*

During his first year and a half as secretary of the navy, Stoddert had dismissed appeals from American merchants for the services of his war-ships in seas other than the Caribbean. He was eager to do what he could for the commercial community whose political and financial support made the navy possible; he was also anxious to see the American flag displayed in foreign waters, but with so few ships available, existing forces had to be concentrated in the Antilles. Requests for protection of American trade in the Baltic and the Mediterranean in mid-1799 could not be met. The projected cruise of the *United States* and *Constitution* to the eastern Atlantic was primarily a symbolic act, but even that had to be canceled.

Nevertheless, Stoddert looked towards a time when new construction would provide him with enough strength to operate beyond the western hemisphere. Murray's cruise to the Canaries and Madeiras was the first such foray, and the extension of the cruise to Gibraltar an unordered one. But by the end of 1799, Stoddert was planning to send a pair of frigates to the Mediterranean the following summer.[1]

He also expected two other frigates to be ready for sea by the end of 1799. At Portsmouth, New Hampshire, the 18-pounder frigate *Congress* 36, a sister of the *Constellation,* was launched on 15 August. The merchants of Salem, Massachusetts, built and launched the 850-ton frigate *Essex* 32, on 30 September 1799. The *Essex* was a small frigate, mounting only 12-pounders on the gundeck, but a smart, fast ship.[2]

Stoddert gave the frigates to two experienced commanders. James Sever, formerly of the *Herald,* commanded the *Congress* to which he had first been appointed in June 1794. Sever had disappointed the secretary in the spring and summer of 1798 by his delays at Boston. During the winter Sever's conduct had drawn criticism, even from fellow New Englanders. He had trouble with his crew and was accused of having not pursued a French privateer of superior force. But Sever found the secretary of the navy an unexpected protector. Stoddert attributed the captain's problems of command to "efforts to introduce proper discipline," and his failure to chase the corsair to a well-founded "total want of confidence in his own vessel the *Herald* whose guns in a heavy sea as was the case would have been totally useless." Even "Admiral Nelson," the secretary wrote Adams, "if his understanding is equal as his bravery would have pursued the very course that Sever did." Had the secretary forgotten his own earlier criticism of the *Herald*'s commander for overarming the ship? Apparently, for by the summer of 1799 Stoddert was ready to "risk my life" on Sever's command abilities. It was undoubtedly through such speculation that the secretary of the navy found himself a near bankrupt. Perhaps Sever's friends, Will Pennock and James Wilkinson had something to do with the captain's resurrection?[3]

Edward Preble captained the *Essex*. As a lieutenant he had commanded the *Pickering* from January to June 1799. In the spring, word reached Stoddert from Commodore Barry that Preble planned to resign on his return to the United States. The secretary held a high opinion of Preble, and believed that his twenty-years' experience should have warranted his posting to a captaincy the previous year. He had served during the Revolution in the Massachusetts state navy, with George Little, now captain of the frigate *Boston*. Stoddert recommended to Adams a promotion, and on 7 June the secretary wrote Preble with the president's approval, enclosing a commission as a captain in the United States Navy backdated to 15 May 1799. There followed promises of a larger command. When Talbot threatened to resign in July 1799, Stoddert considered Preble a possible replacement in the *Constitution*. In October, when it became apparent that Salem's nominee for command of the *Essex*, Captain Richard Derby, would not return in time from a foreign cruise, Stoddert gave the frigate to Preble.[4]

In November the secretary decided that the two New England frigates would escort a convoy bound for the East Indies from Newport, Rhode Island, as far south as the Equator. Where the frigates were then to sail remained uncertain, but they were probably destined for the West Indies. Stoddert ordered that copies of the signals worked out by British and American commanders on that station be sent to Preble and Sever. In fact, the plan was merely an extension of Caribbean operations since the East Indiamen were to be protected from French privateers operating from the Antilles and the Western Islands, rather than from corsairs active in the Indian Ocean.[5]

The Trail of the *Grand Turk*

American trade east of the Cape of Good Hope expanded significantly during the 1790s. Exports that totaled $250,000 before 1793 rose to $1,500,000 in 1796. But as American relations with France soured in 1797, exports suffered, falling to $500,000 in 1798. The cause of the decline lay not in the Indian Ocean itself, but in the general impact of French privateering against American commerce. With the Atlantic safer in 1799 exports rose to $786,000. American merchants involved in the eastern trade, although few in number, looked towards further growth during 1800. (In 1800 exports totaled $1,000,000, and in 1801 rose further to $1,800,000.) But 1799 also witnessed the spread of the *guerre de course* to the Indian Ocean. French warships and corsairs operated from the base at Port Louis, Ile de France [Mauritius], and their activities, Stoddert wrote, caused "great apprehension . . . by the merchants concerned in that trade of danger at and near Batavia [Djakarta, Java]. . . ."[6]

The danger threatening American commerce in the Indian Ocean was more psychological than real. While there was some initial justification for American fears, at the end of 1799 French activity remained limited. Officials in the Mascarenes needed American trade and did their best to prevent the Franco-American embroilment from extending into the Indian Ocean. The British also played a significant part in checking the French east of the Cape of Good Hope, capturing or destroying three fast warships towards the end of the year. Only six privateers remained at large, the most notorious being *la Confiance* 20, commanded by the St. Malo corsair, Robert Surcouf. American losses were slight. Four ships were captured in each of the years 1799 and 1800.[7]

But late in the fall of 1799 the merchants took their concerns directly to the president himself. They wanted more than the outward-bound protection as far south as the Equator that Stoddert had proposed. The merchants generally formed their own convoys late in the spring for a return from Batavia, and they wanted a naval escort for the ships. In early December Adams decided that the *Congress* and *Essex* would sail all the way to Batavia and directed Stoddert to draw up the appropriate orders and make the logistical arrangements. With extra stores carried out in merchantmen, the frigates would escort a convoy to Java, cruise for privateers in the Sunda Strait for a fortnight, and then return with another convoy to the United States in the summer of 1800. Stoddert was confident that Sever and Preble could defeat any force they might meet in the Indian Ocean. And although the secretary had at first resisted the merchants' attempts to have frigates sail as far as Batavia, he now became an enthusiastic supporter of the operation. His excitement infected his staff. Clerk Goldsborough wrote Captain Preble that "a cruise to Batavia, may afford you an opportunity of boxing our fraternal allies by a Quaker squeeze."[8]

2. *The* Congress *Dismasted*

After a rendezvous at Newport, Sever and Preble sailed for Asia on 6 January 1800. Already the plan for the operation had gone awry, for the outward-bound convoy consisted of only three small vessels. The other masters had been more concerned with the passage of the North Atlantic during the winter than with the corsairs at Cayenne, Teneriffe, or beyond. Rather than wait for the escort of the frigates, they had sailed weeks before the *Congress* and *Essex* cleared Block Island.[9]

And for good reason. Not long at sea, the frigates found the North Atlantic inhospitable. High winds, snow, and rain pelted Sever's squadron. On 12 January a gale began to blow out of the southeast. The tarred standing-rigging, set up in the winter, became dangerously slack. Both frigates struggled for survival in a heavy sea.[10]

Faced with gale-force winds, sailing ships generally shortened sail and ran into the wind, pitting the strongest part of the vessel—the bow—against the sea. To run before a gale—scudding—exposed the weaker stern and left the ship a slave to the wind.

Sever gave the order to ride out the gale close-hauled on the wind. But one by one the great masts of the *Congress* gave way, until even the bowsprit was sprung and masts, spars, canvas, and cordage were cut loose and lost to the sea. Proper procedure in a gale under normal conditions was a suicidal course with slack standing-rigging. Completely dismasted, a fortunate *Congress* survived the heavy sea and limped jury-rigged to Hampton Roads.

But the more experienced Preble chose to scud. Under short-sail, with the gale keeping the weather rigging taut, the slack was taken out of the lee standing-rigging. Preble then wore ship, putting the wind on the opposite quarter, and repeated the process. In this fashion the *Essex* weathered the gale with only minor damage in the top.

On his arrival in Norfolk, Sever attributed the near loss of the *Congress* to bad weather and fortune, and not to "negligence" on his part. He feared that the *Essex,* a smaller and more weakly built vessel, had suffered a similar or worse fate. Not until early June did word reach Newport that the *Essex* had survived and anchored at the Cape of Good Hope.[11]

But something was amiss in the *Congress.* In March, Sever wrote Stoddert in an effort to rid himself of Lieutenant John Cordis. Formerly in the *Constitution* under Nicholson, Cordis had been court-martialed in June 1799 on charges of brutality, drunkeness, and sleeping on duty. Though exonerated, Cordis, like Nicholson's other officers, was transferred to a new ship. Sever and Stoddert agreed that rather than try Cordis a second time, it would be best for the service if he resigned.[12]

Whatever his faults as an officer, Cordis was no fool. He struck back at Sever in a letter to Stoddert that questioned the captain's conduct before and during the gale. Cordis stated that he and other officers had warned Sever of the danger posed by the slack rigging, but to no avail. In the midst of the storm, after two masts were already lost, they had proposed that the *Congress* scud, but this suggestion too Sever rejected. Furthermore, Cordis wrote, "it may perhaps have been mentioned to you that the gale was uncommonly boisterous—but rest assured, it was not the case—the sea was very irregular, but the wind by no means so high as seamen in general encounter in most voyages."[13]

The charges might have been dismissed as the ramblings of a disgruntled subordinate had not other events made it clear to Stoddert that there were problems at Norfolk. Only a few days after he received Cordis's letter, word reached the secretary of an unsuccessful attempt by mutineers to seize the frigate at anchor. Stoddert also received a letter from Midshipman John Dubose, who wanted out of the ship. Stoddert agreed to a transfer but asked him not to "mention this to other midshipmen, as there is too much disorder and uneasiness on board the *Congress* already." Two days before Stoddert replied to Dubose's letter, the young man met a fellow midshipman, Samuel Cushing, in a duel and shot him dead through the neck.[14]

Stoddert called for a court of enquiry to decide if Sever's conduct warranted the convening of a formal court-martial. Headed by Truxtun and the Barron brothers, the court took testimony on board the frigate *Chesapeake* on 29 April. Surprisingly, Cordis failed to show, claiming to be sick. But in a written response to questions from the court, Cordis now spoke of an excessively hard gale, and denied that he had offered warnings about the rigging or that there had been a debate about the proper course to pursue during the storm. The court thus found no reason to call a court-martial. Reviewing the proceedings, both Adams and Stoddert expressed "great satisfaction in the result," the secretary adding that he had never doubted the ultimate verdict.[15]

Buy why had Cordis reversed himself in his testimony, in effect branding himself a liar? Apparently, there had been a pre-enquiry deal, and the key figure was Thomas Truxtun, the president of the court. He recognized that Sever *and* the United States Navy were being tried. The *Congress* had been dismasted, almost lost. Her officers wanted out of the frigate. Cordis was under a cloud. Mids dueled and died ashore. The crew mutinied. Not surprisingly, there were many who questioned Sever's command ability. The enquiry, had Cordis stuck to the charges he had made in his letter to Stoddert, would have become a contest in sailing skill between the navy's sixth-ranking captain and a lieutenant with a reputation for drinking and sleeping on duty. Truxtun had no doubt who would prevail. He had concluded that whatever his faults, Cordis was "a good seaman," while Sever was "not a regularly bred seaman." If the court found itself forced to conclude that the *Congress*'s commander was not competent to sail her, the administration's political enemies would certainly question why such a man had been so employed. Truxtun knew full well that there had been doubts voiced about Sever's appointment in 1794. In approaching the myriad problems emanating from the frigate, Truxtun advised Stoddert: "it is best not to disturb the public mind, when it can be avoided without injury to the service, especially at this time." So two days before the enquiry, Truxtun transferred John Cordis to the *Chesapeake*, where he would be first lieutenant to Captain Sam Barron, another of the judges. Saved from dismissal, and perhaps arrest, Cordis recanted. Truxtun went to the length of having the court's proceedings printed and distributed to silence the attacks on Sever, and on the service.[16]

3. To the Sunda Strait

Preble, with a fished mainmast sprung between decks, reached Table Bay at the Cape of Good Hope on 11 March 1800. Spending two weeks anchored with a British squadron under Vice Admiral Sir Roger Curtis, Preble waited in vain for Sever to join him. Not that the time was wasted; the *Essex*'s captain attended almost nightly dinners with British officials and officers while by day his frigate was completely stripped and re-rigged.[17]

With the *Essex* ready for sea, Preble followed Stoddert's instructions concerning "unforeseen events" that might leave but one frigate able to proceed. Leaving a letter at the Cape for Sever, Preble pressed on for the Sunda Strait. Departing on 28 March, he proudly noted in his log that the *Essex* was "the first United States vessel-of-war to double the Cape and show the flag beyond it."[18]

Preble's route to Batavia kept him over 1,500 miles south of Ile de France. On 14 April, he sighted two small French islands in the Indian Ocean—Amsterdam and St. Paul—and noted in his log that the Stars and Stripes flew from the huts of Yankee sealers.[19]

Heading northeast, Preble made landfall off Kolapa Island [Deli] and rounded Java Head into the Sunda Strait on 7 May, falling in with a small

British squadron. Sailing a week in the Strait, the *Essex* anchored in Batavia Roads on the 15th.[20]

Well received at Batavia, Preble waited once again to see if Sever would arrive. In the meantime, he spread word that a convoy would depart for the United States on 10 June. The *Essex* returned to the Strait to cruise for corsairs. Patrolling for two weeks, Preble boarded thirteen ships, all American, but found no French privateers active before returning to Batavia.[21]

Finding twelve ships ready to sail in the Roads, Preble organized the convoy and issued sets of day and night signals to each master. He left instructions that he would wait off Mew Island in the Strait for a few days for any other ships to join him. Drawing on supplies sent from the United States, Preble ordered the excess auctioned off should the *Congress* fail to arrive before 15 July. On 16 June the convoy weighed and sailed for home.[22]

While beating against a contrary wind in the Strait on the 21st, Preble received news from a Dutch proa that Robert Surcouf was cruising nearby. Seeking his quarry, Preble twice caught sight of *la Confiance,* but in each instance light winds gave the edge to the corsair which escaped under sweeps. Having been informed of the presence of the *Essex* beforehand, Surcouf had decided to cruise elsewhere in the Indian Ocean and had no intention of offering battle. Disappointed, Preble reached Mew Bay on the 29th, and there learned from an American ship of Sever's fate. Joined by two additional merchant ships from Batavia, the convoy of fourteen sail escorted by the *Essex* weighed again on 1 July.[23]

Following the southeast trade, the *Essex* was once again battered by violent gales and the convoy was dispersed. Lookouts sighted the Cape on 27 August, and the frigate anchored at St. Helena on 10 September.[24]

Before leaving Mew Bay, Preble had instructed the masters of the ships in his convoy that in the event of their becoming separated, the *Essex* would wait at St. Helena for twenty days for stragglers to rejoin the fold. But by the 21st, with six merchantmen at anchor, three having sailed for home on their own, one dismasted, and only four still missing, the merchant captains petitioned Preble to depart at once. They were more concerned about the perils of the North Atlantic in winter than in running the gauntlet between Cayenne and Teneriffe. Preble agreed, and on the 26th, after the arrival of a seventh vessel, the convoy sailed for the United States.[25]

The *Essex* reached New York on the evening of 28 November 1800, the frigate's company in good health. Only 11 men had died out of a complement of 250, but Preble was himself sick. His health deteriorated and for the remainder of his career he would be racked by illness until his death in April 1807.[26]

Preble's reports to Stoddert bemoaned the fact that only one frigate had reached Batavia. Had two ships arrived safely, one could have escorted the convoy while the other cruised in the Strait. Preble recommended that an American warship be kept on station in the Sunda Strait; in the presence of French privateers, Yankee merchantmen were defenseless in the restricted waters.

Stoddert set in motion a second operation to Batavia, planning to send the *Connecticut,* commanded by Captain Richard Derby who would have had the *Essex* had he returned to the United States sooner, and the *Ganges,* commanded by Lieutenant John Mullowny, formerly John Barry's first in the *United States.* But news of the convention with France led to the cancellation of the expedition.[27]

Stoddert's willingness to launch a second foray into the Indian Ocean is surprising. He spoke again and again of the need to concentrate American forces in the Caribbean. Yet at times his better sense gave way to grandiose schemes beyond the capacity of the small American navy. He planned Barry's and Talbot's cruise through European waters. He failed to reproach Murray when he sailed unordered for Gibraltar. But sending warships to the Indian Ocean was the least sensible of Stoddert's wartime operational plans. Dispatching two frigates to Batavia in December 1799, Stoddert effectively removed the ships from his order of battle for an entire year, of which only two or three months could be spent usefully east of the Cape. Had the ships been able to use Table Bay as they did St. Kitts in the Caribbean, and had enlistments run for two, rather than a single year, a naval effort in the Orient would have been more practicable.

Under the conditions of the Quasi-War, though, the cruise to Batavia was the most ill-conceived operation of the conflict. As valuable as American trade was with the Orient, it totaled only about 2 percent of all commerce. Did it deserve the protection of two frigates? Despite the absence of an American naval presence, only eight ships were lost during the war. The East Indiamen themselves declined to sail in convoy between the United States and the Cape of Good Hope. The *Congress* and *Essex* certainly could have been better employed in the West Indies. Of course, the decision to send Sever and Preble all the way to Batavia had been Adams's, not Stoddert's, but the planned cruise of the *Connecticut* and *Ganges* was the secretary's idea. As for his reasons, it is probably significant that the major proponent of the follow-up cruise was Thomas Fitzsimons of Philadelphia, long a Stoddert associate. But the secretary had shown an enthusiasm for the first foray, whatever its authorship, that demonstrated that he, like so many of the American leaders who followed him, remained determined to pursue the trial of the *Grand Turk.*

11

THE FRENCH BECOME SCARCE

1. Unwarrantable Steps: Truxtun as Tyrant

Having sent the *Congress* and *Essex* to the East Indies in December 1799, Stoddert hoped that 1800 would see answered the requests of other American merchants for naval protection of non-Western Hemisphere commerce. But one by one, battered American frigates began to anchor in the Chesapeake: the *Congress,* dismasted in an Atlantic gale; the *Constellation,* dismasted in her night action with *la Vengeance;* and the *Insurgent,* buffeted by a storm off Cuba, and with a deficient British-made foremast. As a result, work on the *Chesapeake,* outfitting at Norfolk was delayed. Only the *Philadelphia* would soon be ready for sea. "We have so many frigates dismasted," Stoddert wrote, that not one could be spared for service beyond the Caribbean. The *Philadelphia* would be needed to replace Morris at St. Kitts.[1]

As if the burdens of running the navy were not enough, the spring of 1800 was an especially trying time for Stoddert. The struggle between Hamilton and Adams reached fever pitch as the former and his supporters maneuvered to dump the president. Adams struck back in May, demanding McHenry's resignation and firing Pickering when the secretary of state refused to tender his. Stoddert found himself saddled with the administration of the War Department until the new appointee, Stephen Dexter, took office. As a supporter of the president, Stoddert was involved in the political machinations of the Federalists. He was also responsible for outfitting the new capital at Washington and for moving the government south. This work had been shared by the cabinet secretaries, but with the demise of his colleagues on the eve of the transfer, an increasing burden fell on Stoddert.[2]

*   *   *

After ordering Decatur in the *Philadelphia* to take command of the American squadron off Guadeloupe, there was little for Stoddert to do until the situation in the Chesapeake improved. He looked towards his other administrative duties and increasingly left to Truxtun, the senior officer present, the affairs of the navy at Norfolk.[3]

After his "defeat" of *la Vengeance,* Truxtun found himself praised by the Federalist press, Stoddert, and Adams; the Congress passed a resolution honoring him and ordered a medal struck in commemoration of the action of February 1800. Never humble, Truxtun began to think too highly of himself. A marine lieutenant who served under him in 1800 found the captain a man who "accustomed to receive homage, . . . now demands it without bounds." Truxtun had become a "tyrant" who expected "abject submission to his 'supreme will' (to use his own words). . . ."[4]

Truxtun was quite willing to take charge at Norfolk. Stoddert's instructions that the Gosport yard focus its effort on refitting the *Congress* were overridden, Truxtun ordering naval constructor Josiah Fox to ready the *Constellation* by 1 May, writing: "again I desire that you proceed to obey this order—and that I have no excuse in the future." Truxtun's word still being considered "law" at Norfolk, the crews were duly switched to the *Constellation.*[5]

In mid-April, Truxtun received instructions from Stoddert that further fed his ego. With insinuations about his conduct as commander of the *Congress* followed by the attempted mutiny in the frigate, James Sever had turned to Truxtun to convene a court-martial. But he referred Sever to the secretary of the navy. Stoddert felt that Truxtun should have handled the matter himself, without reference to the capital. There were plenty of idle captains about Norfolk to staff a court. He wrote Truxtun on three successive days:

> [14 April] . . . you are the commanding officer in the Chesapeake . . . ;
> [15 April] . . . I do not like this method of appealing to the head of the department, by officers, who are themselves competent to the object of appeal . . . ;
> [16 April] . . . you must assume all authority as if you were already an admiral, as I hope you will quickly be—or as if you had command of the whole navy.[6]

It was no secret that Stoddert had sent a bill to Congress in March calling for the appointment of six admirals. The senior captains in the navy were excited about the prospect of promotion. Decatur, as an example, struck up a sudden correspondence with Timothy Pickering, whose son was a midshipman in the *Philadelphia:* "As I observe . . . that . . . admirals are to be appointed, I have to beg the favor of your friendly interference on my behalf and which will be acknowledged with gratitude by me. . . ." Pickering's own career as secretary of state nearing its end, Decatur's efforts proved pointless, and short-lived.[7]

But Truxtun could be assured of Stoddert's support, for the secretary had personally informed him of the proposal only two days after it was sent to Congress. In the light of the letter of 16 April, it seemed to Truxtun that he would soon be an admiral, and perhaps the senior one and head of the navy. Following the court-martial of the *Congress's* mutineers, Truxtun signed the sentencing instrument: "Truxtun . . . Vested with the powers of Commander in Chief of the Navy of the U.S." But not satisfied with control of local administrative functions, Truxtun took upon himself the operational direction of the navy's ships as well. He ordered Alexander Murray, who had replaced him in command of the *Constellation,* to sail to Guadeloupe. Murray would be joined there later by Sam Barron in the *Chesapeake.* Taking the *Enterprize* under his command, Murray's three-ship squadron was to sail from Guadeloupe to Cayenne, and thence to Curaçao.[8]

Only gradually did the secretary of the navy learn of Truxtun's actions. On 17 May an ambiguously worded letter from Truxtun alerted Stoddert to the possibility that Murray might have sailed "without receiving orders from this Department—I hope this will not turn out to have been the case, it would certainly be very improper." If it were true, Stoddert's plans would be upset. He needed Murray to relieve Talbot at Cap François where an experienced commander was indispensable. The elder Barron was to join Decatur off Guadeloupe where the French *guerre de course* had revived. But now Truxtun had both frigates preparing to sail for the Spanish Main, taking one of Decatur's fastest and most successful schooners with them.[9]

Uncertain about just what had occurred at Norfolk, Stoddert attempted to cover all possibilities. He ordered Barron to Cap François to relieve Talbot if Murray had already sailed for Guadeloupe. If, by chance, the *Constellation* was still at Hampton Roads, Barron was advised to "destroy" the secretary's letter to spare Truxtun embarrassment.[10]

But a second dispatch from Norfolk, confirmed Stoddert's worst fears: Murray had been ordered to sail. To complicate matters further, there was sudden demand for the services of the *Chesapeake* that would prevent her sailing to the West Indies. A large sum of money had to be brought from Charleston to the Bank of the United States in Philadelphia. Also, Senator

Charles Pinckney, a Republican from South Carolina, planned to take passage south in a ship, citing "inability to travel by land." There were occasional reports of French privateers active off the coast, and Stoddert could not afford to take a chance and refuse the services of the navy's ships to protect either the money or the senator. The secretary decided to use the *Ganges* as a naval escort for Pinckney's ship as far as the Chesapeake, where Sam Barron's frigate would then join the cortege and see the senator safely to Charleston. The *Chesapeake* would then transport the specie to Philadelphia.[11]

With Murray already on his way to Guadeloupe, and with Barron retained on the coast, no frigate remained to relieve Talbot at the Cape. An angered Stoddert wrote Truxtun:

> I am extremely mortified at the unwarrantable step which your too great zeal has prompted you to take—I mean, in sending off Murray, without his instructions from the president—It was every way improper—You assumed direction in a case, belonging to the executive exclusively, and God knows what inconveniences may result from it. . . .

But as mortified as the secretary of the navy was, his respect and love of Thomas Truxtun remained unshaken. Letters were ordered destroyed. Nothing was said to the president. And Stoddert provided a cover story for the affair, that "the *Constellation* had sailed from Norfolk . . . in search of the privateer said to have been near" the coast. Two recipients of this tale were Senator Pinckney and Lieutenant Mullowny of the *Ganges.* Perhaps the latter wondered why, if the *Constellation* was off the southern coast, the secretary of the navy had directed that three copies of a letter addressed to Alexander Murray were to be sent "by as many opportunities if such should occur to Saint Kitts." Benjamin Stoddert knew full well where the *Constellation* had sailed.[12]

Murray reached St. Kitts after a "very tedious passage of thirty days" with his instructions from Truxtun in hand. Fortunately, little damage attended the latter's display of initiative and leadership. Decatur, cruising off Guadeloupe, never learned of Murray's arrival until after the *Constellation* had been recalled. Murray himself cruised about the islands, recapturing two brigs while he waited for the arrival of the *Chesapeake.* At St. Kitts on 12 July, he found not his consort, but a letter from Stoddert instructing him to ignore Truxtun's orders and to sail at once for the Cap to relieve Talbot. There, it will be recalled, Murray found the *Constitution* moored in the Roads repairing her badly sprung foremast and in no shape to proceed for home.[13]

2. Final Operations

With Murray at last bound for Cap François to relieve Talbot, Stoddert's major remaining operational problem was to maintain a strong force around Guadeloupe. Elsewhere in the Antilles, French corsairs were quiescent or if active, posed only minor threats to American commerce. But in mid-1800 the situation in the Lesser Antilles remained critical. The resurgence of the Guadeloupean *guerre de course* and the shift of operations into the Atlantic have been discussed. The altered situation placed greater burdens on the ships based at St. Kitts and made the command there once again the most important in the West Indies. Escorts had to remain longer with their convoys to see them to a "safe" latitude. Had the Navy Department possessed as much control over trade as the Admiralty and the Board of Trade held over England's, merchantmen might have been rerouted around the lee of St. Domingo and north through the Windward Passage. Toussaint's control over the coasts of Hispaniola and the Royal Navy concentration in the Passage made this a safer path. No doubt some Americans began to use this latter route on their own, but before any largescale shift in commercial sailing patterns could be organized, the war ended. To meet these demands on the squadron at St. Kitts, Stoddert struggled to build up a force of a dozen warships by the end of the year, seven of which were frigates. He instructed his captains to cruise aggressively, and further to windward where the French privateers threatened not only the West Indian trade, but also the East Indian and Mediterranean as well.[14]

Truxtun, now commanding the *President* 44, resumed command of the American squadron in the Lesser Antilles on 23 September, falling in that day with Decatur and Cross in the *Philadelphia* and the *John Adams* off Montserrat. After seeing the commodore's pendant struck by Decatur, Truxtun sailed for Guadeloupe for a personal reconnaissance, as he had in February 1799 and 1800. But for Truxtun the well had gone dry. He made his way to Basseterre Roads, happy to be back in command and pleased with his ship, which had been Talbot's to build, although he found her draft greater "than an English 74" and a problem in the West Indian anchorages the American navy frequented.[15]

At St. Kitts Truxtun caught up with his administrative duties. He left orders for subordinates to cruise independently and aggressively. He wrote French officials at Guadeloupe promising to hang two of their seamen if the agents followed through on their threat to execute a pair of captured Americans. The men were promptly exchanged. But Truxtun found the French privateers less active than expected, a trend he attributed to the hurricane season. The British appeared to be the more immediate problem. Truxtun interceded with local officials responsible for seizing John Rodgers's recaptured Portuguese brig, but to no avail. Then, on 2 October, Captains Brown and Geddes arrived, turning over to the commodore a packet marked Curaçao papers.[16]

The affair mortified Truxtun. Geddes "pointedly condemned" Watkins's conduct, an opinion with which Truxtun concurred. But what most troubled him was that the events left the United States Navy and the nation itself an object of local derision. He was "hurt at the sneers and horse laughs of some here, at our giving an island to a nation, whose officers instantly set traps to get hold of our property. . . ." To a merchant whose ship and cargo had been seized Truxtun wrote:

> Had I been in the West Indies, when the application from Mr. Phillips
> . . . arrived . . . I should have gone down with the *President,* and such
> other force as appeared to me necessary, and have given a proper
> protection to our citizens, and their property, against such an illegiti-
> mate collection of men, but I should not have suffered a change of the
> government of that island . . . that I should have feared, would have
> become a trap for other of our citizens and property soon after.

In mentioning only Geddes's anger in the relevant dispatch to Stoddert, and in what else he wrote about the affair, it is obvious that Truxtun believed both Brown, the commander on the scene, and Decatur, the commodore at the time, had failed to take appropriate action. "That protection might have been given our citizens without suffering a change of government at Curaçao," Truxtun wrote Stoddert, "no one in my opinion acquainted with the circumstances can doubt."[17]

Complaints about British actions in the West Indies were numerous during 1800. British privateers and warships appeared to be stepping up their searches, seizures, and impressments. The imposition of trade restric- tions injured American commerce. In 1800 exports to the Caribbean fell from $27,300,000 (1799) to $23,500,000. But the greatest losses came in exports to the Dutch West Indies—Surinam and Curaçao—now under British occupation. Exports fell from $5,150,000 in 1799, to $1,296,000 in 1800, and to $625,000 in 1801.[18]

Anti-British agitation increased so that Alexander Hamilton grew con- cerned. He hoped that the stories were Republican "electioneering lies," for they certainly did little to better the chances of the Federalists in the approaching balloting. But even Hamilton came to realize the seriousness of British depredations. Stoddert, too, took note. He hoped that diplomacy would head off a break in relations, but, he wrote Thomas Fitzsimons, "We ought not however to rely solely on this, when we have the means of protecting our commerce from the lawless ravages of British privateers in our own hands." Obviously, the secretary of the navy was not an anglophile.[19]

But the problem of dealing with increasing British spoliations would fall to succeeding administrations. For Stoddert there remained the war with France. Truxtun had assumed command at St. Kitts at a time when the squadron's strength had fallen to eight ships as vessels returned to American ports to refit and recruit new crews. He called for reinforcements which Stoddert did his best to hurry south. In the meantime, Truxtun's commanders would have to make up for their numbers through activity. As Stoddert had written, lone cruising meant risk, but the secretary trusted in the skill and valor of his captains.

One such commander was Lieutenant Charles Stewart, a twenty-two-year-old Philadelphian who had begun his maritime career at the age of thirteen. In the spring of 1798 Captain John Barry had considered Stewart experienced enough to serve as a lieutenant in the *United States* frigate. Stewart was in Philadelphia in July 1800 when Stoddert relieved William Maley as commander of the *Experiment*. The secretary gave the troubled schooner to Stewart, who by then had become Barry's first. The loss of his subordinate, however, did not concern the navy's senior captain who advised Stoddert: "I am perfectly satisfied with your appointment of Lieut. Stewart I hope he will be more active when he comds. than when he is comd."[20]

On 1 October, cruising alone off St. Barts, Stewart sighted two vessels, a brig and a three-masted schooner. The ships were French, two days from Guadeloupe, and bound for France with a convoy loaded with sugar, cotton, and coffee. The brig, sixteen 9-pounders, 150 men, and the schooner, eight 9-pounder carronades and 45 men, left their wards to chase the American. Realizing that he was outgunned, Stewart pointed up the Baltimore-built schooner as close to the wind as she would sail, enabling him to keep out of the reach of his pursuers. Perhaps as he stood on the quarterdeck of the *Experiment* and observed his enemies steadily losing ground, he gave silent thanks to Ben Stoddert. Before leaving Philadelphia, Stewart had attempted to mount several additional cannon in the ship. The secretary had advised that no more than two 6-pounders be taken on board, writing: "I have no doubt your schooner will be injured in her sailing & of course, in her usefulness, by taking in so many guns." Stewart discovered in the course of the action that his ship's speed was of greater importance than her firepower. Neither French vessel could match the *Experiment* to windward, but the fore- and aft-rigged schooner was not falling as far behind as the square-rigged brig. By the early evening when the French gave up the chase, a league separated their ships from each other. Suddenly prey became hunter as Stewart wore and ran down on the schooner. In haste to escape, her commander threw over the side whatever he could to lighten ship, including six of his eight carronades, but his efforts served only to leave him defenseless by the time the *Experiment* came within range. A broadside convinced the French to strike. Lieutenant David Porter took a prize crew to the schooner, while Stewart pressed on after the brig, but it was too late in the evening to overtake a vessel that had continued to flee even while the Americans bore down on her consort.[21]

The capture of *la Diana* made Stewart an "ornament" both in the islands and at home. Among the prisoners was none other than General Rigaud, Toussaint's nemesis in the struggle for Hispaniola. Stewart wrote in a letter published in the United States: "This is the man, Sir, that has wrested millions from my countrymen; the depredations, the piracies, plunder and murders he has committed on my fellow-citizens are but too well known in the United States; and now the supreme ruler of all things has placed him in the hands of that country he has most injured." Commodore Truxtun, to whom the illustrious prisoner was delivered, found Rigaud quite otherwise. "His address and understanding astonished every body here," he wrote friend Moses Myers. Truxtun sent Rigaud to a British prison in Basseterre, under a marine guard, not to prevent an escape, but to protect the man from the Kittians who would have murdered him in the street had they had the opportunity. Rigaud was soon trusted with a parole and exchanged.[22]

As much as Stewart's victory had pleased Truxtun, it had angered the French. Reports reached the *President* that a brig of eighteen guns lay at St. Barts outfitting in preparation to hunt down the *Experiment*. Then came word that Stewart had been captured. Truxtun's regard for his young subordinate is evident in the notation that appears in the log: "we fear many lives has [*sic*] been lost, as we are certain [Stewart] never would have struck while a possibility of saving his vessel remained." But the tale was false. The *Experiment* remained at sea.[23]

* * *

As if directing operations between Puerto Rico and Barbuda and Curaçao and Barbados with but eight ships was not a daunting enough task, Truxtun also faced logistical problems. In mid-August, Stoddert had ordered the brig *Pickering*, Lieutenant Hillar, to sail from Philadelphia to reinforce the squadron at St. Kitts. Accompanying the former Revenue Service cutter was a storeship loaded with "provisions, some cordage & junk" along with a new fore-topmast for the *Philadelphia*. James Long, master of the *Florida*, had made several cruises to Basseterre Roads carry-

ing provisions and stores. The brig's owner, Thomas Fitzsimons, had first
chartered her to the Navy Department in April 1799. But by early October 1800, neither brig had appeared and Truxtun's ships were short of
provisions which were scarce and dearly priced in the islands.[24]

After leaving Philadelphia, the track of the two ships should have taken
them into the cruising area of the American frigate *Insurgent*. Stoddert had
instructed Captain Patrick Fletcher, a former lieutenant in the Continental
Navy and good friend of Moses Brown, to cruise between latitude 38° and
30° north, and longitude 68° and 66° west, before returning to Annapolis
in mid-September. A fourth vessel in the same vicinity in early September
was Truxtun's frigate the *President*. A clue to the fate of the three ships
appears in a report Truxtun prepared for Stoddert: "on the 9th. and 10th.
[of September] I met with a violent gale of wind from the eastward,
accompanied by high & cross seas, but being well prepared to meet this
bad weather, I thank God we weathered it, without any accident or
loss. . . ." The *Insurgent, Pickering,* and *Florida* were apparently not as
fortunate. The brigs were small ships compared to the *President*. And the
Insurgent had been in need of extensive repairs from the time of her
capture. Murray, when he commanded the frigate, had never been satisfied
with her condition, but she had always been rushed out to sea by a
secretary with too few ships at his disposal. For the United States Navy the
loss of two warships and over 400 men was a blow greater than any struck
during the course of the war by the French. But that was the nature of
warfare in the age of sail. Between 1793 and 1815 the Royal Navy lost ten
ships to accidents and the elements for every one that fell to the enemy.[25]

And always forgotten in historical accounts of the Quasi-War is the
Florida which shared the fate of the two men-of-war. Captain Long, his
crew, and the supplies for the American squadron at St. Kitts were lost as
well. Fortunately, a logistical crisis was averted in late October when
Stoddert, unaware that the ships had failed to reach St. Kitts, ordered two
additional storeships to sail from New York to the islands. The provisions
the ships carried were meant for the French prisoners held in Basseterre
jails. Their maintenance had become a financial drain of the Navy Department and Stoddert decided that the captives could be fed more cheaply
with food from the United States. When the vessels reached St. Kitts,
Truxtun ordered the provisions distributed to his men of war. He relieved
himself of the prisoners by dispatching them to Guadeloupe in a cartel.[26]

*   *   *

The *Boston* was a more fortunate reinforcement instructed to join
Truxtun's squadron. Stoddert ordered Captain George Little to cruise off
the American coast and then to windward of Guadeloupe for two or three

weeks before proceeding to St. Kitts. On the morning of 12 October, about 500 miles northeast of Guadeloupe, lookouts sighted a ship of war and a schooner about five leagues to the west-northwest. The pair separated and ran; Little "set every yard of canvas" in pursuit.[27]

Throughout the afternoon Little stalked his quarry and by 4:00 P.M. the range had closed. At his order the *Boston* cleared for action; a gun fired to windward; the colors were run up. Answering with a windward cannon itself, the chase shortened sail in preparation for battle, running up French colors.

She was *le Berceau* 24, Commander Louis André Senes, the same corvette that had accompanied *la Vengeance* to the Antilles from France in the fall of 1799. During the chase Senes had thrown overboard ballast, boats, baggage, spare yards, and whatever else he could in an effort to escape. But finding the American frigate drawing ever nearer, he prepared for the inevitable fight.[28]

As the *Boston* ranged alongside her opponent, George Little hailed the corvette demanding her surrender to "the United States flag." Senes replied that his colors were made too fast to be lowered and responded to the senseless American bombast with his guns. For nearly an hour the two ships exchanged broadsides at pistol-shot range until both drifted apart, their rigging shot away. For the *Boston* it was a poor showing. She mounted twenty-four 12-pounders and twelve 9-pounders, for a one-side weight of metal of 198 pounds. *Le Berceau* carried only twenty-two French 9-pounders and a pair of 12-pounders, for a one-side total of 111 French, or 120 American pounds. Little had made a less than effective use of a 60 percent advantage in firepower.[29]

Both captains set their crews to work repairing the rigging. Little once more drew within pistol-shot range dueling in the darkness with the French. Senes tried to grapple and board. He had 230 men in the corvette and outnumbered the Americans by a score. But Little sheered away presenting his guns. The action continued until 11:00 P.M. when the ships separated again to repair damage.[30]

The battle thus far had been virtually a repetition of the action between the *Constellation* and *la Vengeance,* with the national roles reversed. Both ships were heavily injured in their tops and unable to maneuver. But throughout the night Little somehow managed to keep sight of *le Berceau*. With the dawn the two crippled men-of-war eyed each other as each pressed repairs. At 11:30 A.M. Little saw the French corvette's foremast and mainmast collapse. Two and one-half hours later, the *Boston* limped alongside the battered *le Berceau*. Senes struck. Little took the dismasted prize in tow and returned to Nantasket Roads where he arrived on 15 November.[31]

The French Become Scarce

News of Little's triumph brought praise and congratulations from Stoddert and hopes for "future glory" from John Adams. But the "victory" proved hollow and ultimately put an end to the captain's naval career. Since the engagement had occurred after the signing of the Franco-American convention, the prize had to be returned. For Little and his crew there would be no prize money. To the government would fall the cost of refitting the shattered corvette. And to the administration would fall as well the responsibility for responding to charges of pillaging the crew of *le Berceau*. The corvette's officers charged that Little's lieutenants had personally conducted body searches of the French, even "those parts which delicacy forbids to name," in quest of booty. Prisoners had been held on the orlop deck of the *Boston,* chained on their stomachs, denied food and water, and stripped of all their personal valuables. Stoddert wrote Little that he was certain the allegations were a "misrepresentation—because the conduct complained of would be unworthy of American seamen."[32]

Assembling a court of enquiry fell to the Jefferson administration. Headed by Samuel Nicholson as president, the judges concluded that the charges were "malicious & ill founded" and acquitted Little. Then Secretary of the Navy Robert Smith accepted and supported the decision, agreeing that everything Little had done had been "correct and legal." But in reviewing the proceedings it was obvious to Smith that the French prisoners in the *Boston* had been *"pillaged."* The court had simply failed to demonstrate that Little had been a party to the improper conduct. Coming as it did at a moment when a reduced navy had a surplus of captains, the enquiry spelled professional demise for Little. He had been relieved of command in July 1801 pending the decision of the court in September. The next month Little was discharged, Secretary Smith informing the captain that "the president . . . cannot retain you consistently with the principles of selection that have been adopted."[33]

* * *

Thanks to the aggressive cruising of his ships, the continued efforts of the larger Royal Navy squadron in the Lesser Antilles, and the impact of the shift in French diplomacy in Paris towards the United States finally reaching Guadeloupe, Truxtun began to note a decline in the operations of French corsairs in October 1800. At first he attributed the drop in activity to the hurricane season. He wrote Moses Myers that the squadron sailed "without news or without an enemy." But by early January, it was obvious that the crisis had passed. Over the previous six weeks the privateers had captured only eleven American merchantmen. Truxtun's commanders had retaken three of the prizes and two of the corsairs. But the commodore was disappointed, and wrote Tingey: ". . . with all this cruising my success has been very limited indeed, for the French have become *scarce,* so much so, that what I formerly found (chasing) an amusement, and pastime, is now insipid, irksome & tiresome. . . ." Truxtun was bored, and sick. He longed for "the pure northern air of America." He began to write about his bowels and about "bilious attacks" that had left him "weak and debilitated." He wrote Stoddert:

> If we had an active war, or any particular services of mine could be useful; while I could crawl about, I should ask no indulgence, but as this is not the case, I request you will order me home and without a leeward route [a stop at Kingston or Havana for a convoy], as that would perhaps in my present state be more, than I should get over.

Thomas Truxtun must have been very ill indeed![34]

Had Truxtun's state of body and mind been communicated earlier to the Navy Department, the secretary would have been spared much anxiety. Stoddert had a problem in the fall of 1800. Both John Barry and Silas Talbot were refitting their forty-fours and were eager to assume major commands. Talbot, Stoddert assumed, would have to return to Cap François. "I wish the station was better suited to his activity and bravery," Stoddert wrote Higginson in Boston, "there is but one other station in the W I of importance—that is about Guadeloupe." But the secretary had enticed Truxtun back into the service the previous year by promising not to employ him under Talbot. And if the *Constitution* went to the Leeward Islands, Barry would have to be sent to Hispaniola. While the Guadeloupe station was the larger and more lucrative post, the diplomatic responsibilities that came with the command at Cap François made that position the more demanding. Could Barry be trusted in such a role? In the summer of 1798 he had failed to perform as simple a diplomatic act as the delivery of a letter to the governor of Puerto Rico. Stoddert confessed: "I know not what to do with Barry."[35]

Barry's most recent mission, transporting the envoys to France, had failed to rehabilitate his image at the Navy Department. The poor man had been dogged by bad luck. Because of delays in sending the mission, no fault of Barry's, he had decided to sail a more southerly route to the Tagus, hoping to avoid the worst of the North Atlantic winter. The captain's concern pleased the envoys. But at Lisbon Barry got along poorly with the American minister, William Smith. Sailing north for Corunna, Spain, a violent storm forced Barry to strike his topmasts and moor in a bay between Ferrol and Corunna. But his anchors gave way under a strain that "would not have broken a two inch rope." The *United States* was nearly lost. The envoys were sent ashore in a local fishing boat to proceed

The French Become Scarce

overland to Paris. For Barry it was his second brush with disaster. In the fall of 1798 off the American coast, the frigate had survived a gale that had struck her with the ferocity and effect similar to the one that dismasted the *Congress*. Barry had been at a loss what to do, but Lieutenant James Barron was permitted to attempt what Barry's biographer calls an "experiment." Like Preble, Barron scudded before the storm alternately resetting the standing rigging. How novel was a practice understood by Preble, Barron, and the lackluster John Cordis?[36]

So Barry returned to the Delaware having missed nearly a year and a half of the war, and no better off than when he had left. While he had not displayed incompetence, he had been unlucky. And Stoddert, who had hoped to make his senior captain an admiral on his return, had failed in the interim to convince the Congress of the wisdom of establishing such a high rank in such a small service. That meant further disappointment for proud John Barry, and left Benjamin Stoddert without the means to lure the old veteran ashore and into retirement, or at least the superintendency of a ship of the line. Barry insisted on a fitting command, and that meant either Basseterre Roads or Cap François. Which station would best suit the talents of a commodore who went to sea with a cow to keep his stomach in milk? Stoddert delayed a final decision until he could meet with the president.[37]

Barry had neither a defender nor an admirer in John Adams. The president considered the captain of the *United States* an emigrant foreigner who made "vain boasts" about his service during the American Revolution. But he was the ranking officer, and despite his poor health and that of his wife, he was intent on making another cruise before the war ended. Adams agreed with Stoddert: Talbot would go to Cap François and Barry to St. Kitts. The secretary warned Truxtun of the approaching assumption of authority in the Leeward Islands. "His seniority entitles him to this command, & it could not be denied him," Stoddert wrote, "I need not say more." As a sop, Truxtun received permission to take a ship of his choice from the squadron and cruise independently in the Caribbean until April.[38]

Appropriate orders were on their way to Talbot and Barry as well. Both commodores received the usual instructions, but with new cautions added based on the probability of peace with France. Stoddert advised that they not seek encounters with French national ships, though they were not purposely to "avoid engagements with them, should they show a disposition to attack." Privateers were to be treated as before, but American men-of-war were to be employed "more in convoying our trade than formerly— and of course, less in cruising." Stoddert was ordering his commodores to go over to the defensive, unless the *guerre de course* regained its old vitality, in which case Talbot and Barry were to resume active operations.[39]

Before the *United States* sailed for the islands, Stoddert made two gestures that must have touched and pleased Barry. The secretary assigned his recently warranted son, eighteen-year-old Midshipman Benjamin Forrest Stoddert, to the frigate, advising Barry not "to be too indulgent to him. He has had enough of that at home." Why Stoddert sent his first-born to serve under a captain whom he had criticized for the past two years may appear contradictory. But the war, Stoddert knew, would soon be over and if the new midshipman was to make it to the West Indies before the peace, there was little time to waste. Of the frigates preparing for sea, the *Constitution* was a New England ship and Stoddert who was well aware of regional prejudices, serving as he did a president who considered Pennsylvania "the south," was not about to place a Marylander amongst a pack of wild Yankee youths. The *Constellation* was refitting in the Delaware, but Murray, while he continued to display initiative, was known to rule rather arbitrarily over wardrooms torn by dissension. Whatever Barry's faults, the *United States* seemed to be a happy ship commanded by an officer who either had a good eye for, or produced, talented subordinates. Stoddert had already given commands to three of Barry's lieutenants— James Barron, John Mullowny, and Charles Stewart—and Stephen Decatur, Jr. and Richard Somers remained on board. And the secretary had no need to concern himself with Barry's seamanship, for he had assigned to the *United States* Master Commandant Cyrus Talbot, son of Barry's fellow commodore. Young Talbot had previously commanded his own ship, the *Richmond,* and served now as a de facto flag-captain for the aged Barry. Stoddert had long thought highly of Cyrus Talbot, an experienced officer who had served in the French navy.[40]

Barry received the secretary's appointments to the *United States* with approbation. He would no longer have to fly his "ten shilling pendant" and had the navy secretary's son entrusted to his care. But lest Barry assume he was being rewarded, rather than coddled, Stoddert took one last cruel slap at the man. Mrs. Edward Shippen, wife of a prominent Philadelphian, had requested passage to Antigua in a naval vessel. Stoddert placed the *United States* at her disposal, and enclosed a copy of his letter to her in a note to Barry. Sense of humor or not, John Barry must have been angered and hurt.

Captn. Barry will go to St. Kitts—His ship is a very fine one, and as old as he is, I am sure he would feel as he ought to do, more gratification in landing you safely at Antigua, than in the capture of a French ship of the line.

The French Become Scarce

Such sentiments made public by the secretary of the navy would do little to improve the popular image of the aging commodore whose ill-health was common knowledge. While 181 years later Congress would decree him "the father of the United States Navy," Barry's contemporaries were more restrained in their assessment. Even friend Thomas Tingey, fellow captain and Philadelphian, referred to Barry as the service's "old wife."[41]

* * *

In the meantime, Truxtun made the first overtures towards peace in the islands. Returning from a cruise in early December, he rendezvoused in Basseterre Roads with several ships of his command, reinforcements recently arrived, and the two storeships with provisions for the prisoners. Captain Jewett of the *Trumbull* delivered to the commodore a letter from Stoddert dated 4 October. The secretary had been outraged by the costs of maintaining the French captives and had sent out a new navy agent—Thomas T. Gantt—to replace Clarkson. Reviewing the charges, Truxtun saw the justice of Stoddert's decision and supported it with a nasty letter of his own to Clarkson who had bragged that he made "double" the percentage allowed. For Truxtun it was a "particularly painful" task, because he had appointed Clarkson and had recommended him to Stoddert. But the secretary's desire to feed the prisoners and send them as soon as possible to the United States made little sense to Truxtun. His squadron needed the supplies itself, and rumors of a Franco-American agreement abounded in the islands. To save the department money and the provisions for the American warships, Truxtun made a peaceful gesture to the French. He ordered Basseterre's jails "cleared" of all prisoners and sent them in cartels to Guadeloupe, fully expecting the French to reciprocate.[42]

Returning to the Roads a month later, Truxtun learned that on 6 January cartels had arrived from Guadeloupe with all the Americans held captive there, as well as a proclamation ordering a halt to privateering against American ships. Truxtun's cartel had been well timed, for the French prisoners had reached Guadeloupe almost simultaneously with news from France of a peace settlement. To determine the seriousness of the new French decree, Truxtun sailed for Basse-Terre to make a personal reconnaissance and see if any American merchantmen were being held. "Under easy sail, with . . . colors and broad pendant flying," the *President* stood in to within half-gunshot range of the fort. But the French responded with a vigorous fire and Truxtun withdrew. He expected that they would excuse their behavior as they always had, claiming that they had mistaken the ship for a Royal Navy man-of-war flying United States colors. But, as Truxtun wrote Stoddert, "as no English ship ever went so near to that fort since the war, they must have known it was an American frigate." The

President sailed north, the commodore unsure about how he should respond to the contradictory French actions.[43]

Returning to St. Kitts on 15 January, Truxtun discovered the *United States* at her mooring flying a broad pendant. He struck his own, but unwilling to make any further gesture of deference, remained in the *President.* After ninety minutes, Barry's boat came alongside and the commodore boarded Truxtun's forty-four. He advised Barry of the squadron's dispositions, the change of navy agents, and, most importantly, the proclamation issued from Guadeloupe. Barry had no official word from Stoddert either and the worn-out captain of the *President* "rejoiced" at turning over to his replacement responsibility for what could become a difficult situation. But fully expecting news of a treaty to arrive shortly, Truxtun saw no reason to cruise independently as Stoddert had suggested. He stated to Barry his intention to sail for the United States as soon as possible, taking the *Chesapeake* with him.[44]

Stoddert learned of the treaty on 13 December 1800. Throughout the day clerks drafted letters to be sent to men-of-war outfitting up and down the coast to remain at anchor until further orders. Two days later, Adams transmitted the convention to the Senate with his approbation. Final ratification would not come until 19 December 1801, but administration policies presumed ultimate approval. On 30 December new orders went out to the *Constellation,* one of the vessels detained on the 13th. Captain Murray already held instructions from the secretary for a cruise to the windward of Guadeloupe where Little had met *le Berceau.* He was then to sail to St. Kitts where he was to confer with the commodore before determining where his frigate could best be employed. Murray would operate, as he had throughout the war, under independent command. But he was directed now to sail directly to Basseterre Roads with news of the treaty for Barry and Truxtun. They were to continue to provide escorts for convoys, but were to halt hostilities unless the French unexpectedly continued their depredations.[45]

Murray had an eventful voyage south. Scudding under a reefed foresail in a violent gale, a heavy sea broke upon the *Constellation* and stove in her gunport covers filling her with six feet of water. She barely survived. On a dark mid-January night a week later, lookouts sighted a ship close by that appeared much larger than the American frigate. Murray reasoned that she was not French, for they had nothing so big in the Antilles. The ship was probably British, but she bore down upon the *Constellation* firing her bow cannon. Murray, his crew by this time at quarters, responded with a full broadside before making the night signal for a British ship of war. He received a positive response, followed by a hailed demand that he send a boat on board His Majesty's fifth-rate razee *Magnanime,* commanded by

The French Become Scarce

Captain William Taylor. The forty-four-gun-ship was from the Leeward Islands station. Murray's experiences with the British at Antigua and as commodore at Cap François had made him less willing to accommodate the Royal Navy. He refused and Captain Taylor had to send his boat to the *Constellation.* After determining that neither ship had suffered any serious damage or casualties, Murray sought the latest intelligence from the islands. Had the corsairs halted their depredations against American ships? He was assured they had not.[46]

On 18 January, Murray sighted a three-masted lugger and after a chase lasting several hours captured *le Marrs* 14, a Guadeloupean corsair with a crew of 100. He learned from her master, Prosper Sergente, that France and the United States were no longer at war. Sergente produced a copy of the proclamation ordering a halt to attacks on American ships. Murray released *le Marrs,* giving her master a passport should he fall in with other American cruisers. But the Frenchman chose to accompany the *Constellation,* for Murray had determined to sail directly to Guadeloupe to discuss with the French whether they intended to observe the terms of the treaty while its ratification was discussed. He hoped for a "return to harmony & good will that should ever actuate sister republics."[47]

On 29 January, Murray anchored off Port Liberté, from whence *le Marrs* had sailed. He had sent a note ashore while off Basse-Terre Roads the previous day. The official French reply came in the person of General Jannet, the would-be governor of Curaçao. He invited Murray to come ashore, and insisted that the frigate be moored in the safety of the harbor. That meant under the guns of the fort, but Murray thought the risk offset by the advantages to be derived for American commerce should an effective peace be speedily arranged in the Lesser Antilles. He accepted the offer and worked the *Constellation* into the harbor and moored. As Murray and Jannet were rowed ashore, the American frigate fired a salute; the fort returned the honor. The captain wrote Stoddert:

> when arrived on shore I was received with every mark of civility & attention, & tho I did not contemplate staying more than a few hours, I found such preparations making to celebrate the joyful return of peace, that I was kept two days at the agents, entertained with feasting & bands of music, & no circumstance omited to show the sincerity of their friendship towards the United States, & to place the matter upon solid grounds, I obtained dispatches from the agents, to all the ports, & places where privateers resort, revoking their commissions, to capture American vessels, I have thought this a matter of such great moment, & knowing that our ships can have nothing further to do in this quarter that I shall immediately proceed with them myself, calling first at Puerto Rico, & then down to the Havana,

the consuls of which islands are required to conform themselves strictly to the letter of the treaty so you may now assure the merchants of the United States that their trade will no longer be molested by French cruisers. . . .[48]

Stoddert's instructions gave Murray the latitude to go where he pleased and the captain had the good sense to know that in spreading Jannet's proclamation throughout the islands he was serving the best interests of the United States. After calls at St. Kitts and St. Thomas, the *Constellation* sailed for San Juan, Puerto Rico. Murray sent his first lieutenant ashore with information on the treaty and copies of the decree halting privateering against American ships. On 6 February 1801, Murray left San Juan for Cap François, Santiago de Cuba, and Havana. The *Constellation,* which under Thomas Truxtun epitomized the American spirit in the war with France, now served as the harbinger of peace. In the Lesser Antilles the war was over.[49]

It was over as well off Hispaniola. Toussaint had secured his control of St. Domingo and was well on his way towards dominion over the entire island. Continued cooperation with the general and escorting convoys through the Windward Passage occupied most of the squadron's time. Consul General Edward Stevens viewed his job as finished. Ridden by gout, Stevens feared for his family "in a strange country" should he die. He longed for relief.[50]

Murray, who had relieved Silas Talbot in July 1800, had been himself relieved in September by Captain Sever in the refitted *Congress.* Sever's short command off Hispaniola was marked by lack of discipline and mishap. He charged a lieutenant and his surgeon with court-martial offenses. And the commodore himself embarrassingly collided with a British prize brig. Sever had attempted to sail between the Royal Navy frigate *Tisiphone* and her captive, but he had failed to observe that the brig was being towed.[51]

Talbot resumed command of the station in January 1801, but little remained to be done. Only three privateers were captured by ships of the Cap François station between July 1800 and April 1801.[52]

At Havana the navy faced its last challenge of the Quasi-War. The Cuban station had been left unguarded in mid-1799 after Stoddert received intelligence that the Spanish were about to halt all commercial intercourse with the United States. But the reports were false; despite increased restrictions, trade continued and flourished. Stoddert rushed to scrape together a force for Cuba. He ordered the *Norfolk* over from Hispaniola and later reinforced her with the *Pinckney* and *Warren.*[53]

During the six-week interim French privateering, which had virtually

come to an end, was renewed. Desfourneaux dispatched blank commissions for corsairs from Guadeloupe in a fast schooner. French agents
purchased "several fast American [built] vessels" at Havana and outfitted
them.[54]

Bainbridge's squadron began arriving off Cuba in December 1799 and
through vigilant cruising and convoying drove off the privateers by the
spring of 1800. Bainbridge's own *Norfolk* trapped one French privateer
against the shore and battered her to pieces. The squadron had been so
successful that on their return to the United States the *Norfolk* was refitted
and sent back to St. Domingo while the *Pinckney* was sold off. Left alone
off Cuba, the *Warren* continued her lonely patrols. As one of the ship's
officers wrote: "we see nothing but the stripe."[55]

On 15 June 1800, the *Warren,* a twenty-gun Newburyport-built ship,
moored in Havana harbor, finding there the frigate *General Greene.* Master
Commandant Timothy Newman, nephew of Secretary of State Pickering,
commanded the *Warren.* Newman hoped that Captain Perry bore new
instructions that would take the ship off the Havana station. But Perry,
after leaving Cap François, had sailed to New Orleans to pick up James
Wilkinson and his family. The frigate had called at Havana only to
rendezvous with a convoy due to sail for the American coast. Newman
was disappointed for there was little to be done off the Cuban coast. Perry
suggested that Newman speak with the American consul, John Morton,
for some specie lay at Vera Cruz that merchants wished brought to Havana
and ultimately the United States. Perry, who had delayed so long before
leaving Cap François, could ill-afford any further delay. Ashore, Newman
met with Morton, Perry, and Wilkinson. The amount of money at Vera
Cruz was considerable, some of it Morton's. The three men convinced
Newman that he ought to sail to Vera Cruz despite the fact that is orders
were plainly to the contrary and his was the only ship off the Cuban coast.
There were, of course, the personal financial advantages for Newman
whose prospects of earning any prize money seemed dim. And with no
French activity in evidence for months, there seemed little danger in
undertaking the 1,632 mile roundtrip.[56]

But Newman's fatal error lay not in breaking orders, but in ignoring one
of Stoddert's principal policies: commanders were not to remain in port for
extended periods in the West Indies. Newman should have moored the
Warren off Havana rather than enter the harbor proper, where the ship lay
for eleven days while he debated whether or not to sail for Vera Cruz. Not
long after the *Warren* at last weighed, her crew began to drop from yellow
fever. By the time the ship returned to Havana—15 August—forty-two
men were dead, including Newman and his son.[57]

The *Ganges,* Newman's relief, reached Havana on the 18th. Lieutenant

John Mullowny's ship had been cruising off the Cuban coast for a little over a week, and his men too were falling to Yellow Jack. Nineteen men would die in the *Ganges* and Mullowny decided that the best course was to withdraw both the *Ganges* and *Warren* to the United States. For the first and only time in the war, an American squadron had been driven from its station, not by the French, but by disease. A displeased Stoddert ordered the *Delaware* to Havana to reestablish a naval presence. The sloop of war would remain there until the spring of 1801.[58]

Newman's foolishness and insubordination infuriated both Adams and Stoddert. The secretary would have called for a court-martial if Newman had not "escaped by death." Adams released years of penned-up emotions: "If our ships lie in harbor or suffer their people to make frolics on shore, they infallibly take fevers. The least debauchery or even intemperance on shore, never fails to give them fevers & they have not prudence or fortitude enough to keep out of bad houses & vicious courses if they are allowed to sleep one night on shore."[59]

Not long after the *Ganges* and *Warren* had sailed north, Murray reached Havana in the *Constellation* with copies of the proclamation from Guadeloupe. In Havana, where he met with Spanish officials, he learned that the money he had failed to pick up in March 1800 still lay there awaiting a freight in a frigate. Alexander Murray sailed contentedly for the Delaware with $150,000, a just reward for initiative displayed once again.[60]

3. Stoddert and the New Administration

While the Quasi-War reached its conclusion in the Caribbean, the Federalists were going through their death throes in the United States. On 12 December 1800, the day before news of the Convention of Mortefontaine reached Washington, reports reached the capital of a Republican victory in South Carolina. For John Adams that meant electoral defeat, though whether Thomas Jefferson or Aaron Burr would be the next president remained uncertain until February.[61]

For Stoddert, the news from the south spelled both personal and political disappointment—not that he hoped to stay on in a second Adams administration as secretary of the navy. Since the transfer of the capital to Washington, Stoddert's old Brandywine wound had caused severe pain in his side, and his financial difficulties became embarrassingly obvious to all. Stoddert had expected an Adams victory, which would have allowed him to resign as navy secretary to look after his personal affairs. But with political defeat, a resignation would appear an abandonment of a president

The French Become Scarce

he admired, and leave the navy without a secretary; Adams would have no chance of finding a replacement for the final two months of his administra-tion.[62]

The Federalists were determined to place the navy on a secure footing before yielding power to the Republicans. Detailed proposals were the responsibility of the secretary of the navy, and on 12 January 1801 Stod-dert delivered his plans to Harrison Gray Otis, who presented them to the House of Representatives three days later.[63]

Unlike Adams, who continued to think in terms of cruiser warfare, Stoddert reissued his call for a battleship navy. The United States, he wrote, should "attend principally to a provision for ships of the line and frigates." With the French war nearing its end, only the thirteen frigates should be kept while the other ships could all be sold off. In a crisis the nation could trust that "the enterprising spirit of our citizens will quickly furnish . . . nearly all the small vessels necessary . . ." as they had during the Quasi-War. The savings from this immediate reduction could be di-rected into continued construction of the seventy-four-gun-ships which Congress had authorized in February 1799.[64]

Of the thirteen frigates Stoddert recommended that the government "keep in constant service six . . . ; seven others in port, but always ready for service [in ordinary]." To command the ships he proposed the retention of all commissioned officers and midshipmen, with those not employed maintained on half-pay. Stoddert also believed that the corps of marines should be kept at a strength on 1,100 officers and men.[65]

Stoddert thought his "system . . . so moderate, & so proper, that it would be adopted." But he was disappointed. The reductions in the size of the navy attracted both pro- and anti-navalists and alike, but the sections calling for the maintenance of an officer corps that included 28 captains, 7 master commandants, 110 lieutenants, and 354 midshipmen; a corps of marines 1,100 strong for a nation whose army in 1802 would total less than 3,000; and the construction of battleships met opposition from both cost-conscious Federalists and anti-naval Republicans. Congress accepted the proposals for cuts, but decided to redirect the savings to the Treasury rather than into the seventy-fours.[66]

The act that emerged from Congress was a disappointing compromise for Stoddert. There was not a word about ships of the line or marines. The president was directed to sell the smaller ships and to maintain the thirteen frigates, of which six were to "be kept in constant service," as the secre-tary had recommended. But the officer corps was to be cut to 9 captains, 36 lieutenants, and 150 midshipmen. The remainder would be discharged with four months' pay. Those retained, but not employed, would receive half-pay. Samuel Otis, a navalist who had proposed to the House a measure based upon Stoddert's recommendations, voted against the bill in its final form, while Albert Gallatin voted for it. Thomas Tingey, superintending the construction of seventy-fours at the navy yard in Washington, was the first captain to get a look at the act. He considered it a "paltry bill . . . fraught with imbecility and error." But the measure lay on Adams's desk. His alternatives were to leave the future of the navy to his successors, or to sign the bill and insure by Congressional act that a naval force be maintained and employed. The president, never a proponent of a battleship navy in any case, signed the Peace Establishment Act on 3 March.[67]

Jefferson's inauguration was the next day. Stoddert had tendered his resignation on 18 February, enclosing the letter in one sent to fellow Marylander Robert Smith, whom Stoddert expected would succeed him. But Jefferson had other ideas, although his nominees—Robert L. Livingston, Samuel Smith (Robert's more capable brother), John Langdon, and William Jones—showed little interest in administering a service whose future seemed by no means secure. Jefferson remarked in jest that he would have to advertise for a secretary, and not until 15 July did he finally settle on a willing candidate—Robert Smith.[68]

Jefferson requested that Stoddert remain at the Navy Department until a replacement could be found. Stoddert agreed although he hoped to quit his office by the middle of March. Having known Jefferson since the early 1790s and the first transactions relative to the District of Columbia, Stoddert, as yet, held no personal animosity towards the new president. That would change towards the end of Jefferson's second term when the two men, who until that time had maintained a correspondence, broke irrevocably over the embargo policy. Jefferson considered Stoddert politically moderate and competent, much like his fellow officer Stephen Dexter who also was asked to remain in the cabinet. Both Dexter, whose political views had earned him the nickname "Ambi," and Stoddert were invited to the post-inaugural gala held in Alexandria on 14 March, but the navy secretary chose not to attend, passing up an evening of entertainment at the side of old friend James Wilkinson.[69]

Despite their personal harmony, Stoddert quickly grew frustrated serving a new president. Health and finances continued to distract him, but most importantly, he found himself an executive officer with no orders to execute. Should the ships still on station in the Caribbean be recalled? Should the *Connecticut,* outfitted for a cruise to Batavia, be sent? Should the small vessels in port be sold off? Which of the frigates were to be kept in service and which laid up in ordinary? Should construction continue on the seventy-fours? And which of the officers were to be discharged?[70]

On 21 March, still without direction, Stoddert met with Levi Lincoln, Jefferson's attorney general and acting secretary of state. It was an acrimonious encounter. Stoddert had remained at his post wishing to accom-modate the new administration, but he had been denied free communication with the president and accordingly failed to understand his "system." As a result, "everything in the Navy Dept. stood still." Stoddert recommended "that until a new secy could assume the duties of the Dept. it would be a better arrangement . . . for Mr. Lincoln or Mr. [Henry] Dearborn [secretary of war], to be charged with the duties. . . ." Stoddert assured Lincoln that chief clerk Colonel Thomas "was well acquainted with the whole business of the office—& that Mr. Stoddert would at all times be ready cheerfully to give any information in his power to either of these gentlemen. . . ." He wished to end his official career the next day, but would not insist upon it.[71]

Two days later, Stoddert met with Lincoln again. The president had agreed with the secretary of the navy that the *Herald*, outfitted and prepared for sea, should sail for the West Indies to recall the men of war still on station. The cruise to Batavia was canceled. As for the dispositions of the ships, as they returned to port the smaller vessels were to be sold off, but no decisions had been made relative to the frigates.[72]

Stoddert remained determined to resign. Lieutenant Colonel William Ward Burrows, commandant of the Marine Corps, who met with the secretary on the 23rd noted that "nothing will induce him to stay beyond the end of the month." Jefferson now had to act, for he intended to leave Washington himself on 1 April for Monticello. He met with Samuel Smith and convinced him to take over responsibility for the department under the authority of Dearborn as acting secretary of the navy. Stoddert learned of the arrangement on the 30th. The next day, a Tuesday, he took leave of his staff and rode to his Georgetown home at last a private individual, his service as secretary of the navy at an end after thirty-four months. The orders for Lieutenant Charles C. Russell, commander of the *Herald*, had already reached Boston. The ship sailed on 4 April for the Caribbean with Stoddert's final operational instructions. Commodores John Barry and Silas Talbot were to return to the United States with their squadrons. The Quasi-War had come to an end.[73]

12

CONCLUSIONS

———

Contemplating his return to private life, Benjamin Stoddert wrote not of victory, but of "peace being happily restored between the United States & the French nation. . . ." The undeclared naval war had been the first test of the reborn American navy, a jury-rigged exercise conducted under difficult circumstances. There had been no Aboukir Bays, no Camperdowns, no Cape St. Vincents, no epic victories to herald the end of the war. But the struggle had been waged to effect off the American coast and in the Caribbean. The United States Navy had proven itself a useful instrument of national policy, a hobbyhorse that John Adams rode against the French.[1]

They had sought to use the *guerre de course* to demonstrate to the Americans that French hostility could be more costly than English. Adams and the Congress had responded to force with force to check the ravages of the corsairs while maintaining the neutrality of the nation. Having chastised Europe's preeminent naval power on land during the Revolution, the Americans now determined to do the same on the seas to the world's foremost land power. In Paris the Directors were quick to recognize the failings of their policies. When reports reached France in July 1798 of America's decision to fight, the reversal began. But primitive trans-Atlantic communications, administrative anarchy in the Antilles, and coups that left French officialdom in flux kept an accord two years distant. General Bonaparte, who became first consul in November 1799, understood power. He recognized the wisdom of seeking reconciliation with an armed United States—a greater danger as an enemy and of greater potential as an ally, than an unarmed republic. The Convention of Mortefontaine symbolized a new French policy towards neutrals. Napoleon wished to isolate Britain and saw no purpose in policies that drove allies into her arms.[2]

By establishing a navy and deploying it operationally, Americans had achieved their aims by displaying national resolve. Adams wisely kept the

Conclusions

ends of both foreign and domestic policies limited, neither plunging the country into a full-scale declared war with France, nor yielding to foreign and domestic advocates of a British alliance. The navy was the president's chosen weapon, wielded to serve the interests of the state.

But how well had that force been employed, and how well had its ships and men fought? The final section of chapter 6 examined the administrative and operational shortcomings of the navy evident during the first year of the war. In combination, these problems had caused the fiasco of mid-1799 when only a half-dozen men-of-war remained in the Caribbean in June, after twenty-two had cruised as late as February. But by the end of the year, eighteen American warships were back in the West Indies and during 1800 the number remained between fourteen and twenty-three. These figures indicate administrative improvement and the development of a capacity to conduct sustained operations overseas.

Yet American losses to French corsairs increased significantly during 1800, prompting howls from the merchants directed at Congress and the executive. Stoddert considered the complaints based on expectations of the navy that were too sanguine. He wrote Fitzsimons:

> I know I have discharged my duty to the public with zeal and diligence, and not without judgment, tho I cannot accomplish with less than forty vessels, twenty times as much as the British nation can do with twenty times as many—They cannot with all their force give complete protection in their own channel to their merchant vessels, nor should it be expected that there would not be captures of American vessels in the West Indies, and between the islands and our own coasts. . . .

But most of the merchants, many of whom had owned or sailed in privateers of their own two decades earlier, understood the limits of naval power. Despite the rise in captures, confidence in the navy remained high and the insurance rates within the 10 to 15 percent range to which they had fallen by early 1799.[3]

The upsurge in privateering activity from Guadeloupe during 1800 was caused not by any failure of the part of the American navy, but by the aggressiveness of the new agents sent from France at the end of 1799 and the continued weakening of Great Britain's Leeward Islands command to reinforce the Jamaica station. The British, too, struggled to meet the new onslaught in the Lesser Antilles. Their men-of-war, which had captured ten corsairs in 1799, took nineteen in 1800. But the Royal Navy was too weak to contain the French. Two separate multi-ship flotillas carrying 500 and 1,000 men respectively managed to sail the 514 miles from Guadeloupe to Curaçao, and then return virtually unscathed after being repulsed only with the assistance of two American ships of war. In March 1801, the governor of St. Kitts, fearful of a French expedition against the island, turned to Commodore John Barry for assistance. The last full year and the seventh of the war in the Caribbean had been a difficult one, not only for the United States. In mid-January 1801, Truxtun observed to Stoddert:

> I must not omit to mention here, at the winding up of my West India expeditions, the ravages, that the present European war has occasioned in these distant regions, where distress is depicted in every countenance, and where the decline of commerce cannot be more evident, than by the number of failures, and the few neutrals and American merchantmen, met at sea, in comparison to what there was two years ago. The crops however are very flattering this year to the planters, but the high freights and premiums of insurance, added to the low prices for their produce in Europe, and the high price of provision and Negro clothing &c here, leaves but small proceeds after the yearly sales are closed, &c of course a few years more of war, must be ruinous to many of them, thus all descriptions of people suffer, except such as have nought to lose.

As the Franco-American war came to its end, the European belligerents moved towards peace, if only temporary, themselves.[4]

Rather than failing in the face of the French resurgence, Stoddert's commanders excelled. By any measure the Americans carried more than their share of the struggle in the islands. Like the British, the American navy increased its haul of French corsairs. The 58 privateers taken in 1800 were more than double the 26 captured in 1799. And the Americans owed their success not to greater numbers, but to greater activity. Their average strength in 1799 had been 15, and in the following year only 3 more. Thus, during the two full years of war—1799 and 1800—during which the United States Navy operated in the Caribbean, 86 French privateers were captured by a force that averaged 16 ships, each of the Americans accounting for 5.37 corsairs. Over the same 24 months, the Royal Navy took 29 privateers with a force that averaged 80 ships, each British vessel accounting for .36 corsairs. Statistically, the average American man-of-war was fifteen times as effective as its Royal Navy counterpart.[5]

In weighing such disparate figures, a variety of factors that inhibited British effectiveness must be considered. The Royal Navy had broader responsibilities than the American. The British had to protect their islands and bases from attack. They had to operate not only against the French, but also against the Spanish and Dutch. And they constantly had to search American and other neutral merchantmen to insure that contraband did not find its way into enemy ports. The United States Navy was free from

236

Conclusions

such concerns and able to concentrate its efforts against the French cruisers and privateers. In 1798, when the Royal Navy had focused its West Indian forces on Guadeloupe, rather than Hispaniola, eighty corsairs had been captured. British warships were capable of chasing down privateers when deployed for that purpose.[6]

Nevertheless, the American tally of prizes bears so favorable a comparison, that the effectiveness of the United States Navy's operations can not be questioned. This is not to assert that ship for ship the Americans were superior to the British, but that Stoddert had deployed his warships where they were needed to meet the challenge posed by the French *guerre de course,* and that his commanders and crews had responded. The secretary had trusted to their personal skill and bravery in solo cruising to make up for a deficiency of numbers. He had not been disappointed. Despite the presence of French frigates and corvettes, and several large, well-armed corsairs, the United States Navy had fought two and one-half years in the West Indies losing only a single vessel to the enemy.[7]

* * *

Despite the successes of the Quasi-War, several problems were, or should have been, apparent. The one-year enlistment continually disrupted operations throughout the war and made cruises to Asia impractical. Ships bound for the Caribbean or Mediterranean could expect to spend no more than nine months on station. Stoddert pointed out the handicaps imposed by the limitation to Jefferson, and the new administration, contemplating operations in the Mediterranean against the Barbary states, had enlistments extended to two years when the Republican Congress at last convened in early 1802.[8]

Stoddert was also aware of deficiencies in the American naval officer corps. For every Talbot and Truxtun, there was a Barry and Nicholson. Surprisingly, when he drew up his recommendations for Congress in January 1801, Stoddert passed up an excellent opportunity to prune the corps and suggested that all the officers holding commissions and warrants be retained. The half-pay provision would have allowed a secretary to employ those he considered best suited, but nevertheless would have kept scores of mediocrities on the payroll. Stoddert once more had balked at taking any drastic action against his officers. To them he felt loyalty, and perhaps as an aging, wounded veteran himself, he believed that the older men deserved at least half-pay from the country to which they had devoted much of their adult lives. It fell to Congress to cut the corps, and Stoddert, who considered the number to be retained too small (especially for captains), wrote Murray that "the discrimination therefore will be a most painful duty—fortunately for my feeling it will not fall on me."[9]

But there is evidence that Stoddert's views influenced some early decisions regarding retention and dismissal. He had proffered his advice to the new administration, and Samuel Smith availed himself of the offer. While both Jefferson and Smith were determined to reduce the naval establishment, they did not intend to implement immediately all the provisions of the Peace Establishment Act. Midshipmen and lieutenants would be reduced to 150 and 36 respectively. But while the rank of master commandant had been eliminated by Congress, Smith chose to keep a pair of their number to serve as flag captains in the two squadrons into which the six cruising frigates were to be divided. This was a device first used by Stoddert who sent Cyrus Talbot to serve with Barry in the *United States.* One of Stoddert's final acts as secretary of the navy had been to write Talbot and recommend that he not resign, even if that meant accepting a reduction in rank to lieutenant. "I think your country will one day reap great advantages from your services," Stoddert wrote, "if you consent to this inform Genl. Smith. . . ." The latter bettered Stoddert, offering to retain Talbot in his rank as master commandant and flag captain to the first squadron to be sent to the Mediterranean. Nor were the captains reduced to nine as required by law. The only one dismissed outright was Christopher Raymond Perry on 3 April. The former commander of the *General Greene* frigate had never been recalled to service at the end of his ninety-day suspension by Stoddert. And Samuel Nicholson, whose political friends and family now held power in the capital and lobbied on his behalf, remained ashore where Stoddert had sent him in 1799.[10]

The partisan scythe that swept through the federal bureaucracy after 4 March 1801 spared the naval officer corps. Decisions regarding the retention or dismissal of lieutenants and midshipmen were based on the recommendations of their commanders, who were, of course, mostly Federalists. The most prominent Federalist captain to leave the navy in 1801, Silas Talbot, resigned after being retained. The first Mediterranean command was offered to Truxtun, all of whose lieutenants and midshipmen were retained. The elder Decatur in the *Philadelphia,* and Preble in the *Essex,* both Stoddert favorites, were to accompany the commodore's *President* to North Africa. And Smith ordered the schooner *Enterprize* along as well. Her commander was Lieutenant Andrew Sterett, a former Truxtan lieutenant and the man who had run through Neal Harvey during the engagement between the *Constellation* and *l'Insurgente,* an act for which the Republican press had vilified him. Stoddert would have had few disagreements with Smith's decisions on dismissal, and perhaps this is the best proof of the former secretary's influence. He met with Smith at least once between 3 and 10 April, and kept in touch with Tingey at the Washington navy yard. And most importantly, the corporate memory of the Navy

Conclusions

Department staff, on which any new secretary would have to rely, re-flected Stoddert's thinking. In May when questioned about the professional future of Captain Hugh G. Campbell, Smith responded favorably citing the "high opinion entertained in this department. . . ."[11]

* * *

One of the few weaknesses not only overlooked, but also exacerbated by Stoddert, was the navy's need for small, fast vessels. He allowed his vision of the service's future to obscure more immediate necessities. Stoddert's advocacy of a battleship squadron marks him as one of America's foremost early navalists. But all navies need a balance of ship types, and while the War of 1812 would demonstrate that the United States could have made good use of six or twelve ships of the line, the Barbary Wars would demonstrate that the nation needed schooners. Stoddert, aware of the impending crisis in the Mediterranean, nevertheless recommended and set in motion the sale of the few small ships that had performed well during the war, persisting in his efforts to channel the savings into continued work on the seventy-fours despite the politics of the Jefferson administration.[12]

Silas Talbot's difficulties as commodore at Cap François had made clear the limitations of the large frigates. Swift and strong, the *Constitution* was powerless against corsairs sheltering in shallows. The converted mer-chantmen, while they drew less water, were too slow. The fast schooners and brigs built to carry guns, such as the *Experiment, Enterprize,* and *Eagle,* were the most successful of the American ships, accounting for twenty-five of the captures made during the war. But such vessels were few, and Talbot, with Maley's *Experiment* needed off the south coast of Hispaniola, had been forced to rely upon the impressed prizes *l'Amphi-theatre* and *Sally* to conduct his coastal attacks.

Because of Congressional acts restricting operations to the high seas, the inability of the navy's large ships to engage the enemy near or on the shore was not critically important. Talbot's cutting-out sorties were extralegal at best. But the problems he faced off the northern coast of St. Domingo most resembled those the Americans would confront off the North African littoral during the Barbary Wars. Commodores were not long in the Mediterranean than they began to lament the imbalance in their com-mands. Once again the Navy Department was forced to improvise, leaving the burned wreck of the *Philadelphia* in the harbor at Tripoli, a testament to the dangers of working fifth-rates inshore.

Ironically, in the very navalism that so often gains Stoddert praise, lay the roots of his most serious misjudgments. Lobbying for seventy-fours in the first months of 1799 distracted him from the task at hand: his West Indian commodores needed coordination if their returns to the United

States were to be timely and orderly. Stoddert sent his instructions south too late. His October 1799 recommendation to Adams that the navy needed no more small vessels, was based on a fear that funding for the addition of such ships would come at the expense of the battleship program. While the recommendation appeared justifiable at the time, Stoddert was gambling on the future course of the war. The resurgence of the French *guerre de course* in 1800 taxed the capacity of the squadron in the Lesser Antilles. Stoddert worked to build up the frigate strength at St. Kitts, but Commodore Truxtun was calling for schooners, not fifth-rates.

*   *   *

But men are meant to err, and the organizations to which they give shape can be nothing but imperfect. Even the vaunted Royal Navy's operations were not always successful, nor were all of her admirals Nelsons. By 1801 the United States Navy was a small, fledging, but respectable force. Benjamin Stoddert had proven himself an able administrator, forging a new navy in the midst of war. He successfully directed sustained operations far from American ports in support of the government's policies and the commercial community. His commodores had mostly commanded well. His captains had mostly fought well. His ships had mostly proven their worth. The three forty-fours were the most powerful frigates afloat, although they would have to wait a dozen years to assert their superiority. The men who would command those ships in the War of 1812 all began their naval careers during the Quasi-War. Between 1798 and 1801 the United States Navy had scored a double victory, defeating both the French enemy and the memory of the service's own Continental precursor. The navy had created for itself a new reality. Its successes had displaced the disappointments of the Continental Navy in the popular and political mind. Those who hoped in 1801 that the government would shortly be selling off once again its last frigate, as it had in 1785, were chapfallen. The "anti-navy" Jeffersonians took power facing another crisis in the Mediterranean. They expected the navy, albeit in reduced form, to serve their policies as competently as it had their predecessor's. The United States Navy's frigates were soon on their way, not to the auction block, but to the Barbary coast.

APPENDIX A

American and British Naval Deployments,
January 1798–December 1800

American deployments have been matched to the Royal Navy's stations (North America here combined with Newfoundland). "West Indies" includes ships in columns 2 and 3. For the Royal Navy "Total" equals the sum of columns 1 through 3. For the Americans the difference between "Total" and the sum of columns 1 through 3 represents ships refitting or deployed elsewhere than off the American coast or in the Caribbean.

Year	North America	Jamaica	Leeward Islands	West Indies	Total
1798	1	2	3	4	5
	RN/USN	RN/USN	RN/USN	RN/USN	RN/USN
JAN	20/0	23/0	59/0	82/0	102/0
FEB	17/0	24/0	67/0	91/0	108/0
MAR	17/0	23/0	67/0	90/0	107/0
APR	16/0	22/0	68/0	90/0	106/0
MAY	20/2	22/0	71/0	93/0	113/2
JUN	22/3	20/0	70/0	90/0	112/3
JUL	26/3	20/0	71/2	91/2	116/5
AUG	20/4	26/2	67/2	93/4	113/9
SEP	22/5	30/2	60/2	90/4	112/11
OCT	19/9	26/0	55/0	81/0	100/15
NOV	19/11	31/1	45/3	76/4	95/16
DEC	15/6	31/4	49/10	80/14	95/21

American and British Naval Deployments

Year	North America	Jamaica	Leeward Islands	West Indies	Total
1799	1	2	3	4	5
	RN/USN	RN/USN	RN/USN	RN/USN	RN/USN
JAN	15/0	35/6	46/13	81/19	96/22
FEB	14/0	32/6	48/16	80/22	94/22
MAR	13/0	35/5	47/16	82/21	95/22
APR	16/0	37/5	47/14	84/19	100/22
MAY	17/0	35/1	52/7	87/8	104/22
JUN	21/1	37/1	52/5	89/6	110/19
JUL	22/1	38/2	50/6	88/8	110/20
AUG	21/3	37/3	46/7	83/10	104/20
SEP	21/2	42/7	35/10	77/17	98/24
OCT	21/2	43/7	32/7	75/14	96/25
NOV	22/2	42/6	31/10	73/16	95/25
DEC	19/1	41/7	36/11	77/18	96/26
1800					
JAN	15/0	40/8	35/10	75/18	90/28
FEB	—/0	—/10	—/13	—/23	—/29
MAR	15/0	39/10	40/10	79/20	94/30
APR	15/0	42/9	36/10	78/19	93/30
MAY	16/0	42/6	37/12	79/18	95/31
JUN	16/1	43/8	39/11	82/19	98/32
JUL	20/2	45/9	38/13	83/22	103/32
AUG	22/2	42/7	46/9	88/16	110/32
SEP	18/4	49/8	36/8	85/16	103/32
OCT	16/1	44/7	34/9	78/16	94/30
NOV	17/0	42/4	33/10	75/14	92/30
DEC	14/0	40/5	39/9	79/14	93/31

APPENDIX B

The Reports of Captains Isaac Phillips and John Loring[1]

The documents are reproduced here for two reasons: first, to make them as accessible as the other important papers relative to the Quasi-War compiled by the Navy Department during the 1930s under the direction of Dudley W. Knox; and second, to demonstrate conclusively that Phillips's 1825 account of the Havana incident is, with regard to the major points in dispute, a fabrication. In that work, written in the belief that his report had been consumed by the fires that raged through the Washington Navy Yard in 1814, Phillips denied having ordered the convoy to halt, stated that his crew had been mustered before his return from the *Carnatic,* and claimed to have struck his colors. Philips literally took an oath, "on the Holy Evangels of Almighty God," that Stoddert's charges were false. But Phillips's entire defense is contradicted in his own, and Loring's reports.[2]

The Honble. Benjamin Stoddert Esquire

Sir,

I herewith send you a historical account of events which took place on the 17th November 1798 at sea within two and six leagues distance from—Havana—between Commodore John Loring commander of his Britannic Majesty's ship the *Carnatic,* with four other British men of war as follows—the *Queen* 98, the *Thunderer* 74, the *Maidstone* 32, and the *Greyhound* 36 guns, under his command, and Isaac Phillips commander of the United States ship *Baltimore.*

242

Having under my convoy nine sail of American merchantmen from
Charleston bound to Havanna, on the day of the above date at 8. A.M. I
descried five sail of Ships bearing about N.W. and found they were
standing close upon a wind to the southward and eastward, with Spanish
colours flying, in order to cut me off together with my convoy, from
entering the Port of Havana, which bore S.W. from me about 4 leagues
distance, at about half past 8 A.M. I discovered the said ships to have
English colours flying, and the Frigate *Maidstone* fired a Gun to leeward,
which I soon answered in the same way, having my colours flying, and
about fifteen minutes after, there was another gun fired to leeward from
the Ship *Carnatic,* who had a broad red Pendant flying at her main Top
gallant Mast Head. I then had no doubt, but that it was a British Squadron, and as I did not wish to enter the Port of Havanna, I wore ship and
stood towards the Frigate *Maidstone,* the nighest to me, and in about ten
minutes that Frigate hove about and stood off the same length of time, then
hove about and stood in.—I at this time observing the Commodore laying
too, made the best of my way to speak him, which I did in about three
quarters of an hour.—he then ordered me from his Cabin windows to hoist
the signal for the Convoy to heave too, which I immediately obeyed, and at
the same moment observed the Frigate *Maidstone* to fire a shot a head of
the ship *Eliza,* and another a head of the Brig *Norfolk,* who together with
the Brig *Friendship,* hauled their wind towards the British Fleet.—At this
moment Commodore Loring sent his boat on board the *Baltimore,* with two
officers, one of which, I took to be a marine officer, the other a large
unpolished man, with coat and trousers on, which last informed, that the
Commodore wanted to speak with me, and that I might go in their boat,
which I accordingly did, and when I went along side his ship, the side was
manned with two men. Captain Loring received, and treated me politely
while on board his ship (except that he told me he should impress my
men).—The following is the conversation as nigh as I can recollect that
passed between Captain Loring, and myself respecting the impressment of
my men; this is a subject which Captain Loring did not broach to me, but a
few moments before I left his ship—He first asked me how many men I
had. I told him about one hundred & fifty; he said that was a great number
for my ship; he then asked me, what countrymen they were, I told him I
believed they were of all nations; he then asked me, if I had any Englishmen on board I told him I did not know them to be Englishmen, but
that they might be; he then asked me if they had any protections, I told him
I did not know, but that I believed not, and that I thought private
protections on board a Public Ship were not necessary; as I considered our
Flag, a sufficient protection to our men; he then said, that I misconceived
the matter, and that he should take all the men that appeared to him to be

Englishmen.—I then told him it was a difficult matter to say who were, and who were not Englishmen, as the men of the two nations were very much alike, and further asked him suppose he should find fifty or an hundred men, who appeared to him to be Englishmen, whether he should take them. his answer was in the affirmative, and that he would give me all the Americans he had in his ship, and the other ships in his Fleet in exchange.—I then asked him how many American seamen he had, he told me he thought he had four on board his ship, and that there were about six more, on board his Fleet. I then told him, that if he took so many of my men, as to distress my ship, that I thought I should be under the disagreeable necessity of abandoning my ship to him, at which he smiled.—I further observed to him that our Navy was in its infant state, and a transaction of this kind would have a tendency to destroy it, and defeat the objects of our Government in the protection of the commerce of the United States.—all this he said he could not help, and that his Ship was distressed for men, and that he must have them, at which reply I must confess I did not feel at my ease, which I supposed Captain Loring discovered, and kindly asked me whether I would dine with him, or go on board the *Baltimore,* and from a disposition to relieve my feelings I chose the latter; he then ordered his boat manned and waited on me to the Gangway, where I was accosted by some unfortunate Americans, who with protections in their hands said they were Americans, and pushed one of them into my hands, which out of delicacy to Captain Loring I again returned to him without reading it or speaking to the man.—I then went in the Boat and proceeded on board the *Baltimore,* whom I found my officers, who are worthy the name considered as mere Cyphers, and had no command of the Ship in my absence, owing to the officers of the *Carnatic* taking the command on themselves, and even after I was on the quarter deck of the *Baltimore,* a Mr. Smith, the fifth Lieutenant of the *Carnatic* came on board with a verbal message from Captain Loring, to take all the men who had not protections, and stood in my Lee gangway ordering the maneuvres of the ship. This Mr. Smith is the man whom I have already mentioned as having trousers on, when I have not an officer who walks my quarter deck in any such habit; Mr. Wright the second Lieutenant of the *Carnatic* at this time requested I would have all hands called, and give him a list of their names, which I accordingly did, he then commenced calling their names without paying any more respect to the officers than the common sailors, asking them all except my first officers, for their protections, and many of my petty officers were ordered into the Boat, and sent on board Commodore Loring, the officers and men sent on board his Ship was to the number of fifty five; among which was my Cabin Steward, a native of Maryland, and had been a resident of Annapolis; this man had the Keys of my liquors, and when my dinner was on the table, I had nothing to drink but water.—At this time I had two gentlemen Mr. Lewis Trazvant, and Mr. Timmons both of Charleston, South Carolina on board my ship, the Brig *Norfolk* in which they were passengers, was considered as captured, and I sent my boat for them to come on board the *Baltimore;*—in order to render their situation more comfortable as Mr. Trazvant was an invalid,—but instead of its having that effect, I believe it had a different one, seeing me treated with so much disrespect, and my flag so much dishonored. Both of those Gentlemen I believe, have wrote to their friends on this disagreeable subject.—As dinner was now on the Table, and I had nothing to give those Gentlemen but water, I set down, and wrote Commodore Loring the following note.—

Commodore Loring
Sir, ·
   You have taken my Cabin Steward who had got the key of my closet where my wine is, and I am now going to dinner, I should be glad to drink a glass of wine if you please.

Your humble svt.
Isaac Phillips

I sent the letter by my first Lieutenant William Speak,[3] who gave it to Captain Loring, and after he read it, he made use of this language "that it was a damned insulting Letter."—I am very sorry that I am so situated, in order to do myself justice, as that it becomes necessary for my pen to be the medium through which such language is to be conveyed.—Mr. Speak then returned on board the *Baltimore,* and in a short time after, there came an officer from Captain Loring requesting I would come, or send an officer on board his ship, to point out such as were and such as were not Englishmen, among the men which he had taken out of the *Baltimore.*—My reply to his officer was as follows. Sir, I generally make it a practice to speak the truth, and if I were to go on board your ship, and say such men were Englishmen, and such were not, I might expose myself to being charged with telling untruths,—as such is the situation, I decline going myself, or sending my officers.—In about one hour after this Commodore Loring sent back fifty of the men he had taken from the *Baltimore,* with a verbal requisition by one of his officers that I should pay up the balance of the wages due the five men, he thought proper to detain, and that if I had not the money, a bill on some of my friends, or some respectable gentleman in Charleston would answer the purpose.—I then told Mr. Wright that I had not any money, but that I would write the Commodore on the subject which I did as follows.

Appendix B

Commodore Loring
Sir,
   I wish to know whether you make a demand of the wages due the
men, you have thought proper to take from me, as the Government of
the United States makes no provisions for any such occurrence.

> I remain with respect
> Your most humble servant
> Isaac Phillips

United States Ship
Baltimore 17 Novemr. 1798

At the time of writing this letter a Midshipman or cockswain came from
the *Thunderer* and imposed 10, or 11, Spanish prisoners on board the
Baltimore without my consent, or any message whatever.—
   In a short time after this there came the second Lieutenant (Mr Ross) of
the *Thunderer,* on board the *Baltimore* with a verbal order from Captain
Loring to let him have three Englishmen that were on board the *Baltimore,*
and I would observe that Mr Ross behaved himself the most becoming on
this business of any person with whom I had to do;—he requested, I would
point out to him three men of that discription: I told him, I could do no
such thing, and observed that my men were subject to his examination, and
that if he chose to take any number, I should not oppose it, but requested
he would not consider it as a voluntary surrender of my men; he then said,
as that was the situation he should not take any, but that he would again
go on board the Commodore, which he did, but did not again return on
board the *Baltimore.*—By this time night was coming on, and the wind
blowing fresh, I wished to know whether I was to be dismissed, or
detained, and I sent Mr Speake (my first Lieutenant) on board Commodore
Loring, for information on that point. Captain Loring told Mr Speake that
I was at liberty to do as I thought proper, but that he should send me a
letter by his Boat, which he did and was as follows.—

> *Carnatic* at Sea
> Novemr. 17th 1798

Sir
   Being informed by the men, whom I have already on board (taken
out of the American States Ship *Baltimore*) *you command,* that there
are four more seamen on board, subjects of Great Britain; I do hereby
demand them as such, and every other British subject you may have
on board the Ship you command. From the conversation I had with
you this morning on board his Majesty's Ship I have the honor to
command, I have every reason to suppose, there are many still remaining, and from the two very extraordinary notes received from you, I

am led to suppose, it is your wish to detain them.—I shall therefore lay your conduct before the Commander in chief in order that it may be represented to the Executive Government of the United States of America, particularly as I have offered you a very fair exchange of American seamen, if any were on board the Squadron under my command.—

> I am Sir
> Your humble servant
> Jno. Loring

To
Capt. Isaac Phillips,
American States ship *Baltimore*
This letter was brought by one of the Lieutenants of the *Carnatic,* and by whom I returned the following answer.—

> United States Ship *Baltimore*
> 17 Novemr. 1798

Sir,
    Your letter of this evening I have received, and note the contents.— With respect to the four men you mention, I have now on board my ship, I have to observe that I do not know them as British subjects, and am at a loss to know what four men you allude to, neither can I as an officer of the United States give up my men voluntarily,—but if you send an officer to take them I shall not oppose it.—With respect to my conduct this day, I think I can justify it, and shall fully make it known to the Government of the United States.—

> I remain with sentiments of esteem
> Your humble servant
> Isaac Phillips

Commodore Loring
Commander of his Majesty's
ship *Carnatic*
    Norfolk 28th December 1798

    The preceeding is an exact statement of the occurrences which took place between Commodore Jno. Loring and myself.

> Isaac Phillips

Appendix B

Carnatic, Port Royal Harbour
20th. Febry 1799

Sir,

In reply to your Letter under date the 19th. Instant, enclosing a Copy of a Letter of complaint against me from Timothy Pickering Esqr. Secretary of State to the United States addressed to Robert Liston Esqr. Envoy Extraordinary and Minister Plenipotentiary from the said United States to the Court of Great Britain,[4] I have to acquaint you with the Circumstances of the transaction, which, it seems, has given rise to that complaint; and I hope and trust I shall make it fully appear that my inclination as well as my duty lead me to conduct myself as becoming the Character of a British Naval Officer.

On the 16th. of November last, cruizing off the Havana in the Ship I command together with the *Queen, Thunderer, Maidstone* and *Greyhound,* we descried a fleet of nine Sail standing along shore endeavouring to gain that Port, and accordingly gave chace to them. Upon our approach, we perceived them to be under charge of an armed Vessel, which seemed to keep between them and us, and so far from having an inclination to come towards us, when her Captain saw we were British Ships of War (as stated in the Complaint) the *Maidstone* fired two Shot at her, and the *Carnatic* two more before she would put her head towards us. This conduct gave me just cause to suspect they were not Americans, but Spaniards under false Colours: or that, if they were Americans, they were laden with Naval or Military Stores, contrary to the Treaty subsisting between the British Court and the American States. I therefore made the *Maidstone'*s signal to examine the Strangers; and Captain Donnelly informed me he hailed the armed Ship and requested she would go to the *Carnatic.* In the mean time the rest of the Convoy were using every effort to gain the Port of the Havana, and five of them actually got in: and as it appears from the information of Captain Whyte[5] late of His Majesty's Sloop *Musquito,* who was a Prisoner there, my Suspicions were fully justified; as he saw them land Naval stores of every description and the Master of one of them told him (I make use of his own expression) "If we escape the vigilance of your Cruizers, the profits of two Voyages with Naval Stores will repay the capture of the third; therefore no *catchee* no *havee.*" The other three Vessels were cut off by the *Maidstone* and so delicate were we in searching them that we permitted two to go away, and Captain Whyte affirms that they landed a large quantity of Naval stores and made their boast that they outwitted our Squadron. The other Vessel was detained and brought into this Port, where a quantity of Canvas was found on board her and accordingly condemned by the Court of Vice Admiralty, and an appeal is made for the whole of the Cargo and Hull.

So far I hope, Sir, I have incontrovertibly justified myself for having stopped and examined those Vessels at the mouth of an Enemy's Port. I shall now proceed to relate my conduct towards the armed ship and to justify my doubts whether she was under the Public Flag of the United States or not. When she approached us, I thought it a compliment, in the event of her being an American Man of War, to send my own boat to her; and her Captain (Phillips) came on board the *Carnatic*. It became a delicate question with me to know whether she was so or not, more especially as we well know from various instances the American Merchant Ships armed themselves and convoyed others with Naval stores, &c. to the Enemy's ports: and as she had more the appearance of an armed Merchant Ship, and as Captain Phillips himself acknowledged she really had been a Merchant Ship before, so far was I justified in asking if he had a Commission. His answer was that he had *not,* but that he had an Order from the American Secretary of War to see those Vessels in safety to the Havana. I then asked him if he had any British Seamen on board his Ship: he said he *had.* I then told him that the Squadron had some Americans who expressed a wish to return to their own Service and that I was not only well inclined to give them up in exchange for the British Seamen in his Ship; but that I had pledged my word of honor to Mr. Talbot the American Commissioner appointed to inspect their Seamen in the English Service that I would, if I met any Vessels of that Nation at Sea, exchange every American that I had for an equal number of British Seamen. To this fair proposition he gave me an evasive negative answer; but I, however, kept up an amicable conversation with him, still saying it was my duty to obtain the British Seamen he acknowledged he had on board his Ship. So far from seeming offended & suffering insult and abuse (as mentioned in a Baltimore paper) he took some refreshment and returned to his Ship. I then sent an Officer to get such British Seamen as were on board the *Baltimore;* in the execution of which duty it was scarcely unavoidable that, as his Officers would hold no communication with mine, some Americans might have been sent with them. But I was determined that no improper transaction should take place; and therefore sent my first Lieutenant (the greatest mark of respect I could offer) to request that he would either come or send and point out such as were Americans and I would instantly deliver them back. To that message he returned an answer, "That he would not comply with my request." A written correspondence then ensued, of which the enclosed Letters No. 1, 2, 3 & 4 are Copies:[6] the result of which was finding he would neither lead nor drive, my duty compelled me, contrary to my inclination, to find out those who were British. And it is a positive fact which can be proved, as they are now alive and on board the Ship I command that the Boatswain, about whom the Complaint has been alledged, was born in the County of Down in Ireland, and that three others also were Irish, and another entered.

Appendix B

No Officer in His Majesty's Navy hath a greater respect for the observance of proper conduct towards the Friends or Allies of the British Nation, and more particularly the United States, than I have; and I am satisfied the Government of that Country would not knowingly protect the Ships of its Merchants while carrying on an unlawful Trade contrary to the Treaties subsisting between the two Countries and to the Law of Nations. Neither do I think it would allow of British Subjects being detained in its Ships of War. But if, in the course of things, their executive Officers will transgress the rules of propriety, and unnecessarily complain when the fault really lies at their own Door, I humbly conceive that that complaint should have been thoroughly sifted before it came officially to you. Far be it from me to complain of their conduct. I only mention it in my own justification of a charge, than which no Man living would be more averse to subject himself to than myself. If required, the Captains of the respective Ships under my Command are willing to attest to the truth of the above representation; and I am perfectly willing, nay I should rejoice if a Court Martial were ordered for the purpose of convincing the World that my conduct was proper in every respect.

> I have the honor to be
> Sir,
> Your most obedient
> and very humble Servant,
> (Sign'd) Jno. Loring
> A Copy
> H Parker

Sir Hyde Parker Knt.
Vice Admiral of the Red,
Commander in Chief,
&c.&c.&c.

ABBREVIATIONS

Adm.	Admiralty
ASP	*American State Papers*
BW	*Naval Documents Related to the United States Wars with the Barbary Powers*
DAB	*Dictionary of American Biography*
DLC	Library of Congress
DNA	National Archives
FO	Foreign Office
JCC	*Journals of the Continental Congress*
LCC	Letters of the Continental Congress
LCP	Library Company of Philadelphia
NDAR	*Naval Documents of the American Revolution*
NDL	Navy Department Library
NHi	New-York Historical Society
PHi	Historical Society of Pennsylvania
PRO	Public Record Office
QW	*Naval Documents Related to the Quasi-War with France*
RG	Record Group
SDA	State Department Archives

NOTES

Frontispiece

1. Benjamin Stoddert to John Templeman, 29 June 1798, Philadelphia Maritime Museum, Manuscript Collection, Benjamin Stoddert.

Preface

1. Gardner W. Allen, *Our Naval War with France* (Boston, 1909).
2. United States Navy Department, Office of Naval Records and Library, *Naval Documents Related to the Quasi-War with France: Naval Operations, February 1797–December 1801*, Dudley W. Knox, ed., 7 vols. (Washington, D.C., 1935–1938).

Introduction

1. Quoted in Robert Greenhalgh Albion and Jennie Barnes Pope, *Sea Lanes in Wartime: The American Experience, 1775–1945* (New York, 1942), p. 65.
2. Ben J. Wattenberg, ed., *The Statistical History of the United States from Colonial Times to the Present* (New York, 1976), pp. 750–51, 760–61.
3. United States Department of the Navy, Office of Naval Records and Library, *Naval Documents Related to the United States Wars with the Barbary Powers: Naval Operations, 1785–1807*, Dudley W. Knox, ed., 6 vols. (Washington, D.C., 1939–1944), I: 69–70; and Alfred Thayer Mahan, *The Influence of Sea Power upon the French Revolution and Empire*, 2 vols. (London, 1892; reprint ed., St. Clair Shores, Mich., 1970), II: 219–20, 228–29, 232. For the diplomacy of the 1790s see Carnegie Endowment for International Peace, *The Controversy over Neutral Rights between the United States and France, 1797–1800*, James Brown Scott, ed. (New York, 1917); Gerard H. Clarfield, *Timothy Pickering and American Diplomacy, 1795–1800* (Columbia, Mo. 1969); Alfred Hall Bowman, *The Struggle for Neutrality: Franco-American Diplomacy during the Federalist Era* (Knoxville, Tenn., 1974); Alexander DeConde, *Entangling Alliance: Politics and Diplomacy under George Washington* (Durham N.C. 1958); and DeConde's *The Quasi-War: The Politics and Diplomacy of the Undeclared War with France, 1797–1801* (New York, 1966); Felix Gilbert, *To the Farewell Address: Ideas of Early American Foreign Policy* (Princeton,

N.J., 1961); Charles S. Hyneman, *The First American Neutrality: A Study of the American Understanding of Neutral Obligations during the Years 1792–1815* (Urbana, Ill., 1914); James A. James, "French Opinion as a Factor in Preventing War between France and the United States, 1795–1800," *American Historical Review* 30 (October 1924): 44–55; E. Wilson Lyon, "The Franco-American Convention of 1800," *Journal of Modern History* 62 (September 1940): 305–33; and Lyon's "The Directory and the United States," *American Historical Review* 43 (April 1938): 514–32; and Bradford Perkins, *The First Rapprochement: England and the United States, 1795–1805* (Berkeley, Calif., 1967). For a French view of the diplomatic and maritime issues see Ulane Bonnel, *La France, les États-Unis et la guerre de course, 1797–1815* (Paris, 1961).

4. United States Congress, *American State Papers: Documents, Legislative and Executive, of the Congress of the United States . . . Selected and Edited under the Authority of Congress*, 38 vols. (Washington, 1832–1861), Class I, *Foreign Relations*, I: 577. See also DeConde, *Entangling Alliance*, pp. 457, 483; Bowman, *Struggle for Neutrality*, pp. 237–47; and Bonnel, *Guerre de course*, p. 51.

5. *ASP, Foreign Relations*, II: 30–31, 169–82.

6. Ibid., pp. 28–65.

7. Ibid., p. 182; *QW*, I: 7–9; *ASP, Foreign Relations*, II: 153–63. For a discussion of the affair see William Stinchcombe, *The XYZ Affair* (Westport Conn., 1980).

8. Wattenberg, *Statistical History*, pp. 750, 907; *ASP*, Class IV, *Commerce and Navigation*, I: 362–84; Albion and Pope, *Sealanes*, pp. 70, 83; William H. A. Carr, *Perils Named and Unnamed: The Story of the Insurance Company of North America* (New York, 1967), pp. 21–25; Harrold E. Gillingham, *Marine Insurance in Philadelphia, 1721–1800* (Philadelphia, 1933), pp. 100–2; Charles W. Goldsborough, *The United States Naval Chronicle* (Washington, D.C., 1824), pp. 108–10; Bonnel, *Guerre de course*, pp. 319–67; United States Congress, Senate, "The French Spoliation Claims," George A. King, Senate Document 451 (Washington, D.C., 1916), pp. 51–52; and *ASP*, Class VI, *Naval Affairs*, I: 67–69.

Chapter 1

1. Leonard D. White, *The Federalists: A Study in Administrative History* (New York, 1948), pp. 145–55.

2. William Bell Clark, *Gallant John Barry, 1745–1803: The Story of a Naval Hero of Two Wars* (New York, 1938), p. 394; Martin I. J. Griffin, *Commodore John Barry, "Father of the American Navy": The Record of His Services for Our Country* (Philadelphia, 1903), p. 336.

3. Alexander Hamilton, *The Papers of Alexander Hamilton*, Howard C. Syrett, ed., 26 vols. (New York, 1961–79), XXI: 449; ibid., XXII: 64–65, 168, 221–22; ibid., XIX: 395–97; White, *Federalists*, pp. 237–52.

4. *ASP, Naval Affairs*, I: 33–34, 37–39.

5. United States Congress, *The Debates and Proceedings in the Congress of the United States . . .* , Fifth Congress, 15 May 1797–3 March 1799 (Washington, D.C., 1851), pp. 534, 535, 541, 1426, 1522, 1545–54; *QW*, I: 59–60.

6. Robert G. Albion, "The First Days of the Navy Department," *Military Affairs* 12 (Spring 1948): 4; Charles Oscar Paullin, *Paullin's History of Naval Administration, 1775–1911* (Annapolis, Md., 1968), p. 102; Henry Cabot Lodge, *Life and Letters of George Cabot* (Boston, 1878), pp. 155–56.

7. Ibid., pp. 156–58; *Hamilton Papers*, XIX: 435–41; George Washington, *The Writings of George Washington from the Original Manuscript Sources, 1745–1799*, John C. Fitzpatrick, ed., 39 vols. (Washington, D.C., 1931–44), XXXVI: 393–95.

8. *Hamilton Papers*, XXI: 465–66.

9. *QW*, I: 78; commission of Benjamin Stoddert as secretary of the navy, 21 May 1798, National Archives, Record Group 59, General Records of the Department of State, Miscellaneous Permanent Commissions, Vol. B, 1789–1802; *Hamilton Papers*, XIX: 435–41; Stephen G. Kurtz, *The Presidency of John Adams: The Collapse of Federalism, 1795–1800* (Philadelphia, 1957), p. 282; John Adams, *The Works of John Adams, Second President of the United States; with a Life of the Author*, Charles Francis Adams, ed., 10 vols. (Boston, 1850–56), VIII: 645–46; Dumas Malone, *Jefferson and His Time*, vol. 3: *Jefferson and the Ordeal of Liberty* (Boston, 1962), pp. 320–21.

10. Lodge, *Cabot*, p. 144; Goldsborough, *Naval Chronicle*, p. 86; Harold and Margaret Sprout, *The Rise of American Naval Power, 1776–1918* (Princeton, N.J., 1939), pp. 42–43; Robert Greenhalgh Albion, *Makers of American Naval Policy, 1798–1947*, Rowena Reed, ed. (Annapolis, Md., 1980), p. 38.

11. Biographical sketches of Stoddert are few. The most notable are his great-granddaughter Harriot Stoddert Turner's "Memoirs of Benjamin Stoddert, First Secretary of the United States Navy," *Records of the Columbia Historical Society* 20 (1917): 141–66; John J. Carrigg, "Benjamin Stoddert," in Paolo E. Coletta, ed., *American Secretaries of the Navy*, 2 vols. (Annapolis, Md., 1980), I: 59–75; and the entry by Curtis W. Garrison in *Dictionary of American Biography*, 20 vols. (New York, 1928–36), XVIII: 62–64. For details of Stoddert's family see Bessie Wilmarth Gahn, *Original Patentees of Land at Washington Prior to 1700* (Washington, D.C., 1936), pp. 15, 45; the will of James Stoddert, 29 March 1726, typed transcript from the original at the Hall of Records, Annapolis, Md., Wills 19: Folio, 61–65, at the Historical Society of Pennsylvania, Stoddert Family Notes; Benjamin Stoddert file, Navy Department Library, Naval Historical Center, Washington; Turner, "Memoirs," pp. 141–43; J. Thomas Scharf, *History of Maryland, from the Earliest Period to the Present Day*, 3 vols. (Baltimore, 1879), I: 471, 481–82; George Washington, *The Papers of George Washington: Colonial Series*, William Abbot, ed., 2 vols. (Charlottesville, Va., 1983–   ), II: 305–8, 309n; *Washington's Writings*, I: 364–65, 366–67.

12. Stoddert to John Templeman, n.d., Library of Congress, Benjamin Stoddert Papers; Turner, "Memoirs," p. 143; Howard Jenkins, ed., "Journal of Sally Wister," *The Pennsylvania Magazine of History and Biography* IX: no. 3 (1885): 325–26. The Stoddert referred to in the journal is misidentified by the editor as Benjamin Stoddert, ibid., p. 323. Stoddert's cousin, William Trueman Stoddert, served in Smallwood's brigade, the general whose staff was quartered in the Wister home. Benjamin Stoddert's regiment was attached to Wayne's brigade. Francis B. Heitman, *Historical Register of the Officers of the Continental Army during the War of the Revolution, April 1775, to December 1783*, revised edition (Washington, D.C., 1914), pp. 522, 592; James Ripley Jacobs, *Tarnished Warrior: Major-General James Wilkinson* (New York, 1938), pp. 7, 26; James Wilkinson, *Memoirs of My Own Times*, 3 vols. (Philadelphia, 1816), I: 158; Robert K. Wright, Jr., *The Continental Army* (Washington, D.C., 1983), p. 322; Charles J. Stillé, *Major-General Anthony Wayne and the Pennsylvania Line in the Continental Army* (Philadelphia, 1893), pp. 73–102; Anthony Wayne to the court of enquiry regarding the Paoli massacre, 25 October 1777, PHi, Anthony Wayne Papers, IV, #23 and #24. Stoddert com-

manded the videttes the night of the massacre; Piers Mackesy, *The War for America, 1775–1783* (Cambridge, Mass., 1965), p. 129; George R. Prowell, *History of York County Pennsylvania*, 2 vols. (Chicago, 1907), I: 207–8; Thomas Hartley to Wayne, 12 and 21 February 1778, PHi, Wayne Papers, IV: #83 and #86; William R. Reed, ed., "Orderly Book of General Edward Hand," *The Pennsylvania Magazine of History and Biography* 41 (1917): 466.

13. Bernhard Knollenberg, *Washington and the Revolution, a Reappraisal: Gates, Conway, and the Continental Congress* (New York, 1968); Paul David Nelson, *General Horatio Gates: A Biography* (Baton Rouge, La., 1976), pp. 174–75, 182–85; Jacobs, *Tarnished Warrior*, p. 52; Wilkinson, *Memoirs*, I: 386–89; Stoddert to Gates, 25 February 1778, New-York Historical Society, Horatio Gates Papers. Gates and Wilkinson eventually dueled nonetheless, see Nelson, *Gates*, pp. 195–96; and Jacobs, *Tarnished Warrior*, p. 57.

14. Ibid., p. 186; Heitman, *Historical Register*, p. 592; Pickering to Henry Laurens, 24 June 1778, DNA, RG 247, Letters of the Continental Congress, reel 157, item 147, vol. 2, p. 121; Prowell, *York County*, I: 208; and the United States Continental Congress, *Journals of the Continental Congress, 1774–1789*, Worthington C. Ford, ed., 34 vols. (Washington, D.C., 1904–1937), XII: 1077, 1101, 1107.

15. David Craft, "The Expedition of Col. Thomas Hartley against the Indians in 1778, to Avenge the Massacre of Wyoming," *Wyoming Historical and Genealogical Society, Proceedings and Collections* 9 (1905): 189–216; Prowell, *York County*, I: 208–9; Don Higginbotham, *The War of American Independence: Military Attitudes, Policies, and Practice, 1763–1789* (Bloomington, Ind., 1977), pp. 325–27; *Pennsylvania Archives*, Series I, Samuel Hazard, ed., 9 vols. (Philadelphia, 1853–54), VI: 773–74; ibid., VII: 3–4, 5–9, 81–82, 86–87, 87, 258, 336; *Washington's Writings*, XIV: 249–50, 321–22, 354–55; JCC, XIII: 472; and Stoddert to John Jay, 16 April 1779, DNA, LCC, RG 247, reel 102, item 78, vol. 21, p. 39.

16. JCC, XI: 555; ibid., XIV: 1009; Stoddert to John Davis, 6 August 1779, Library of Congress, Peter Force Collection, Series 8D, No. 32, reel 5; Erna Risch, *Supplying Washington's Army* (Washington, D.C., 1981), pp. 101, 106–108.

17. Harry M. Ward, *The Department of War, 1785–1795* (Pittsburgh, Pa., 1962), pp. 2–3, 5, 11; Octavius Pickering, *The Life of Timothy Pickering*, 4 vols., vols. 2–4 by Charles W. Upham (Boston, 1867–1873), II; 27; JCC, XIX, 126, 145–46; Stoddert to Richard Peters, 14 February 1781, DNA, RG 247, LCC, reel 160, vol. 6, #157; and Stoddert to Samuel Huntington. 6 February 1781, ibid., reel 102, item 78, vol. 21, #17.

18. Stoddert to Templeman, n.d., DLC, Stoddert Papers; Gaius Marcus Brumbaugh, *Maryland Records: Colonial, Revolutionary, County and Church from Original Sources* (Baltimore, 1915), I: 133; Robert Barnes, ed., *Maryland Genealogies: A Consolidation of Articles from the Maryland Historical Magazine*, 2 vols. (Baltimore, 1980), I: 187–90; Forrest to Stoddert, 26 March 1783, DLC, Miscellaneous Manuscripts Collection, Uriah Forrest.

19. Stoddert to Templeman, n.d., DLC, Stoddert Papers; Grace Dunlop Ecker, *A Portrait of Old Georgetown* (Richmond, Va., 1937), p. 12; NDL, Stoddert file; Stoddert to Thomas Fitzsimons, 11 February 1784, PHi, Simon Gratz Autograph Collection, Case 4, Box 23; Wilhelmus Bogart Bryan, *A History of the National Capital: From Its Foundation through the Period of the Adoption of the Organic Act*, 2 vols. (New York, 1914), I: 97, 100–1; Rhoda M. Dorsey, "The Pattern of Baltimore Commerce during the Confederation Period," *Maryland Historical Mag-*

azine 62 (June 1967): 133–34; Richard K. MacMaster, ed., "The Tobacco trade with France: Letters of Joseph Fenwick, Consul at Bordeaux, 1785–1795," ibid., 60 (March 1965): 33, 38.

20. The Junior League of Washington, *An Illustrated History: The City of Washington,* Thomas Francek, ed. (New York, 1977), pp. 41–45; Ecker, *Old Georgetown,* pp. 4, 77–79; E. James Ferguson, *The Power of the Purse: A History of American Public Finance, 1776–1790* (Chapel Hill, N.C., 1961), pp. 275–76; JCC, XXXIV: 17; *Washington's Writings,* XXXI: 218–19; Thomas Jefferson, *The Papers of Thomas Jefferson,* Julian P. Boyd, ed., 21 vols. (Princeton, N.J., 1950–   ), XX: 73–74. Most of Washington's correspondence with Deakins and Stoddert was, in fact, drafted by Jefferson, see ibid., *n.* Stoddert to Clement Biddle, 20 March 1798, DLC, Stoddert Papers.

21. Ellis Paxson Oberholtzer, *Robert Morris, Patriot and Financier* (New York, 1903), pp. 308, 324–25, 332; Bryan, *National Capital,* I: 16, 428, 430, 505; Proof of debt to Benjamin Stoddert, DNA, RG 21, Bankruptcy Act of 1800, Eastern District of Pennsylvania, M 933, the case of Robert Morris, Roll 7, case 42; Stoddert to Templeman, n.d., DLC, Stoddert Papers; Jacob M. Price, *France and the Chesapeake: A History of the French Tobacco Monopoly, 1694–1791, and of Its Relationship to British and American Tobacco Trades,* 2 vols. (Ann Arbor, Mich., 1973), II: 841–42; Doresy, "Baltimore Commerce," p. 134; ASP, Class III, *Finance,* I: 666–67; and Bryan, *National Capital,* I: 96–97.

22. Stoddert to Elias Dayton, 27 December 1803, DLC, Stoddert Papers; Stoddert to William Whann, 4 March 1809, PHi, Manuscript Collection of the Library Company of Philadelphia.

23. Marshall Smelser, *The Congress Founds the Navy, 1787–1798* (Notre Dame, Ind., 1959), p. 157; Bernard C. Steiner, *The Life and Correspondence of James McHenry, Secretary of War under Washington and Adams* (Cleveland, 1907), p. 303; Stoddert to Benjamin Lowndes, 26 May 1798, DLC, George Washington Campbell Papers; *QW,* I: 91.

24. Adams, *Works,* IX: 582–83.

25. Ibid., X: 126–31; *Rules for the Regulation of the Navy of the United Colonies of North-America* (Philadelphia, 1775, reprint ed., Washington, D.C., 1944); *QW,* I: 7–9; and Page Smith, *John Adams,* 2 vols. (Garden City, N.Y., 1962), II: 967.

26. White, *Federalists,* p. 517; *Hamilton Papers,* XXI: 494–95; *QW,* I: 96–97, 111–12, 115, 251; *BW,* I: 280–83.

27. *Hamilton Papers,* XXI: 465–66; Irving H. King, *George Washington's Coast Guard: Origins of the U.S. Revenue Cutter Service, 1790–1801* (Annapolis, MD., 1978), pp. 145–53; *QW,* I: 56.

28. Ibid., pp. 74–75.

29. *Hamilton Papers,* XXI: 461–62; *QW,* I: 77.

30. Ibid., I: 88, 90.

31. Steiner, *McHenry,* p. 303.

32. *Hamilton Papers,* XXI: 491–92; *QW,* I: 115.

33. Steiner, *McHenry,* pp. 303–4.

34. *QW,* I: 122–23, 123, Stoddert to Clement Biddle, 20 March 1798, DLC, Stoddert Papers; Oberholtzer, *Morris,* p. 350.

35. United States Congress, *The Public Statutes at Large of the United States of America, from the Organization of the Government in 1789 to March 1845 . . . ,* Richard Peters, ed., 8 vols. (Boston, 1861–67), I: 565–66, 587; *QW,* I: 123, 198–99.

Chapter 2

1. Adams, *Works*, X: 126–31; *QW,* I: 139–41; DeConde, *Quasi-War,* pp. 84–89.
2. *QW,* I: 77, 92–93.
3. Ibid., pp. 133–34, 135, 139.
4. Ibid., 63–64, 72–73; Homer C. Votaw, "The Sloop of War *Ganges,*" The United States Naval Institute *Proceedings* 98 (July 1972): 82.
5. Ibid., p. 83; Molly Elliot Seawell, *Twelve Naval Captains: Being a Record of Certain Americans Who Made Themselves Immortal* (New York, 1900), pp. 28–41.
6. For the army and military expansion in general during the period see Richard H. Kohn, *Eagle and Sword: The Federalists and the Creation of the Military Establishment in America, 1783–1802* (New York, 1975), pp. 193–256. For the development of, and challenges to war powers, see Abraham D. Sofaer, *War, Foreign Affairs and Constitutional Power: The Origins* (Cambridge, Mass., 1976), pp. 131–66.
7. *QW,* I: 58.
8. The vessels were purchased between May and September 1798, except for the brig *Augusta,* acquired in the spring of 1799.
9. *QW,* VII: 364–71.
10. The *George Washington,* Captain William Bainbridge, was sent to the Mediterranean in 1800 on a diplomatic mission to Algiers.
11. *QW,* III: 344–55; ibid., IV: 31, 54–55, 65–66; and Moses Myers to Truxtun, 19 September 1799, PHi, T. Truxtun Hare Collection.
12. Russell was discharged on 10 December 1801, see *QW,* VII: 348.
13. Ibid., II: 210. More guns necessitated more crew, which also meant the quicker consumption of provisions, reducing the time a ship could remain at sea. Overarming also accelerated the processes of wear and tear on the ship and exacerbated the problem of finding enough cannon early in the war. See ibid., p. 232. Stoddert wrote concerning the cutter *Virginia* 14, Francis Bright: "the vessels which injure our commerce in the West Indies carry one and two guns—vessels carrying four, six, or eight guns, are the most useful kind we can employ—and if Captain Bright's vessel be reduced to 6 or 8, and 30 or 35 men, she will be more formidable than in her present situation." The *Virginia* at the time carried fourteen guns and seventy men.
14. Ibid., III: 38, 507–8.
15. Ibid., I: 101. The emphasis is Dale's.
16. Eugene S. Ferguson, *Truxtun of the Constellation: The Life of Commodore Thomas Truxtun, U.S. Navy, 1755–1822* (Baltimore, 1956), pp. 39–42; Thomas Truxtun, *Remarks, Instructions, and Examples Relating to the Latitude and Longitude* (Philadelphia, 1794); and Truxtun's *Instructions, Signals, and Explanations Offered for the U.S. Fleet* (Baltimore, 1797).
17. *QW,* I: 92–93, 118–19.
18. Ibid., p. 134–35.
19. Ibid., pp. 156–58, 158, 160.
20. Ibid., pp. 152, 232–33, 291.
21. Ibid., pp. 304–6, 365; Ferguson, *Truxtun,* pp. 145–47; for the *Hermione* mutiny see Dudley Pope, *The Black Ship* (Philadelphia, 1964); and W. M. P. Dunne, "The *Constellation* and the *Hermione,*" *Mariner's Mirror* 70 (August 1984): 82–85.
22. The *President* 44, at New York, the *Congress* 36, at Portsmouth, N.H., and the *Chesapeake,* 36, at Norfolk, would not be completed until later in the war.

23. Howard I. Chapelle, *The History of the American Sailing Navy: The Ships and Their Development* (New York, 1949), pp. 117–22.

24. Ibid., pp. 118–28; and Joshua Humphreys to Robert Morris, 6 January 1793, PHi, Joshua Humphreys Papers, Letterbook, 1793–97.

25. William James, *The Naval History of Great Britain from the Declaration of War by France in 1793 to the Accession of George IV,* 2nd ed., 6 vols. (London, 1850), I: 224–26; G. J. Marcus, *Heart of Oak: A Survey of British Sea Power in the Georgian Era* (London, 1957), p. 67.

26. Chapelle, *American Sailing Navy,* p. 132. Live oak, *Quercus virens,* grew in a twenty-mile-wide strip along the southern coast of the United States from Norfolk to the Mississippi, see Robert Greenhaigh Albion, *Forests and Sea Power: The Timber Problem of the Royal Navy, 1652–1862* (Cambridge, Mass., 1926), p. 23; and Virginia Steele Wood, *Live Oaking: Southern Timber for Tall Ships* (Boston, 1981), pp. 23–44.

27. Chapelle, *American Sailing Navy,* p. 134; and *QW,* I: 160.

28. Ibid., pp. 211–12, 300–2; and Chapelle, *American Sailing Navy,* p. 132.

29. *QW,* I: 132, 300–2; ibid., I: 3. Truxtun had previously written Stoddert: "You mention six months' provisions to be put on board this ship, none of our frigates can carry it, this is one of the mistakes that I foresaw in the plan, before the keel of any one of them was laid." Ibid., I: 568.

30. Chapelle, *American Sailing Navy,* pp. 130–31. For an amusing example of the peculiar qualities of the *United States,* see Herman Melville, *White-Jacket, or the World in a Man-of-War* (Chicago, 1970), pp. 268–73. Melville served in the *United States* and noted that for maximum speed the captain of the *Neversink* (the *United States*) crowded the crew forward holding 24-pound shot.

31. Charles R. Fisher, "The Great Guns of the Navy, 1797–1843," *American Neptune* 36 (October 1976): 281–82. Truxtun wrote that the total length of the masts and yards of the *Constellation* was only twenty-seven feet short of that of an English sixty-four gun ship of the line, see *QW,* I: 300–2; ibid., II: 336. Also, compare the spar dimensions of the *Constellation* and the *Congress* given in Chapelle, *American Sailing Navy,* p. 483. Truxtun replaced the 24-pounders with 18-pounders in June 1799, *QW,* III: 394.

32. Ira N. Hollis, *The Frigate Constitution: The Central Figure of the Navy under Sail* (Boston, 1901), p. 39; Chapelle, *American Sailing Navy,* p. 263. Compare the plans of the forty-four-gun frigate of 1794, after page 121, with the plan of the *President* 44, made by the British after her capture in 1815, after page 264. Note the absence of waist ports on the spar deck. See also *QW,* VII: 295.

33. Ibid., I: 67–68, 116–18, 141–42; *DAB,* V: 186–87.

34. *QW,* I: 149, 150, 177–79.

35. Ibid., pp. 175–76.

36. *La Croyable* was a recently built Baltimore schooner, probably one of the many ships seized in the Caribbean by the French during 1797. Off the American coast for only a few days before her capture, she had plundered the *Alexander Hamilton* and seized two other ships. See ibid., p. 175. The government purchased *La Croyable* for $7,000 and rechristened her the *Retaliation,* see ibid., pp. 261–62.

Chapter 3

1. *QW,* I: 161–62; Clark, *Barry,* p. 412.

2. Ibid., pp. 382–86, 390–92.

3. McHenry to Wolcott, 13 September 1796, DNA, RG 45, Correspondence on Naval Affairs when the Navy was under the War Department, 1790–1798, Entry 374, pp. 185–88; McHenry to Samuel Hughes, 20 May 1796, ibid., p. 168.

4. Clark, *Barry,* p. 387; Josiah Fox to Truxtun, 7 August 1797, DNA, RG 45, Correspondence on Naval Affairs, p. 275.

5. Clark, *Barry,* p. 393, 404; George Gillasspy to Barry, 21 November 1797, NHi, Barnes Collection, John Barry Papers; Gillasspy to Barry, 26 November 1797, ibid.; McHenry to Jay, 19 March 1798, DNA, RG 45, Correspondence on Naval Affairs, p. 287; McHenry to Jay, ibid., p. 299.

6. Clark, *Barry,* pp. 399–400; 410; *QW,* I: 122–23.

7. Ibid., II: 129–34; ibid., I: 320–21; ibid., VI: 491; and Perkins, *First Rapprochement,* pp. 95–96.

8. *ASP, Naval Affairs,* I: 128–29; Wolcott to King, 3 July 1798, DNA, RG 59, Records of the Department of State, Miscellaneous Letters; Ralph W. Hidy, *The House of Baring in American Trade and Finance: English Merchant Bankers at Work, 1763–1861* (Cambridge, Mass., 1949), p. 32; *QW,* III: 324, 353, 354; ibid., IV: 368.

9. Ibid., V: 58–61; ibid., I: 303–4.

10. Pickering to Samuel Hodgdon, 24 November 1795, DNA, RG 45, Correspondence on Arming and Equipping Early Frigates and Ships of War, When the Navy was under the War Department, 13 May 1795–26 July 1798, Entry 375, pp. 1–2; McHenry to Harris, 3 May 1797, ibid., p. 5; McHenry to Hughes, 20 May 1796, DNA, RG 45, Correspondence on Naval Affairs, p. 168; Fox to Truxtun, 7 August 1797, ibid., p. 275; McHenry to Samuel Nicholson, 23 June 1797, ibid., p. 251; *QW,* II: 21, 22; and Stoddert memo, 3 August 1798, DNA, RG 59, SDA, Miscellaneous Letters.

11. *QW,* I: 161–62, 163.

12. Clark, *Barry,* p. 412; *QW,* I: 174, 175, 181–82, 187, 189–91, 192–93.

13. Ibid., pp. 189–91.

14. Ibid., pp. 203–4, 232.

15. Ibid., pp. 200, 255–56. The frigates at Cap François were reportedly commanded by Joshua Barney.

16. Clark, *Barry,* p. 418.

17. Ibid., p. 420; *QW,* I: 265.

18. Ibid., pp. 325, 327.

19. Ibid., p. 331.

20. Ibid., p. 334.

21. Ibid., pp. 363, 369, 375.

22. Ibid., p. 377.

23. Ibid., pp. 381, 384, 430, 438; and Clark, *Barry,* p. 423.

24. *QW,* I: 430. Stoddert mentioned in a letter to Adams dated 30 July that Barry could be expected to leave the islands about the end of August, ibid., pp. 255–56.

25. Ibid., pp. 190–92.

26. The term "hurricane" is derived from a native Caribbean word meaning "big wind." For a history of Caribbean hurricanes see Ivan Ray Tannehill, *Hurricanes: Their Nature and History, Particularly Those of the West Indies and the Southern Coasts of the United States* (Princeton, N.J., 1956). Beaufort scale 12 means winds greater than 75 miles per hour; ibid., pp. 143–47. The connection between the hurricane season and the West Indian and North American theaters is discussed in Marcus, *Heart of Oak,* p. 27.

27. *QW*, I: 255–56, 58; ibid., III: 385–86.

28. Tannehill, *Hurricanes,* p. 248.

29. Bonnel, *Guerre de course,* pp. 319–67.

30. Clark, *Barry,* p. 368.

31. Ibid., p. 416; and James Fenimore Cooper, *History of the Navy of the United States,* 3rd ed., 2 vols. (Cooperstown, N.Y., 1848), I: 150.

32. Clark, *Barry,* p. 241, 243; *DAB,* XIII: 506–7; and Stephen Tallichet Powers, "Robert Morris and the Courts-Martial of Captains Samuel Nicholson and John Manley of the Continental Navy," *Military Affairs* 44 (February 1980): 13–17. See also Fletcher Pratt, *Preble's Boys: Commodore Preble and the Birth of American Sea Power* (New York, 1950), pp. 14–15.

33. Barry to Nicholson, 24 June 1794, NHi, Barry Papers.

34. *QW*, I: 96–97, 102; and Tyrone G. Martin, *A Most Fortunate Ship: A Narrative History of "Old Ironsides"* (Chester, Conn., 1980), pp. 22–23.

35. Nicholson to Barry, 15 July 1794, PHi, Gratz Collection, Case 5, Box 28; *QW*, I: 106–7, 111–12.

36. James Lowell to Wolcott, 22 June 1798, DNA, RG 59, SDA, Miscellaneous Letters.

37. Joseph H. Nicholson to Samuel Nicholson, 12 January 1800, DNA, RG 45, Area File 7.

38. *QW*, I: 197–98, 236, 295–96.

39. Ibid., 377.

40. Ibid., pp. 383, 393–6.

41. Ibid., pp. 414–17.

42. Ibid., pp. 448–49, 449, 468–69, 555–56.

43. Ibid., pp. 493, 495, 502. On Stoddert's 5 October letter is inscribed: "This Letter was not delivered to Captn Nicholson, but returned by Mr Pennock at the desire of the Secy of the Navy G[arrett] C[ottringer]."

44. *QW*, I: 555; Moses Myers to Barry, 5 October 1798, NHi, Barry Papers. Myers believed that Nicholson had captured a bad bargain in the *Niger.* For British comments see Robert Liston to Lord Grenville, 27 September 1798, Public Record Office, Foreign Office 5/22, #57 [DLC transcript]; Liston to Grenville, 7 November 1788, ibid.,#65; Liston to Grenville, 2 April 1799, ibid., #26; and *Statutes,* II: 723–24.

Chapter 4

1. *QW*, I: 193, 197.

2. Ibid., pp. 120–21.

3. Knox to Sever, 18 July 1794, DLC, James Sever Papers; Knox to Sever, 8 August 1794, ibid., McHenry to Sever, 4 June 1796, ibid., Wolcott to Higginson, 17 May 1798, DNA, RG 45, Area File 11; Wolcott to Sever, 17 May 1798, ibid.

4. *QW*, I: 111–12; ibid. IV: 143; Heitman, *Historical Register,* p. 489; Wright, *Continental Army,* p. 216; *Washington's Writings,* XXVIII: 91–94; Allen, *Naval War,* p. 131; Fred T. Jane, *The Imperial Russian Navy: Its Past, Present, and Future* (London, 1899), pp. 714–24; Knox to Sever, 18 July 1794, DLC, Sever Papers.

5. *QW*, I: 111–12.

6. Ibid., VII: 135–39; ibid., I: 254, 327, 328–29, 349, 350.

7. Ibid., p. 356.

8. Ibid., pp. 111–12.

9. Ibid., pp. 96–97, 158–59.

10. King, *George Washington's Coast Guard*, pp. 172–73; and see Florence Kern's series of short histories of the early cutters and their commanders, listed individually in the bibliography.

11. *QW*, I: 7–9.

12. King, *George Washington's Coast Guard*, pp. 146, 147–49; and Chapelle, *American Sailing Navy*, pp. 182–83.

13. *QW*, I: 367–68.

14. Archibald Henderson, *Washington's Southern Tour, 1791* (Boston and New York, 1923), p. 155; United States Navy Department, *Naval Documents of the American Revolution*, William Bell Clark et al., eds., 8 vols. to date (Washington, D.C. 1964–   ), III: 1043–46; Florence Kern, *Robert Cochran's U.S. Revenue Cutter South Carolina, 1793–1798* (Washington, D.C., 1978); *Hamilton Papers*, VIII: 331, 349–50.

15. *QW*, I: 252, 372, 386, 387, 401, 523–24; Liston to Grenville, 27 September 1798, PRO, FO 5/22, #57; Liston to Grenville, 7 November 1798, ibid., #65.

16. *QW*, I: 516; ibid., II: 399–400.

17. King, *George Washington's Coast Guard*, pp. 162–63.

18. Ibid., pp. 176–77; *QW*, IV: 3.

19. Ibid., I: 255–56.

20. Ibid., p. 251.

21. Ibid., pp. 291, 292, 295–96, 335.

22. Ibid., pp. 284–85, 288.

23. Ibid., pp. 319, 336.

24. Ibid., pp. 333–34, 335, 337–38.

25. Ibid.

26. David Syrett, "The Organization of British Trade Convoys during the American War, 1775–1783," *Mariner's Mirror* 62 (May 1976): 169–81. See also Mackesy, *War for America*, p. 396. Secrecy, even when intended, was rarely attained.

27. *QW*, I: 359.

28. Ibid., p. 341.

29. Ibid., pp. 363, 364, 370, 431, 475.

30. Ibid., pp. 480, 482, 508–9.

31. Ibid., p. 506.

32. Ibid., p. 541.

33. Ibid., pp. 550, 559; ibid., II: 1–2.

34. John F. Campbell, "The Havana Incident," *American Neptune* 22 (October 1962): 269–76, states that Nicholson received orders, since lost, to sail to Havana, but existing documents make it clear that no such orders were issued. See *QW*, I: 295–96, 504, 538.

35. Ibid., p. 365; ibid., II: 1–2; ibid., IV: 504; ibid., V: 249.

36. Ibid., I: 569–70.

37. Ibid., II: 26, 26–27; Dudley Pope, *The Great Gamble* (New York, 1972), pp. 5–14; Sir Hyde Parker to Evan Nepean, 10 February 1799, PRO, Adm. 1/249; and Parker to Nepean, ibid. Loring's squadron had been patrolling between the Dry Tortugas and Cape San Antonio to intercept an expected Spanish convoy from Vera Cruz.

38. North Callahan, *Flight from the Republic: The Tories of the American Revo-

lution (Indianapolis, 1967), p. 110; Hugh Edward Egerton, *The Royal Commission on the Losses and Services of American Royalists, 1783–1785* (New York, 1971), pp. 327, 328–29; *NDAR*, IV: 1171; ibid., V: 764, 764–65n; ibid., VII: 217–18; and Liston to Grenville, 16 January 1799, PRO, FO 5/25, #3.

39. Phillips to Stoddert, 28 December 1798, DNA, RG 59, SDA, Miscellaneous Letters.

40. Ibid., Loring to Parker, 20 February 1799, PRO, Adm. 1/249; and *QW*, II: 30–32. Phillips's report is given in Appendix B.

41. Ibid.,

42. Ibid., pp. 26–27, 135.

43. Ibid., pp. 29–30.

44. Liston to Grenville, 16 January 1799, PRO, FO 5/25, #3; and Loring to Parker, 20 February 1799, PRO, Adm. 1/249.

45. Scott Thomas Jackson, "Impressment and Anglo-American Discord, 1787–1818" (Ph.D. dissertation, University of Michigan, 1976), pp. 136–47; Perkins, *First Rapprochement*, p. 99; King to Pickering, 14 March 1799, DNA, RG 59, SDA, Diplomatic Dispatches from Great Britain, #28; King to Pickering, 15 March 1799, ibid., #29; King to Pickering, 22 March 1799, ibid., #39; and King to Pickering, 22 March 1799, ibid., #33. In the latter King noted that the British were defending their conduct in part by arguing that Phillips had "acquiesced in or consented to *all* that was done [in code in the original]."

46. Ibid.,

47. *QW*, II: 276–77.

48. Stoddert to Pickering, 11 January 1799, DNA, RG 59, SDA, Miscellaneous Letters; Pickering to Fisher Ames, 28 November 1799, DNA, RG 45, Area File 11; and Liston to Grenville, 16 January 1799, PRO, FO 5/25, #3.

49. *QW*, II: 243.

50. Ibid., pp. 30, 32–34.

51. Isaac Phillips, *An Impartial Examination of the Case of Captain Isaac Phillips, late of the Navy, And Commander of the United States Sloop of War Baltimore, in 1798. Compiled from Original Documents and Records, with the Proceedings upon his application to be restored to his rank in the United States Navy* (Baltimore, 1825). Leonard F. Guttridge and Jay D. Smith in *The Commodores* (New York, 1969; reprint ed., Annapolis, Md., 1984), pp. 37–39, follow Phillips's defense and assail Stoddert's cousin, the *Baltimore*'s first lieutenant, Josias Speake, "who yielded the muster role in Phillips's absence." For a historiographic treatment see Michael A. Palmer, "The Dismission of Captain Isaac Phillips," *American Neptune* 45 (Spring 1985): 94–103.

52. David Steel, *Original and Correct List of the Royal Navy* (London, 1801); and C. A. Pengelly, *The First Bellerophon* (London, 1966), pp. 135, 144.

53. *QW*, I: 430.

54. Ibid., p. 433.

55. Ibid., pp. 442–43, 462–63, 483–84, 503, 538–39; *Appleton's Cyclopaedia of American Biography*, James Grant Wilson, ed., 6 vols. (New York, 1888–89), I: 513; and Hugh G. Campbell to Jones & Clarke, 4 November 1798, PHi, Jones & Clarke Papers, Box 2, Correspondence.

56. *DAB*, XIII: 357–58; John Howard Brown, *American Naval Heroes, 1775–1812–1861–1898: Being Biographical Sketches of the Brave Men Who Have Glorified the American Navy by Their Deeds of Heroism* (Boston, 1899), pp. 157–68.

57. *QW*, I: 407, 435, 542–43; ibid., II: 491–92; ibid., III: 267; and Truxtun to B.

Dayton, 6 March 1799, DLC, Thomas Truxtun Papers, Miscellaneous Manuscripts Collection.

58. *DAB*, I: 504–507; Seawell, *Twelve Naval Captains*, pp. 53–82; and David F. Long, *Ready to Hazard: A Biography of Commodore William Bainbridge, 1774–1833* (Hanover, N.H., and London, 1981).

59. *QW*, II: 40–42.

60. Marcus, *Heart of Oak*, pp. 20–23; and Mahan, *French Revolution and Empire*, I: 100–3, 342–80.

61. Ibid., 247–49; James, *Naval History*, I: 247–49; and Bonnel, *Guerre de course*, p. 96.

62. *QW*, II: 40–42.

63. Goldsborough, *Naval Chronicle*, pp. 127–29. The story is repeated in Seawell, *Twelve Naval Captains*, pp. 56–57; Edgar Stanton Maclay, *A History of the United States Navy from 1775 to 1901*, 3 vols. (New York, 1910), I: 166–67; Copper, *History*, I: 164; as well as his *Lives of Distinguished American Naval Officers*, 2 vols. (Philadelphia, 1846), I: 15–17; Howard P. Nash, *The Forgotten Wars: The Role of the U. S. Navy in the Quasi-War with France and the Barbary Wars, 1798–1805* (New York, 1968), p. 93; Allen, *Naval War*, p. 74; Long, *Ready to Hazard*, pp. 225–27; and is reprinted in *QW*, II: 42–43.

64. Ibid., p. 57.

Chapter 5

1. *QW*, I: 457, 481.

2. Ibid., pp. 460–61, 566–58; and Benjamin Harkin to Nathaniel Shaler, 2 November 1798, PHi, Shaler Papers, Correspondence, Envelope #1.

3. *QW.*, I: 538–40.

4. Ibid.

5. *DAB*, VI: 444–45; *QW*, V: 59, 109; *BW*, I: 486–87.

6. See photostats in DLC from the PRO, Adm. 1/3985. For an example of the exchange of intelligence in the Caribbean between British and American commanders see *QW*, II: 240, 258–59. For other sources of information see ibid., I: 485–86; and ibid., II: 57.

7. Bonnel, *Guerre de course*, pp. 319–67.

8. Hugh Thomas, *Cuba: The Pursuit of Freedom* (New York, 1971), pp. 76–77, 1560; and *ASP, Commerce and Navigation*, I: 384, 417, 431.

9. H. J. K. Jenkins, "The Heyday of French Privateering from Guadeloupe, 1796–1798," *Mariner's Mirror* 64 (August 1978): 245–50; and Jenkins, " 'The Colonial Robespierre': Victor Hugues on Guadeloupe, 1794–1798," *History Today* 27 (November 1977): 734–40.

10. Ibid.; Mahan, *French Revolution and Empire*, II: 213.

11. James, *Naval History*, I: 332; Bonnel, *Guerre de course*, pp. 96–98; and *ASP, Foreign Relations*, II: 222–23.

12. See chapter 19, section 2.

13. Bernard Mayo, ed., *Instructions to the British Ministers to the United States, 1791–1812* (Washington, D.C., 1941), pp. 155–60; Carnegie Endowment for International Peace, *Diplomatic Correspondence of the United States: Canadian Relations, 1784–1860*, William R. Manning, ed., 3 vols. (Washington, D.C., 1940–43),

I: 136–39; Liston to Grenville, 27 September 1798, PRO, FO 5/25, #55; and Liston to Grenville, 7 November 1798, ibid., #64.

14. Stoddert to Pickering, 14 July 1798, DNA, RG 59, SDA, Miscellaneous Letters; Pickering to Liston, 18 July 1798, ibid., Domestic Letters; *QW*, I: 227, 235; Pickering to Liston, 27 July 1798, DNA, RG 59, SDA, Domestic Letters; and George Vandeput to Nepean, 9 November 1798, PRO, Adam. 1/494. The 20 July 1798 letter from Stoddert to Pickering is misdated and should be 23 July. Perkins, *First Rapprochement*, p. 98, suggests that Vandeput stole Stoddert's idea, but the concept of a system of recognition signals was arrived at by the two men independently. Stoddert's plan was not forwarded to Liston until 18 July. Vandeput's signals reached Philadelphia on the 22nd or 23rd. The admiral was in Halifax at the time and no dispatches could have traveled from Philadelphia to Nova Scotia and back within five days.

15. See chapter 7, section 3.

16. *QW*, I: 336; and Appendix C.

17. *QW*, I: 433–34.

18. Ibid., 566–68; ibid., II: 77–78, 140–41, 200–1. Throughout the summer the two cutters had been patrolling between Long Island and Cape Henry.

19. Ibid., I: 336.

20. Ibid., pp. 542–43. The order of ranking in 1794 stood Barry, Nicholson, Talbot, Dale, Truxtun, and Sever.

21. Ibid., p. 510.

22. Ibid., pp. 542–43.

23. Ibid., II: 300, 313.

24. Ibid., p. 300, 516–17.

25. Ibid., I: 367–68, 408.

26. *DAB*, XVIII: 560–61; Carr, *Perils Named and Unnamed*, p. 52; Truxtun to Biddle, 24 October 1801, PHi, LCP, Truxtun-Biddle Letters, Box I, folio #42. Little is known of what, exactly, Tingey did during the American Revolution. Truxtun wrote Biddle, in the letter cited above, that Tingey had been "an Englishman and a Tory last war." Tingey had commanded the *Ganges* on an Asian voyage before Dale, see *Ganges* journal, DLC, Thomas Tingey Papers.

27. *QW*, II: 87–88, 88.

28. King, *George Washington's Coast Guard*, p. 160; Allen, *Naval War*, p. 83; Nash, *Forgotten Wars*, p. 97; Cooper, *History*, I: 167–68; and Maclay, *History*, I: 176, place the ships in the Windward Passage with Tingey. See also *QW*, II: 406–407, 497; ibid., III: 42, 107, 110–11.

29. Ibid., 343–44.

30. Ibid., II: 519–20; ibid., III: 90–91.

31. Ibid., II: 70–72.

32. Ibid., pp. 59–60, 60, 65, 93, 100, 222–23, 230–31, 250, 274.

33. Ibid., pp. 72, 73–74, 76, 244; and Stoddert to Truxtun, 10 December 1798, DNA, RG 45, Entry 00, Box 1, Operations of U. S. Ships against the French.

34. See chapter 2, section 1.

35. *QW*, I: 476–77.

36. Ibid., II: 116–21.

37. Ibid., V: 125–26, 209–10, 295–96.

38. Ibid., II: 203–4, 204, 233, 241–42, 243, 251.

39. Ibid., pp. 251–52, 252, 299.

40. Ibid., pp. 257, 258–59, 265, 267, 303–4, 400, 533; ibid., III: 57; ibid., IV: 80, 81; ibid., VI: 387; ibid., VII: 374–75.

41. Ibid., I: 39.
42. For the use of the system in Asian waters see chapter 10. For the Mediterranean during the Barbary Waters and after see James A. Field, Jr., *America and the Mediterranean World, 1776–1882* (Princeton, N.J., 1969), pp. 55–56.
43. *QW*, II: 421, 422–23; and Nash, *Forgotten Wars*, p. 116.
44. *QW*, II: 241, 322; Liston to Grenville, 2 April 1799, PRO, FO 5/25, #26. Decatur identified the captain of the British frigate, the *Solebay*, as "Rowiod." Stephen Poyntz is listed by Steel as commanding the frigate, but she may have been cruising under Captain Edward Riou who was serving on Parker's station at the time.
45. *QW*, III: 216.
46. Ibid., II: 283–85.
47. Ibid.
48. Ibid., pp. 366–69; and Michael A. Palmer, "The Quasi-War and the Creation of the American Navy, 1798–1801" (Ph.D. dissertation, Temple University, 1981), p. 206n.
49. *QW*, II: 412.
50. Ibid., pp. 366–69, 382 (emphasis in the original). For the official Navy Department reaction to Tingey's conduct see ibid., pp. 429–30. Stoddert wrote: "your . . . letters . . . have been communicated to the president, who highly approves of the conduct you pursued with regard to the British frigate you fell in with."
51. Ibid., pp. 302, 366–69.
52. Ibid., pp. 389–90, 417, 479–80, 529.
53. Ibid., p. 139.
54. Ibid., IV: 92–97.
55. Ibid., II: 241–42, 266.
56. Ibid., pp. 19, 213.
57. Ibid., p. 247.
58. Ibid., pp. 253, 307–8.
59. Ibid., p. 447; Liston to Grenville, 2 April 1799, PRO, FO 5/25, #26.
60. *QW*, II: 276, 281.
61. Ibid., pp. 332, 372.
62. Ibid., pp. 304–5, 310; Allen, *Naval War*, p. 90; and Clark, *Barry*, p. 455.
63. *QW*. II: 380–82.
64. Ibid., 253; ibid., VI: 412; and Ferguson, *Truxtun*, p. 20.
65. *QW*, II: 257.
66. Ibid., pp. 258–59.
67. Ibid., pp. 269–70, 303–4. Clark, *Barry*, p. 438, argues that Barry eventually complied with Truxtun's request, further stretching his resources, and making a detachment to the south impossible.
68. Ibid.
69. *QW*, II: 238, 241, 366.
70. Ibid., pp. 212, 237, 243.
71. Ibid., p. 240.
72. Ibid., pp. 307–8, 328; and John Hoxse, *The Yankee Tar: An Authentic Narrative of the Voyages and Hardships of John Hoxse and the Cruises of the U. S. Frigate Constellation* (Northampton, Mass., 1840), p. 52.
73. *QW*, II: 326–27.
74. Ibid., p. 328.
75. Maclay, *History*, I: 183–86n.

76. Hoxse, *Yankee Tar,* p. 52.

77. Maclay, *History,* I: 183–86n.

78. *QW,* II: 376–77.

79. O. Troude, *Batailles Navales de la France,* 4 vols. (Paris, 1867–68), III: 167–70.

80. Maclay, *History,* I: 183–86n.

81. Ibid.

82. *QW,* II: 376–77.

83. Troude, *Batailles Navales,* III: 169.

84. Maclay, *History,* I: 183–86n. The Truxtun-Barreaut conversations are drawn from their official reports, the indirect being converted into direct discourse.

85. *QW,* II: 326–27, 356–58.

86. Ibid., pp. 329–30, 354, 379.

87. David Le Pere Savageau, "The United States Navy and Its Half War Prisoners, 1798–1801," *American Neptune* 31 (July 1971): 168–69; *QW,* II: 432, 379.

88. Ibid., pp. 329–30, 345. The midshipman was James Macdonough, older brother of Thomas. For the killing of Neal Harvey, see ibid., pp. 334–35 (emphasis in the original); and ibid., I: 304–16. Some among the political opposition considered Sterett's action murder, see John Wood, *The Suppressed History of the Administration of John Adams (from 1797 to 1801) as printed and suppressed in 1802* (Reprint, New York, 1968), p. 193. For a sketch of the twenty-one-year-old Sterett see *DAB,* XVII: 584–85.

89. *QW,* II: 439, 444–45.

90. Ibid., p. 463.

91. Ibid., pp. 380–82.

92. Ibid., pp. 383, 387, 473–75.

93. Ibid., III: 24–25.

94. Ibid., II: 451.

95. Ibid., p. 374.

96. Ibid., pp. 476–77.

97. Ibid., III: 110–11.

Chapter 6

1. *QW,* III: pp. 86, 176.

2. Ibid., II: 459, 467–68, 522; ibid., III: 52, 149, 150–51. While in pursuit of a French privateer that had been forced to come to, Williams changed course and chased a Swedish merchant vessel. See ibid., 491–92.

3. Ibid., 144, 168, 176–77, 234–35. The latter was never sent.

4. Ibid., pp. 244, 252, 272–73.

5. The strength of the navy dropped temporarily in the spring of 1799 because of the return of the cutters *Virginia, Diligence, Governor Jay,* and *General Greene* to the Treasury Department.

6. *QW,* III: 272–73, 285.

7. Ibid., p. 293; ibid., IV: 162.

8. Ibid., II: 467–68, 473–75; ibid., III: 47.

9. Clark, *Barry,* p. 444; *QW,* III: 77, 217–18. Stoddert had hoped that Truxtun would remain longer in the Caribbean, see ibid., p. 185.

10. Ibid., 13–14.

11. *QW*, II: 313; ibid., III: 66–67.

12. Ibid., pp. 120–21, 131–32; ibid., II: 519–20.

13. Ibid., pp. 264–65; ibid., II: 519–20.

14. Ibid., III: 185, 264–65, 285–86, 340; Malone, *Ordeal of Liberty*, pp. 473–74.

15. James Wilkinson to Nicholson, 6 November 1799, DNA, RG 45, Area File 7; *DAB*, XIII: 506–7.

16. Ibid., XVIII: 280; Perkins, *First Rapprochement*, pp. 63–65; and Henry T. Tuckerman, *The Life of Silas Talbot: A Commodore in the Navy of the United States* (New York, 1859).

17. *Hamilton Papers*, XXII: 152; *QW*, I: 367–78, 351–52; ibid., II: 519–20; ibid., III: 265–66.

18. Ibid., pp. 157–58, 273, 400, 401, 463, 490–91, 491–92, 495; and Ferguson, *Truxtun*, p. 179.

19. *QW*, III: 479.

20. Ibid., 528–32, 533.

21. Michael Lewis, *England's Sea-Officers: The Story of the Naval Profession* (London, 1939), pp. 60–76.

22. QW, III: 567–68; ibid., IV: 20, 51; and Truxtun to McHenry, 5 August 1799, United States Naval Academy Museum, Manuscript Collection, Thomas Truxtun.

23. *QW*, III: 516.

24. Ibid., II: 478–80; ibid., III: 218–20.

25. Ibid., pp. 248–49, 267–68, 385–86, 495–96.

26. Ibid., pp. 423–24.

27. DeConde, *Quasi-War*, pp. 128–30; and Bonnel, *Guerre de course*, pp. 97–99.

28. Ibid.,

29. *QW*, III: 26–28, 51–52, 153–54, 192, 357–58.

30. Ibid., pp. 280–81, 294–95, 304, 366, 475.

31. Ibid., pp. 5–6.

32. Ibid., pp. 108–9.

33. Ibid., I: 58; K. Jack Bauer, "Naval Shipbuilding Programs, 1794–1860," *Military Affairs* 29 (Spring 1965): 30–31; *DAB*,XIV: 484; and Richard Dillon, *We Have Met the Enemy: Oliver Hazard Perry, Wilderness Commodore* (New York, 1978), pp. 1–14.

34. *QW*, III: 150–51.

35. Ibid., 258–59, 260, 293, 457–58, 513, 566, 569. Murray and some of the *Montezuma's* men had contracted yellow fever during their brief stop at Havana in April 1799.

36. *QW*, III: 408–9, 409–10, 421.

37. Ibid., pp. 294–95, 341–42.

38. Ibid., pp. 179–80. The ship and Blakely's property were eventually released by the French under Spanish pressure.

39. *QW*, III: 340–41, 402–403, 459–60.

40. Bauer, "Naval Building Programs," p. 31; *QW*, II: 97; ibid., III: 223–24 (emphasis in the original).

41. Stoddert to Pickering, 9 August 1798, DNA, RG 59, SDA, Miscellaneous Letters; *QW*, I: 217, 290; Pickering to Sever, 14 May 1795, DNA, RG 45, Area File 11; Perkins, *First Raaprochement*, p. 96; *QW*, IV: 112; ibid., VII: 80–84, 246–47; ibid., III: 194; ibid., V: 100–1, 289–90, 517–18. See also R. J. B. Knight, "The

Introduction of Copper Sheathing into the Royal Navy, 1779–1786," *Mariner's Mirror* 59 (August 1973): 299–309; Maurer Maurer, "Coppered Bottoms for the Royal Navy: A Factor in the Maritime War of 1778–1783," *Military Affairs* 14 (April 1950): 57–61; Maurer Maurer, "Coppered Bottoms for the United States Navy, 1794–1803," United States Naval Institute *Proceedings* 71 (June 1945): 693–99; and Palmer, "Quasi-War," pp. 311–14.

42. *QW*, II: 310–111; ibid., III: 55, 451–52; ibid., IV: 114–15.

43. Ibid., III: 463.

44. Ibid., pp. 362, 534.

45. Ibid., pp. 428–29, 462; Clark, *Barry*, p. 456. Barry actually left the Delaware on 6 July.

46. *QW*, III: 362.

47. Ibid., pp. 112, 161–62.

48. Ibid., pp. 85–86, 93–94, 161.

49. Ibid., pp. 399–400..

50. Ibid., pp. 274–75, 349–50, 412–20, 480–81. Cordis was exonerated. Carmick's description of the *Constitution's* marines was: "I think it is not possible to produce such another shabby set of animals in this world. . . ."

51. Ibid., pp. 559–60.

52. Rebecca Stoddert to Eliza Gantt, DLC, Rebecca Lowndes Stoddert Papers; and *QW*, III: 476.

53. George Gibbs, *Memoirs of the Administration of Washington and John Adams, Edited from the Papers of Oliver Wolcott, Secretary of the Treasury*, 2 vols. (New York, 1846), II: 313–18.

54. *QW*, VII: 80–84.

55. Palmer, "Quasi-War," p. 284; and Cornelius William Stafford, *The Philadelphia Directory for 1800* (Philadelphia, 1800), p. 120, and the appendix on government officers, p. 25.

56. Gibbs, *Wolcott*, II: 115, 115–17; Adams, *Works*, IX: 604–8; *QW*, II: 129–34. For a discussion of Stoddert's and Adams's naval policies see Frederic H. Hayes, "John Adams and American Sea Power," *American Neptune* 25 (January 1965): 35–45; Russell F. Weigley, *The American Way of War: A History of United States Military Strategy and Policy* (New York, 1973), pp. 43–44; the Sprouts, *American Naval Policy*, pp. 25–44; Craig L. Symonds, *Navalists and Antinavalists: The Naval Policy Debate in the United States, 1785–1827* (Newark, Del., 1980), pp. 51–81; Robert F. Jones, "The Naval Thought and Policy of Benjamin Stoddert, First Secretary of the Navy, 1798–1801," *American Neptune* 24 (January 1964): 61–69; and Palmer, "Quasi-War," pp. 294–305.

57. Alfred Thayer Mahan, *The Influence of Sea Power upon History, 1660–1783* (Boston, 1918), pp. 1–89 passim.

58. Palmer, "Quasi-War," pp. 314–25; *ASP, Finance*, I: 752–54; Paullin, *Naval Administration*, p. 139; United States Navy Department, *American Ships of the Line* (Washington, D.C. 1969), pp. 12–13; My belief that Stoddert's plans were the source of Hamilton's recommendations is based on a close comparison of Stoddert to Parker, 29 December 1798, *QW*, II: 129–34, with Paul Hamilton to Langdon Cheves, 3 December 1811, United States Navy Department, Naval Historical Center, *The Naval War of 1812: A Documentary History*, William S. Dudley, ed., vol. I (Washington, D.C. 1985), pp. 53–56.

59. The most successful of the cutters were the *Pickering* and *Eagle*.

60. *QW*, IV: 313–14.

61. Ibid., I: 350.

62. Robert Morris to Thomas Pinckney, 18 March 1795, State Historical Society of Wisconsin, Archives Division [Naval Historical Division photostat]; Pickering to Washington, 14 March 1795, Massachusetts Historical Society, Timothy Pickering Papers, Vol. 35, #193; *QW*, III: 248.

63. Ibid., p. 274.

64. Ibid., VI: 287–88.

65. Stoddert also considered dispatching small squadrons to the Mediterranean and the Far East.

66. Adams, *Works*, VIII: 599; Savageau, "Half War Prisoners," pp. 159–76; Jenkins, "Heyday," p. 249; and Bonnel, *Guerre de course*, p. 112.

67. Kenneth Schaffel, "The American Board of War, 1776–1787" (Ph.D. dissertation, City University of New York, 1983), pp. 197–218.

68. *QW*, III: 453; Savageau, "Half War Prisoners," p. 170.

69. *ASP, Naval Affairs*, I: 68–70.

70. Truxtun to Biddle, 3 December 1799, PHi, LCP, Truxtun-Biddle Letters, Box I, folio #25.

Chapter 7

1. *QW*, III: 429.

2. Ibid., pp. 538–39.

3. Ibid., pp. 559–60.

4. Ibid., pp. 550–51.

5. Ibid., pp. 505, 551–52.

6. Ferguson, *Truxtun*, pp. 175–76.

7. Nominal difference because French pounds were one-twelfth heavier than English pounds, while American shot was usually one-eighteenth underweight. Thus the *Constellation*'s 792 pound broadside actually weighed less, while *l'Insurgente*'s 564 French pounds equaled 611 English, see James, *Naval History*, I: 45–46; and Cooper, *History*, I: 270–71.

8. *QW*, III: 480.

9. Ferguson, *Truxtun*, p. 176; *QW*, III: 386.

10. Ibid., pp. 551–52.

11. Ibid., pp. 550–51.

12. Ibid., IV: 30–31.

13. Ibid., pp. 21, 60–61.

14. Ibid., pp. 373–74.

15. Ibid., pp. 182, 188, 190–91.

16. Ibid., pp. 184–85, 216.

17. Ibid., pp. 229–30, 257, 278–79, 324–25. Two French privateers were active in the Canaries in the fall of 1799; Murray simply missed them.

18. Ibid., pp. 29, 104–5.

19. Adams, *Works*, IX: 10–12; *QW*, IV: 87–88.

20. Ibid., pp. 189, 241–42, 246, 291.

21. Ibid., pp. 342–43. The *George Washington* had been slated for the auction block.

22. Ibid., p. 304.

23. Ibid., pp. 24, 25, 29, 41, 64–65, 121–22.

24. Ibid., pp. 106, 107–10, 130, 149–51, 193, 243–44.

25. Ibid., pp. 2, 21, 47, 73, 129, 144–45, 204.

26. Palmer, "Quasi-War," pp. 326–28; *QW,* I: 77–78, 118–19, 328–29, 210, 244, 442–43, 462–63; ibid., III: 310, 332–33. Paullin, *Naval Administration,* pp. 110–11; and Reuben Elmore Stivers, *Privateers & Volunteers: The Men and Women of Our Reserve Naval Forces, 1766–1866* (Annapolis, Md., 1975), p. 50, claim that little difficulty was encountered during the Quasi-War in recruiting. Paullin states that "enough men to man a frigate could usually be enlisted in a week's time." I have yet to discover a single such case.

27. *QW,* III: 100; ibid., IV: 41, 121–22.

28. Ibid., pp. 20, 35. Samuel was the brother of James Barron, see *DAB,* I: 649–51; and *Appleton's,* I: 179. For Truxtun's remarks on Decatur see Truxtun to Biddle, 3 December 1799, Phi, LCP, Truxtun-Biddle Papers, Box I, folio #25.

29. *QW,* IV: 35, 69, 217–18; and Ferguson, *Truxtun,* pp. 182–83.

30. *QW,* IV: 311–12; Ferguson, *Truxtun,* pp. 184–86; and Charles Biddle, *Autobiography of Charles Biddle, Vice-President of the Supreme Executive Council of Pennsylvania, 1745–1821* (Philadelphia, 1883), pp. 281–82.

31. *QW,* IV: 333, 361–62, 564; and Ferguson, *Truxtun,* pp. 186–87.

32. *QW,* IV: 72–73, 82.

33. Ibid., pp. 170–71, 178; and *DAB,* XIII: 219.

34. *QW,* IV: 270.

35. Cross to William Jones, 23 August 1798, PHi, Jones and Clarke Papers, Correspondence; *QW,* IV: 101–102, 243; ibid., I: 342–43.

36. *QW,* IV: 217, 240.

37. *DAB,* XII: 149–50; *QW,* III; 304, 475.

38. Ibid., IV: 53–54.

39. Ibid., III: 357; ibid., IV: 241.

40. James, *Naval History,* II: 420–21; *QW,* IV: 66–67.

41. Ibid.

42. Ibid.

43. *The Naval Chronicle Containing a General and Biographical History of the Royal Navy of the United Kingdom; with a Variety of Original Papers on Nautical Subjects,* 40 vols. (London, 1799–1818), III: 139.

44. Mayo, *Instructions,* pp. 179–80; Liston to Grenville, 2 February 1799, PRO, FO 5/25, #4. Liston characterized McNeill as "a foolish intemperate old man," a description that he had probably taken from Stoddert. The American secretary of the navy and Liston got along quite well, the British minister reporting to Grenville that Stoddert's "conduct since his entry into office has been uniformly candid and friendly. . . ." See Liston to Grenville, 31 December 1799, ibid., #67.

45. *QW,* IV: 431, 464–66.

46. Ibid., p. 158.

47. Charles Oscar Paullin, *Commodore John Rodgers: Captain, Commodore, and Senior Officer in the Navy, 1773–1838* (Cleveland, 1910); and *QW,* II: 29–31.

48. The original account comes from Goldsborough, *Naval Chronicle,* pp. 132–37, but is repeated in most histories of the war and in Paullin's biography of Rodgers on pages 46–47. The battle was fought on 9 February, Williams commanding the *Norfolk* brig fell in with the frigates in company on 11 February, and the next day Truxtun noted that the ships anchored at Basseterre, see *QW,* II: 335–37, 343–44, 346.

49. Ibid., III: 285–86; ibid., IV: 159–60, 437–38, 441–42. The *Maryland* was a 380-ton sloop of war mounting twenty-six cannon, with a crew of 180.

50. Ibid., pp. 189, 195–96, 373–74.

51. Ibid., p. 126.

52. Ibid., pp. 92–97, 132–34; Truxtun to Biddle, 3 December 1799, PHi, LCP, Truxtun-Biddle Letters, Box 1, folio #25.

53. *QW,* IV: 92–97.

54. Ibid., pp. 153, 215.

55. Bonnel, *Guerre de course,* pp. 319–67; *QW,* IV: 29, 229; ibid., VII: 372–73.

56. Ibid., IV: 52; *Appleton's,* I: 409; and Edgar Stanton Maclay, *Moses Brown, Captain U. S. N.* (New York, 1904).

57. *QW,* IV: 201–2.

58. Ibid., pp. 216, 229.

59. Ibid., pp. 169, 170–72, 409, 410.

60. Ibid., pp. 83, 199–200.

61. Ibid., pp. 187–88, 218–19.

62. Ibid., pp. 286, 278–88, 288.

63. Ibid., pp. 337, 403.

64. M. Clarke, *The Memoirs of the Celebrated and Beautiful Mrs. Ann Carson, Daughter of an Officer of the U.S. Navy, and Wife of Another, Whose Life Terminated in the Philadelphia Prison,* 2 vols. (Philadelphia, 1838;; reprint ed. in 1 vol., New York, 1980), pp. 15–26.

65. *QW,* IV: 403. Baker endorsed the letter at the bottom, agreeing with the recommendations therein.

66. Ibid., pp. 387, 394, 441–42, 454.

67. Troude, *Batailles Navales,* III: 183, 186, 210, 213, 218, 220; and James, *Naval History,* II: 387.

68. *QW,* IV: 165, 467, 468–69, 476–77, 487–88.

69. Ibid., pp. 404–5, 519.

70. Ibid., pp. 227, 432, 445, 463, 477–79, 500–2, 559, 565, 577–78, 589; ibid., VII: 373–73.

71. Ibid., IV: 295.

Chapter 8

1. Charles Callan Tansill, *The United States and Santo Domingo, 1798–1873: A Chapter in Caribbean Diplomacy* (Baltimore, 1938), pp. 1–9; and John H. Coatsworth, "American Trade with European Colonies in the Caribbean and South America, 1790–1812," *William and Mary Quarterly,* 3rd Ser. 24 (April 1967): 245–46, 263.

2. John W. Fortescue, *A History of the British Army,* 13 vols. (London, 1889–1930), IV: 76–77, 325–33, 339; and James, *Naval History,* I: 251.

3. Fortescue, *History,* IV: 340; and James, *Naval History,* I: 247–49.

4. Fortescue, *History,* IV: 560.

5. Ibid., pp. 496, 545–46. The money and manpower saved in the Caribbean were to be deployed instead in Europe, the maritime and colonial strategy of Henry Dundas, secretary of state for war, giving way to the continental strategy of Lord Grenville. For an excellent discussion of British strategy between 1798 and 1802,

and a more sympathetic view of Dundas, much maligned by Fortescue, see Piers Mackesy's *Statesmen at War: The Strategy of Overthrow, 1798–1799* (London, 1974), and *War without Victory: The Downfall of Pitt, 1799–1802* (Oxford, 1984).

6. Fortescue, *History*, IV: 550–51.

7. Ibid., pp. 551–52.

8. *Dictionary of National Biography*, 63 vols. (London, 1885–1900), XXXV: 374–76.

9. Fortescue, *History*, IV: 554–55.

10. Ibid., pp. 551–56. The convention is reprinted in Rayford W. Logan, *The Diplomatic Relations of the United States with Haiti, 1776–1891* (Chapel Hill, N.C., 1941), pp. 65–66. There are undocumented claims that Maitland offered to make Toussaint a king, see ibid., p. 64; and C. L. R. James, *The Black Jacobins: Toussaint L'Ouverture and the San Domingo Revolution* (New York, 1963), pp. 211–12.

11. Fortescue, *History*, IV: 562–63.

12. Ibid., pp. 565–66. Hyde Parker complained about Thomas Maitland in January 1798, two months before his return to St. Domingo from London, see Parker to Lord Spencer, extracted in Spencer to Henry Dundas, 4 April 1798, DLC, Melville Papers. Parker noted that he disliked "the necessity of making an application to a lieutenant-colonel. . . ." For Parker's reaction to Maitland's decision to evacuate the whole of St. Domingo see Navy Records Society, *Private Papers of George, Second Earl Spencer, First Lord of the Admiralty, 1794–1801*, Julian S. Corbett and H. W. Richmond, eds., 4 vols (London, 1913–1924), III: 266–68, 269–70. The cabinet, however, supported Maitland's decision and reasoning, not Parker's see ibid., pp. 271, 272.

13. For Parker's view of the importance of the Môle see ibid., pp. 266–67.

14. Fortescue, *History*, IV: 559.

15. Tansill, *The United States and San Domingo*, pp. 37–46; Perkins, *First Rapprochement*, pp. 106–8; Logan, *The United States and Haiti*, pp. 68–71; and Ludwell Lee Montague, *Haiti and the United States, 1714–1938* (New York, 1966), pp. 29–30.

16. Tansill, *The United States and San Domingo*, pp. 44–46.

17. Logan, *The United States and Haiti*, pp. 73–74; James, *Black Jacobins*, pp. 266–67; and *QW*, II; 216–17.

18. Perkins, *First Rapprochement*, pp. 108, 110; Logan, *The United States and Haiti*, pp. 81–90, 110; and Montague, *Haiti and the United States*, pp. 38–39.

19. Adams, *Works*, IX: 634–35; and *QW*, III: 453.

20. Ibid., IV: 217.

21. Tansill, *The United States and San Domingo*, pp. 58–65.

22. *QW*, IV: 84–85, 412–20; ibid., III: 122–28.

23. Ibid., pp. 389–93; ibid., IV: 84–85; and Tansill, *The United States and San Domingo*, p. 67n.

24. *QW*, III: 389–93; ibid., IV: 157–58, 194, 209–10, 235; Thomas Wentworth Higginson, *Life and Times of Stephen Higginson* (Boston, 1907), pp. 163–68. The possibility remains that the cargo was, in fact, shipped to Cap François despite Stoddert's disagreement with the plan. It was at this time that the secretary of the navy found himself in a disagreement with Higginson at Boston over the proposed replacement of the larger *Herald* with the *Augusta* brig, see chapter 2, section 2. Stoddert never named the "pressures" which forced to give in to Higginson. Perhaps Pickering convinced Stoddert to allow the cargo to be sent unofficially, for

such a decision would be consistent with the secretary of state's handling of affairs, and his relationship with Higginson.

25. *QW*, IV: 71–72, 458–59.

26. Ibid., III: 174–75; ibid., IV: 222–23, 400–2, 468–69, 481, 503; ibid., V: 119–20.

27. Ibid., III: 389–93; Tansill, *The United States and San Domingo*, p. 67n.

28. *QW*, IV: 476–77, 555–56.

29. James, *Naval History*, II: 414–15; and Liston to Grenville, 6 February 1800, PRO, FO 5/25, #7.

30. *Spencer Papers*, III: 282–83.

31. Ibid., pp. 284–85; and *Naval Chronicle*, III: 152.

32. *QW*, IV: 570–71; ibid., V: 281–82.

33. Ibid., IV: 555–56; ibid., V: 286.

34. Ibid., pp. 94, 208–9.

35. Ibid., pp. 250–51, 318.

36. Ibid., VI: 139–40, 314, 382–83.

37. Ibid., V: 286.

38. Ibid., pp. 309–10, 336–37, 349–50, 355; and Logan, *The United States and Haiti*, p. 106. Logan implies that the plan was executed, but as late as April Talbot was still undecided, see *QW*, V: 381–83. The log of the *Constitution* makes clear that the frigate never sailed to Jacmel.

39. Ibid., p. 473; ibid., VI: 321–22, 422–23.

40. Logan, *The United States and Haiti*, p. 104; and Montague, *Haiti and the United States*, p. 40, consider the assistance of the American decisive. James, *Black Jacobins*, fails to mention the operations of the United States Navy in support of Toussaint.

41. *QW*, III: 294–95, 500; ibid., IV: 84–85, 191, 193. For a view of Bainbridge's alleged brutality see John Rea, *A Letter to William Bainbridge Esqr. Formerly Commander of the United States' Ship George Washington; relative to Some Transactions, on Board Said Ship, during a Voyage to Algiers, Constantinople, &c.* (Philadelphia, 1802). Long, *Ready to Hazard*, pp. 54–58, offers a rejoinder.

42. *QW*, IV: 503–6.

43. Ibid., pp. 480, 547–48, 561; ibid., V: 82–83.

44. Ibid., VII: 372–73.

45. Ibid., V: 488–90. The French frigate *l'Africaine* briefly stopped at Cap François to debark officials in May 1800.

46. The account is drawn from ibid., pp. 1–3, 4, 5–6.

47. David Dixon Porter, *Memoir of Commodore David Porter of the United States Navy* (Albany, 1875), pp. 29–32. D. D. Porter also repeats the tale of Rodgers and Porter battling the French crew of *l'Insurgente*, ibid., pp. 22–23. Long, *Nothing Too Daring*, p. 13, repeats the D. D. Porter version of the action in the Bight. Allen, *Naval War*, pp. 146–47, presents both versions. William M. Fowler, Jr., in *Jack Tars and Commodores: The American Navy, 1787–1815* (Boston, 1984), p. 52, also makes Porter out to be the hero of the day.

48. "Biographical Memoir of Captain David Porter," *Analetic Magazine* 4 (September 1814): 226; Cooper, *Naval History*, I: 183; *QW*, V: 208–209; ibid., VI: 41–43.

49. Ibid., pp. 43–45.

50. Ibid., pp. 373–74.

51. Ibid., V: 183–84, 185–89.

52. Linda and Christopher McKee, "An Inquiry into the Conduct of Joshua Blake," *American Neptune* 21 (April 1961): 130–41.

53. *QW,* VI: 548; ibid., VII: 315–61. Information on Pickering's squadron in the Mediterranean appears in *BW,* I: passim. Maley's prize agent was Benjamin Hodgdon whose brother Samuel was the Intendant for Military Stores and an old friend of Pickering. Hodgdon kept Pickering posted on the fate of Maley, see *QW,* VI: 133.

54. For Maley's court of enquiry see DNA, RG 45, Naval Records, Court Martials, 1799–1861, Case 25B. See also *QW,* VI: 293–99, 373.

55. Ibid., pp. 389–90.

56. Carnegie Endowment for International Peace, *Prize Cases Decided in the United States Supreme Court, 1789–1918,* James Brown Scott, ed., 3 vols. (Oxford, 1923), I: 245–69 (William Maley v. Jared Shattuck); and *QW,* VI: 548.

57. Ibid., V: 241, 389.

58. Ibid., pp. 394–95, 440–41.

59. Ibid., pp. 443, 446–47, 447–48, 457–59, 461–62, 462, 463.

60. Ibid., pp. 459–60, 460.

61. Ibid., VI: 238–39, 263–64, 380, 472–73, 559; and Dillon, *We Have Met the Enemy,* p. 12.

62. DNA, RG 45, Courts Martials, #6.

63. *QW,* VII: 559.

64. For a contemporary biographical sketch of Parker see *Naval Chronicle,* V: 281–307.

65. *QW,* V: 94.

66. Ibid., pp. 183–84, 184–85, 252.

67. Ibid., pp. 183–84.

68. Ibid., III: 40–41, 49–51, 84.

69. Ibid., V: 333–34, 337–38.

70. Ibid., VI: 317–18.

71. Ibid., V: 252, 259, 533. The charges against the Bosses are drawn from Maley's court of enquiry, DNA, RG 45, Courts Martial, #25B.

72. *QW,* V: 263–64.

73. Ibid., pp. 503–4.

74. Cooper, *History,* I: 91; *Hamilton Papers,* XXII: 60–61, 152. Robert W. Hamilton was Alexander Hamilton's first cousin and an Englishman.

75. *QW,* V: 468, 470, 474.

76. Ibid., p. 474.

77. Ibid., pp. 503–4.

78. Ibid., p. 471, 496.

79. Ibid., pp. 481, 483, 485, 491.

80. Ibid., pp. 495, 496.

81. Ibid., 499.

82. Ibid., pp. 501–3.

83. Ibid., pp. 503–4.

84. Ibid.

85. Ibid., pp. 500–1, 504–5.

86. Ibid.

87. Ibid., VI: 9.

88. Ibid., pp. 10, 16, 17.

89. Ibid., p. 32.

90. Ibid., pp. 35, 35–36.
91. Ibid., pp. 39, 163.
92. Ibid., pp. 139–40, 153–54, 165–66.
93. Martin, *Most Fortunate Ship*, pp. 17–18.
94. *QW*, VI: 210–11.
95. Ibid., pp. 94, 314, 387, 388.
96. Ibid, pp. 79, 150, 274–75, 317–18, 411.
97. Ibid., pp. 150, 210–11, 320; and John Paul Russo, "Hull's First Victory: One Painting, Three Famous Men," *American Neptune* 25 (January 1965): 32.

Chapter 9

1. *QW*, V: 44, 112.
2. Ibid., p. 115; and Hoxse, *Yankee Tar*, p. 66.
3. *QW*, IV: 377–80.
4. Truxtun's decision to sail alone for Guadeloupe could be passed over if he were merely a captain of an American frigate, but he was the commodore of the squadron operating in the whole of the Lesser Antilles. Even by contemporary standards, Truxtun's behavior was inexcusable. As an example, late in 1813 Captain Stephen Decatur, Jr., issued a challenge to the British squadron blockading New London, Conn. Decatur proposed that the American frigates *United States* and *Macedonian* meet the *Endymion* and *Statira*. The British commodore, Captain Thomas Masterman Hardy in the *Ramillies*, agreed to the duel in principle, but declined the matchup proposed by Decatur, which favored the Americans. The commander-in-chief, Admiral Sir John Borlase Warren, was relieved to learn that the meeting had been aborted. He wrote to Secretary of the Admiralty Sir John Wilson Croker: "I am very glad the matter terminated in the manner it did . . . thinking it extremely improper that private feeling should interfere in such points with public service, and be the means of affording the enemy an opportunity to advance his small force upon an equality with ours in the present superiority." See Warren to Croker, 2 February 1814, PRO, Adm. 1/505.
5. *QW*, V: 143, 157, 176, 176–77.
6. The account of the action is drawn from ibid., pp. 159, 160, 160–61, 162, 164–66, 166–69, 169–70, 170–72, 196–97, 198; ibid., VII: 401; James, *Naval History*, III: 1–3; Frank Donovan, *The Tall Frigates* (New York, 1962), pp. 44–47; Maclay, *History*, I: 193–98; Nash, *Forgotten Wars*, pp. 159–62; Allen, *Naval War*, pp. 163–76; Ferguson, *Truxtun*, pp. 187–98; Cooper, *History*, I: 172–75; Troude, *Batailles Navales*, III: 200–1.
7. According to Pitot's accounts the American fire stopped first and only the battered state of *la Vengeance* saved Truxtun from capture. But the first lieutenant of the French frigate told Stoddert's brother-in-law in 1808 that Pitot had struck twice during the action, the surrenders going unnoticed in the darkness. See *QW*, V: 170–72.
8. The figure of 160 is frequently dismissed, but is probably accurate. The crew of *la Vengeance* totaled 320 during the action, exclusive of soldiers and passengers. But at the time of her capture by the British *Seine* frigate in August 1800, only 160 of the crew remained on board, see ibid., VI: 267.
9. The disparity in casualties is not unusual considering the French tactic of firing into the masts, and the American of firing into the hull. The *Seine* lost

thirteen killed and twenty-nine wounded in taking the half-crewed French frigate in August, see ibid., p. 270. For American casualties see ibid., V: 208. One of the Yankee casualties was John Hoxse, whose arm was amputated, see Hoxse, *Yankee Tar*, pp. 70–71. Hoxse's account of the battle, ibid., pp. 69–70, is in fact a plagiarized account taken directly from Truxtun's journal for 2 February 1800, see *QW*, V: 160–61. Hoxse took Truxtun's report of the battle and substituted "Captain Truxtun" wherever Truxtun had used the first person singular pronoun. Hoxse most likely went into shock as the result of his wound and the amputation and may have remembered very little about the engagement.

10. Goldsborough, *Naval Chronicle*, pp. 168–69.

11. The loss of the *Chesapeake* to the well-drilled crew of Captain Philip Bowes Vere Broke's *Shannon* on 1 June 1813 is a good example, see Peter Padfield, *Broke and the Shannon* (London, 1968).

12. *QW*, V: 159.

13. Ibid., pp. 183, 193, 209–10.

14. Ibid., pp. 31–33.

15. Ibid., p. 28.

16. Ibid., pp. 68, 89–90, 90.

17. Ibid., pp. 125–26.

18. Ibid., IV: 384; ibid., V: 176.

19. Ibid., pp. 209–10.

20. Ibid., pp. 249, 300–2.

21. Ibid., pp. 145–46, 386, 473–74, 563.

22. Ibid., pp. 199, 386; ibid., VI: 174–75.

23. Ibid., II: 248.

24. DeConde, *Quasi-War*, p. 215.

25. Charles Maurice de Talleyrand-Périgord, *Memoirs of the Prince de Talleyrand*, Duc de Broglie, ed., 5 vols. (London, 1891–92), I: 209, 213; Bonnel, *Guerre de course*, p. 91; *QW*, IV: 584–87 (enclosing a copy of the law of 26 July 1778).

26. The American envoys reached France after the coup.

27. *QW*, VI: 1–2, 176–77.

28. Steel, *Naval Chronologist*, pp. 67–70.

29. *QW*, V: 377–79.

30. Ibid., VI: 532–33.

31. Ibid., V: 154–57, 181–82, 200–1 (emphasis in the original); and ibid., VI: 364–65.

32. Ibid., V: 103–4.

33. By April Stoddert realized that Rodgers was not sailing north on his own and would have to be recalled. The secretary instructed Decatur to do so, noting that the *Maryland* could "do nothing" off Surinam, see ibid., p. 386. See also Truxtun to Biddle, 19 January 1811, PHi, LCP, Truxtun-Biddle Letters, Box 2, folio #92; and *QW*, VII: 292.

34. Ibid., V: 121, 237, 323–24, 342; and Clarke, *Ann Carson*, pp. 25–26.

35. *QW*, V: 377–79.

36. Ibid., VI: 63–64; and Michael O'Quinlivan, "Setting the Pattern: The Navy and the Marine Corps at Curaçao, 1800," *Navy* 2 (May 1959): 58.

37. *QW*, VI: 81.

38. Ibid., p. 236.

39. Ibid., pp. 218–19, 267.

40. Ibid., pp. 322–23; and news item on Curaçao that appeared in the Virginia

Argus, 7 October 1800, Marine Corps Historical Center, Chronological File, transcript.

41. *QW,* VI: 341–42.

42. Ibid., pp. 337–41.

43. James, *Naval History,* III: 38; *Spencer Papers,* III: 264–65, 268–69; *Naval Chronicle,* IV: 505–6, 506, 506–7.

44. Ibid., p. 519; news report that appeared in the Massachusetts *Mercury,* 28 October 1800, Marine Corps Historical Center, Chronological File, transcript.

45. *QW,* VI: 500–1.

46. Ibid., p. 372.

47. Ibid., pp. 337–41, 500–1.

48. Ibid., IV: 288.

49. Ibid., VI: 372.

50. Ibid., pp. 337–41.

51. Ibid., pp. 451–52, 500–2; *Naval Chronicle,* IV: 506–7.

52. Ibid., pp. 439–40; and Edward Thornton to Grenville, 29 December 1800, PRO, FO 5/29, #28.

53. Perkins, *First Rapprochement,* pp. 133–34. For a biographical sketch of Watkins see John Marshall, *Royal Naval Biography; or, Memoirs of the Services of all the Flag-Officers, Superannuated Rear-Admirals, Retired Captains, Post-Captains, and Commanders, . . .* 8 vols. in 12 (London, 1824), III: 9–12. William Savage, the American agent for impressed seamen at Jamaica noted the changed atmosphere that came with Seymour's replacement of Parker. Savage reported on 1 November 1800: "The conduct of the navy here, so far as respects the impressing and detaining of American seamen, is widely different on the score of humanity from what was pursued during the administration of Admiral Parker." See *QW,* VI: 519. In Phillips's letter of 25 October 1800, ibid., pp. 500–1, the American consul wrote of the arrival at Curaçao of Seymour on 23 October expecting "several excesses & improper transactions" to be redressed. One of Lord Seymour's first actions was to return to Phillips the specie Watkins had seized, see ibid., p. 337.

Chapter 10

1. The new frigates *Philadelphia* 36, and *Chesapeake* 36, were never sent to the Mediterranean as intended, see *QW,* IV: 516, 564–65.

2. Ibid., pp. 75–77, 239. See also Philip Chadwick Foster Smith, *The Frigate Essex Papers: Building the Salem Frigate, 1798–1799* (Salem, Mass., 1974).

3. *QW,* III: 495, 503; Pennock to Sever, 20 July 1800, DLC, Sever Papers.

4. For a biography of Preble see Christopher McKee, *Edward Preble: A Naval Biography, 1761–1807* (Annapolis, Md., 1972). See also *QW,* III: 248, 252–53, 315; and Smith, *Essex Papers,* pp. 161–63.

5. *QW,* IV: 397–98, 400, 407, 409, 456–57, 474.

6. *ASP, Commerce and Navigation,* I: 317, 362, 384, 417, 431, 453, 489; Alfred W. Crosby, Jr., "American Trade with Mauritius in the Age of the French Revolution and Napoleon," *American Neptune* 45 (January 1965): 5–17; and *QW,* IV: 475–76.

7. Bonnel, *Guerre de course,* p. 376; *QW,* IV: 56–57, 531–33. Robert Surcouf's skill can be attested to by an action he fought on 9 October 1800 in the Indian Ocean. *La Confiance,* twenty 8-pounders, measuring 490 tons, captured the East

India Company ship *Kent* 26, which carried twenty 12-pounders and six 6-pounders and measured 820 tons. Surcouf's crew outnumbered the British by 250 to 100, however, see James, *Naval History*, III: 31; Charles Marie Cunat, *Histoire de Robert Surcouf, Capitaine de Corsaire* (Paris, 1842), pp. 136–47.

    8. *QW*, IV: 474, 475, 475–76, 483, 485, 490–91, 491, 520–23, 577.

    9. Ibid., pp. 494–95, 578–79; ibid., V: 47, 50; and McKee, *Preble*, p. 70.

    10. *QW*, V: 53, 62–63, 65–66, 70, 70–71, 110.

    11. Ibid., VI: 12–13.

    12. Ibid., V: 322; ibid., III: 412–20; and James E. Valle, *Rocks and Shoals: Order and Discipline in the Old Navy, 1800–1861* (Annapolis, Md., 1980), p. 204. Valle makes a minor error in reference to the year of the court-martial.

    13. *QW*, V: 65–66.

    14. Ibid., pp. 449, 450. For details of the mutiny see Valle, *Rocks & Shoals*, p. 112.

    15. *QW*, V: 451–56, 492.

    16. Ibid., p. 462; Truxtun to Stoddert, April 1800, DNA, RG 45, Courts Martial, #1. The record of the enquiry is appended to Cordis's court-martial. A copy of the proceedings as printed by Truxtun in Norfolk in 1800 is in DLC, Sever Papers.

    17. *QW*, V: 128, 294, 305, 335, 345; and McKee, *Preble*, p. 71.

    18. *QW*, V: 299–300, 346, 347; ibid., IV: 520–23.

    19. Ibid., V: 423.

    20. Ibid., pp. 474, 486, 521.

    21. Ibid., pp. 498, 534; ibid., VI: 224.

    22. Ibid., pp. 33, 53, 57.

    23. Ibid., pp. 50, 68, 96–97, 224, 411; McKee, *Preble*, pp. 77–78. Learning of the presence of the *Essex* at Batavia, Surcouf's biographer notes that the corsair "judged it prudent to change his cruising grounds and to proceed to another part of the Indian Ocean." See Cunat, *Surcouf*, pp. 127–28.

    24. *QW*, VI: 299, 343.

    25. Ibid., pp. 351, 371–72, 384, 388.

    26. Ibid., pp. 415–18, 557; ibid., VII: 46–47; McKee, *Preble*, pp. 347–48.

    27. *QW*, VII: 3, 168, 203.

Chapter 11

    1. *QW*, IV: 516, 564–65; ibid., V: 242, 339–40, 343, 353, 360.

    2. Kurtz, *Adams*, pp. 323, 392–93; DeConde, *Quasi-War*, pp. 183, 217–18, 270–73; Robert L. Scheina, "Benjamin Stoddert, Politics, and the Navy," *American Neptune* 36 (January 1976): 62; and John B. Boles, "Politics, Intrigue, and the Presidency: James McHenry to Bishop John Carroll, May 16, 1800," *Maryland Historical Magazine* 69 (Spring 1974): 69–85. McHenry wrote Carroll of the secretary of the navy: "Stoddert you know is pretty dexterous at intrigue." During his two-week tenure as secretary of war Stoddert had the assistance of James Wilkinson, see Jacobs, *Tarnished Warrior*, p. 193. The stockade building at the junction of the Alabama and Tombigbee rivers was given the name Fort Stoddert, see *Dictionary of American History*, James Truslow Adams, ed., 5 vols. (New York, 1940), II: 184–85. A naval fruit of the connection of the two men took the form of a

midshipman's warrant issued at Wilkinson's behest for Joseph Israel, who died when the *Intrepid* infernal exploded prematurely in Tripoli harbor in 1804. See Wilkinson to Stoddert, 7 December 1800, Naval Historical Center, Operational Archives, ZB Files, Joseph Israel.

3. *QW,* V: 377–79.

4. Ferguson, *Truxtun,* p. 201; *QW,* VI: 239–41.

5. Ibid., V: 280, 334–35, 373, 373–74, 430.

6. Ibid., pp. 414–15, 419, 421–22.

7. Ibid., pp. 287–88, 449.

8. Ibid., pp. 295–96, 427–28, 511, 538, 544, 545–46; ibid., VI: 71, 72; and Ferguson, *Truxtun,* p. 204.

9. *QW,* V: 511, 522–23, 526–27.

10. Ibid., pp. 526–27.

11. Ibid., pp. 557, 561–62, 567.

12. Ibid., pp. 545–46, 555, 556, 559, 561–62, 573.

13. Ibid., VI: 71, 71–72, 72, 86–87, 138.

14. Ibid., pp. 271–72.

15. Ibid., pp. 378, 389, 537.

16. Ibid., pp. 391, 419–20, 423–24, 425, 427.

17. Ibid., pp. 508–9; ibid., VII: 11–12.

18. *ASP, Commerce and Navigation,* I: 431, 453, 489.

19. *QW,* V: 418; ibid., VII: 188, 518–19.

20. Ibid., VI: 198. For sketches of Stewart's career see Pratt, *Preble's Boys,* pp. 317–43; and "Biographical Notice of Captain Charles Stewart," *Analectic Magazine* 7 (February 1816): 132–41.

21. *QW,* VI: 183–84, 422–23; Pratt, *Preble's Boys,* pp. 321–22; and Cooper, *History,* I: 183–84.

22. *QW,* VI: 430–31, 506–7.

23. Ibid., pp. 476, 496.

24. Ibid., pp. 257, 258, 418–19; ibid., III: 56.

25. Maclay, *Brown,* p. 13; *QW,* VI: 149; ibid., VII: 86–90; Christopher McKee, "The Pathology of a Profession: Death in the United States Navy Officer Corps, 1797–1815," *War & Society* 3 (May 1985): 6–7, 22n. McKee's findings are similar to Michael Lewis's for the Royal Navy in his *A Social History of the Navy, 1793–1815* (London, 1960), pp. 348, 441, and passim.

26. *QW,* VI: 487–88, 489; ibid., VII: 4–5.

27. Ibid., VI: 271–72, 457.

28. Maclay, *History,* I: 208–9.

29. Troude, *Batailles Navales,* III: 218–19; *QW,* VI: 457.

30. Maclay, *History,* I: 209–212, reprints the official report of Lieutenant Louis Marie Clerment of *le Berceau.*

31. Ibid.; *QW,* VI: 456–57, 351–32.

32. Ibid., pp. 458–59, 555.

33. Ibid., VII: 246, 266, 293.

34. Ibid., pp. 506–7; ibid., VII: 1–3, 34–35, 69–70.

35. Ibid., VI: 514–15.

36. Ibid., V: 178, 384. For the near loss of the *United States* in 1798 see Clark, *Barry,* pp. 428–29; William Oliver Stevens, *An Affair of Honor: The Biography of Commodore James Barron, U.S.N.* (Norfolk, Va., 1969), pp. 25–27; and the entries for 18–21 October 1798 in "A Journal of the cruises of the *United States* and

Patapsco, 1798–1801," kept by Freeborn Banning, United States Naval Academy Museum.

37. Joseph H. Nicholson to Samuel Nicholson, 12 January 1800, DNA, RG 45, Area File 7; and Barry to Sarah Barry, 8 October 1798, NHi, Barnes Collection, Barry Papers.

38. Adams, *Works,* X: 27–28; *QW,* VI: 522–23; ibid., VII: 20.

39. Ibid., pp. 14–15; ibid., VI: 536–37.

40. Joseph Gurn, *Commodore John Barry: Father of the American Navy* (New York, 1937), p. 380; McKee, "Pathology of a Profession," pp. 18–19, 25n; *QW,* III: 252–53; ibid., VII: 23.

41. Ibid., VI: 557–58; and Truxtun to Biddle, 24 October 1801, PHi, LCP, Truxtun-Biddle Letters, Box I, folio #42.

42. *QW,* VII: 19, 86–90.

43. Ibid.

44. Ibid., pp. 90–91, 92.

45. Ibid., pp. 29, 56; ibid., VI: 558.

46. Ibid., VII: 112–14; and Christopher McKee, ed., "*Constitution* in the Quasi-War with France: The Letters of John Roche, Jr., 1798–1801," *American Neptune* 27 (April 1967): 147–48.

47. *QW,* VII: 96, 97, 107–8.

48. Ibid., pp. 110, 112–14.

49. Ibid., pp. 119, 127.

50. Ibid., VI: 170–71, 215; and Stevens to Pickering, 31 May 1800, Naval Historical Center, Operational Archives, ZB Files.

51. *QW,* VI: 107–8, 425–26, 426; ibid., VII; 48–49, 259–61; and Valle, *Rocks & Shoals,* pp. 112–14.

52. *QW,* VI: 536; ibid., VII: 372–73.

53. Ibid., IV: 126, 191, 193.

54. Ibid., pp. 508–9.

55. Ibid., V: 134, 142, 221–22, 240, 335–36, 370, 371, 416, 527.

56. Ibid., VII: 244–45.

57. Ibid., VI: 56, 255, 259–60.

58. Ibid., V: 558; ibid., VI: 195, 261, 379.

59. Ibid., pp. 345–46, 381–82.

60. Ibid., pp. 389, 449.

61. Malone, *Ordeal of Liberty,* p. 492.

62. Gibbs, *Wolcott,* II: 409–10; and Stoddert to Jefferson, 18 February 1801, DLC, Thomas Jefferson Papers.

63. *ASP, Naval Affairs,* I: 74–80.

64. Adams, *Works,* IX: 143–47. Adams spoke of "a navy adapted to defensive war" and the fortification of seaports. Stoddert's conceptions were more fully developed, see *ASP, Naval Affairs,* I: 74–80.

65. Ibid.

66. *QW,* VII: 140; Symonds, *Navalists and Antinavalists,* pp. 83–86; and Russell F. Weigley, *History of the United States Army* (New York, 1967), p. 566.

67. *QW,* VII: 134–35; *Statutes,* II: 122–23; Symonds, *Navalists and Anti-navalists,* pp. 83–86; and Truxtun to Biddle, 24 October 1801, PHi, LCP, Truxtun-Biddle Letters, Box I, folio #42. The strength of the Marine Corps in 1803 was 524, see Allan R. Millet, *Semper Fideles: The History of the United States Marine Corps* (New York, 1980), p. 628; Wattenberg, *Statistical History,* p. 1143.

68. Stoddert to Jefferson, 18 February 1801, DLC, Jefferson Papers; and Paullin, *Naval Administration*, pp. 119–21.

69. Jefferson to Stoddert, 21 February 1801, DLC, Jefferson Papers; Stoddert to Jefferson, 25 January 1809, ibid.; Stoddert to Jefferson, 14 January 1809, ibid.; Jefferson to Stoddert, 18 February 1809, ibid.; and Dumas Malone, *Jefferson and His Time*, vol. 4; *Jefferson the President: First Term, 1801–1805* (Boston, 1970), pp. 35–36.

70. *QW*, VII: 144. At this stage Jefferson intended to deploy the six frigates to be kept in service thus: two in the West Indies, two in the Mediterranean, and two in the Indian Ocean, see Thomas Jefferson, *The Works of Thomas Jefferson*, Paul Leicester Ford, ed., 12 vols. (New York, 1904–1905), I: 365.

71. Memo in Stoddert's handwriting dated 21 March 1801, DLC, Jefferson Papers.

72. *QW*, VII: 145–46. A final decision to send a squadron to the Mediterranean was not made until the cabinet meeting of 15 May 1801, see Ford, *Works of Jefferson*, I: 365–66.

73. *QW*, VII: 153, 154, 155–56, 193; Jefferson to Stoddert, 30 March 1801, DLC, Jefferson Papers; Malone, *First Term*, p. xxv.

Chapter 12

1. *QW*, VII: 148.

2. *Hamilton Papers*, XXII: 1–4. King wrote from London: "It is at least ten days since the spirited measures pursued in America, must have been known at Paris; we are therefore anxious to learn the effect they have produced." On 23 September 1798 came the answer: "You will have no war," he wrote Hamilton. See ibid., pp. 187–88. Claude François, Baron de Menéval, served as secretary to Joseph Bonaparte, who handled the negotiations with the Americans. Menéval wrote of the Franco-American convention: "It was a victory over England." See Menéval's *Memoirs of Napoleon Bonaparte: The Court of the First Empire*, 3 vols. (New York, 1910), I: 40–42.

3. *QW*, VI: 174–75.

4. Ibid., VII: 86–90.

5. Steel, *Naval Chronologist*, pp. 67–74; and *QW*, VII: 372–73.

6. Jenkins, "Heyday of Privateering," pp. 248–49; and Steel, *Naval Chronologist*, pp. 61–67.

7. Bainbridge's *Retaliation* was the only American warship captured by the French.

8. *Statutes*, II: 129–30; and *QW*, VII: 145–46.

9. Ibid., p. 158.

10. *BW*, I: 434–35, 443, 488–89; and *QW*, VII: 164, 177.

11. Carl E. Prince, "The Passing of the Aristocracy: Jefferson's Removal of the Federalists, 1801–1805," *Journal of American History* 57 (December 1970): 563–75; *BW*, I: 426–27, 428–29, 443.

12. Ibid., p. 558. Smith, who had begun his duties as secretary of the navy, pressed Tingey and the naval agents in ports where Stoddert had begun construction of seventy-four-gun ships to keep the work proceeding.

Appendix B

1. Phillips to Stoddert, 28 December 1798, DNA, RG 59, SDA, Miscellaneous Letters; and Loring to Parker, 20 February 1799, PRO, Adm. 1/249. The latter transcript of Crown-copyright records in the Public Record Office appears by permission of the Controller of H. M. Stationery Office.

2. Phillips, *Impartial Examination*, pp. 11, 24, 41–43.

3. Phillips' first lieutenant's name was Josias M. Speake, a cousin of Stoddert who was obviously not on a first-name basis with his captain.

4. Liston, of course, was the British minister to the United States; not vice-versa.

5. Lieutenant Thomas White commanding the *Mosquito* had earlier clashed with the American Revenue Service brig *Unanimity*. The *Mosquito* had been captured by a Spanish frigate.

6. The four enclosures match those in Phillips's report to Stoddert, a copy of which can also be found in the PRO.

GLOSSARY

This is not intended to be an all-inclusive glossary of nautical terms, but rather a simple user's guide to terms that appear in the book.

Braces: lines running from the ends of the yards to the deck, used to traverse the yards on the masts.

Brig: A two-mastered, square-rigged vessel.

Cable's length: 120 fathoms or 720 feet.

Cannon: Shipboard artillery firing a sold shot or ball.

Careen, to: To heave a ship down by one side to clean or repair her bottom.

Carronade: Ordnance capable of firing a heavy ball at short range. Well-suited to the upper decks of frigates and smaller ships. Also called "smasher," a term derived from the carronade's ability to smash the timbers of wooden ships.

Commodore: In the United States and Royal navies during the last years of the eighteenth century, commodore was an administrative/command title given to the senior captain of a multi-ship force in the absence of an admiral. Commodores flew broad pendants from their ships. An "established" commodore had another junior captain or officer to run the flagship. If the commodore had to administer both ship and squadron, he was said to fly a "ten shilling pendant."

Corsair: A privateer.

Corvette: A flush-decked, three-masted, square-rigged warship. Also referred to as ship, sloop of war, and occasionally sloop.

Crank: A vessel liable to heel or capsize.

Cutter: A single-masted, fore and aft-rigged vessel. Used as a general term to describe the ships of the United States Revenue Cutter Service during the period. By the Quasi-War the "cutters" were in fact mostly schooners and brigs.

Fathom: Six feet.

Fore and aft rigged: Rigged in line with the keel. Schooner or sloop rigged.

Forecastle: A partial deck over the gun deck in the fore part of the ship.

Frigate: A three-masted, square-rigged warship mounting between 20 and 28 cannon (sixth-rate) and 30 to 50 cannon (fifth-rate) on more than one deck.

Gangway: A walkway extended from the forecastle to the quarterdeck.

Guerre de course: Warfare directed against the enemy's commerce with cruisers—smaller warships and privateers.

Heel, to: To lean over to one side.

Larboard: The left or port side of a ship.

League (marine): Three nautical miles.

Lee: The side of a ship away from the direction of the wind.

Leeward: The direction away from the wind.

Glossary

Luff, to: To put the tiller to the lee side to have the ship to sail closer to the wind.

Orlop deck: Lower deck of a warship below the gun deck.

Port: In the age of sail port usually referred to the direction of the left, rather than the larboard side itself.

Privateer: Vessel of war owned, manned, and armed privately, but commissioned by a country to cruise against the enemy's ships.

Quarterdeck: Partial deck over the gun deck in the after part of the ship.

Rake, to: To cannonade along the axis of a ship's keel.

Range: Pistol shot—50 yards or less,

Musket shot—200 yards,

Point blank—range within which cannon fire can fire with flat trajectory,

Random—greater than 200 yards.

Rates: Approximate number of cannon carried:

1st—over 100,
2nd—over 80,
3rd—over 60,
4th—over 50,
5th—over 30,
6th—over 20.

Rigging: All the ropes used to support the masts (standing) or work the yards and sails (running).

Schooner: A two-masted, fore and aft-rigged vessel.

Scud, to: To run before the wind, in the direction towards which the wind blows.

Ship: A three-masted, square-rigged, flush-decked vessel.

Sloop: A single-masted, fore and aft-rigged vessel.

Sloop of war: A three-masted, square-rigged, flush-decked warship. Sometimes referred to as a sloop.

Spanker: A fore and aft sail on the mizzen mast. Also called a driver.

Spar deck: A near complete deck connecting the quarterdeck and forecastle. On the American frigates such as the *Constitution* this deck gave the ship a virtual second gun deck. The American frigates were often called spar-decked fifth-rates.

Square-rigged: With the yards running at right angles to the keel.

Stay, to: To arrange the sails and work the rudder to bring the ship's bow towards the wind preparatory to tacking. To miss stays is to fail in the attempt.

Stopper: Short pieces of rope used to repair or provide redundant support for a yard or sail.

Tack, to: To change course bringing the bow across the direct path of the wind.

Tonnage: A measurement of internal area. Not displacement in the age of sail.

Wear, to: To change course turning the stern to windward.

Weather: The side of a ship or direction from which the wind is blowing.

Weather gauge: To hold a position upwind of another ship in battle. Also termed wind-gauge.

Weigh, to: To heave up the anchor.

Windward: The direction from which the wind is blowing.

BIBLIOGRAPHY

MANUSCRIPT SOURCES

United Kingdom
Public Record Office, Kew, Richmond, Surrey
    Adm 1/249. Admirals' Dispatches, Jamaica
    Adm 1/494. Admirals' Dispatches, North America (Photostats, DLC)
    Adm. 1/505. Admirals' Dispatches, North America (Photostats, DLC)
    Adm. 1/3985. Letters of Intelligence (Photostats, DLC)
    FO 5/25. America, Correspondence (Transcripts, DLC)
    FO 5/26. America, Correspondence (Transcripts, DLC)
United States
Historical Society of Pennsylvania, Philadelphia
    John H. Dilkes Papers, William Jones Section
    Dreer Collection
    Gratz Collections
    Joshua Humphreys Papers
    Jones and Clarke Papers
    Library Company of Philadelphia: Miscellaneous Manuscript Collection,
        Truxtun-Biddle Letters
    William Shaler Papers
    T. Truxtun-Hare Collection
    Anthony Wayne Papers
Library of Congress, Washington, D.C.
    George Washington Campbell Papers
    Peter Force Collection
    Naval Historical Foundation: Thomas Tingey Papers
    James Sever Papers
    Benjamin Stoddert Papers
    Rebecca Lowndes Stoddert Papers
    Miscellaneous Manuscript Collection: Uriah Forrest, Thomas Truxtun
Massachusetts Historical Society, Boston
    Timothy Pickering Papers
National Archives, Washington, D.C.

Bibliography

Record Group 21. Bankruptcy Act of 1800
Record Group 45. Records of the Office of Naval Records and Library
Record Group 59. Records of the Department of State
Record Group 247. Letters of the Continental Congress.
Naval Historical Center, Washington, D.C.
Operational Archives, ZB Files
New-York Historical Society, New York
John S. Barnes Collection (John Barry Papers)
Horatio Gates Papers
Philadelphia Maritime Museum, Philadelphia
Hepburn Collection, John Barry Papers
Manuscript Collection
United States Naval Academy Museum, Annapolis, Maryland
Freeborn Banning's Journal of the cruises of the *United States* and *Patapsco,*
1798–1801
Manuscript Collections (Thomas Truxtun)

PRINTED DOCUMENTS

Adams, John. *The Works of John Adams, Second President of the United States; with a Life of the Author.* Charles Francis Adams, ed., 10 vols. Boston: Little Brown and Company, 1850–56.

Brumbaugh, Gaius Marcus. *Maryland Records: Colonial, Revolutionary, County and Church from Original Sources.* Vol. I. Baltimore: Williams & Wilkins Company, 1915.

Carnegie Endowment for International Peace. *Diplomatic Correspondence of the United States: Canadian Relations, 1784–1860.* William R. Manning, ed. 3 vols. Washington, D.C.: Carnegie Endowment for International Peace, 1940–43.

——. *Prize Cases Decided in the United States Supreme Court, 1789–1918.* James Brown Scott, ed. 3. vols. Oxford: Clarendon Press, 1923.

Hamilton, Alexander. *The Papers of Alexander Hamilton.* Howard C. Syrett, ed. 26 vols. New York: Columbia University Press, 1961–79.

Hazard, Samuel, ed. *Pennsylvania Archives.* Series I. 9 vols. Philadelphia: Joseph Severns & Co., 1853–54.

Jefferson, Thomas. *The Papers of Thomas Jefferson.* Julian P. Boyd, ed. 21 vols. to date. Princeton, N.J.: Princeton University Press, 1950–   ).

——. *The Works of Thomas Jefferson.* Paul Leicester Ford, ed. 12 vols. New York and London: G. P. Putnam's Sons, 1904–05.

Mayo, Bernard, ed. *Instructions to the British Ministers to the United States, 1791–1812.* Washington, D.C.: United States Government Printing Office, 1941.

Navy Records Society. *Private Papers of George, Second Earl Spencer, First Lord of the Admiralty, 1794–1801.* Julian S. Corbett and Herbert W. Richmond, eds. 4 vols. Printed for the Naval Records Society, 1913–24.

United States Congress. *American State Papers: Documents, Legislative and Executive, of the Congress of the United States . . . Selected and Edited under the Authority of Congress.* 38 vols. Washington, D.C.: Gales and Seaton, 1832–61.

——. *The Debates and Proceedings in the Congress of the United States . . . Fifth Congress, Comprising the Period May 15, 1797, to March 3, 1799, Inclusive.* Washington, D.C.: Gales and Seaton, 1851.

——. *The Public Statutes at Large of the United States of America, from the Organization of the Government in 1789, to March 1845. . . .* Richard Peters, ed. 8 vols. Boston: Little, Brown, and Company, 1861–67.

United States Continental Congress. *Journals of the Continental Congress, 1774–1789.* Worthington C. Ford, ed. 34 vols. Washington, D.C.: United States Government Printing Office, 1904–1937.

———. *Rules for the Regulation of the Navy of the United Colonies of North-America.* Philadelphia: William and Thomas Bradford, 1775; reprint ed., Washington, D.C.: Naval Historical Foundation, 1944.

United States Navy Department. *Naval Documents of the American Revolution.* William Bell Clark, William James Morgan, and William S. Dudley eds. 8 vols. to date. Washington, D.C.: United States Government Printing Office, 1964–

———. *The Naval War of 1812: A Documentary History.* William S. Dudley, ed. 1 vol. to date. Washington, D.C.: United States Government Printing Office, 1985–

———. *Naval Documents Related to the United States War with the Barbary Powers: Naval Operations Including Diplomatic Background, 1785–1807.* Dudley W. Knox, ed. 6 vols. Washington, D.C.: United States Government Printing Office, 1939–44.

———. *Naval Documents Related to the Quasi-War with France: Naval Operations, February 1797–December 1801.* Dudley W. Knox, ed. 7 vols. Washington, D.C.: United States Government Printing Office, 1935–38.

Washington, George. *The Papers of George Washington: Colonial Series.* W. W. Abbott, ed. 2 vols. Charlottesville: University Press of Virginia, 1983–

———. *The Writings of George Washington from the Original Manuscript Sources, 1745–1799.* John C. Fitzpatrick, ed. 39 vols. Washington, D.C.: United States Government Printing Office, 1931–44.

MEMOIRS AND MONOGRAPHS

Albion, Robert Greenhalgh. *Makers of Naval Policy, 1798–1947.* Rowena Reed, ed. Annapolis, Md.: Naval Institute Press, 1980.

———. *Forests and Sea Power: The Timber Problem of the Royal Navy, 1652–1862.* Cambridge, Mass.: Harvard University Press, 1926.

——— and Jennie Barnes Pope. *Sea Lanes in Wartime: The American Experience, 1775–1945.* New York: W. W. Norton & Co., Inc., 1942; reprint ed., Hamden, Conn.: Archon Books, 1968.

Allen, Gardner W. *Our Naval War with France.* Boston and New York: Houghton Mifflin Company, 1909.

Appleton's Cyclopaedia of America Biography. James Grant Wilson and John Fiske, eds. 6 vols. New York: D. Appleton and Company, 1888–89.

Barnes, Robert, ed. *Maryland Genealogies: A Consolidation of Articles from the Maryland Historical Magazine.* 2 vols. Baltimore: Genealogical Publishing Company, Inc., 1980.

Barnett, E. *The West India Pilot.* 2 vols. London: The Hydrographic Office, Admiralty, 1872.

Bemis, Samuel Flagg. *Jay's Treaty: A Study in Commerce and Diplomacy.* New York: Macmillan Company, 1924.

———. *Pinckney's Treaty: America's Advantage from Europe's Distress, 1783–1800.* New Haven, Conn.: Yale University Press, 1960.

Biddle, Charles. *Autobiography of Charles Biddle, Vice-President of the Supreme Executive Council of Pennsylvania, 1745–1821.* Philadelphia: E. Claxton and Company, 1883.

Bibliography

Bonnel, Ulane. *La France, les Etats-Unis et la guerre de course, 1797–1815*. Paris: Nouvelles Editions Latines, 1961.

Bowman, Albert Hall. *The Struggle for Neutrality: Franco-American Diplomacy during the Federalist Era*. Knoxville: University of Tennessee Press, 1974.

Brown, John Howard. *American Naval Heroes, 1775—1812—1861—1898: Being Biographical Sketches of the Brave Men Who Have Glorified the American Navy by Their Deeds of Heroism*. Boston: Brown and Company, Publishers, 1899.

Bryan, Wilhelmus Bogart. *A History of the National Capital: From Its Foundation through the Period of the Adoption of the Organic Act*. 2 vols. New York: Macmillan Company, 1914.

Callahan, North. *Flight from the Republic: The Tories of the American Revolution*. Indianapolis: Bobbs-Merrill, 1967.

Carothers, Bettie Stirling, ed. *1776 Census of Maryland*. Chesterfield, Miss.: Privately printed, n.d.

Carnegie Endowment for International Peace. *The Controversy over Neutral Rights between the United States and France, 1797–1800*. James Brown Scott, ed. New York: Oxford University Press, 1917.

Carr, William H. A. *Perils Named and Unnamed: The Story of the Insurance Company of North America*. New York: McGraw-Hill Book Company, 1967.

Chapelle, Howard I. *The History of the American Sailing Navy: The Ships and Their Development*. New York: W. W. Norton & Co., Inc., 1949; reprint ed., New York: Bonanza Books, n.d.

Clarfield, Gerard H. *Timothy Pickering and American Diplomacy, 1795–1800*. Columbia: University of Missouri Press, 1969.

Clark, M. *The Memoirs of the Celebrated and Beautiful Mrs. Ann Carson, Daughter of an Officer of the U.S. Navy, and Wife of Another, Whose Life Terminated in the Philadelphia Prison*. 2 vols. Philadelphia, 1838; reprint ed., 2 vols in 1, New York: Arno Press, 1980.

Clark, William Bell. *Gallant John Barry, 1745–1803: The Story of a Naval Hero of Two Wars*. New York: Macmillan Company, 1938.

Coletta, Paolo E., ed. *American Secretaries of the Navy*. 2 vols. Annapolis, Md.: Naval Institute Press, 1980.

Colledge, J. J. *Ships of the Royal Navy: An Historical Index*. 2 vols. New York: Augustus M. Kelley, Publishers, 1969–70.

Congressional Quarterly. *Guide to Congress*. 3rd ed. Washington, D.C.: Congressional Quarterly Inc., 1982.

Cooper, James Fenimore. *History of the Navy of the United States*. 3rd ed. 2 vols. Cooperstown, N.Y.: H. & E. Phinney, 1848.

———. *Live of Distinguished American Naval Officers*. 2 vols. Philadelphia: Carey and Hart, 1846.

Cunat, Charles Marie. *Histoire de Robert Surcouf, Capitaine de Corsaire*. Paris: Jules Chapelle et Cie, 1842.

DeConde, Alexander. *Entangling Alliance: Politics and Diplomacy under George Washington*. Durham, N.C.: Duke University Press, 1958.

———. *The Quasi-War: The Politics and Diplomacy of the Undeclared Naval War with France, 1797–1801*. New York: Charles Scribner's Sons, 1966.

Department of Commerce and Labor, Bureau of the Census. *Heads of Families at the First Census of the United States Taken in the Year 1790: Maryland*. Washington, D.C.: United States Government Printing Office, 1907.

Dictionary of American Biography. Allen Johnson et al., eds. 20 vols. New York: Charles Scribner's Sons, 1928–36.

Dictionary of American History. James Truslow Adam, ed. 5 vols. New York: Charles Scribner's Sons, 1940.

Dictionary of National Biography. Stephen Leslie et al., eds. 63 vols. London: Smith, Elder, & Co., 1885–1900.

Dillon, Richard. We Have Met the Enemy: Oliver Hazard Perry, Wilderness Commodore. New York: McGraw-Hill Book Company, 1978.

Donovan, Frank. The Tall Frigates. New York: Dodd, Mead & Company, 1962.

Ecker, Grace Dunlop. A Portrait of Old GeorgeTown. Richmond, Va.: Garrett & Massic, Inc., 1933.

Egertown, Hugh Edward, ed. The Royal Commission on the Losses and Services of American Royalists, 1783–1785. New York: Burt Franklin, 1971.

Emmons, George F. The Navy of the United States, from the Commencement, 1775–1853; with a Brief History of Each Vessel's Service and Fate as Appears upon Record. Washington, D.C.: Gideon & Co., 1853.

Fairburn, William Armstrong. Merchant Sail. Center-Lovell, Me.: Fairburn Marine Education Foundation, Inc., 1945–55.

Falconer, William, and William Barney. A New Universal Dictionary of the Marine. . . . London, 1815; reprint ed., New York: Library Editions, Ltd., 1970.

Ferguson, E. James. The Power of the Purse: A History of American Public Finance, 1776–1790. Chapel Hill: University of North Carolina Press, 1961.

Ferguson, Eugene S. Truxtun of the Constellation: The Life of Commodore Thomas Truxtun, U.S. Navy, 1755–1822. Baltimore: Johns Hopkins Press, 1956.

Field, James A., Jr. America and the Mediterranean World, 1776–1882. Princeton, N.J.: Princeton University Press, 1969.

Fordyce, Alexander Dingwall. Outlines of Naval Routine. London: Smith, Elder & Co., 1837.

Fortescue, John W. A History of the British Army. 13 vols. London: Macmillan, 1889–1930.

Fowler, William M., Jr. Jack Tars and Commodores: The American Navy, 1783–1815. Boston: Houghton Mifflin Company, 1984.

Gahn, Bessie Wilmarth. Original Patentees of Land at Washington Prior to 1700. Washington, D.C.: Published by the Author, 1936.

Gibbs, George, ed. Memoirs of the Administrations of Washington and John Adams, Edited from the Papers of Oliver Wolcott, Secretary of the Treasury. 2 vols. New York: Printed for the Subscribers, 1846.

Gilbert, Felix. To the Farewell Address: Ideas of Early American Foreign Policy. Princeton, N.J. Princeton University Press, 1961.

Gillingham, Harold E. Marine Insurance in Philadelphia, 1721–1800. Philadelphia: Published by the Author, 1933.

Goldsborough, Charles W. An Original and Correct List in the United States Navy. . . . Washington, D.C.: Printed by the Author, 1800.

———. The United States Naval Chronicle. Vol. I. Washington, D.C.: James Wilson, 1824.

Great Britain, Admiralty. The Commissioned Sea Officers of the Royal Navy, 1660–1815. David B. Smith et al., eds. 3 vols. 1954.

Griffin, Martin I. J. Commodore John Barry, "The Father of the American Navy": The Record of His Services for Our Country. Philadelphia: Published by the Author, 1903.

Gurn, Joseph. Commodore John Barry: Father of the American Navy. New York: P. J. Kennedy & Sons, 1933.

Bibliography

Guttridge, Leonard F. and Jay D. Smith. *The Commodores.* New York: Harper & Row, 1969; reprint ed., Annapolis, Md.: Naval Institute Press, 1984.

Heitman, Francis B. *Historical Register of Officers of the Continental Army during the War of the Revolution, April 1775, to December 1783.* Revised ed. Washington, D.C.: The Rare Book Shop Publishing Company, Inc., 1914.

Henderson, Archibald. *Washington's Southern Tour, 1791.* Boston and New York: Houghton Mifflin Company, 1923.

Henderson, James. *The Frigates: An Account of the Lesser Warships of the Wars from 1793–1815.* New York: Dodd, Mead & Co., 1971.

———. *Sloops and Brigs: An Account of the Smallest Vessels of the Royal Navy during the Great Wars, 1793–1815.* Annapolis, Md.: Naval Institute Press, 1972.

Hourigan, P. W. *Manual of Seamanship for the Officer of the Deck: Ship Under Sail Alone.* Annapolis, Md.: United States Naval Institute, 1903; reprint ed., 1980.

Hidy, Ralph W. *The House of Baring in American Trade and Finance: English Merchant Bankers at Work, 1763–1861.* Cambridge, Mass.: Harvard University Press, 1949.

Higginbotham, Don. *The War for American Independence: Military Attitudes, Policies, and Practice, 1763–1789.* New York: Macmillan Publishing Co., 1971; paperback ed., Bloomington: Indiana University Press, 1977.

Higginson, Thomas Wentworth. *Life and Times of Stephen Higginson.* Boston: Houghton, Mifflin and Company, 1907.

Hollis, Ira N. *The Frigate Constitution: The Central Figure of the Navy under Sail.* Boston: Houghton, Mifflin and Company, 1901.

Hoxse, John. *The Yankee Tar: An Authentic Narrative of the Voyages and Hardships of John Hoxse and the Cruises of the U.S. Frigate Constellation.* Northampton, Mass.: Printed by John Metcalf for the Author, 1840.

Hutchins, John G. B. *The American Maritime Industries and Public Policy, 1789–1914.* Cambridge, Mass.: Harvard University Press, 1941.

Hyneman, Charles S. *The First American Neutrality: A Study of the American Understanding of Neutral Obligations during the Years 1792–1815.* Urbana: University of Illinois, 1914.

Jacobs, James Ripley. *Tarnished Warrior: Major-General James Wilkinson.* New York: Macmillan Company, 1938.

James, C. L. R. *The Black Jacobins: Toussaint L'Ouverture and the San Domingo Revolution.* 2nd ed. New York: Vintage Books, 1963.

James, William. *The Naval History of Great Britain from the Declaration of War by France in 1793 to the Accession of George IV.* 2nd ed. 6 vols. London: Richard Bentley, 1850.

Junior League of Washington. *The City of Washington: An Illustrated History.* Thomas French, ed. New York: Alfred A. Knopf, 1977.

Kern, Florence. *Hopley Yeaton's U.S. Revenue Cutter Scammel, 1791–1798.* Washington, D.C.: Alised Enterprises, 1975.

———. *James Montgomery's U.S. Revenue Cutter General Greene, 1791–1797.* Washington, D.C.: Alised Enterprises, 1977.

———. *Jonathan Maltbie's U.S. Revenue Cutter Argus, 1791–1804.* Washington, D.C.: Alised Enterprises, 1976.

———. *John Foster Williams' U.S. Revenue Cutter Massachusetts, 1791–1792.* Washington, D.C. Alised Enterprises, 1976.

———. *John Howell's U.S. Revenue Cutter Eagle, 1793–1799.* Washington, D.C.: Alised Enterprises, 1978.

————. *Patrick Dennis' U.S. Revenue Cutter Vigilant, 1791–1798.* Washington, D.C.: Alised Enterprises, 1976.

————. *Richard Taylor's U.S. Revenue Cutter Virginia, 1791–1797.* Washington, D.C.: Alised Enterprises, 1977.

————. *Robert Cochran's U.S. Revenue Cutter South Carolina, 1793–1798.* Washington, D.C.: Alised Enterprises, 1978.

————. *Simon Gross's U.S. Revenue Cutter Active, 1791–1798.* Washington, D.C.: Alised Enterprises, 1977.

————. *William Cooke's U.S. Revenue Cutter Diligence, 1792–1798.* Washington, D.C.: Alised Enterprises, 1979.

King, Irving H. *George Washington's Coast Guard: Origins of the U.S. Revenue Cutter Service, 1794–1801.* Annapolis, Md.: Naval Institute Press, 1978.

Knollenberg, Bernhard. *Washington and the Revolution, A Reappraisal: Gates, Conway, and the Continental Congress.* New York: Macmillan Company, 1940; reprint ed., Archon Books, 1968.

Knox, Dudley W. *A History of the United States Navy.* New York: G. P. Putnam's Sons, 1936.

Kohn, Richard H. *Eagle and Sword: The Federalists and the Creation of the Military Establishment in America, 1783–1802.* New York: Free Press, 1975.

Kurtz, Stephen G. *The Presidency of John Adams: The Collapse of Federalism, 1795–1800.* Philadelphia: University of Pennsylvania Press, 1957.

Lever, Darcy. *The Young Sea Officer's Sheet Anchor: or a Key to the Leading of Rigging and to Practical Seamanship.* 2nd ed. London, 1819; reprint ed., New York: Edward W. Sweetman Co., 1963.

Lewis, Michael. *A Social History of the Navy, 1793–1815.* London: George Allen & Unwin Limited, 1960.

————. *England's Sea-Officers: The Story of the Naval Profession.* London: George Allen & Unwin Limited, 1939.

Lodge, Henry Cabot. *Life and Letters of George Cabot.* Boston: Little, Brown & Company, 1878.

Logan, Rayford W. *The Diplomatic Relations of the United States with Haiti, 1776–1891.* Chapel Hill: University of North Carolina Press, 1941.

Long, David F. *Nothing Too Daring: A Biography of Commodore David Porter, 1780–1843.* Annapolis, Md.: United States Naval Institute, 1970.

————. *Ready to Hazard: A Biography of Commodore William Bainbridge, 1774–1833.* Hanover, N.H., and London: University Press of New England, 1981.

McKee, Christopher. *Edward Preble: A Naval Biography, 1761–1807.* Annapolis, Md.: Naval Institute Press, 1972.

Mackesy, Piers. *Statesmen at War: The Strategy of Overthrow, 1798–1799.* London: Longman Group Limited, 1974.

————. *War without Victory: The Downfall of Pitt, 1799–1802.* Oxford: Clarendon Press, 1984.

————. *The War for America, 1775–1783.* Cambridge, Mass.: Harvard University Press, 1965.

Maclay, Edgar Stanton. *A History of the United States Navy from 1775 to 1901.* Enlarged ed. 3 vols. New York: D. Appleton and Company, 1910.

————. *Moses Brown, Captain U.S.N.* New York: Baker and Taylor Company, 1904.

Mahan, Alfred Thayer. *The Influence of Sea Power upon the French Revolution and*

Empire. 2 vols. London: Sampson: Sampson Low, Marston & Company, Limited, 1892; reprint ed., St. Clair Shores, Mich.: Scholarly Press, 1970.

———. *The Influence of Sea Power upon History, 1650–1783.* Boston: Little, Brown and Company, 1918.

Malone, Dumas. *Jefferson and His Time.* Vol. 3: *Jefferson and the Ordeal of Liberty.* Boston: Little, Brown and Company, 1962.

———. *Jefferson and His Time.* Vol. 4: *Jefferson the President: First Term, 1801–1805.* Boston: Little, Brown and Company, 1970.

Marcus, G. J. *Heart of Oak: A Survey of British Sea Power in the Georgian Era.* London: Oxford University Press, 1975.

Marshall, John. *Royal Naval Biography; or, Memoirs of the Services of all the Flag-Officers, Superannuated Rear-Admirals, Retired Captains, Post-Captains, and Commanders, . . .* 8 vols. in 12. London: Longman, Hurst, Rees, Orme, Brown, and Green, 1824.

Martin, Tyrone G. *A Most Fortunate Ship: A Narrative History of "Old Ironsides."* Chester, Conn.: Globe Pequot Press, 1980.

Melville, Herman. *White Jacket or the World in a Man-of-War.* Evanston, Ill.: Northwestern University Press, 1970.

Menéval, Claude François, Baron de. *Memoirs of Napoleon Bonaparte: The Court of the First Empire.* 3 vols. New York: P. F. Collier & Son, 1910.

Millet, Allan R. *Semper Fidelis: The History of the United States Marine Corps.* New York: Macmillan Publishing Co., 1980.

Montague, Ludwell Lee. *Haiti and the United States, 1714–1938.* New York: Russell & Russell, 1966.

Nash, Howard P. *The Forgotten Wars: The Role of the U.S. Navy in the Quasi-War with France and the Barbary Wars, 1798–1805.* New York: A. S. Barnes and Company, 1968.

The Naval Chronicle: Containing a General and Biographical History of the Royal Navy of the United Kingdom; with a Variety of Original Papers on Nautical Subjects. 40 vols. London: J. Gold, 1799–1818.

Nelson, Paul David. *General Horatio Gates: A Biography.* Baton Rouge: Louisiana State University Press, 1976.

Oberholtzer, Ellis Paxson. *Robert Morris, Patriot and Financier.* New York: Macmillan Company, 1903.

Padfield, Peter. *Broke and the Shannon.* London: Hodder and Stoughton, 1968.

Paullin, Charles Oscar. *Commodore John Rodgers: Captain, Commodore, and Senior Officer in the Navy, 1773–1838.* Cleveland: The Arthur H. Clark Company, 1910.

———. *Paullin's History of Naval Administration, 1775–1911.* Annapolis, Md.: United States Naval Institute, 1968.

Pengelly, C. A. *The First Bellerophon.* London: John Baker, 1966.

Perkins, Bradford. *The First Rapprochement: England and the United States, 1795–1805.* Berkeley: University of California Press, 1967.

Phillips, Isaac. *An Impartial Examination of the Case of Captain Isaac Phillips, late of the Navy, And Compiled from Original Documents and Records, with the Proceedings upon his Application to be Restored to His Rank in the United States Navy.* Baltimore: Benjamin Edes, 1825.

Pickering, Octavius and Charles W. Upham. *The Life of Timothy Pickering.* 4 vols. Boston: Little, Brown and Company, 1867–73.

Pope, Dudley. *The Black Ship.* Philadelphia: J. B. Lippincott Company, 1964.

————. *The Great Gamble*. New York: Simon and Schuster, 1972.

Porter, David Dixon. *Memoir of Commodore David Porter of the United States Navy*. Albany, N.Y.: J. Munsell, 1875.

Pratt, Fletcher. *Preble's Boys: Commodore Preble and the Birth of American Sea Power*. New York: William Sloane Associates, 1950.

Price, Jacob M. *France and the Chesapeake: A History of the French Tobacco Monopoly, 1674–1791, and of Its Relationship to the British and American Tobacco Trades*. 2 vols. Ann Arbor: University of Michigan Press, 1973.

Prowell, George R. *History of York County Pennsylvania*. 2 vols. Chicago: J. H. Beers & Co., 1907.

Rea, John. *A Letter to William Bainbridge Esqr. Formerly Commander of the United States Ship George Washington; Relative to Some Transactions, on Board Said Ship, during a Voyage to Algiers, Constantinople, &c.* Philadelphia: Printed for the Author, 1802.

Risch, Erna. *Supplying Washington's Army*. Washington, D.C.: Center for Military History, 1981.

Robison, Samuel S. and Mary L. Robison. *A History of Naval Tactics from 1530 to 1930: The Evolution of Tactical Maxims*. Annapolis, Md.: The United States Naval Institute, 1942.

Rogers, John G. *Origins of Sea Terms*. Mystic, Conn.: Mystic Seaport Museum, Inc., 1984.

Scharf, J. Thomas. *History of Maryland from the Earliest Period to the Present Day*. 3 vols. Baltimore: John B. Piet, 1879.

Seawell, Molly Elliot. *Twelve Naval Captains: Being a Record of Certain Americans Who Made Themselves Immortal*. New York: Charles Scribner's Sons, 1900.

Smelser, Marshall. *The Congress Founds the Navy, 1787–1798*. Notre Dame, Ind.: University of Notre Dame Press, 1959.

Smith, Page. *John Adams*. 2 vols. Garden City, N.Y.: Doubleday & Co., Inc., 1962.

Smith, Philip Chadwick Foster. *The Frigate Essex Papers: Building the Salem Frigate, 1798–1799*. Salem, Mass.: Peabody Museum of Salem, 1974.

Sofaer, Abraham D. *War, Foreign Affairs and Constitutional Power: The Origins*. Cambridge, Mass.: Ballinger Publishing Company, 1976.

Sprout, Harold and Margaret. *The Rise of American Naval Power, 1776–1918*. Princeton, N.J.: Princeton University Press, 1939.

Stafford, Cornelius William. *The Philadelphia Directory for 1800*. Philadelphia: William V. Woodward, 1800.

Steel, David. *Original and Correct List of the Royal Navy*. London: Printed for David Steel, 1798–1801.

————. *Steel's Naval Chronologist of the War: From Its Commencement in Feb. 1793, to Its Conclusion in 1801*. London: Printed for David Steel, 1802.

Steiner, Bernard C. *The Life and Correspondence of James McHenry, Secretary of War under Washington and Adams*. Cleveland: The Barrows Brothers Company, 1907.

Stevens, William Oliver. *An Affair of Honor: The Biography of Commodore James Barron, U.S.N.* Chesapeake, Va.: Norfolk County Historical Society, 1969.

Stillé, Charles J. *Major-General Anthony Wayne and the Pennsylvania Line in the Continental Army*. Philadelphia: J. B. Lippincott Company, 1893.

Stinchcombe, William, *The XYZ Affair*. Westport, Conn.: Greenwood Press, 1980.

Stivers, Reuben Elmore. *Privateers & Volunteers: The Men and Women of Our Reserve Naval Forces, 1766 to 1866*. Annapolis, Md.: Naval Institute Press, 1975.

294

Bibliography

Symonds, Craig L. *Navalists and Antinavalists: The Naval Policy Debate in the United States, 1785–1827.* Newark: University of Delaware Press, 1980.

Syrett, David. *Shipping and the American War, 1775–1783: A Study of British Transport Organization.* London: The Athlone Press, 1970.

Talleyrand-Périgord, Charles Maurice de, Prince de Bénévent. *Memoirs of the Prince de Talleyrand.* Duc de Broglie, ed. 5 vols. London and Sydney: Griffith Farron Okeden and Welsh, 1891–92.

Tannehill, Ivan Ray. *Hurricanes: Their Nature and History, Particularly Those of the West Indies and the Southern Coasts of the United States.* Princeton, N.J.: Princeton University Press, 1956.

Tansill, Charles Callan. *The United States and Santo Domingo, 1798–1873: A Chapter in Caribbean Diplomacy.* Baltimore: Johns Hopkins Press, 1938.

Thomas, Hugh. *Cuba: The Pursuit of Freedom.* New York: Harper & Row, 1971.

Troude, O. *Batailles Navales de la France.* 4 vols. Paris: Challamel Aime, 1867–68.

Tuckerman, Henry T. *The Life of Silas Talbot: A Commodore in the Navy of the United States.* New York: J. C. Riker, 1859.

United States Congress. *Biographical Directory of the American Congress, 1774–1961.* Washington, D.C.: United States Government Printing Office, 1961.

United States Navy Department. *American Ships of the Line.* Washington, D.C.: United States Government Printing Office, 1969.

United States Navy Department. *Dictionary of American Naval Fighting Ships.* James L. Mooney, ed. 8 vols. Washington, D.C.: United States Government Printing Office, 1959–81.

Valle, James E. *Rocks & Shoals: Order and Discipline in the Old Navy, 1800–1861.* Annapolis, Md.: Naval Institute Press, 1980.

Virta, Alan. *Prince George's County: A Pictorial History.* Norfolk, Va.: Donning Company, 1984.

Ward, Harry M. *The Department of War, 1781–1795.* Pittsburgh, Pa.: University of Pittsburgh Press, 1962.

Wattenberg, Ben J., ed. *The Statistical History of the United States From Colonial Times to the Present.* New York: Basic Books, 1976.

Weigley, Russell F. *The American Way of War: A History of United States Military Strategy and Policy.* New York: Macmillan Publishing Co., 1973.

———. *History of the United States Army.* New York: Macmillan Company, 1967.

White, Leonard D. *The Federalists: A Study in Administrative History.* New York: Macmillan Company, 1948.

Wilkinson, James. *Memoirs of My Own Times.* 3 vols. Philadelphia: Abraham Small, 1816.

Wood, John. *The Suppressed History of the Administration of John Adams (from 1797 to 1801) As Printed and Suppressed in 1802.* Reprint ed. New York: Burt Franklin, 1968.

Wood, Virginia Steele. *Live Oaking: Southern Timber for Tall Ships.* Boston: Northeastern University Press, 1981.

Wright, Robert K., Jr. *The Continental Army.* Washington, D.C.: Center for Military History, 1983.

ARTICLES

Albion, Robert Greenhalgh. "The First Days of the Navy Department." *Military Affairs* 12 (Spring 1948): 1–11.

Baurer, K. Jack. "Naval Shipbuilding Programs, 1794–1860." *Military Affairs* 29 (Spring 1965): 29–40.

Boles, John B. "Politics, Intrigue, and the Presidency: James McHenry to Bishop John Carroll, May 16, 1800." *Maryland Historical Magazine* 69 (Spring 1974): 64–85.

Campbell, John F. "The Havana Incident." *American Neptune* 22 (October 1962): 269–76.

Coatsworth, John H. "American Trade with European Colonies in the Caribbean and South America, 1790–1812." *William and Mary Quarterly* 3rd Ser. 24 (April 1967): 243–66.

Craft, David. "The Expedition of Col. Thomas Hartley Against the Indians in 1778, to Avenge the Massacre of Wyoming." *Wyoming Historical and Geneological Society Proceedings and Collections* 9 (1905): 189–216.

Crosby, Alfrew W., Jr. "American Trade with Mauritius in the Age of the French Revolution and Napoleon." *American Neptune* 45 (January 1965): 5–17.

Dorsey, Rhoda M. "The Pattern of Baltimore Commerce during the Confederation Period." *Maryland Historical Magazine* 62 (June 1967): 119–34.

Dunne, W. M. P. "The Constellation and the Hermione." *Mariner's Mirror* 70 (August 1984): 82–85.

Fisher, Charles R. "The Great Guns of the Navy, 1797–1843." *American Neptune* 36 (October 1976): 276–95.

Harrod, Frederick S. "Jim Crow in the Navy, 1798–1941." United States Naval Institute *Proceedings* 105 (September 1979): 47–53.

Hayes, Frederic H. "John Adams and American Sea Power." *American Neptune* 25 (January 1965): 35–45.

[Irving, Washington]. "Biographical Memoir of Captain David Porter." *Analectic Magazine* 4 (September 1814): 225–43.

———. "Biographical Notice of Captain Charles Stewart." *Analectic Magazine* 7 (February 1816): 132–41.

James, James A. "French Opinion as a Factor in Preventing War between France and the United States, 1795–1800." *American Historical Review* 30 (October 1924): 44–55.

Jenkins, H. J. K. "'The Colonial Robespierre': Victor Hugues on Guadeloupe, 1794–98." *History Today* 27 (November 1977): 734–40.

———. "The Heyday of French Privateering from Guadeloupe, 1796–1798." *Mariner's Mirror* 64 (August 1978): 245–50.

Jenkins, Howard, ed. "Journal of Sally Wister." *The Pennsylvania Magazine of History and Biography* 9 (No. 3, 1885): 318–33; (No. 4, 1885): 463–78; (No. 1, 1886): 51–60.

Jones, Robert F. "The Naval Thought and Policy of Benjamin Stoddert, First Secretary of the Navy, 1798–1801." *American Neptune* 24 (January 1964): 61–69.

King, George A. "The French Spoliation Claims." Senate Document No. 451, 64th Congress, 1st Session.

Knight, R. J. B. "The Introduction of Copper Sheathing into the Royal Navy, 1779–1786." *Mariner's Mirror* 59 (August 1973): 299–309.

Lyon, E. Wilson. "The Directory and the United States." *American Historical Review* 43 (April 1938): 514–32.

———. "The Franco-American Convention of 1800." *Journal of Modern History* 62 (September 1940): 305–33.

296
Bibliography

McKee, Christopher, ed. "*Constitution* in the Quasi-War with France: The Letters of John Roche, Jr., 1798–1801." *American Neptune* 27 (April 1967): 135–49.
———. "The Pathology of a Profession: Death in the United States Navy Officer Corps, 1797–1815." *War & Society* 3 (May 1985): 1–25.
McKee, Linda and Christopher. "An Inquiry into the Conduct of Joshua Blake." *American Neptune* 21 (April 1961): 130–41.
MacMaster, Richard K., ed. "The Tobacco Trade with France: Letters of Joseph Fenwick, Consul at Bordeaux, 1787–1795." *Maryland Historical Magazine* 60 (March 1965): 26–55.
Maurer, Maurer. "Coppered Bottoms for the Royal Navy: A Factor in the Maritime War of 1778–1783." *Military Affairs* 14 (April 1980): 57–61.
———. "Coppered Bottoms for the United States Navy, 1794–1803." United States Naval Institute *Proceedings* 71 (June 1945): 693–99.
O'Quinlivan, Michael. "Setting the Pattern: The Navy and Marine Corps at Curacao, 1800." *Navy* 2 (May 1959): 58–59.
Palmer, Michael. "The Dismission of Capt. Isaac Phillips." *American Neptune* 45 (Spring 1985): 94–103.
Powers, Stephen Tallichett. "Robert Morris and the Courts-Martial of Captains Samuel Nicholson and John Manley of the Continental Navy." *Military Affairs* 44 (February 1980): 13–17.
Prince, Carl E. "The Passing of the Aristocracy: Jefferson's Removal of the Federalists, 1801–1805." *Journal of American History* 57 (December 1970): 563–75.
Read, William B., ed. "Orderly Book of General Edward Hand, Valley Forge, January, 1778." *The Pennsylvania Magazine of History and Biography* 41 (No. 2, 1917): 198–223; (No. 3, 1917): 257–73; (No. 4, 1917): 458–67.
Russo, John Paul. "Hull's First Victory: One Painting, Three Famous Men." *American Neptune* 25 (January 1965): 29–34.
Savageau, David Le Pere. "The United States Navy and Its 'Half War" Prisoners, 1798–1801." *American Neptune* 31 (July 1971): 159–76.
Scheina, Robert L. "Benjamin Stoddert, Politics, and the Navy." *American Neptune* 36 (January 1976): 54–68.
Syrett, David. "The Organization of British Trade Convoys during the American War, 1775–1783." *Mariner's Mirror* 62 (May 1976): 169–81.
Turner, Harriot Stoddert. "Memoirs of Benjamin Stoddert, First Secretary of the United States Navy." *Records of the Columbia Historical Society* 20 (1917): 141–66.
Votaw, Homer C. "The Sloop-of-War *Ganges.*" United States Naval Institute *Proceedings* 98 (July 1972): 82–84.
Wood, David N. "The All-Volunteer Force in 1798." United States Naval Institute *Proceedings* 105 (June 1979): 45–48.

DISSERTATIONS

Carrigg, John Joseph. "Benjamin Stoddert and the Foundation of the American Navy." Ph.D. dissertation, Georgetown University, 1952.
Jackson, Scott Thomas. "Impressment and Anglo-American Discord, 1787–1818." Ph.D. dissertation, University of Michigan, 1976.
Palmer, Michael A. "The Quasi-War and the Creation of the American Navy, 1798–1801." Ph.D. dissertation, Temple University, 1981.
Schaffel, Kenneth. "The American Board of War." Ph.D. dissertation, City University of New York, 1983.

INDEX

297

Index

302

Index

Truxtun, John Williams, 102
Truxtun, Thomas: commands the
Constellation, 19; examines the Augusta,
22; prewar career of, 24; initial cruise of,
25–26; on the Constellation's design
problems, 29; overguns the Constellation,
29–30, 33; prepares for Havana cruise,
57; the Nancy incident, 59; takes convoy
to Havana, 59–60; angered by Nicholson,
60; merchants request convoy from
Havana, 61; reports on French activity
off American coast, 72–73; recommends
use of small ships off Cuba, 79; seniority
of, 79–81, 112–14; Dale's leave of
absence, 80; commands squadron in
Caribbean, 83; to regroup with Barry, 83;
reaches St. Kitts, 94; vessel from
requested by Barry, 94; meets with
British officials, 95; establishes convoy
routine in Leeward Islands, 96;
disappointed by Barry's failure to
cooperate, 96–97; reconnoiters
Guadeloupe, 97; captures l'Insurgente,
98–103; captures l'Union, 103; Barry
requests to send force to the Spanish
Main, 104; to take command of Murray's
squadron, 105; return of, 109–10; resigns,
114, 139; on Stoddert, 131; prize award
for capture of l'Insurgente, 133–34;
manning difficulties, 138; favors S. Barron
as replacement, 139; on Decatur, 139; to
relieve Tingey, 139; returns to duty, 139–
40; health of, 140, 221; use of tenders,
173–74; relieves Morris, 183; seeks to
engage French, 183–85; battle with la
Vengeance, 185–88; unable to find Morris,
188; falls in with Murray, 189–90;
opinion of Rodgers, 195; chairs the
Congress enquiry, 206–7; overrules
Stoddert, 211; personality of, 211; U.S.
Congress honors, 211; runs navy at
Norfolk, 211; Sever court of enquiry, 211;
acts as commander in chief, 212; seeks
admiralcy, 212; relationship with
Stoddert, 213; captured prisoners, 214;
commands the President, 214; commands
in Caribbean, 214; negotiates with
British officials, 215; weathers storm,
218; reinforcements for, 218–19;
command of, 221; overture to French,
224; confers with Barry, 225
Tryon, Moses: reinforces Morris, 149
Tufts, Turrell: as navy agent, 86; reports
shift in privateering activity, 194

Unanimity: commanded by Cochran, 54;
run in with the Mosquito, 54

L'Union: captures by the Constellation, 103
United States: early misfortune of, 32; initial
orders for, 32; ordnance for, 32–35;
grounds in the Delaware, 35; leaves the
Delaware, 35; orders for Caribbean, 36–
38; encounter with the Thetis, 38;
captures the Sans Pareil, 39; captures la
Jalouse, 40; rotting provisions of, 41;
heads Barry's squadron, 83; captures
l'Amour de la Patrie, 94; captures le
Tartuffe, 94; premature return of, 109–10;
European cruise of, 122–24, 133; mission
to France, 137; disabled, 221; survives
storm, 222; officer relations in, 223
United States Navy: see Navy, United
States
Ushant, 69

Vandeput, George: devises signals for
British and American ships, 77
La Vengeance: reaches Guadeloupe, 149;
engages the Constellation, 185–88;
captured by the Seine, 187; at
Willemstad, 196
Vera Cruz, Mexico: the Merrimack cruises
to, 146–47; money at, 228
Virgin Islands, 96
Virginia: taken into Navy, 55; with
Truxtun, 83; premature return of, 108
Le Volontaire: captures the Retaliation, 71;
threat of to Tingey's squadron, 115

War Department: and naval affairs, 7–8,
15–16; and armament shortage, 33–34
War of 1812, 30, 38, 138, 195, 238, 239
Warren: command of given to Newman,
169; yellow fever decimates, 228; actions
off Cuba, 228
Washington, D.C., 38, 172, 201, 229, 232;
capital moves to, 169; Stoddert plans for
transfer of government to, 210–11
Washington Navy Yard, 66, 91, 127, 231,
237, 242
Washington, George: appoints Dale captain,
20; and Barry, 43; appoints Nicholson
captain, 45; and Truxtun's resignation,
139; mourned in France, 192
Watkins, Frederick: operations at Curaçao,
197–201
Watson, John: foments mutiny in the
Constellation, 26
Welles, Gideon, 10
Wellington, Duke of, 152
West Indies: see Caribbean
Western Squadron, 69
Western Islands, 135, 203
Wharton, John, 27